Human Rights in Development Yearbook

Human Rights and Local/Living Law

Human Rights in Development
Yearbook 2003

Human Rights and Local/Living Law

Edited by

Lone Lindholt and Sten Schaumburg-Müller

A Human Rights Project involving the following institutions:

Chr. Michelsen Institute, Bergen, Norway
Danish Institute for Human Rights, Copenhagen, Denmark
Icelandic Human Rights Center, Reykjavik, Iceland
Institute for Human Rights, Åbo Akademi University, Turku/Åbo, Finland
Ludwig Boltzmann Institute of Human Rights, Vienna, Austria
Netherlands Institute of Human Rights, Utrecht, The Netherlands
Norwegian Centre for Human Rights, Oslo, Norway
Raoul Wallenberg Institute of Human Rights and Humanitarian Law, Lund, Sweden

Martinus Nijhoff Publishers
Leiden/Boston

Nordic Human Rights Publications
Oslo

A C.I.P. Catalogue record for this book is available from the Library of Congress.

Printed on acid-free paper.

ISSN 0801-8049
ISBN 90-04-13876-5

Distribution in Scandinavia
Norwegian Centre for Human Rights
Grensen 18
N-0159 Oslo
Norway
Tel. 47-22-42-1360
Fax 47-22-42-2542

Printed and bound in The Netherlands

PREFACE

The volumes published in the *Human Rights in Development* series, which for historical reasons still carry the word Yearbook in their title, are the result of a long-term collaboration between human rights research institutes and centres. Currently, the partners in the project include the Cristian Michelsen Institute, Bergen; the Danish Institute for Human Rights, Copenhagen; the Icelandic Human Rights Centre, Reykjavik; the Ludwig Boltzman Institute of Human Rights, Vienna; the Netherlands Institute of Human Rights, Utrecht; the Norwegian Centre for Human Rights, Oslo; the Raoul Wallenberg Institute of Human Rights and Humanitarian Law, Lund; and the Åbo Akademi University Institute for Human Rights, Turku/Åbo.

The *Human Rights in Development* series takes its starting point in a development perspective and aims to be topical, comprehensive, and multi-disciplinary, exemplifying the "cross-fertilization" of theoretical and practical approaches. Contributions are sought from researchers and practitioners in both donor and recipient countries. To ensure an increased focus on Southern perspectives, participation in the editorial work and inclusion of authors from a broad geographical scope has been, and is continuously, sought.

In recent years the volume has increasingly moved from the concept of a traditional yearbook or journal, towards a thematic anthology. Thus, instead of comprising freestanding articles on unrelated issues, the current design rests on a common theme bringing together a diversity of authors and contributions to address one common topic. To facilitate this, the overall responsibility for the continuation of the project rests with one of the participating institutions, which from 2001 through 2004 has been the Danish Institute for Human Rights.

The task of thematically editing this volume, the fifteenth in the series and bearing the heading "Yearbook 2003", has also been the responsibility of the Danish Institute for Human Rights. It was originally foreseen to be published as volume fourteen, but because of delays in the extensive editorial process of preparing this particular volume, it was decided to publish it later than the previous volume (now 2002) edited by the Åbo Akademi and entitled "Empowerment, Participation, Accountability and Non-Discrimination: Operationalizing a Human Rights-Based Approach to Development".

As the title of this volume, "Human rights and local/living law", indicates, its focus is on the various forms of local, informal and/or customary law and their interaction with human rights. In this respect the Danish Institute for Human Rights wishes to thank Sten Schaumburg-Müller for his extensive and most valuable contribution to the fairly extensive editorial process of this particular volume. Similar thanks go to our two capable and efficient language editors Andrew George and Grethe Johansen, as well as to Adam Frederik Nissen Feldt who handled the technical aspects of the editing with great speed and accuracy.

Finally, on behalf of all of the participating institutions we wish to thank the following development agencies, whose contributions made the production of this volume possible: the Danish Foreign Ministry (DANIDA), the Swedish Foreign Ministry (SIDA), the Norwegian Ministry of Foreign Affairs, and the Department of Development Policy of the Finnish Ministry for Foreign Affairs.

LONE LINDHOLT
GENERAL EDITOR
DANISH INSTITUTE FOR HUMAN RIGHTS

STEN SCHAUMBURG-MÜLLER
THEMATIC EDITOR
UNIVERSITY OF AARHUS

TABLE OF CONTENTS

CONTRIBUTORS

Lone Lindholt, Ph.D. and Master of Law. Senior Legal Analyst and Head of Civil Society Programme, International Department Danish Institute for Human Rights. Working in the area of human rights in developing and transitional countries, local and traditional law.

Sten Schaumburg-Müller, Ph.D. and Master of Law, B.A. in philosophy. Professor at Department of Jurisprudence, University of Aarhus, Denmark. Research interests include human rights, jurisprudence and mass media law.

Mireya Maritza Peña Guzmán, M.A. equivalent and Ph.D in Public Law, University of Paris, LL.M equivalent, EHESS, France. Currently holding a position as UNV/Human Rights Officer in the United Nations Mission in Ethiopia and Eritrea (UNMEE). Works in the are of the Study of the Person in the Law and Intercultural Human Rights (Miami, Florida, United States of America).

Are Knudsen, social anthropologist. Senior researcher at the Chr. Michelsen Institute for Development and Human Rights (CMI), Bergen, Norway. Current research interests include retributive justice, Islamist movements and post-war societies & peace building.

Tiina Saaresranta, M. Pol. Sc. Researcher at the Institute of Human Rights of Åbo Akademi University, Finland. Currently working in Bolivia with Education on the Rights of Indigenous Peoples in Bolivia and Ecuador.

Boipuso Nkwae, B.Sc(Hons), MSc. Research Assistant/Ph.D. Candidate, Department of Geodesy & Geomatics Engineering, Land & Coastal Studies Research Group, University of New Brunswick,Fredericton, Canada. Research focus on land tenure and land administration issues in Southern Africa, with particular emphasis on customary tenure in transition, on San/Khoikhoi indigenous rights issues in Southern Africa and on First Nations issues in North America.

Ragnhild L. Muriaas, M.A., PhD Candidate, Department of Comparative Politics, University of Bergen, Norway. Current PhD project, financed by the Norwegian Research Council, is a comparative analysis of the position of traditional authorities in local communities in Uganda and South Africa.

Sulistyowati Irianto, Ph.D. and M.A., legal anthropology from University of Indonesia and University of Leiden, the Netherlands, respectively. Teaches legal anthropology at the Faculty of Law and at the School of Law and Women's Studies Graduate Program, University of Indonesia. In charge of the Convention Watch Working Group and head of the Center for Women and Gender's Studies, University of Indonesia.

Stener Ekern, Social Anthropologist (Cand. Polit. from the University of Bergen, Norway). Currently a researcher at the Norwegian Centre for Human Rights in Oslo. Main topics of interest are political and legal anthropology, and Central and South America.

Lillian Tibatemwa-Ekirikubinza, LL.B (Makerere); LL.M (Bristol, UK); PH.D(University of Copenhagen). Associate Professor of Law and Deputy Vice-Chancellor (Academic Affairs)Makerere University Uganda. Crime and Criminology. Working in areas of Children's Rights, Gender, Law.

Karin Ask, social anthropologist at Chr. Michelsen Institute for Development and Human Rights, Bergen, Norway.

Michelo Hansungule, LL.M, Ph.D. Professor of Human Rights Law, Center for Human Rights, Faculty of Law, University of Pretoria. Visiting Professor, Raoul Wallenberg Institute of Human Rights and humanitarian Law, University of Lund, Sweden.

Introduction

Lone Lindholt

INTRODUCTION

1. Background

Over the last decades donor agencies and organisations have focussed on the formal legal system in relation to development processes. However, increasingly attention is being paid to the importance of ensuring that other structures as well are taken into account, and exploring the possibilities of supporting them as well as the advantages in the process of ensuring access to justice for all. The main question is whether, and how, donors should support these structures and alternative systems.

In addition to formal legal systems, based on Constitutions, statutes and legal jurisprudence adopted by the official court system, numerous countries have a supplementary regime of norms and practices which serve a similar or complimentary role at the local level and in relation to daily life of members of the community. These systems may be more or less formalised and/or codified, and often their claim for legitimacy is directly based on or indirectly referring to tradition and custom, but go beyond these in the sense that they are adhered to and sanctioned in a manner resembling that of the official national legal system.

The objective of this volume has been to reflect in a research-based manner on some of these issues, with the aim to compare and analyse the extent of the compatibility of the balancing human rights concerns. The research on which most of the papers are based, takes its outset in concrete empirical material relating to the issues relating to local/living law, i.e. using particular systems and cases as a basis, and could very well do so in a comparative perspective with a common outset in specific human rights standards or issues. In addition, the papers encompass a theoretical framework as well, for instance by being ex- or implicitly based on law and development theory, legal pluralism, or legal polycentricity, with empirical reflection based on one or more concrete examples. Finally, the papers also address some theoretical aspects relating to human rights - for instance the question of universality/cultural relativity of human rights, and the definition and criteria relating to the concept of access to justice.

Both in terms of empirical scope and in the recruitment of contributors, the editors have aimed towards ensuring a global perspective. Thus, the volume represents views from Europe, Asia, Africa and Latin America.

Ultimately, the publication should contribute to a further discussion on the applicability of customary norms and institutions in a post-traditional context, including the extent and nature of compatibility with human rights principles, and in this respect pointing towards areas of particular concern as well as opportunities for utilising such norms as a means of ensuring and implementing human rights principles and access to justice in a given context.

2. Issues and questions addressed

In terms of terminology, they have been titled "informal" or "customary", or more recently, "post-traditional". However, another term, which is the one we will apply in this context as suggested by *Sten Schaumburg-Müller*, is simply, "local" or "living law", signifying that this is a normative structure operating below the state level and closely related to regulating conflict and/or behaviour at the level of every day life in the community. The argument for using the term "local/living law" is to imply that we are interested in local law as opposed to state law and in living law as opposed to norms not in use. On the other hand the notion of 'living law' has a tendency to obscure the relation between norms and behaviour, not being able to point out the difference between living law and actual behaviour. Finally, by using the term *'law'*, we imply that norms and law are not exactly identical. He rejects the use of other common terms such as *"post-traditional"*, because he views it as "- simply not apt to catch any difference between various systems of law or levels of law", and *"customary law"* as "- an ambiguous term with several contradictory meanings and because of its connotation of tradition, habit and behaviour", as well as mainly being viewed as a colonial construct.

Tiina Saaresrantaa deliberately in the same vein uses the term "indigenous law" rather than "indigenous customary law", stressing that "in the Latin-American context the latter term has acquired a negative connotation, that is, understood to describe a system of inferior value, a system that is static, inflexible and with limited possibilities of development. This use of concepts also corresponds to the preferences of indigenous organizations of the Andean region". In addition, "the vindication of their own systems of law as *law* is part of the ongoing process of de-colonialisation". *Ragnhild Muriaas* brings a similar perspective from South Africa, however with the added complication that the codification of customary law had an impact on its regulation e.g. by the local courts, although this did not prevent further development of these "living laws", named so by the South African Law Commission in 1997. *Sulistyowati Irianto* analyses another version, the Indonesian doctrine Unity in Diversity, establishing the spirit of multiculturalism and diversity, which is upheld widely through rights to promote different cultures, including custom (local law, customary law).

Lillian Tibatemwa-Ekirikubinza applies the term "living law", which she views as "- a rough combination of practices, attitudes, ideas, cultures and norms that are more or less a compromise to the social dictates". *Stener Ekern* uses the term "customary legislative system" about a parallel system of local and state legal system, based on a bi-ethnic tradition with separate Mayan communal self-rule, with a system of dual government, and with Canton autonomy, as it is practiced through the maintenance of a local, Mayan polity. *Karin Ask* uses the term "local law" with a primary reference to "Pashtunwali, the customary unwritten law (*riwaj*) that is also living law in the border regions of Pakistan". She contrasts this to the Sharia law, but at the same time stresses that "(d)ifferent layers of religious law and local law were activated as regulatory norms of gender interaction in every day life during the war and exile" of the Afghan population. Finally, *Michelo Hansungule* also uses the term "living law" to illustrate various aspects of family law, using relevant examples from selected African cultures and traditions, and in particular he illustrates how the African family emphasizes distinctive roles and responsibilities of individuals, adding in some cases a human rights perspective.

In addition, these terms in particularly also indicate at least some degree of dynamics, serving as a reminder that a basis in tradition does not mean that such structures remain static. In addition, they are often the result of influences from several different norm and legal cultures and systems, as e.g. illustrated by *Are Knudsen* in relation to tribal and Islamic law, as well as by both *Ragnhild Muriaas* and *Tiina Saaresrantaa* with respect to colonial and post-colonial legal systems, often in a process of intercultural dialogue. *Sulistyowati Irianto* adds that even the co-existence of national and local law with international human rights norm presents a case of legal pluralism, stressing that the concept of "*Pancasila* is thus considered as basic law, the highest source of law for any kind of Indonesian laws", thus examining how the law may be observed against its political, economical, cultural, and historical background." *Lillian Tibatemwa-Ekirikubinza* maintains that "Formal laws influence living laws although they too generate their own rules and norms (... and) living law is influenced by, but does not necessarily conform to the formal legal system." *Karin Ask* illustrates the complexity added in the case of Afghanistan by the presence of the international community bringing the principle of human rights standards, as well as the constitutional law, to challenge the norms upheld by groups of actors including the Taliban, local and religious authorities.

<u>The institutions mandated to deal with them</u> may include the ordinary courts and other complaints bodies recognised by the official state system. *Mireya Pena* e.g. illustrates how the Constitutional Court of Colombia is mandated to settle conflicts between the indigenous and state law systems. However, most often these norms are administered by other bodies at the communal level, which are similarly more or less formalised but usually operate with a wide degree of recognition by the community. In the context of Afghanistan, *Karin Ask* stresses the role of the tribal councils (*Jirga/Shura*) in upholding the authority of local law, defining the *Jirga* as "- a local/tribal institution of decision-making and dispute settlement. This is an informal institution which utilises local customary law to arrive at a collective decision about the resolution of a dispute or local problem, a decision that is binding on the parties involved."

The indigenous legal system is part of the general organisational structure of the community, and therefore the same authority has the faculty to create, implement and reform the law, *Tiina Saaresrantaa* points out that such norms may be viewed as having <u>supreme validity</u> by members of society, to whom the official court system and imported norms in the form of legislation and a Constitution seem inaccessible and remote - especially in a post-colonial society. *Stener Ekern* exemplifies the norm according to which "- the Communal Mayor of a canton in Totonicapán, will act in this way or that because he considers himself to be—as the common expressions go—a "son of the community" and a "respectable" man that "shows respect". Leadership is temporarily bestowed upon him because he has demonstrated the necessary personal qualities, and moreover he has consistently "put the community before his own interest [of personal gain]"".

Also, the fact that the norms are flexible and may be adapted to particular circumstances, and even individuals, may be an advantage, particularly if those persons given the authority to administer them are themselves aware of this. E.g *Tiina Saaresrantaa* stressed this aspect in relation to indigenous peoples in Colombia and Ecuador. Also *Ragnhild Muriaas* stresses, in the context of South Africa, that "(f)eatures speaking in favour of traditional justice systems are that they are easily accessible, few costs are involved, they are informal, they use the same language as the disputants, and their proceedings are reasonable".

In many instances the preference for using traditional systems of redress and conflict resolution, may simply be that state law and the official administration hereof, may be ineffective, i.e. affected by corruption, inefficiency and lack of accessibility, especially in rural areas, as illustrated by *Are Knudsen*, and by *Ragnhild Muriaas* in relation to South Africa.

Finally, their ability to handle conflicts at the immediate level, thus contributing to ensuring that they do not escalate, makes them valuable both for securing order and peace in the community, as well as cost-effective medium particularly needed in a developing country with over-burdened and under-funded courts. *Are Knudsen* illustrates this in relation to killings in Pakistan.

However, from a human rights point of view, the same character of intimacy, informality and adaptability also has serious drawbacks, particularly as they tend to perpetuate existing inequalities in society by enforcing discriminatory practices and norms, for instance against women. This may particularly evident in areas relating to economic and social rights, for example against widows, and in areas of family, inheritance and property law. Also, as illustrated by *Are Knudsen* in relation to honour killings in Pakistan, it will have a negative gender bias, leading to increased violation of women's rights. Also *Tiina Saaresrantaa* analyses this in relation to the two particular cases of the rights of indigenous women, and the prohibition of torture, cruel and inhuman treatment. She illustrates, in the case of Latin America, that the inequality may persevere not just at an individual but also at a collective level, where "the long history of inequality has resulted in three consequences for indigenous peoples: the undervaluing of their own culture by indigenous peoples themselves and by the others, uncontrolled contamination by the other culture as a strategy of invasion or survival, and the production of silence by force". The same does *Boipuso Nkwae* in relation to the land tenure system in Botswana. *Sulistyowati Irianto* illustrates that in the context of Indonesia, the ethnic Chinese women, in spite of legal principles recognising their rights, are still subject to multi-dimensional discrimination, i.e. on the basis of race religion and gender. *Stener Ekern* illustrates, with an outset in the Maya of Guatemala, how "- in the totality of the authority and the absence of a division of powers - one perceives a lack of concern for those that in one way or another are different or simply unable to comply with the role of a "respectable person". A fundamental contrast seems to be located in the concepts of citizenship ("respectable persons" v. "human beings") of the two communities". *Michelo Hansungule* discussed a similar issue in relation to manifesting the duty of respect based on age, stating that "It may be a question of maintaining the power of the elders, but it is first and foremost a question of dignity".

There are areas where traditional/local systems in particular may serve as a means to securing human rights; see e.g. *Boipuso Nkwae* in relation to land rights of the indigenous San in Botswana, where "(f)orcing the comparison of San land tenure to the Bantu forms of tenure - has not helped the San hunter-gatherers in protecting and reclaiming their land rights", ultimately with a bearing on e.g. poverty alleviation and from a human rights perspective with an impact on e.g. economic and social rights, the right to equality, and freedom of residence in contrast to the villagisation schemes imposed on the San by the Botswana government. *Lillian Tibatemwa-Ekirikubinza* illustrates how, in the area of juvenile justice, and based on the principle of diversion, Uganda's 1996 Statute provides alternatives to the formal justice system through the Local Committee Courts. The rule is thus calling for informal as opposed to formal social control, and the focus of the restorative justice paradigm is on reparation of the harm suffered by the victim. The need to keep a child's contact with the formal justice system at the very minimum is also apparent in the fact that almost all the orders re-channel the child back into the community. A slightly critical approach is adopted by *Michelo Hansungule*, who emphasizes that "(f)rom an African perspective, the state fulfils its duty only when it balances its protection mandate between the individual and the collective (...) Modern approaches are flawed to the extent that they overemphasize the individuality aspect at the expense of the collective. On the other hand, individualistic approaches conflict with collectivistic strands."

When such norms and processes are applied to cases where members of society have violated them, i.e. similar to the process of trial of an accused in the official system, the principles of fair trial may not be fulfilled. This includes such aspects as equality of arms, access to and choice of representation, presumption of innocence, the right to remain silent, impartiality of the judge, separation of powers and freedom from cruel, inhuman or degrading punishment or treatment.

The key focus of this volume is how to balance the customary or traditional practices with human rights interests. *Sten Schaumburg-Müller* characterises the relationship in the way that "The human rights environment and the local sub-state law environment apparently share a mutual distrust toward one another. From the human rights point of view, local/living law is often perceived negatively, as an obstacle to development and a potential violator of human rights (...) Local/living law is not merely traditional dysfunctional human rights violating mores, but in some cases they may contain good solutions to human problems – From the local/living law point of view, human rights may be conceived as at best irrelevant but more often intruding, destructive of local culture and norms, unfit for solving local problems, individualistic and even dangerously protective of criminal offenders etc.". He sees the dichotomy as "understandable, but not insurmountable". With a similar focus on human rights, *Ragnhild Muriaas* discusses how South African governments have encountered in their efforts to balance policies designed to accommodate customary law and traditional courts with policies aimed to protect universal human rights, and with a view to ensuring compatibility with the post-apartheid Constitution. This includes in particular all persons' rights to equality before the law, and the rights of women to equality, especially in view of their status as minors under customary law. *Stener Ekern* maintains that "It follows that in societies where other collective identities and norms predominate, human rights language will not produce the same resonance. It is worth noting that the Mayan languages lack a word for expressing "right" as something that can be claimed in the abstract without reference to the fulfilment of an obligation. Human rights activists therefore typically resort to the Spanish word *derecho*". *Michelo Hansungule* mentions that especially the traditional rituals of a person moving into adulthood, e.g. circumcision of teenagers, has serious human rights implications.

This includes e.g. looking at examples of mutual interaction between these systems and state and civil society, for instance illustrating examples of how attempts have been made to shape the norms within the informal systems to ensure that they remain dynamic and reflective of society's processes, for instance towards increasing recognition of human rights values.

Other research questions offered to the authors include:

How can plural legal systems be brought into a common field, i.e. examining the conditions for co-existence of local/living law and state law? *Sten Schaumburg-Müller* states that the basic condition is dynamic and interactive, i.e. that "(n)o set of norms can be totally autonomous, and it is not an option not to change. The challenges are how to interact with other sets of norms and how to develop". *Mireya Pena* illustrates through examples from a number of Latin American countries the growing trend towards "constitutionalisation", i.e. the adoption of a distinct legal framework for the indigenous population within state law. The same does *Tiina Saaresrantaa* in relation to Ecuador, where the essential limitations relate to respect for the constitution, domestic laws and international standards, and that jurisdiction is limited to internal matters. In the case of Pakistan, *Are Knudsen* concludes that "The Qisas and Diyat Act elevates elements of traditional justice to statutory law and encourages out-of-court settlements in accordance with local customs", and that often "tribalisation" and "islamisation" of the penal code have made prosecuting honour killings ineffectual and provided legal sanction for traditional justice, and that "customary law takes precedence over jural law, encouraging the offended party to seek private justice", at the same time concluding that "the jural system and traditional justice tend to reinforce rather than counteract each other." *Ragnhild Muriaas* indicates that the original intent of the colonial regime in South Africa was to integrate the customary system into formal law and make it an official sub-category of a formal plural legal system. *Sulistyowati Irianto* analyses the context of Indonesia, where on the one hand the Constitution is guided by "a spirit of multiculturalism and diversity" by giving members of society the right to promote differences in culture including recognition of custom, local and customary laws. In contrast, *Lillian Tibatemwa-Ekirikubinza* states that in Uganda "(i)n regard to criminal law, statutes have specifically provided that customary law has no place in the criminal justice system and it is in fact a crime to settle criminal cases outside the formal justice system".

How systemic in nature is local/living law, i.e. do they have the form of structures and hierarchies, rather than being a looser framework of processes and mechanisms with a high degree of flexibility? *Ragnhild Muriaas* maintains that "The codification of customary law was a colonial attempt to systematise customary rights by seeking to provide a legal definition of the rules applied in traditional courts". *Michelo Hansungule* takes a slightly different approach, describing the traditional African family structure as composed of a number of "individuals (...) glued to one another and each one of them to the community in terms of a carefully elaborated set of duties and responsibilities recognized and enforceable by living law."

What is the understanding of justice within state versus local systems, and what is their role (especially remedial) in relation to dealing with human rights violations, such as genocide? Are Knudsen points to the right to revenge and the preference for retaliation, and that "(b)ringing a killing to court is locally construed as dishonourable and a breach of tradition".

Lillian Tibatemwa-Ekirikubinza analyses the principle of restorative justice in relation to the law and practice of juvenile justice in Uganda, and argues for a revisiting of indigenous justice traditions in order to ensure that the resulting model is cognisant of cultural sensitivities and is appropriate and acceptable to the community. This takes its outset in an approach to law, which depends on what the actors perceive to be the accepted norms and values as well as on what is contained in the statutes. She further emphasizes the recognition of retribution as the main objective for achieving justice, and the involvement of the parents and the rest of the community in relation to redressing wrongdoing by juveniles and children. *Karin Ask* illustrates how the difference between the local/customary institution Jirga and a court of Sharia in Afghanistan may be summarised as the difference between negotiations to restore an equilibrium between two contestants and adjudication to restore justice.

And, *Michelo Hansungule* stresses "a need for Africa to re-invent its position in relation to the concepts of law and justice (...)analysing critically the traditional elements of law and justice so as to ensure that the valuable elements are preserved", and that "the original process of justice in Africa is woven around the principles of inclusiveness, participatory and substantive justice", while adding also that e.g. concepts such as defence and appeal, even though they make take different forms, are still inherent aspects of African concepts of justice.

And, finally, how do local systems such as these relate to such issues as balance and separation of powers, gender issues, governance, conflict prevention, crime prevention issues, and the re-building of societies in transition from violent conflict or dictatorship?

E.g. *Tiina Saaresrantaa* reflect the thinking that the indigenous system does not recognise separation of powers, and *Ragnhild Muriaas* raises the issue whether, within a system of legal pluralism, states *do* in fact or *ought to* have a monopoly of law enforcement in society.

She examines the three dilemmas (capacity, ethical and strategic), which are supposed to affect the process of balancing the accommodation of customary law and the judicial function of traditional leaders with fundamental human rights, illustrating how they have "caused an incoherent process, which has not managed to transform the complex legal system in local communities to a sufficient degree". She furthermore illustrates how the early codification of customary law in South Africa by the colonialist not just made them static (formally but still not in practice), but also served to keep existing power relations, i.e. dominance by elder men, in place.

3. Perspectives

A range of issues are addressed in this volume, and we hope that it can contribute to the understanding of local/living law and to the improvement of human rights performance in societies with strong elements of non-state local/living law.

Certainly, there are still many theoretical and not least practical problems to be addressed as regards the relation between international human rights and local/living law. Further analyses of local legal and normative structures and their internal as well as external relations are required. Not only should these more local phenomena not be ignored, but their implications for human rights issues still need further research, elaboration and theorising. This is the case even more so as the role of the state is changing due to various globalisation processes, as a result of which local/living law may be further suppressed as it is not formally recognised in international law. On the other hand it may also be strengthened in the same process that weakens the nation state. Neither development is foreseeable, and both scenarios have implications for the implementation of human rights. As is seen from the various articles of this volume, local practices, norms and customs may be detrimental to human rights as well as supportive and in a better position than state law to provide human rights to the local population.

With this volume we have focused on the analysis of the relation between local/living law and international human rights standards, and hopefully we have contributed to the development of an interest in this field, even to the development of theoretical analyses and – in the longer perspective – contributed to the improvement of human rights performance in the world.

The Global and the Local. Reflection on Human Rights and Local/Living Law

Sten Schaumburg-Müller

INTRODUCTION

Dealing with human rights and sub-state norms, such as the norms of a more or less specified ethnic group, requires an understanding of human rights as well as an understanding of such sub-state norms and the respective societies. It is probably correct to state that to a large extent the two fields have developed their own tradition, concepts, discourses etc., without much interaction. Human rights are dealt with mainly on the international field and mainly by lawyers who tend to have a normative approach. The relations of human rights to other normative levels are mainly dealt with in relation to state law, including questions such as how do states implement their international obligations etc. Sub-state norms, on the contrary, are mainly dealt with by anthropologists with a descriptive approach even to legal issues, and the sub-state level is usually contrasted to state level and/or "Western" law, not to the purportedly universal human rights law. The need for bringing these traditions together is obvious: Sub-state communities simply do play a role, in some countries probably a larger role than state norms. Ignoring the local level when dealing with human rights, is therefore tantamount to ignoring vital elements of human rights, including the important aspect of implementation. Similarly, ignoring human rights aspects when dealing with sub-state norms, is tantamount to leaving out important normative questions: Does the specific local normative order violate human rights, support human rights or even contribute to the understanding of universal morality? No community is isolated, all communities are actors on the global scene, whether the participants like it or not, or whether they are aware of it or not, and human rights are one of the global parameters.

In the following I shall deal with some conceptual issues, attempting to prepare the way for a joint human rights local/living law approach.

HUMAN RIGHTS AS MORE THAN INTERNATIONAL PUBLIC LAW

The term 'international public law' designates law dealing with relations between states[1] as opposed to the law prevailing within each state. States make all sorts of agreements dealing with war and peace, trade, borders etc., and agreements can be either bilateral, involving only two states, or multilateral,

[1] Inter-national = between nations; equals the terms 'ius gentium' and 'Völkerrecht'.

involving many states. Human rights are often seen as a set of multilateral international agreements obliging states to treat their citizens in a certain specified manner. Thus, human rights are understood as part of international public law. This is of course true, the UN-charter and the many human rights conventions are parts of the international public law as the specific area of law dealing with relations between states and states' obligations towards other actors. However, this is not the only truth, and therefore a misrepresentation. The 'international human rights vis a vis state law' picture is far from covering all human rights aspects.

Firstly, human rights are more than a set of international rules and are not restricted to the international level. As a matter of fact, implementation of human rights would be impossible, if human rights were solely a question of international law. National constitutions often have a chapter on human rights, and in fact most legal areas do contain human rights aspects: criminal law (the prohibition of retroactive criminalization), criminal procedure (presumption of innocence), family law (right to marry) and even civil law (rights to property). In this way, human rights are crosscutting the traditional divisions of legal areas.

Secondly, even international human rights do not have states as the sole actors. It is obvious that human rights involve the individual person as a bearer of rights, and this is often used as an example of persons being subjects of international law.[2] However, states are not the necessary bearers of obligations when dealing with human rights. The Universal Declaration of Human Rights of 1948 is rather vague – or open – as to the obliged subjects. The follow-up Conventions, such as the twin Covenants on social, economic and cultural rights and civil and political rights, respectively, the Convention Against Racial Discrimination [3] etc., naturally have states as the central actors: Conventions are agreements between states, and it is a fundamental principle that parties can only bind themselves. But from the outset, universal human rights do *not* stipulate that the only possible parties to human rights agreement

---

[2] Peter Malanczuk, *Akehurst's Modern Introduction to International Law*, 7th ed., Routledge, 1997, p. 100 f.

[3] International Covenant on Social, Economic and Cultural Rights (CESCR) finalized in 1966, in force 1976, presently with 146 members, International Covenant on Civil and Political Rights (CCPR), finalized 1966, in force 1976, presently with 151 members, and respectively, the Convention on the Elimination of Racial Discrimination (CERD), finalized 1965, in force 1969, presently with 169 members (www1.umn.edu/humanrts).

are states. States are important, but not all-important, and other actors do have an important role to play, including any sub-state norm generating entity.

There are several complicated issues at stake here, such as the question of individual duties and the rights and duties of other collective entities than states, operational criteria for defining such entities and the relationship between individuals and these entities.[4] Time and space do not allow me to go into these questions, although relevant. For the present purpose it suffices to emphasize that human rights cannot be adequately grasped within the framework of international public law.

HUMAN RIGHTS ARE NOT NATURAL

Human rights are often seen as a kind of natural law:[5] Human rights are not connected to any existing state and human beings have rights, no matter where or who they are. Consequently, those rights are not societal by nature, human rights stem from the very fact that humans are humans, are embedded in human nature so to speak. In this sense human rights are natural, and therefore human rights are conceived as a kind of natural law. This view is based on two partly intertwined ideas.

Firstly, in European history and legal philosophy human rights are definitely of a natural law character. John Locke, the English 17th century philosopher, based his conception on human rights – right to life, liberty, security and property – in the state of nature. Even here humans have rights, only they are not well protected. Therefore, humans decide to join a society in order to

[4] As regards individual duties, see Gudmundur Alfredsson & Asbjørn Eide (eds.), *The Universal Declaration of Human Rights. A Common Standard of Achievement*, Martinus Nijhoff Publishers, 1999, p. 637 f.; Lone Lindholt, *Questioning the Universality of Human Rights*, Ashgate, 1997, p. 238 f.; as regards minorities, see Asbjørn Eide, "The Non-Inclusion of Minority Rights. Resolution 217C (III)" in *The Universal Declaration of Human Rights*, op.cit., p. 701 f.; and as regards business, see Michael Addo (ed.), *Human Rights Standards and the Responsibility of Transnational Corporations*, Kluwer Law International, 1999.

[5] As an example see David Forsythe, *Human Rights in International Relations*, Cambridge University Press, 2000, p. 28 ff. In an anthropological article it is claimed that "human rights (have) … inescapable natural law connotations", Marie-Bénédicte Dembour, "Human Rights Talk and Anthropological Ambivalence. The Particular Context of Universal Claims", Olivia Harris (ed.), *Inside and Outside the Law,* Routledge, 1996. As I shall argue, they are by no means inescapable.

obtain a better protection of their natural rights. The mutual acknowledgement of rights is prevalent in society, and therefore it is for the benefit of each human being to give up some of his freedom in order to have it accepted and secured by the community. Locke has had a tremendous influence on European legal thought, and the US Declaration of Independence is written on the basis of a Locke'an concept of human rights.

Secondly, when introducing new law, partly in a new way, it is tempting to postulate a natural basis. As law is somehow connected to justice (although the connection is precarious as many examples in this volume show), law is in need of justification, and when introducing new law there appears to be a need for legitimising this new way of prescribing the order of society. One way of legitimising is by referring to nature. If human rights are natural endowments as opposed to contingently ascribed legal positions, there is no room for recalcitrant governments or legislatures for that matter to dismiss human rights. In this way, differing on human rights issues is not simply a question of different opinions and preferences. Going against human rights is tantamount to acting against nature – in much the same way as disliked sexual behaviour is referred to as acts against nature rather than acts against the mores of society.

When Locke and others introduced a new way of legal thinking based on individual rights, this was sought justified in nature and natural law. Therefore, the tendency to conceive human rights as natural law is understandable.

However, it is not recommendable. Even though a natural law view of human rights is a widespread assumption, it is nevertheless wrong, misleading and even dangerous.

Firstly, it is philosophically unfounded. Human rights are not a preset number of rules, discovered by outstanding lawyers. The main problem is that there is no method of *finding* the specific naturally existing human rights. Human rights are – as any other type of law – man-made.[6] Secondly, a natural law approach tends to lead to wrong questions and doubtful activities. Rather than asking how to solve a problem – and the post 1945 human rights were pretty much an answer to the question of how to avoid another devastating war and outrageous atrocities – the natural law approach invites for questions of how to

---

[6] This does *not* entail that human beings can make whatever laws they wish, nor does it entail that any man-made law is as good as any other. But I shall leave out this discussion here.

establish a correct and coherent set of natural rights. Lastly, the natural law approach dangerously bypasses democratic and participatory approaches to law: If human rights are natural, it is up to specifically skilled persons (such as human rights lawyers and maybe human rights activists) to find them. Engaging in human rights thus becomes a one-way monologue, and the ones with human rights knowledge can simply require others to tune in. In this way, human rights become procedurally exclusive rather than inclusive, and élitist rather than participatory. It is no incident that post-1945 human rights include democracy,[7] are universal in scope and explicitly non natural – in contrast to the 17th and 18th century human rights conception that was based on natural law, national sovereignty and limited to local implementation.

MUTUAL PREJUDICES

The human rights environment and the local sub-state law environment apparently share a mutual distrust toward one another. From the human rights point of view, local/living law is often perceived negatively, as an obstacle to development and a potential violator of human rights, especially in the fields of equal treatment of sexes.

As an example CEDAW, art. 5 (a) provides that "States Parties shall take all appropriate measures to modify the social and cultural patterns of conduct of men and women, with a view to achieving the elimination of prejudices and customary and all other practices which are based on the idea of the inferiority or the superiority of either of the sexes or on stereotyped roles for men and women." No doubt, many cultural patterns are based on stereotyped roles of the sexes and no doubt, the relationship is often highly unequal. The now abandoned age-old Chinese custom of binding girls' feet is just one obvious example. In this way, there is nothing wrong in wanting to modify cultural patterns and conduct, on the contrary. Human development is also about changing dysfunctional behaviour. But several problems are involved.

Firstly, and most relevant in this context, article 5 depicts tradition as a problem and human rights as the answer. There is no counterbalancing provision supporting good local traditions and ways of dealing with the intricate relation between the sexes. The very idea that local ways and

[7] Universal Declaration of Human Rights, art. 21.

solutions may have good answers is simply not part of the approach. I am not suggesting that local/living law always has good ways of dealing with the relation between the sexes, on the contrary, but it is not convincing to leave out totally this possibility. This approach cuts off information and dismisses local ways as inferior by definition, and leaves no room for bringing in experience. Besides, the drafters obviously did not feel any need to warn against modern practices, even though modernization and development may entail a deterioration of the situation of women.[8]

Secondly, the approach seems to preclude any complementary concept, the idea that there are differences between men and women. I should be the first to emphasize that a "different, but equal" conception very easily leads to discrimination, not only in terms of different treatment but in terms of unfair treatment and hierarchical ordering of the different entities. In fact, the US Supreme Court's "separate, but equal" decision[9] regarding the status of races in USA has provided a legal basis for discriminatory practices. The problem, of course, when dealing with sexes is that there *are* differences and that it is not self-evident which social consequences those differences do or ought to have, and it is even not precisely clear which differences are natural (such as the different roles in procreation) and which are societal (such as binding of the feet).

Apparently, local/living law often has a complementary view on the relation between genders,[10] and it is highly problematic if the answer to this situation from a human rights point of view is simply to dismiss the state of affairs as violating human rights and requiring it to be adjusted to the universal level. Stener Ekern reports from Mayan communities in Guatemala that they have a complementary conception of the sexes and that widows and single mothers are in a precarious situation, living without the complementarity and therefore outside the good way of life.[11] The human rights answer to this situation, obviously in need of improvement, is important. One way is to focus on the

[8] Ester Boserup, *Woman's Role in Economic Development*, George Allen and Unwin, 1970; Agnete Weis Bentzon, "Afrikanske sædvaner i historisk perspektiv" [African customs in a historical perspective], *Den Ny Verden*, 1997, vol. 30, p. 13-34.

[9] Plessy v Ferguson, 163 US 537 (1896).

[10] Signe Arnfred, "Polygami og brudepris i Mocambique" [Polygamy and bride price in Mozambique], *Den Ny Verden*, 1997, vol. 30, p. 35-55.

[11] Stener Ekern, "Visions of the Right Order. Contrasts between Mayan Communitarian Law in Guatemala and International Human Rights Law", (present volume).

connection between the complementarity and the plight of widows and single mothers with a requirement to mount the human rights non-discrimination track. This would be an exclusive, non-participatory approach, based on a conception of human rights as a given, unquestionable entity. Another way is to forward the question: How can the situation of the widows and single mothers be improved – thereby leaving the situation open (not in the way of accepting *any* kind of answer, but accepting that there may be several solutions to the problem)[12] and thus even participatory. The solution is not deducted from pre-exstisting concepts, but proposed on the basis of considerations where human rights as well as local/living law are taken into account.[13]

My favourite example is from Zambia: According to customary law, a husband has a right to claim damages from his wife's lover. Traditionally, the wife has no claim for compensation from the husband's lover, probably connected to the fact that customary marriages are potentially polygynous. However, local court justices dealing with these kinds of cases, have been discussing the option of awarding damages to the wife as well, based on "unlawful interference in marriage", and some, especially the younger, would actually use it.[14] A strict human rights approach could lead to a simple dismissal of the institute of granting compensation in adultery cases, this not being modern, but it seems more wise to use the local, living concept of law and moral and combine this with the human rights requirement of non-discrimination.

In this way, research on local/living law becomes important also in a human rights set-up: Local/living law is not merely traditional dysfunctional human rights violating mores, but in some cases they may contain good solutions to human problems.

From the local/living law point of view, human rights may be conceived as at best irrelevant but more often intruding, destructive of local culture and norms,

---

[12] Inspired by John Rawls' concept of "reasonable pluralism": There may be several and even conflicting values in a society (pluralism), but not *all* values are acceptable (reasonable). John Rawls, *Political Liberalism*, Columbia University Press, 1993.

[13] Ekern categorizes the approach as pragmatic to which I very much agree. Philosophical pragmatism, as advocated by e.g. John Dewey, focuses on solving problems rather setting up principles.

[14] Afronet, *Local Court Study*, Lusaka, 1999, p. 12, and own observations and discussions with Zambian local court justices.

unfit for solving local problems, individualistic and even dangerously protective of criminal offenders etc.

The proponents of such a view, however, often do not distinguish between what human rights prescribe and what is actually being done. Many abhorrent acts of states are not done *because of* human rights but in spite of such rights, as clear-cut human rights violations.

Secondly, many human rights critics do not grasp the magnitude of the post-1945 revolution in human rights conception. Taking off with the 1945 UN Charter and the 1948 Universal Declaration, human rights became universal (in concept, not necessarily in practice), inclusive of social rights and vested in the global community.[15] It should be noted that many human rights proponents have not grasped the development either, and tend to stick to a narrow concept of human rights, at the risk of totally disregarding local/living law.

Before human rights were nationally based, to a large extent based in natural legal thought, they did not, at least not systematically, include social and economic rights. Thus, the 1789 Locke-inspired French Declaration of Rights of Man and Citizen[16] was only for the French, mentioned only civil and political rights, and vested sovereignty with the nation, thus excluding a large part of humanity, most of whom is not French, and many of whom are in need of social and economic rights, in comparison to the drafters who thought it natural to be French and wealthy. Besides, limiting human rights to the (French) nation opened the door for the mission, excluding other concepts and cultures as wrong, and for the military, making this exclusion effective.

What I am arguing here is that the mutual distrust between human rights and local/living law is understandable, but not insurmountable. The underlying assumption of this approach is that human rights as well as local/living law must be open. Human rights are not truly human if they dismiss any subjective feeling on part of an individual or a group that their norms are not taken into consideration. By definition, human rights are not pre-exclusive, and self-

[15] I shall not at present go further into the complicated discussion on whether even the post 1945 human rights implicitly presumed a world consisting of strong nation states. By any measure, the Universal Declaration of Human Rights *is* more universal than the French Declaration, even if it may be debatable whether it is sufficiently universal.

[16] "Déclaration des droits de l'homme et du citoyen". The addition "et du citoyen" [and of the citizen] is often left out in references to the French Declaration.

determination is an inseparable part of human rights. In the same manner, local/living law is only living if it is open to change and improvement. No set of norms can be totally autonomous, and it is not an option not to change. The challenges are how to interact with other sets of norms and how to develop. No matter how well-rooted local custom and practices may seem (and often they are of a far younger and more dynamic nature than usually perceived), they cannot avoid contact with other sets of norms, including human rights. To the extent that either system is closed, the mutual distrust is logical. Hence, they must be open in order to be able to improve, thereby improving the situation of the involved people.

CONSIDERATIONS ON TERMINOLOGY

For this volume we have chosen the concept 'local/living law' as a working term to imply that we are interested in local law as opposed to state law and in living law as opposed to norms not in use.

The concept of *'local'* does not seem to be very problematic. It simply points out a geographical element and distinguishes it from other types of law. It is neither global nor regional, it is not attached to the state level, and it connotes a perception of being attached to a smaller group of people on the sub-state level (or cross state, as the case may be).

'Living' implies that it is alive and in use, in the sense that it is not merely historical or otherwise not in use. Living implies actually prevailing norms.

Still, 'living law' is not an unproblematic concept. It may imply, in simple terms, that it is what people do rather than what they ought to do, but as a matter of fact do not do, or it may imply prevailing norms rather than what is prescribed by black letter law, i.e. "law in action vs law in books".

In both ways, the notion of 'living law' has a tendency to obscure the relation between norms and behaviour, not being able to point out the difference between living law and actual behaviour. The confusion of law and behaviour has troubled living law proponents, from Eugen Ehrlich's introduction of the concept, over the realists' emphasis on law in action rather than law in books and to many legal pluralism proponents.[17] These authors definitely have a point by criticizing the traditional legal focus on law in books and formal state law by insisting on the relevance of what is actually going on. But they regularly overdo their point and end up with not being able to distinguish between norms and behaviour and with dismissing law as irrelevant.

As an example, we could mention the ban on torture, prevalent in international human rights as well as in many national constitutions, and one of the most absolutely maintained and clearly defined human rights standards. Still, in too many countries, the police use force as a way of investigating crime. From a living law point of view one could claim that black letter law is not very interesting, when as a matter of fact suspects are beaten up in police custody anyway, and it is definitely a point that we do not get sufficient knowledge by merely looking at the law according to which torture is forbidden.

But the living law approach may take us too far, implying that the prevailing norms (the living law) are beating up detainees rather than a ban on torture (the black letter law). In this way, the beating becomes yet another type of law, and even a more important type. They even risk legitimizing torture by categorizing this phenomenon as law.

To my perception, living law proponents have got very valid points in emphasizing the necessity of looking at reality and the necessity of bringing in other normative fields, such as the norms prevailing at a local police station. But they go astray when they do not realize that law is a counterfactual phenomenon, not meant to describe reality (what is going on at the police station etc.), but meant to be prescriptive (what ought to go on at the police station and which norms ought to prevail). Insisting on reality risks ending up in insisting on the irrelevance of anything non-real, such as law which is not factual, but counterfactual in nature. After all, law does not describe regular behaviour, but is about what some people want others to do.[18]

---

[17] Eugen Ehrlich, *Grundlegung der Soziologie des Rechts*, München, 1913; Roscoe Pound, "Law in Books and Law in Action", *American Law Review*, 1910, vol. 44, p. 12-36; John Griffiths, "What Is Legal Pluralism?", *Journal of Legal Pluralism*, 1986, vol. 24, p. 1-55; Sten Schaumburg-Müller, "Pursuing Theory in Law on Loose Ground", *Retfærd*, 2002, no. 99, p. 33-51.

[18] Martin Chanock, *Law, Custom and Social Order. The Colonial Experience in Malawi and Zambia*, Cambridge University Press, 1985, p. 17.

The example is meant to emphasize the importance and relevance of distinguishing between practices (what is actually going on at the local police station) and prevailing norms (do the policemen actually feel obliged to behave in a brutal manner, because that is what their colleagues do or what their superiors require). The example may be controversial – hardly anybody would call the beating of detainees 'law' – but nevertheless it focuses on the distinction which is relevant when dealing with all kinds of law, human rights law as well as local/living law. The behaviour within an indigenous group may or may not qualify as law, even though we do not have pre-set criteria for the categorization.

By entertaining the concept of local/living law we therefore only intend to imply that norms are in some way prevailing, meaning that the law has actual normative power. Actual behaviour is another, albeit relevant, matter, and we do not have any set of standardized procedure to check whether a certain norm is actually prevailing or not.

By using the term *'law'*, we imply that norms and law are not exactly identical. There may be norms, such as shaking hands when meeting, that are definitely not law, even though the distinction is not always clear. Insisting on a possible distinction between law and norms does not entail any necessary link between law and state as in the legal positivist tradition with their central tenet that only norms backed by the forces of the state are law. There may be non-state law as well as non-state norms. Insisting on the difference does not entail any hierarchical order either.

In this way, the concept of local/living law provides us with the opportunity to take non-state norms into consideration, not merely as violations of (state) law, but as relevant normative orders that cannot be ignored simply because they are operating, and probably more importantly even may have good solutions to prevalent problems. Besides, the approach leaves us with the option of evaluating the local norms, not - as many living law and legal pluralism proponents do – merely giving an account of any prevalent practice as a matter of fact, but combining knowledge of local norms with a normative approach.

We have deliberately chosen not to use the term *'post-traditional'* which is used by some authors and organisations. Firstly, the concept implies that (a system of) law used to be traditional and that the particular entity has now developed or emerged out of that tradition. The problem is that 'tradition' is a highly controversial concept,[19] various traits of society being deified into tradition whereas others being rejected as alien and not belonging to the society (un-American behaviour, non-African values etc).

Secondly, the term implies that only some types of law were traditional, in contrast to other historical types that consequently cannot be understood as traditional. The implicit idea is that certain historical types of law were based on tradition (such as African customary law) in contrast to other historical types that did not include tradition (such as European law). This does not make much sense. It seems to be linked to the misconception that the normative systems which the colonizers met in Africa and other places were stagnant and traditional, whereas the colonizers' law was dynamic and changing.[20] Even if it were possible to generalize some differences between 19th century English[21] and French law and the law prevailing in the colonies, 'tradition' is not a useful bench marker. Thus, English law was clearly much more traditional than post-revolutionary French law, and the prevailing law in colonized countries was certainly not static.

Thirdly, the term 'post-traditional' may connote that not all contemporary law is modern. Only some types of law have developed into modern law, human rights probably being the prototype of a more rational, liberating way of ordering society. According to this understanding not all law has modernized, and some has diverged into something non-modern, away from tradition but without modernity. This does not make much sense, either. Modern Western law is not, solely or always, modern, but always reflects a tradition from which it has developed. Distinguishing this local (European or Western) tradition from the modern aspects is difficult but necessary when dealing with universalizing law, with the ever-present risk of universalizing local traditions.

In conclusion 'post traditional' is simply not apt to catch any difference between various systems of law or levels of law. All legal systems contain some traditional elements although to a different degree, and all legal systems

---

[19] Eric Hobsbawm and Terence Ranger (eds.), *The Invention of Tradition*, Cambridge University Press, 2002.

[20] Henry Sumner Maine, *Ancient Law*, 1861. Se also below on the concept of 'customary law'.

[21] The British Empire introduced mainly English common law rather than other types of law prevailing in the United Kingdom.

have the capacity to develop and do actually develop, geared by internal as well as external factors. Thus, all law is more or less post-traditional.

Especially in an African context the term *'customary law'* is applied, even to extend that statutes provide for the use of "African customary law"[22] – as if such an entity were a distinct and recognizable feature.[23] The problem is that the concept is highly dubious because of its ambiguity with several contradictory meanings and because of its connotation of tradition, habit and behaviour.

As for the ambiguity, the term is sometimes used to characterize prevailing law in pre-colonial societies.[24] It makes some sense to use the term with this reference, even though the term is problematic as the pre-colonial normative system (to the extent that it was really a system) was not necessarily customary. More problematic is the fact that it is very difficult to gather knowledge on this type of law, as we do not have very reliable sources of information mainly because of the oral tradition. Some authors naïvely infer that knowledge of the pre-colonial law can be extracted from colonial times, which is of course not necessarily the case.[25]

Secondly, the term may connote that whatever people do is customary law. If 60% of the population carry out female circumcision, then this habit may be described as being customary (law).[26] Certainly, if no one carries out a certain act, nobody would call this act customary law, but this does not entail that even if everybody is doing the same thing, such acts are necessarily customary law. Think of the shaking hands example mentioned above, and even though there may not be a strict line between habits and law, and even though different societies – and even different strata of one society - may draw the line differently, all societies (as far as I know) have the idea that some norms are more important than others. This leads to the conclusion that prevailing habits

[22] As an example, the Zambian Courts can use "African customary law" as a legal source, Local Courts Act, sec. 12, Subordinate Courts Act, sec. 16.

[23] The idea that customary law is an identifiable entity links to what I have called the second generation, see below.

[24] As an example see John Hatchard & Muna Ndulo, *Readings in Criminal Law and Criminology in Zambia*, Multimedia Publications, Lusaka and James Currey, London, 1994.

[25] Ibid. In the section on "Pre-colonial Law" they refer to court cases from the colonial time.

[26] Agnete Weis Bentzon,"Den hvide jurists byrde" [White Lawyer's Burden], Peter Blume, Kirsten Ketscher og Steen Rønsholdt (eds.), *Liv, arbejde og forvaltning. Til Ole Krarup på 60 års dagen*, GadJura, 1995, p. 371.

are not necessarily law. In addition, it should be noted that the categorization of some norms as 'law' is never a purely descriptive activity, as it contains a normative element.

Thirdly, the term is used to refer to the particular type of law, developed in the colonial era. In this way, 'customary law' is seen as a colonial construct.[27] The analysis is connected to the British indirect rule, leaving local decisions to local chiefs, etc. The point is that with the advent of the colonizers the kings and chiefs were provided with the backing of an enormous foreign military power (unless of course they did not want to cooperate in which case they were deported or otherwise had their power diminished) and thereby became less dependent on the backing of their own society.The advent of the colonial power thus changed significantly the society by distorting existing power relations including prevailing checks and balances[28] and thereby changed the law of the society, the emerging law being labelled 'customary law'. As a minor but illustrative example Martin Chanock mentions that native courts in Central Africa imposed heavier penalties for offences committed against chiefs, headmen and even elders than offences committed against other persons, the point being that now – as distinct from the situation in pre-colonial times - they had the chance to secure their position with the combined backing of courts and executive powers.[29] Another example is a colonial court's refusal to accept the status of 'customary marriage' for African couples living together in the urban centres, the argument being that this was immoral behaviour, not sanctioned by the elders of the home tribe.[30] Even though we may disagree with the Victorian minded local courts officer, the latter example illustrates the difficulty in equating habits with law. According to this approach 'customary law' cannot be a reflection of pre-colonial "indigenous" law, but is a type of law that evolved during colonial times. Nor is it a mere reflection of contemporary local habits, as the colonial power has played its part in granting the status of law to only some of these habits. These points are probably exacerbated in South Africa, having had an apartheid-regime up to 1990 in

[27] Chanock, op.cit.; John L. Comaroff & Simon Roberts, *Rules and Processes. The Cultural Logic of Dispute in an African Context*, University of Chicago Press, 1981.

[28] T. Olawale Elias emphasizes that the chief was in a constant risk of being ignored and that despotism was not an option. *The Nature of African Customary Law*, Manchester University Press, 1956, p. 192.

[29] Chanock, op.cit., p. 74.

[30] Ibid., p. 174.

which customary law officially was the law of the tribes, but in effect as much a result of the overall apartheid regime.[31]

Apart from the problem that the term has no specific meaning with the consequence that we do not know what we are talking about when talking about customary law, the term has an unfortunate connotation of tradition and habit. The term implicitly assumes the idea of law building on local habits and practices in contrast to Western or modern law that builds on legislation and court decisions, without realizing that habits are rarely clear-cut (and if they are, they are rarely disputed in court), but plastic, changeable and even contestable, that decisions from chiefs or various gatherings in the community may play a role in moulding the law and that power relations do play a role. Thus, the term 'customary' tends to depict a situation with a group living according to their unconscious habits with no disturbances from neither deliberate decisions for the well-being of the group, nor from the machinations of individuals and subgroups trying to shape the laws to their favour.

In conclusion the term 'customary law' is ambiguous, imprecise and overburdened and should therefore be avoided.

The problem, of course, is that the term is actually being used. The suggestion is therefore twofold: For scholarly use the meaning should be clarified, not just using 'customary law' as though it had a precise and obvious reference.[32]

As regards the use in normative texts, such as national acts and international conventions, one can of course regret the use. The 1991 ILO Convention no. 169 concerning Indigenous and Tribal Peoples in Independent Countries thus provides that "These peoples shall have the rights to *retain* their own customs and institutions" (art. 8, my italics), and "the methods customarily practised by the peoples ... dealing with offences committed by their members shall be respected" (art. 9), implying that new methods developed by the same people

[31] See the discussion in Ragnhild Muriaas, "Dilemmas Connected to Recognising Customary Law and Courts in South Africa" (present volume) with use of T.W. Bennett, *A Sourcebook of African Customary Law for Southern Africa*, Juta & Co., 1991, and Sandra B. Burman, "The Interaction of Legislation relating to Urban Africans and the Laws Regulating Family Relationships", in T.W. Bennett et al., *Urban Black Law*, Juta & Co., 1984.

[32] Ragnhild Muriaas may serve as a good example. In her contribution she has to deal with 'customary law' simply because it is an important and widely used concept in a South African context, but the term is analyzed, not just used as an unproblematic matter of fact.

are not protected. The solution to this unfortunate wording must be an updated interpretation, taking the purpose of the Convention into consideration, which is to support vulnerable people and not to exile them into living museums.

Other terms may be considered. When dealing with the issue in Ecuador and Columbia in this volume, Tina Saaresranta uses the term 'indigenous law' ("derecho indígena") which makes sense in a Latin American context. In Africa, however, the concept of being 'indigenous' is problematic and contested and applies only convincingly to peoples like the San, thus leaving out a lot of local/living law that by no definition is indigenous. Are Knudsen[33] uses the term 'traditional justice' when dealing with honour killings in Pakistan. If this is the conception of the participants who may claim that they act according to their traditions, the term is not inappropriate. The problem, however, is that 'tradition' is rather a matter of interpreting, legitimizing and even inventing more than a referral to historical facts. Often 'tradition' is used as an attempt to legitimize behaviour that may otherwise be judged immoral.[34] As with 'customary law', it is recommendable to clarify the meaning, not just applying it as if it had a distinct and unproblematic content.

THREE GENERATIONS OF LITERATURE

When dealing with African local/living law, one may distinguish between three generations of literature. I have no systematic knowledge of the literature dealing with local/living law in Asia and the Americas, but despite significant historical differences, in the internal development as well as colonial history, I believe that the three generation division may provide relevant points to any consideration of local/living law.

The first generation could be called the difference theory and the proponents the dichotomy lovers as they stress the systematic difference between (African) local/living law and Western or European law. The most well known

[33] Are Knudsen, "Traditional (In)justice. Honour Killings in Pakistan", (present volume).

[34] From my own experience in Zambia, I could mention the habit of 'property grabbing', a derogatory term referring to the appropriation of the deceased's property by his blood family, leaving nothing to the widow and children. Often the appropriators would justify their act by referring to tradition even though 1) tradition could not have dealt with the distribution of refrigerators, title deeds etc., and 2) no research supported the view that previously it was a habit to leave widows and children without any protection.

proponent is probably Henry Sumner Maine (not writing specifically on African law) who stresses the difference between status and contract, where "ancient" societies (such as his contemporary India and the Roman Empire) are built upon the preset status of persons whereas modern law is based on contracts and free agreements between individuals.[35]

The Danish author Karen Blixen, who was running a coffee farm in Kenya from 1913 to 1931 wrote: "The idea of justice of Europe and Africa are not the same and those of the one world are unbearable to the other,"[36] and narrates a story of two parents who claimed compensation from her as their daughter died while working on the farm. According to Blixen, the parents based their claim on compensation, whereas Blixen dismissed the claim as she had no guilt. In this way Blixen depicts the African/European dichotomy as two incompatible systems based on two incompatible principles, compensation and guilt.

Likewise, J.H. Driberg concludes his description of African law: "The conflict with our own ideas is fairly obvious: on the one side a system which is a living, sentient organism, part of the general cultural complex, based on a collectivistic society, depending on sanctions of its own which are not penal; on the other a penal code, which is not intrinsically one with the rest of our culture but can be arbitrarily imposed, and which is naturally individualistic in character."[37]

The dichotomy lovers may be neutral in their approach – there are insurmountable differences, but no system is superior to the other – but it is difficult. Even Blixen, who is fully aware that her sense of justice may seem as weird to the parents as their claim for compensation seems to her, compares the parents' incapacity to understand her innocence to the incapacity to understand the theory of relativity, thus implying that her own – European - conception of justice is as natural and unquestionable as Einstein's theory.[38]

---

[35] Maine, op.cit.

[36] Karen Blixen, *Out of Africa*, Penguin Books, 1954, p. 93. (1st ed. 1937).

[37] J.H. Driberg, "The African Conception of Law", *Journal of Comparative Legislation and International Law*, 1934, 3rd Series, vol. XVI, part II, p. 230 ff., citation from p. 245.

[38] Which of course it is not: By contemporary European standards Blixen would be liable, not because of guilt but because of the undertaking. She was the employer in whose interest the work was carried out.

In colonial times the general and common view was that of European superiority, the civilizing mission of European law and justice, but in more recent times one can observe a new or reversed type of the first generation literature, now praising the virtues of African indigenous law versus the alienating and morally inferior but unfortunately more powerful Western law. Thus, one author speaks of the pre-colonial times as "uniform, harmonious and consistent" [39] and deplores the status of African customary law as an endangered species,[40] and another describes the chiefs' courts as harmonious, mediating and enforcing familiar values without any problems and similarly regrets the whittling away of African indigenous legal systems.[41]
The fallacy of this first generation is of course not to try to point out differences, and there is nothing wrong in pointing out advantages of local/living law courts (accessible, cheap, known language, etc.),[42] on the contrary. The problem is that differences are dichotomized into two opposed set of systems or even values,[43] and secondly, in case of a more biased dichotomy, to glorify one set as superior, as if pre-colonial Africa was "the golden and good pre-colonial age of African innocence",[44] or Western law by nature superior to any other type. No society is completely harmonious, although certain groups may have an interest in depicting it as such, and it is probably not possible to put up a reasonable diagram listing the features of living/local law systems in one category and Western law in the other.

This is where *the second generation* comes in, with two major points: First, 'customary law' is an entity of law as good – or as bad – as any Western or

---

[39] Martin Okany, *The Role of Customary Courts in Nigeria*, Fourth Dimension Publishing Co., 1984, p. 145, quoted from Joseph Otteh, "African Customary Law", *Materialesamling fra Advokatseminar 1994*. Landsforeningen af Beskikkede Advokater og Det Danske Center for Menneskerettigheder, p. 86.

[40] Otteh, op.cit., p. 83.

[41] Carlson Anyangwe, "The Whittling Away of African Indigenous Legal and Judicial Systems", *Zambia Law Journal*, Special Edition, 1998, p. 46-67.

[42] Ibid.

[43] Rudolfo Stavenhagen, *Derecho Indígena y Derechos Humanos en América Latina*, México, Instituto Interamericano de Derechos Humanos, 1988, as refered by Mireya Peña, "Legal Pluralism as an Approach to Indigenous Peoples' Rights", present volume.

[44] Robert Thornton, "Chiefs. Power in a Political Wilderness", Donald I. Ray & P.S. Reddy (eds.), *Grassroots Governance? Chiefs in Africa and the Afro-Caribbean,* University of Calgary Press, 2003, p. 139, quoted from Ragnhild Muriaas, "Dilemmas connected to recognising customary law and courts in South Africa", (present volume).

European type, and second, that there are many similarities across the barrier and as many differences internally in each category.

The second generation includes many outstanding scholars with a production of monographs on the laws of a certain tribe, such as Max Gluckman's *The Judicial Process among the Barotse of Northern Rhodesia* [45] and Isaac Schapera's *A Handbook of Tswana Law and Custom*,[46] just to mention a few. It is based on more thorough research,[47] the main idea being that the various African customary law jurisdictions are as intricate and differentiated as any other legal system and that they differ like European jurisdictions differ.[48]
The Nigerian lawyer T.O. Elias deserves mentioning with his intricate knowledge of African as well as European law. His *The Nature of African Customary Law* is a well written and convincing rejection of the tenets of the first generation:[49]

Firstly, African customary law *is* law – in contrast to anthropologists as Evans-Pritchard[50] who depicted the Nuer as having no law at all. Evans-Pritchard thus belongs to a previously rather common subcategory of the first generation, holding that the norms of local tribes did not even amount to law. Apparently, the situation in Latin America as regards the indigenous peoples' normative systems belonged to that category up to around 1990.

---

[45] Max Gluckman, *The Judicial Process Among the Barotse of Northern Rhodesia*, Manchester University Press, 1955.

[46] Isaac Schapera, *A Handbook of Tswana Law and Custom,* Oxford University Press, 1955.

[47] It should be mentioned that Driberg actually calls for more research.

[48] Second generation authors are critical towards any rigid dichotomization and unfounded generalizations. Thus, in criminal law there is hardly any basis for pointing out sets of differences as suggested by Donna Lee Van Cott, "Legal Pluralism and Informal Community Justice Administration in Latin America", as quoted by Mireya Peña in the present volume. The "set of differences" allegedly lies in the fact that indigenous law criminalizes certain acts, and "Western" law criminalizes others. Read according to the second generation, these are no *sets* of differences, but mere differences, just as Danish law criminalizes fraud committed by an agent on his principal ("mandatsvig"), whereas British law does not, and German law criminalizes Holocaust denial, whereas Danish law does not. The categories of 'indigenous' and 'Western' do not seem to have convincing explanatory power.

[49] Elias, op.cit., Chapter 3 has the appropriate title: "Common Errors About Customary Law".

[50] E.E. Evans-Pritchard, *The Nuer. A Description of the Modes of Livelihood and Political Institutions of a Nilotic People,* Clarendon, 1960 (1st ed.1940).

Secondly, the dichotomies simply do not hold water when scrutinized more thoroughly. Thus, Elias critizices the status/contract dichotomy as forwarded by Maine and the above-mentioned Driberg by pointing out that status is also prevalent in European law, the status of citizenship and of minority being obvious examples.[51] The other way round status is not the only feature in various African 'customary' legal systems, as acquired status can be changed. Another, probably even more common dichotomy is the idea that Western or European law is individualistic, whereas customary law is collectivistic. In the same manner, Elias points out the dubious nature of this idea: Collective entities are very important in European law, the state and the company to mention the most important ones, whereas e.g. 'collective liability' according to customary law on closer examination turns out to be vicarious liability, the individual being the primary liable and the family or eventually the clan as only vicariously liable.[52]

In conclusion, the difference between the systems is therefore in degree and not in kind[53] and the main difference is rather between centralized societies on the one hand and acephalous societies on the other.

The third generation opposes the second with two major points: First, African customary law is not so much African as it is colonial, a product of the meeting between the colonial power and local norms, systems, interests and powers.[54] The writing down of the existing legal systems is therefore not something particularly African (let alone indigenous), but is a peculiar colonial product. Understood this way, local/living law is not specifically indigenous in the sense of original. Local/living law is a mix, as any other type of law. Second, those depicted legal systems are not really systems, they do not constitute a coherent jurisdiction, a corpus juris, but are much more loosely constructed as a rather incoherent bunch of norms, as a normative repertoire.[55]

Comaroff and Roberts, basing their thesis on research from Botswana, criticize Schapera and dismiss the idea of having a Handbook of Tswana Law and Custom. According to these authors a handbook mispresents the Tswana

---

[51] Elias, op.cit., p. 95.
[52] Elias, op.cit., Chapter 6: "Status and the Individual".
[53] Ibid., p. 33.
[54] Chanock, op.cit. This point has been further elaborated above.
[55] Comaroff & Roberts, op.cit.

norms that do not fit into a telephone directory kind of handbook, but are much more like a musician's repertoire from which s/he can choose an appropriate piece of music without any compelling reasons to do so. The repertoire consists of a continuum of norms from mere etiquette to more strict rules, and the norms are divergent with often two or more conflicting rules to cover the situation at hand. In other words, the idea of a system of rules is not very appropriate.

Besides, they are quite skeptical towards the idea that the customary law process is more reconciliatory and mediating in an often alleged contradiction to the Western court procedure which creates antagonism and designates a winner and a looser. Like everybody else Tswanas are interested in winning their case[56] and the processes going on before the actual court case (seen as mediatory attempts) are as much attempts to gather the necessary support.[57] As for the content of the law, the problem in conceiving local/living law as a body of law is the lack of accuracy in legal concepts and lack of a precise definition of facts forming the basis for legal consequences. As an example, according to Western law marriage implies certain legal consequences relating to property, maintenance, inheritance etc. with distinct differences to non-married persons. In Tswana law there seems to be a continuum from being engaged, living together and being married[58] with no precise criterion to determine whether one status or the other is preveailing, with the result that there is no certainty in legal positions. In this way the local/living law is more plastic than assumed by the second generation scholars and may be open to machinations, the outcome of a legal conflict depending more on bargaining powers than on the legal position.[59]

These features are not necessarily true for all other kinds of local/living law, but I believe it indicates a pertinent problem, namely that there is no easily identifiable 'prevailing law', and that attempts to identify and clarify the prevailing living/local law inevitably involve elements of decisions and of politics.

---

[56] Ibid., p. 130.

[57] Ibid., p. 111.

[58] "Bonyatsi, ba dula mmogo, nyalo", Comaroff & Roberts, op.cit., p. 134.

[59] See also Anne Griffiths, "Between Paradigms. Differing Perspectives on Justice in Molepolole, Botswana", *Journal of Legal Pluralism*, 1996, p. 195-214.

This is of course not to say that claims for recognizance are irrelevant or illegitimate. On the contrary, the legitimacy of local/living law does not lie in its purported originality, indigenousness or purity. The freedom and equality in dignity and rights, as stipulated in the Universal Declaration of Human Rights art. 1, is incompatible with a downright rejection of local/living law, perceived by the participants to be morally correct and binding. Neither a local set of norms nor the law of any nation state is a priori superior to any other set of norms. However, the authors of the third generation do indicate problems when the task is to operationalize and implement the living/local law.

GENERATIONS AND CHALLENGES

The three generations can be seen as an expanding field of knowledge. The Europeans, when confronted with "native law", at first conceived it to be totally different from their own, often even not worth the term law. However, as shown by e.g. Malinowski,[60] this was simply not true. Also societies that the Europeans regarded as "savage" had norms much on equal terms with the Europeans. This acknowledgement resulted in profound studies of the normative systems of other civilizations, inferring that the structure was similar, only the content somewhat different. However, this understanding was not unproblematic, and new research showed that the concept of a local/living corpus juris was highly doubtful and that the local/living law was neither fully local as it was generated by the meeting of local and colonial powers, nor fully living. The writing down by anthropologists and court decisions used as precedents, tended to petrify the law, creating an ever increasing gap between the living and the law.

However, the 'expansion of knowledge' conception is not the only relevant perspective. It may be rather a question of need. Thus, the first generation can be seen as the scientists of the conquering power, in need of understanding the local norms as well as legitimizing their conquest. Admitting that local law was as a relevant/consistent/well developed/reflecting justice as their own, simply did not fit with the tenets of colonialism. In the same manner, the reversed first generation, the one lamenting the withering away of customary law as the disappearing of a harmonious, paradise-like society has the purpose

[60] Bronislaw Malinowski, *Crime and Custom in Savage Society*, Routledge and Kegan Paul, 1961 (7th impr.). Belonging to the second generation, but not writing from Africa.

of defending local/living law. However noble this project may be, the strategy is not convincing. The only way of surviving is adaptation to the present conditions, not clinging to good old times that were never there anyway.

The second generation can be seen as the scholars of the colonial administrators. Not that they sided with the patriarchal ideology of colonialism, but there was a need of profound knowledge of local/living law, a practical need in a situation where divergent legal systems must cooperate.

The third generation were the scholars of the post-colonial period, with little political influence. The leaders of the independent states focused on modernization and normally did not care much about local/living law, unless of course it could be used in the power struggle.[61] Thus, the third generation authors have had less practical impact, although their points are of great practical value.

What is needed now, is a new generation to ask questions like: How is local/living law able to improve people's lives, in which ways is local/living law supporting human rights, civil and political as well as social, economic and cultural, and where do discrepancies exist between local/living law and human rights and how can those problems be solved?

This should not be an approach that rejects living/local law as traditional or in any other way as an obstacle to development,[62] nor supporting a deification of living/local law as the golden age. What is needed is: 1) research with an understanding of the positive and negative aspects of these norms (not that these are defined or definable beforehand, but this does not entail that the distinction is defunct); and 2) research that in itself suggests or at least allows for suggestions possible for the improvement of the lives of the people who live with living/local law, and who are at the same time very often among the poor people on the earth, living in developing societies.

---

[61] In Malawi the late president Banda used the "traditional courts" to deal with political opponents, as these courts did not entertain legal principles such as due process of law, nulla poena sine lege, in dubio pro reo, etc.

[62] See also Bonny Ibwawoh, "Cultural Tradition and National Human Rights Standards in Conflict", Kirsten Hastrup (ed.), *Legal Cultures and Human Rights. The Challenge of Diversity*, Kluwer Law International, p. 85-102.

As the field of human rights illustrates, no society is an island, and all societies have connections and ties with other, sometimes quite different societies. This is true for nation states as well as sub-state communities, and as a matter of fact even for regional and global communities. And it is bound to create challenges. When people – individuals as well as peoples - interact, there is an inherent need for common norms, not uniformity, but at least *some* common ground. In this way, human rights can be seen as an answer to globalization: Which norms could serve as our common norms, as a way of common normative communication? Such indispensable common norms are not self-evident, as the philosophers of the enlightenment believed, and they are not natural. They are human, and humans are bound to err, and there is no other way to develop common norms than trial and error. The process of creating global common norms will cause frictions at all levels, human rights vis-à-vis nation state law as well as local/living law.

Thus, human rights constitute a challenge for local communities to enter the global scene. No society is perfect and all can be improved. Human rights are also about that improvement. But the challenge is twofold (at least), as local communities pose a challenge to human rights. All societies have ways of doing things and ways of solving problems. Those kinds of solutions should be brought to the global scene for others to profit from. As part of this process, research and dissemination of information is necessary, research not only on 'human rights' or 'local/living law', but also on the relations and frictions between the levels (as contributions in this volume show). And it is vital that the information process is also a two way communication, information on human rights at the local level *and* information on local problems and solutions at the global level.

BIBLIOGRAPHY

Addo, Michael (ed.): Human Rights Standards and the Responsibility of Transnational Corporations, Kluwer Law International, 1999.

Afronet, *Local Court Study*, Lusaka, 1999, p. 12.

Alfredsson, Gudmundur & Asbjørn Eide (eds.): *The Universal* Declaration *of Human Rights. A Common Standard of Achievement*, Martinus Nijhoff Publishers, 1999.

Anyangwe, Carlson: "The Whittling Away of African Indigenous Legal and Judicial Systems", *Zambia Law Journal*, Special Edition, 1998, p. 46-67.

Arnfred, Signe: "Polygami og brudepris i Mocambique" [Polygamy and bride price in Mozambique], *Den Ny Verden*, 1997, vol. 30, p. 35-55.

Bennett, T.W.: A Sourcebook of African Customary Law for Southern Africa, Juta & Co., 1991.

Bentzon, Agnete Weis: "Den hvide jurists byrde" [White Lawyer's Burden], Peter Blume, Kirsten Ketscher og Steen Rønsholdt (eds.), *Liv, arbejde og forvaltning. Til Ole Krarup på 60 års dagen*, GadJura, 1995, p. 357-376.

Bentzon, Agnete Weis: "Afrikanske sædvaner i historisk perspektiv" [African customs in a historical perspective], *Den Ny Verden*, 1997, vol. 30, p. 13-34.

Blixen, Karen: *Out of Africa*, Penguin Books, 1954, p. 93. (1st ed. 1937).

Boserup, Ester: *Woman's Role in Economic Development*, George Allen and Unwin, 1970.

Burman, Sandra B.: "The Interaction of Legislation relating to Urban Africans and the Laws Regulating Family Relationships", T.W. Bennett et al., *Urban Black Law*, Juta & Co., 1984.

Chanock, Martin: Law, Custom and Social Order. The Colonial Experience in Malawi and Zambia, Cambridge University Press, 1985.

Comaroff, John L. & Simon Roberts: Rules and Processes. The Cultural Logic of Dispute in an African Context, University of Chicago Press, 1981.

Dembour, Marie-Bénédicte: "Human Rights Talk and Anthropological Ambivalence. The Particular Context of Universal Claims", Olivia Harris (ed.), *Inside and Outside the Law,* Routledge, 1996.

Driberg, J.H.: "The African Conception of Law", *Journal of Comparative Legislation and International Law*, 1934, 3rd Series, vol. XVI, part II, p. 230 ff.

Ehrlich, Eugen: Grundlegung der Soziologie des Rechts, München, 1913

Eide, Asbjørn: "The Non-Inclusion of Minority Rights. Resolution 217C (III)", Gudmundur Alfredsson & Asbjørn Eide (eds.), *The Universal Declaration of Human Rights. A Common Standard of Achievement*, Martinus Nijhoff Publishers, 1999.

Elias, T. Olawale: *The Nature of African Customary Law*, Manchester University Press, 1956.

Evans-Pritchard, E.E.: The Nuer. A Description of the Modes of Livelihood and Political Institutions of a Nilotic People, Clarendon, 1960 (1st ed.1940).

Forsythe, David: *Human Rights in International Relations*, Cambridge University Press, 2000.

Gluckman, Max: The Judicial Process Among the Barotse of Northern Rhodesia, Manchester University Press, 1955.

Griffiths, Anne: "Between Paradigms. Differing Perspectives on Justice in Molepolole, Botswana", *Journal of Legal Pluralism*, 1996, p. 195-214.

Griffiths, John: "What Is Legal Pluralism?", *Journal of Legal Pluralism*, 1986, vol. 24, p. 1-55.

Hatchard, John & Muna Ndulo: *Readings in Criminal Law and Criminology in Zambia*, Multimedia Publications, Lusaka and James Currey, London, 1994.

Hobsbawm, Eric and Terence Ranger (eds.): *The Invention of Tradition*, Cambridge University Press, 2002.

Ibwawoh, Bonny: "Cultural Tradition and National Human Rights Standards in Conflict", Kirsten Hastrup (ed.), *Legal Cultures and Human Rights. The Challenge of Diversity*, Kluwer Law International, p. 85-102.

Knudsen, Are: "Traditional (In)justice. Honour Killings in Pakistan", (present volume).

Lindholt, Lone: Questioning the Universality of Human Rights, Ashgate, 1997.

Maine, Henry Sumner: *Ancient Law*, 1861.

Malanczuk, Peter: Akehurst's Modern Introduction to International Law, 7th ed., Routledge, 1997.

Malinowski, Bronislaw: *Crime and Custom in Savage Society*, Routledge and Kegan Paul, 1961 (7th impr.).

Muriaas, Ragnhild: "Dilemmas Connected to Recognising Customary Law and Courts in South Africa" (present volume).

Okany, Martin: *The Role of Customary Courts in Nigeria*, Fourth Dimension Publishing Co., 1984.

Otteh, Joseph: "African Customary Law", *Materialesamling fra Advokatseminar 1994*. Landsforeningen af Beskikkede Advokater og Det Danske Center for Menneskerettigheder.

Pound, Roscoe: "Law in Books and Law in Action", *American Law Review*, 1910, vol. 44, p. 12-36.

Rawls, John: *Political Liberalism*, Columbia University Press, 1993.

Schapera, Isaac: *A Handbook of Tswana Law and Custom,* Oxford University Press, 1955.

Schaumburg-Müller, Sten: "Pursuing Theory in Law on Loose Ground", *Retfærd*, 2002, no. 99, p. 33-51.

Stener Ekern, "Visions of the Right Order. Contrasts between Mayan Communitarian Law in Guatemala and International Human Rights Law", (present volume).

Thornton, Robert: "Chiefs. Power in a Political Wilderness", Donald I. Ray & P.S. Reddy (eds.), *Grassroots Governance? Chiefs in Africa and the Afro-Caribbean,* University of Calgary Press, 2003, p. 139.

Legal Pluralism as an Approach to Indigenous and Tribal Peoples' Rights*

*By Mireya Maritza Peña Guzmán***

* This article is dedicated to Natalia, my younger sister and best friend, who contributed with ideas, criticism and research to this article...She, my immortal, passed away on December 21, 2003 when I was working on a revised version of this article.

** The author wants to express her sincere and deep gratitude to Professor Martin Scheinin, director of the Human Rights Institute at the Åbo Akademi University (Finland), the architect of the idea to write in English on this topic. The author would also like to thank Dr. Sten Schaumburg-Müller from Aarhus University, (Denmark), Dr. Lone Lindholt from the Danish Institute for Human Rights and Professor Roy Balleste, Associate Law Library Director at Nova Southeastern University in Fort-Lauderdale, Florida (United States) for their insightful comments and editorial suggestions on the first drafts of this article. An earlier version of this paper was presented in a thematic working group within the framework of the 2003 Advance Course on the International Protection of Human Rights at the Institute for Human Rights at the Åbo Akademi University in Turku/Åbo, Finland. The author wants to thank Angelika Kartush (Austria), Daiva Stepaniene (Lithuania), Diana Kovatcheva (Bulgaria), Liisa Valjento (Finland) and Sabelo Gumedze (Swaziland), whose questions and comments helped her to clarify some aspects of the topic.

> Where, after all universal human rights begin?
> In small places close to home-so close and so small
> that they cannot be seen on any map of the world.
> *Eleanor Roosevelt*

One of the cornerstone features of contemporary law is the recognition of indigenous peoples as new and special subjects of concern at international, regional and domestic legal levels. International concern about indigenous peoples formally began within the United Nations Organization in the 70s; since then, the UNO has exerted an important influence over regional and domestic developments in this matter.

Regional concern about indigenous peoples formally began in Africa in the 80s and in Europe and the Americas in the 90s. Within the African context, the adoption of the African Charter on Human and Peoples' Rights (Banjul Charter) by the member States of the Organization of the African Unity (currently the African Union) on June 27, 1981 constitutes a major breakthrough in the recognition of the rights of peoples, including tribal peoples.[1] Within the European context, the Council of Europe does not account yet neither on legal instruments nor on formal policies dealing specifically with indigenous peoples. In contrast, the European Union concern on this matter began in the late 90s. Within the framework of the European Community's development cooperation, the European Commission on May 11th, 1998 tabled a Working Document supporting indigenous peoples, which accounted on their direct involvement. The adoption of a EU Council resolution on November 30th, 1998 providing the main guidelines for supporting indigenous peoples follows this EU initiative. [2] Within the

[1] See for example article 21.5, which affirms that "States parties to the [...]Charter shall undertake to eliminate all forms of foreign economic exploitation particularly that practiced by international monopolies so as to enable their peoples to fully benefit from the advantages derived from their national resources". [the underline is mine] In provision, the use of the term peoples is clearly not assimilated to that of States and within the African context has to be understood as including tribal peoples. 'The African Charter on Human and Peoples' Rights is available in OAU Doc.CAB/LEG/67/3 rev. 5, at: http://www.africa-union.org/Official_documents/Treaties_%20 Conventions_%20Protocols/Banjul%20Charter.pdf

[2] A summary of recent European developments including the European policy on indigenous peoples is available at: http://193.194.138.190/html/racism/minorpam14.doc, and a synthesis of the Developments of the European Union on indigenous peoples within the

Americas' context, the Organization of American States has, in turn, taking some steps to the formal recognition of Indigenous peoples within the interamerican system of human rights protection. In this sense, the Inter-American Commission on Human Rights approved a "Proposed American Declaration on the Rights of Indigenous Peoples" in February 1997. It is clearly inspired by the UN Draft Declaration on Indigenous Peoples and if adopted, it will be the first regional legal instrument dealing specifically with indigenous peoples. [3]

At the domestic level, concern about indigenous peoples is reflected in a wide range of constitutional changes and/or amendments recognizing the rights of indigenous individuals and groups in different countries around the globe. The Latin American countries are among the best examples of this trend that began in the 1970s with Equador (Constitutional change in 1978) in the vanguard. In the last two decades constitutional changes and or amendments have taken place in, *inter alia*, Guatemala (1985), Nicaragua (1987 and 1995), Brazil (1988), Colombia (1991), Paraguay (1992), Peru (1993), Bolivia and Argentina (1994), and Venezuela (1999). In the present decade the 1917 constitution of Mexico and the 1992 Constitution of Paraguay were amended in 2000 and 2001 respectively in favour of the protection of the indigenous individuals, groups and peoples. [4]

The Nordic region has also been active. Despite the fact that the current Swedish Constitution does not mention explicitly the Sami people, [5] it recognizes in Chapter 1 article 2(4) the rights of *"ethnic, linguistic and religious minorities to preserve and develop a cultural and social life of their*

framework of the policy on Human Rights and Democratization is available at: http://europa.eu.int/comm/external_relations/human_rights/ip/index.htm

[3] A working document comparing the original draft with the proposals by the States, indigenous representatives, and the Chair of the Working Group to prepare the Draft American Declaration on the Rights of Indigenous peoples (OAS, Doc GT/DADIN/doc.53/02) is available at: www.oas.org/consejo/CAJP/docs/cp09193e11.doc. Other significant continental policy-making activities in this field may be found at:
http://www.summit-americas.org/Quebec-Indigenous/indigenous-archives-eng.htm.

[4] The Latin American constitutions are available at Georgetown university's web site http://www.georgestown.edu> in the official language of the respective countries.

[5] The Sami peoples, commonly known as Lapps in English and Lapons in French, are indigenous peoples that inhabit Fennoscandia (Finland, Sweden and Norway) and the Kola Peninsula in Russia.In 1992 it was estimated that the total population of Sami was between 60.000 and 100.000 individuals, with 70.000 being the most accurate figure. See: Elina Helander, Les Sami de Norvège [The Sami of Norway], Ministry of Foreign Affairs the Information document UDA309FRA.

own."[6] The *Storting* passed an amendment to the Norwegian Constitution - article 110a - in April 1988, to recognize explicitly the rights of the Sami people,[7] and the 2000 Finnish Constitution expressly mentions the Sami as an indigenous people holder of rights in section 17(3).[8] This trend is also reflected, *inter alia,* in the constitution of the Russian Federation as approved by the National Referendum of December 12th, 1993,[9] the Constitution Act, 1982 of Canada,[10] the Constitution of Indonesia,[11] and the Constitutional acts of New Zealand.[12] Concerning the recognition of tribal peoples, we can mention, *inter alia,* article 81.3 of the 1963 Kenyan Constitution as amended in 1999, articles 3, 4, 8, 10, 39, 40, 43 and 86 of the 1994 Ethiopian Constitution, article 35.5 of the 1992 Constitution of the Republic of Ghana, and some of the African

---

[6] The Swedish constitution is available in English at: http://www.uni-wuerzburg.de/law/sw00c___.doc?

[7] The Constitution of the Kingdom of Norway provides in article 110a: *"It is the responsibility of the authorities of the State to create conditions enabling the Sami people to preserve and develop its language, culture and way of life."* The Norwegian constitution is available in English at: http://odin.dep.no/odin/engelsk/norway/system/032005-990424/.

[8] Section 17 (3) of the Constitution of Finland states: *"[t]he Sami, as an indigenous people, as well as the Roma and other groups, have the right to maintain and develop their own language and culture. Provisions on the right of the Sami to use the Sami language before the authorities are laid down by an Act. The rights of persons using sign language and of persons in need of interpretation or translation aid owing to disability shall be guaranteed by an Act."* The Finish Constitution is available in English at: http://www.uni-wuerzburg.de/law/fi00c___.doc?

[9] The Constitution of the Russian Federation as approved by the National Referendum of December 12th, 1993 establishes in article 69 that *"the Russian Federation guarantees the rights of small indigenous peoples in accordance with the generally accepted principles and standards of international law and international treaties of the Russian Federation".* The Constitution of the Russian Federation ratified on December 12th, 1993 is available in English at: http://www.departments.bucknell.edu/russian/const/constit.html.

[10] The Canadian constitution Act, 1982, explicitly recognized in article 35.1 *"the existing aboriginal and treaty rights of the aboriginal peoples of Canada"* and in article 35.2 it specifies that the expression "aboriginal peoples of Canada" includes the Indian, Inuit and Métis peoples of Canada. The Canadian Constitution Act, 1982 is available at: http://www.solon.org/Constitutions/Canada/English/ca_1982.html#1

[11] The 1945 Constitution of the Republic of Indonesia mentions in article 32 that *"[t]he old and indigenous cultures which were the peak of cultural life in all the regions of Indonesia, together form the national culture..."* The 1945 Constitution of the Republic of Indonesia is available at: http://inic.utexas.edu/asnic/countries/indonesia/ConstIndonesia.html

[12] The Constitution Act, 1986 is the principal formal legal document of the Constitution of New Zealand. However, the Constitution consists of a number of formal legal documents, named conventions (decisions of the courts and customary law and some written documents) Thus, the Treaty of Waitangi signed by English residents and Maori Chiefs in 1840 is regarded as a founding document of the government in New Zealand. See: http://www.archives.govt.nz/holdings/treaty_frame.html

constitutions which have recognized the African Charter of Human and Peoples rights

The recognition of indigenous peoples in a legal context is a demanding challenge for the domestic legal regimes of ethnically diverse societies. International indigenous peoples' rights include both individual and collective rights and must be applied in the domestic context respecting indigenous peoples' cultural distinctiveness. The question at stake is, therefore, how to accommodate cultural differences within the State?

The states' answers to this question have varied in a historical perspective. Cultural differences were traditionally accommodated within policies of tolerance[13] and non-discrimination.[14] These two policies were combined in the 70s in the models of 'consociational democracy'[15] and 'control'[16] that were developed to deal with conflicting ethnic demands in pluralist societies.[17] The recent international rejection of cultural assimilation motivated the development of multiculturalism as a policy involving measures of promotion

[13] The liberal policy of tolerance implies that minority communities can freely develop themselves and act as they wish without being punished, as long as they do not interfere with the majority culture. See: Yvonne M. Sonders, *Towards a Right to Cultural Identity*, School of Human rights Research Series, Volume 15, Maastricht, 2002.

[14] Under non-discrimination policies, individual freedom is founded upon the principle of universal equality subject to specific hegemonic cultural values. Accordingly, cultural identities should neither be supported nor penalized by public policy but should instead be left to the private sphere. Will Kymlicka (ed.) *The Rights of Minority Cultures*, Oxford University Press, 1996, at page 9.

[15] The term "consociational democracy" was first introduced by Arend Lijphard and denotes a model of democracy that seeks to resolve political differences through consensus rather than majority rule. It is characterized by the ability of leaders of competing subcultures within a pluralistic society to avoid dangers of inter-groups conflict through a continual striving for both the cooperation among the respective subcultures and a degree of commitment to the unity of the country. See: Arend Lijphart, *Democracy in Plural Societies. A comparative Exploration,* London, 1977, at page 53 and "Typologies of Democratic Systems" in *Comparative Political Studies 1*, April 1968, pages 3-44.

[16] The 'control' model was first presented by Ian Lustick to be applied in situations where a majority dominates and reduces any other segment of the national population to a position of subordination. It was developed to explain political stability in "deeply divided" societies lacking of the conditions of consociationalism. See: Ian Lustick, "Stability in Deeply Divided Societies: Consociationalism versus Control", in *World Politics,* No.31, 325-344, at page 325.

[17] See: Lennard Sillanpää, *Political and Administrative responses to Sami Self-determination. A comparative Study of Public Administration in Fennoscandia on the Issue of Sami Land Title as an aboriginal Right,* Societas Scientiarum Fennica [The Finish Society of Sciences and Letters], 1994, at pages 4-7.

and protection of ethno-cultural identity.[18] The key issue in this context is how to enjoy the benefits of both multiculturalism and international human rights, and subsequently, how to implement this at the domestic level.

"Legal Pluralism" [19] is one of the phenomena associated with the accommodation of indigenous peoples within domestic legal systems through policies of multiculturalism. It is rooted in "legal monism" as a contingent reality, which characterized the creation of modern states between the 16th and the 19th centuries.

Thus, legal pluralism emerged as an approach that recognizes domestic legal systems are influenced by a plurality of "infra" and "supra" systems that frequently overlap.[20] In this context, "infra-legal systems" are to be understood as a set of rules created by local communities and/or tribal or indigenous groups, which is intended to be applicable within those communities or groups as being the legal rules. The expression "supra legal systems" is, in turn, to be understood as the body of rules adopted by the international community, which is intended to be applicable to the States.

In its earliest version, legal pluralism holds that there are innumerable autonomic sources of Law as well as centres generating rules of Law, which compete *de facto* with the State for the production, implementation, and application of legal rules.[21] The Sociologists of Law used legal pluralism as a hypothesis explicative of the domestic legal systems' dynamism by admitting

---

[18] Kymlicka, 1996, *op. cit.,* at pages 9-10; See also: Nathan Glazer, "Individual Rights against Group Rights", in Kymlicka, 1996, *op. cit.*, pp 123-138, at page 133 and Michael Walzer, "Pluralism: A Political Perspective", in Kymlicka , 1996, *op. cit.*, pp. 139-154 pp, at pages 148-151.

[19] Legal pluralism has been used as a valid approach to a variety of social and legal phenomena. Accordingly, legal pluralism has found support in academic contributions mainly stemming from anthropological, sociological and legal studies. Two comprehensive studies reviewing the literature on legal pluralism are: Merry S.E. "Legal Pluralism", *Law and Society Review 22:* 869-96 and Woodman G.R., "The Idea of legal pluralism", *Legal Pluralism in the Arab World* (Chapter 1), Kluwer Law International, 1999: 3-19.

[20] From a systemic point of view I differ from the conception of professor Jean-André Arnaud, who considers that legal pluralism is characterized only by the presence of infra-legal systems within the domestic legal system. See: Jean-André Arnaud, *Introduction à l'Analyse Sociologique des Systèmes Juridiques* [Introduction to the Legal Systems' Sociological Analysis], Bruyllant, Brussels, 1998, at page 297.

[21] See: Georges Gurvitch, L'Expérience Juridique et la Philosophie Ppluraliste du Droit [The Legal Experience and the Pluralistic Philosophy of Law] Paris, 1935.

the existence of concurrent legal systems of different levels (domestic, supra-domestic and infra-domestic) within the same geopolitical space.[22] Through the years the notion of legal pluralism has been associated with the existence of plural normative orders within modern western societies in particular[23] and nowadays, it connotes the simultaneous existence of distinct normative systems within a single geopolitical space.[24]

From a theoretical point of view, critics could suggest that "legal pluralism" is a faulty analytical concept. As described by Chris Fuller, the coexistence of plural legal or normative orders is a universal fact of the modern world. The concept of legal pluralism points to nothing distinctive since from every perspective it only highlights that homogenous societies do not exist. In addition, legal pluralism as a legal concept may merely serve "to reproduce the law-centred misconstructions" which have been strongly criticized.[25] This assumption may itself, however, be misleading. Whereas legal pluralism as a theory may justifiably be open to criticism, as a living concept legal pluralism highlights a way to accommodate a plurality of legal orders within a single geopolitical space, as I shall discuss further in this article.

From a pragmatic point of view, critics could also suggest that legal pluralism is currently only apparent since decision-makers have a tendency to protect domestic legal systems' monopoly on normative production and application of law. They might also argue that the final decision on the relationship between international law and domestic law[26] is always taken at the domestic level usually through the constitution, i.e. the so-called *bloc de constitutionnalité*.[27] Experience, however, denies this interpretation.

---

[22] See: Jean, Carbonnier, *Sociologie Juridique* [Sociology of Law], PUF, 1978.

[23] Chris Fuller, "Legal Anthropology, Legal Pluralism and Legal Though" in *Anthropology Today*, Vol.10, No.3, June 1994, pages 9-12, at page 10.

[24] Donna Lee Van Cott, "A political Analysis of Legal Pluralism in Bolivia and Colombia", *Journal of Latin American Studies,* No. 32, Cambridge University Press, 2000, pp 207-234, at page 209.

[25] *Ibidem*

[26] The most common theoretical approaches to the relationship between international law and domestic law are the so-called dualism and monism.

[27] The doctrinal expression *bloc de constitutionnalité* [bloc of constitutionality] was created for pedagogical purposes in the 70s. It means that the constitution is not limited to the articles it enumerates including the different international instruments mentioned in its preamble, as it operates in France, or, in one of its articles as it operates in most of the Latin American constitutions.

The internationalisation of issues traditionally considered as domestic affairs illustrates that international law brings an important influence on domestic legal systems. Nowadays, international human rights law imposes positive States' obligations for the implementation of individuals' protection, which is no longer considered to be an internal affair insulated from external influence. International concern about indigenous individuals and groups has exerted a notable influence on domestic legal regimes, as inferred from the constitutional and/or legislative recognition of indigenous peoples and their rights in different countries around the globe.

The same argument may be advanced with regard to communal, informal and indigenous approaches to justice.[28] Their validity stems from local and social values having great authority within communities.[29] These mechanisms have shown to be more efficacious than some of the state mechanisms because of their flexibility and dynamism. The *Rondas Campesinas*[30] in Peru and the indigenous judicial authorities in some indigenous communities [31] are exemplary on the influence that "infra-domestic legal system" may bring to State law.

---

[28] Communal and indigenous mechanisms of justice are said to be "alternative mechanisms of justice", because they stem from the communities to satisfy their necessity of local justice and then, they are usually disregarded, or legally ignored by the state. See: André-Jean Arnaud, *Dictionnaire encyclopédique de théorie et de sociologie du droit* [Encyclopaedic Dictionnary of Legal Theory and Sociology], second edition, LGDJ, Paris, 1993.

[29] Rachel Sieder, "Customary Law and Local Power in Guatemala" in Rachel Sieder (ed.), *Guatemala After the Peace Accords*, Institute of Latin American Studies, London, pp.97-115 quoted by Donna Lee Van Cott, *op.cit.*, 2003, at page 25.

[30] The *Rondas Campesinas* were formed in Peru as a communal reaction to the theft of livestock. They began to function in 1976 as a form of private collective security system. The Peruvian army used the Rondas Campesinas as a model to organize country men in the 1980s and, they were finally legalized in 1986 by the Law No.24571 promulgated by the Peruvian ex-president Alan García. See: Orin Starn, *Con los llanques todo barro: reflexiones sobre rondas campesinas, protesta rural y nuevos movimientos sociales* [Reflexions on *the Rondas Campesinas*, rural protest and new social movements], Lima, Peru, 1991.

[31] Fernando García Serrano found in the 1990s that the indigenous systems of justice administration had completely replaced the state legal system in some of the Quichua communities of Equator. See: Fernando García Serrano, "Formas Indígenas de Administración de Justicia: Tres estudios de caso de la Nacionalidad quichua de la sierra y amazonía ecuatoriana" [Indigenous Forms of Justice Administration: Three study- cases on the Quichua nationality of the Sierra and the Equatorian Amazon.], in García Fernando et al. *De la Exclusion a la Participación: Pueblos Indigenas y sus Derechos Colectivos en el Ecuador* [From Exclusion to Participation: Indigenous Peoples and their Collective Rights in Equator], Quito, 2000, pp. 71-104.

I shall argue that the implementation of legal pluralism illustrates a way to accommodate indigenous peoples aspirations about law within States, thereby effecting interaction between international human rights law and indigenous peoples' law. **Part II** presents a theoretical background of the topic by providing an approach to the concept of indigenous peoples and their core claims. **Part III** introduces the conflicting claims involving indigenous peoples and State and non-state actors at both the domestic and the international levels. **Part IV** examines past trends in decisions in respect of indigenous peoples. **Part V** highlights some emerging trends in the Americas in the context of legal pluralism. **Part VI** illustrates legal pluralism in practice through the presentation of the implementation of the legal recognition of indigenous judicial authorities within the Colombian legal system. Finally, **Part VII** presents a general appraisal of the topic and some recommendations in the quest for protecting indigenous peoples rights, in particular their right to legal autonomy.

II. IDENTIFYING INDIGENOUS PEOPLES AND THEIR CLAIMS

There is no formal and universal definition of indigenous peoples. Nevertheless, they have been identified taking into consideration a number of criteria. The permanence of their claims in the legal scenario has permitted several authors to identify core claims that include the recognition of indigenous peoples' legal systems as part of their demand for autonomy and self-determination. I shall first present the main criteria used to identify indigenous peoples and then, I shall refer to the *problematique* that is inherent to the recognition of indigenous peoples' law and legal systems.

Global Criteria to Identify Indigenous Peoples

Despite the lack of formal definition, indigenous peoples have been identified according to criteria developed within the framework of the UN System. The most widespread approaches are those proposed first in the so-called *Martínez Cobo Report,* secondly by Mrs. Erica-Irene Daes for the UN Working Group on Indigenous populations and, thirdly in the Convention concerning Indigenous and Tribal Peoples in independent countries (No.169) adopted by the International Labour Organization (ILO) in 1989.[32] The Study of the Problem of Discrimination against Indigenous Populations presented to the UN Sub-Commission on the Prevention of Discrimination of Minorities by the Special Rapporteur José Martínez Cobo in 1986, frames the concept of indigenous peoples in the context of colonization. It takes into consideration some elements already introduced by the Convention on Tribal and Indigenous populations in independent countries (No.107) adopted by the ILO in 1957. According to the Martínez Cobo Report :

> indigenous communities, peoples and nations are those which, having a historical continuity with pre-invasion and pre-colonial societies that developed on their territories, consider themselves distinct from other sectors of the societies now prevailing in those territories, or parts of them. They form at present non-dominant sectors of society and are determined to preserve, develop and transmit to future generations their ancestral territories, and their ethnic identity, as the basis of their continued existence as peoples, in accordance with their own cultural patterns, social institutions and legal systems.

This definition highlights that historical continuity, self-identification, non-dominance at present[33] and continued existence are the main features of indigenous communities, peoples and nations.[34] Evaluating this approach, Mrs. Erica-Irene A. Daes[35] suggested some additional elements to be considered when defining indigenous peoples. These elements are indigenous peoples' special relation with their ancestral lands and voluntary cultural distinctiveness.[36] However, the most widely used criteria in the Working

---

[32] The complete text of the ILO convention 169/1989 is available in English at: http://www.ilo.org/ilolex/cgi-lex/convde.pl?C169.

[33] The element of "non-dominance at present" is to be understood as the fact that indigenous groups have been placed, even if only formally, under a State's structure which incorporates national, social and cultural characteristics alien to theirs. [Erica-Irene Daes, *Interview*, Miami, FL (USA), September, 2002] It does not imply that "if as a result of measures taken for the full realization of the indigenous group rights, it becomes no longer non-dominant, the group ceases to be "indigenous" but that "some form of discrimination or marginalization exits" and therefore, it justifies, the action by the international community. See: Erica-Irene Daes, UN. Doc. E/CN.4/Sub.2/AC.4/1996/2, at par. 26.

[34] See: José Martínez Cobo (Special Rapporteur), "Study of the Problem of Discrimination against Indigenous Populations" presented to the UN Sub-Commission on the Prevention of Discrimination of Minorities, 1986, in *UN Doc. E/CN.4/Sub.2/1986/7/Add.4*, United Nations Publication, Sales No.E.86.XIV.3, at par.379.

[35] Mrs. Erica-Irene A. Daes was the founding Chairperson and Special Rapporteur of the United Nations Working Group on Indigenous Populations for almost two decades (1984-2002).

[36] Erica-Irene Daes, UN. Doc. E/CN.4/Sub.2/AC.4/1996/2, at par. 26.

Group on Indigenous Populations' practice were indigenous peoples' historical continuity, cultural distinctiveness and non-dominance at present. [37]

The most recent approach to the notion of indigenous peoples is that proposed in ILO Convention 169. It distinguishes between tribal and indigenous peoples in an attempt to ameliorate international protection problems encountered by some black communities in Latin America as well as by some African and Asian tribal and indigenous groups whose governments do not recognise them as such. The ILO Convention 169 mentions different objective criteria and a common subjective criterion to identify tribal and indigenous peoples. Indigenous Peoples may be identified as those groups who are regarded as such "on account of their descent from the populations which inhabited the country, or a geographical region to which the country belongs, at the time of conquest or colonization or the establishment of present State boundaries and who, irrespective of their legal status, retain some or all of their own social, economic, cultural and political institutions". [38] The objective criteria that identify tribal peoples are social, cultural and economic distinctiveness and a particular status determined by their own customs or traditions or by special laws or regulations. Self-identification is considered a subjective criterion crucial for determining both tribal and indigenous peoples.

The Core of Indigenous Peoples Claims

Despite the lack of a formal clear-cut internationally agreed definition of indigenous peoples, they and their representatives and organizations have asserted a set of defined claims to States and more recently to the international community.[39] They may be considered "classic indigenous peoples' claims", because of their recurring nature as demands in the legal scenario. These are also the principal themes that recur in the many and various types of indigenous movements. As pointed out by Rodolfo Stavenhagen, they may be grouped in five main categories: the definition and legal status of the category "indigenous"; land rights and agrarian aspects; the cultural identity of

[37] Erica-Irene Daes, *Interview*, Miami, FL (USA), September, 2002

[38] ILO Convention No.169, article 1.1 (a).

[39] The expression « international community » is very controversial given its abstract and ambiguous character. For a definition, see: Patrick James Flood, *The Effectiveness of UN Human Rights Institutions"*, Praeger Publishers, 1998, 168p. at page 3.

indigenous peoples; their social organization and juridical recognition of their customs, and the participation of their organizations in politics.[40]

The first category of indigenous peoples claims is the legal (and more recently, constitutional) recognition of the indigenous existence and entitlement to be holders of subjective rights, such as individual international human rights and collective international peoples' rights. The second claim is the right of indigenous peoples to freely dispose of the economic and cultural resources required for their social development and economical growth. This claim includes the preservation, recovery and enlargement of their ancestral lands, profit sharing of the economic exploitation of natural resources and the preservation of the quality of their collective habitat. The third claim of indigenous groups and peoples is the right to practice and develop their culture. This right includes the incorporation of their languages and cultural values in domestic educational paradigms as well as the access to the national cultural goods and their participation of the national set of cultural values. The fourth category of claims is the right to social and political autonomy and the profit sharing of development in order to compensate historical wrongdoings. The fifth claim is the implementation of policies, which facilitate and ensure the effectiveness of the rights aforementioned.[41] Of these categories, Diego Iturralde says that it is linguistic and territorial claims on which all the claims are based; because these are in effect pre-requisites for all the others[42]

III. CONFLICTING CLAIMS

The identification of conflicting claims is a *sine qua non* condition for understanding the recognition of legal pluralism as a means to accommodate indigenous peoples within the State. Conflicting claims at the domestic level are different from those at the international level. Even if the core of indigenous peoples' claims still remains, these claims have evolved through the years and new actors, such as international organizations, are playing roles

[40]See: Rodolfo Stavenhagen, "Indigenous Organizations: rising actors in Latin America", *Cepal Review* No.62, August 1997, pages 63-75.

[41] See: Rodolfo Stavenhagen and Diego Iturralde (eds.) *Entre la ley y la costumbre. El derecho consuetudianrio indígena en América Latina* [Between Law and Custom. Indigenous Customary Law in Latin America], Mexico, 1990.

[42] See: Iturralde, 1990, *op. cit.*

of increasing importance. I shall present the conflicting claims at both domestic and international levels.

Conflicting Claims at the Domestic Level

Conflicting claims between indigenous peoples and States at the domestic level could be described as a dichotomy between state sovereignty and indigenous autonomy[43] and internal self-determination.[44] At the domestic level, the coexistence of socio-political and legal indigenous peoples' systems with those of the State is said to yield conflicting parallel systems.[45]

The State - sovereign entity and legitimate centre of power – is the holder of the monopoly on normative production and implementation of law. However, the indigenous customs of social, political and legal regulation continue to be applicable within the indigenous groups that insist on their validity within the territories they inhabit and which are within the territorial jurisdiction of the State.

For States, indigenous systems of social, political and legal regulation do not represent a risk if those systems remain in compliance with the hegemonic legal regime. If they do not, it is clear for the states that their legal regime must prevail. For indigenous peoples, the legal regime of the State is, often, perceived as a residual system of formal mechanisms they eventually could have recourse to, to attain their rights within their own communities as well as *vis-à-vis* the dominant society. Indigenous peoples however used to have their own systems of social and political organization as well as justice

[43] The concept of autonomy changes meaning depending on the context in which it is used. Derived from the Greek « autos » (self) and « nomos »(law), one then understands « self-governing » or « self-governmental ». For a summary on the legal meanings of the term autonomy see: W. Schick, *Staatslexikon*, Volume I, Pages 490-491, and *Der Grosse Brockhaus,* Volume 2, Quoted by Oskar Peterlini, *Autonomy and the protection of ethnic minorities in trentino-South Tyrol. An overview of the history, law and politics,* Collection Ethnos 48, Braumuller editors, 1997, at page 194.

[44] The distinction between « internal » and « external » self-determination is based on the idea that self-determination may take different ways including Statehood but also many other including effective participation within a State and autonomy arrangements i.e. regional or cultural self-government. See: Antonio Cassese, *Self-determination of peoples. A legal reappraisal,* Cambridge University Press, 1995, 375 p.

[45] Mireya Maritza Peña Guzmán, "The Emerging System of International protection of Indigenous Peoples' Rights", in *St.* Thomas Law Review, Vol.9, Fall, 1996, at page 253.

administration. Accordingly, they claim their right to freely determine their destiny as a group without being denied of their right to participate in the life of their national societies.

Conflicting Claims at the International Level

Conflicting claims at the international level may be described in the following way. Indigenous peoples claim before international organizations that States have failed to respect their core claims. This is frequently extrapolated to the international community in which indigenous peoples demand involvement and cooperation. Over the years, this claim has evolved into the general demand of indigenous peoples for the establishment of effective international and/or regional mechanisms, which enable them to present their complaints and to find a legal settlement to their claims before an impartial supra-national body.

States are reluctant to agree the direct involvement of both international organizations and the international community in the settlement of disputes concerning indigenous peoples. For them, it is clear that the international legal order is based upon the respect of their right to sovereignty and non-intervention in domestic affairs. In addition, they argue that indigenous peoples are not recognised as such under international law, and therefore, domestic policies concerning them are a domestic matter. Nevertheless, as pointed out by the Permanent Court of International Justice (PCIJ) [46]

> the jurisdiction of the State is exclusive within the limits fixed by international law- using this expression in its wider sense, that is to say, embracing both customary law and general as well as particular treaty law".[47]

---

[46] The Permanent Court of International Justice (PCIJ) was established in 1920 as the jurisdictional body of the League of Nations. It dealt with contentious cases and advisory opinions up to 1942. In 1945, with the establishment of the United Nations Organization, the PCIJ was replaced by the International Court of Justice. See, *inter alia*: Bimal N. Patel, *The World Court Reference Guide Judgment, Advisory Opinions and Order of the Permanent Court of International Justice and the International Court of Justice*, 1922-2000, Kluwer Law International, 2002; Manley O. Hudson, *World Court Reports, 1922-1942: Permanent Court of International Justice, Oceana Publications, 1969*; Manley O. Hudson, *World Court, 1922-1929: A Handbook of the Permanent Court of International Justice*, Gaunt Incorporated, 2001.

[47] PCIJ, Advisory Opinion, *Nationality Decrees Issued in Tunis and Morocco*, Series B, N° 4, p. 24; italics in the original text, quoted by Allan Pellet in "State Sovereignty and the protection of fundamental human rights: an international law perspective" available at: http://www.pugwash.org/reports/rc/pellet.htm.

This has prompted international organizations to increase their involvement in the protection of indigenous peoples utilising the international dimension of human rights protection. International organizations have begun to seriously question the position of States concerning policies towards indigenous peoples and the extent of their rights as recognised by States. Intergovernmental international organizations are however conscious of their political character and need to build upon the will of the States, as the legitimate actors in international relations. Accordingly, they adopt the position that access to international bodies should be gained via State involvement[48] with limited exceptions concerning special procedures under international human rights law framed by the United Nations.[49]

IV. PAST TRENDS IN DECISIONS

The recognition as such of indigenous peoples laws and legal systems is not a common feature in the four stages that have characterized the interaction between law and indigenous peoples. The first stage, may be described as "offensive-defensive", was characterized by an incipient struggle intended to recognize the existence of indigenous peoples. The second, a stage of "submission", was characterized by the colonization. The third, a stage labelled as of "reconciliation" was characterized by the quest for the political integration of the State, the Law and the Indigenous peoples through assimilation policies. The fourth and current stage may be considered as "evolution toward the recognition of multicultural states". [50]

This last stage grows out of multiculturalism, which implies the equal value of norms and cultural practices between different societies thereby enabling separate communities to keep distinct cultural identities and to coexist harmoniously within a given geopolitical space. [51] It is characterized by

[48] See: Alexander Orakhelashvili, "The Position of the Individual in International Law", in *California Western International Law Journal*, Vol . 9, 2001.

[49] For a presentation of the United Nations System for the protection of human rights, see: Thomas Buergenthal, David P. Steward, Dinah Shelton, *International Human Rights in a Nutshell,* Nutshell Series, third edition, January 2002.

[50] Peña Guzmán, 1996, *op. cit.*, p. 259

[51] Yvonne M. Sonders, *Towards a Right to Cultural Identity*, School of Human rights Research Series, Volume 15, Maastricht, 2002

policies oriented towards the integration of indigenous peoples in States' development processes so that States respect indigenous peoples' customs and traditions while promoting their participation in the political life of the State.[52]

At the international level, we are certainly in the fourth stage. In contrast, domestic policies concerning indigenous peoples flow between the first, the third and the fourth stages. I shall in what follows consider past trends in decision at the international level and some of the current trends at the domestic level.

Past Trends in Decision at the International Level

The International Labour Organization was the first intergovernmental organization that included indigenous individuals and groups on its agenda by adopting three conventions on indigenous workers in the 1930s.[53] Later in the 1950s, following a study on the conditions of life and work of indigenous populations in independent countries carried out in 1953, the ILO, adopted in 1957, two international instruments dealing with indigenous peoples: The Convention No. 107 and the Recommendation No. 104 both of them on "Indigenous and Tribal populations." The ILO Convention 107 was the first international instrument that set standards for the treatment of indigenous peoples.[54] The 1960s were characterized by assimilation policies toward indigenous peoples that were promoted in these international instruments.

In the 1970s, a very significant movement began at the United Nations regarding indigenous peoples, as a result of pressing demands made by indigenous peoples themselves, their representatives and human rights activists. Since then, international policy-making on indigenous peoples has been very dynamic although international standard setting has not achieved an ideal system of protection of indigenous peoples, as I shall consider next.

---

[52] Peña Guzmán, 1996, *op. cit.*, p. 259

[53] Those conventions are: (1)The ILO Convention No.50 on "Recruiting of Indigenous Workers, June 20 1936; (2)The ILO Convention No.64 on "Contracts of Employment (Indigenous Workers), June 27, 1939 and (3) ILO Convention No. 65 on "Penal Sanctions (Indigenous Workers), June 27, 1939. All these international instruments have been set aside because of their assimilationist tendencies.

[54] The complete text of the ILO Convention 107/1957 is available at: http://www.ilo.org/ilolex/cgi-lex/convde.pl?C107.

International Policy-making in Respect of Indigenous Peoples

In 1971, the Economic and Social Council (ECOSOC) adopted the resolution 1589 authorizing the Sub-commission on the Prevention of Discrimination and Protection of Minorities (now the Sub-Commission on the Promotion and Protection of Human Rights) to undertake a complete and comprehensive *Study of the Problem of Discrimination Against Indigenous Populations.* This study, prepared by the Special Rapporteur José Martínez Cobo, highlights the precarious and discriminatory conditions being faced by indigenous peoples. In the light of this Study and because of indigenous initiatives, in 1982 the Sub-commission was authorized to set up a "Working Group on Indigenous Populations" with the aim of dealing exclusively with issues concerning the recognition and protection of the rights and freedoms of the indigenous populations of the World.

In the 1980s, the Working Group and the ILO initiated a process of revision of the ILO Convention 107, which entered in its final stage at the ILO General Conference in 1988. Accordingly, on June 27, 1989 the ILO adopted the Convention concerning Indigenous and Tribal Peoples in Independent Countries (No.169).

The 1990s were characterized by the recognition of indigenous peoples' rights to environmental security pursuant to the Earth Summit in Rio de Janeiro (Rio Summit) in 1992. [55] Additionally, the year 1993 was designated as the International Year of the World's Indigenous People. This was a reaffirmation of the commitment of the international community to ensure the enjoyment by indigenous peoples of human rights and fundamental freedoms and to respect the value and diversity of their cultures and identities. Likewise, the Vienna Declaration and Programme of Action[56] adopted the same year in the World

[55] The UN conference on Environment and Development was the result of the UN desire to help Governments to rethink economic development finding ways to halt the destruction of irreplaceable natural resources and earth pollution. In the Summit, Governments recognized the need to redirect international and national plans and policies to ensure that all economic decisions fully took into account any environmental impact. The UN Conference on Environment and Development (1992) is available at: http://www.un.org/geninfo/bp/enviro.html

[56] The Vienna Declaration and Programme of Action is Available in English at: http://www.unhchr.ch/huridocda/huridoca.nsf/(Symbol)/A.CONF.157.23.En?OpenDocument

Conference on Human Rights,[57] reaffirmed, *inter alia*, the importance of the above-mentioned International Year pointed to the inherent dignity and the unique contribution of indigenous peoples to development, the plurality of societies as well as calling upon States to ensure respect for human rights and fundamental freedoms of indigenous peoples. It also recommended to the UN General Assembly to proclaim an International Decade of the World's Indigenous People (1994-2004), which began on December 10, 1994. One of the main goals of the Decade was to create within the United Nations' System a Permanent Forum for the Indigenous Peoples. As part of this goal, the Working Group proposed the "Draft Declaration,"[58] a document setting forth the rights of indigenous peoples.

The current Decade began with the establishment of the Permanent Forum on indigenous Issues[59] by means of the ECOSOC resolution 2000/22. It serves as an advisory body to the Council and has a mandate to discuss indigenous issues relating to economic and social development, culture, the environment, education, health and human rights. In 2002, one of the main highlights was the use of the term "peoples" to refer to "indigenous peoples" in an official document of the United Nations without making further declarations on the way the term peoples should be understood. In September 2002, the Johannesburg Declaration[60] adopted within the framework of the UN World Summit [61] by reaffirming *"the vital role of the indigenous peoples in sustainable development"* in paragraph 25, became such a historical international legal instrument. In this sense, it is noteworthy to bear in mind that the ILO Convention 169 affirms in article 1.3. that the term 'peoples' should not be understood as having any implications concerning the rights attach to the term under contemporary international law; these implications concern mainly to the right of peoples to self-determination as recognized in article 1 common to the two 1966 Covenants on Human Rights.

---

[57] Information on the World Conference on Human Rights is available at: http://www.unhchr.ch/html/menu5/wchr.htm

[58] The text of the UN Draft Declaration is available at: http://www.usask.ca/nativelaw/ddirplain.html.

[59] All information concerning the Permanent Forum on Indigenous Issues is available on line on the official website for the Permanent Forum on Indigenous Issues at http://www.un.org/esa/socdev/pfii/

[60] The text of the Johannesburg Declaration on Sustainable Development is available at: <www.johannesburgsummit.org/html/documents/ summit_docs/1009wssd_pol_declaration.doc>.

[61] Information on the World Summit on Sustainable Development is available at: http://www.johannesburgsummit.org/

Another of the major highlights of 2002 was the celebration of the Permanent Forum's first session held in May 13-24, 2002. The second meeting of the Permanent Forum was held from 12 to 23 May 2003 and the third meeting in May 2004.

International Standard Setting with Respect to Indigenous Peoples

International standard setting is relatively recent within the United Nations Organization. In fact, indigenous peoples account *de lege lata* on a Convention adopted by the International Labour Organisation and they also account *de lege ferenda* on a Universal Declaration expected to be approved before the end of the International Decade of the World's Indigenous People (1994-2004). I shall refer hereinafter to both *lex lata* and *lex ferenda.*

Lex Lata

The ILO Convention 169 codified the classic claims of indigenous peoples within its provisions. It is divided into ten parts and forty-four articles. Part I deals with the General Policy applicable to indigenous peoples. It determines the groups to which the Convention applies by distinguishing between indigenous and tribal peoples. It also highlights that the use of the term 'peoples' in the Convention is not to be understood as "having any implication as regards the rights which may attach to the term under international law".[62]

Responsibility for the protection of the rights of indigenous peoples lies with governments, which, with the participation of indigenous peoples must coordinate and maintain systematic action for the protection of rights and integrity of these peoples by ensuring and promoting their rights. The participation of indigenous peoples in both policy-making and decision-making processes is recognized through their right to be consulted before the adoption of policies and decisions on matters of their direct concern - see articles 6 and 7 of the Convention.

The first set of rights ascribed to indigenous peoples basic and universal human rights and fundamental freedoms[63] and their right to citizenship[64] both

[62] ILO Convention No.169, article 1.3.
[63] ILO Convention No. 169, articles 3 and 8.3.

without discrimination,[65] in particular between male and female members of these peoples.[66] The Convention also emphasizes the special protection and recognition of social, cultural, religious and spiritual values and practices.[67] It points to the requirement of respect for indigenous customary law in the application of national laws and regulations relating to these peoples[68] and for the compliance with domestic fundamental rights and internationally recognized human rights.[69] Moreover, respect for the methods customarily practiced by them to deal with the offences committed by their members is also to be granted to indigenous as and when possible.[70] When it is not possible punishments applied to them must take into consideration their economic, social and cultural characteristics; methods of punishment alternative to prison are to be preferred.[71]

Part II is concerned with land rights. It provides that the term "land" is to be understood as comprising "the concept of territories, which covers the total environment of the areas which the peoples concerned occupy or otherwise use".[72] It recognizes the right of ownership and possession of indigenous peoples over traditional lands and imposes on governments the obligation to take all necessary steps to identify the lands traditionally occupied by indigenous peoples, as well as to guarantee effective protection of land rights.[73] It also recognizes their right to participate in the use, management and conservation of natural resources pertaining to their lands.

Part III deals with recruitment and conditions of employment and part IV with vocational training, handicrafts and rural industries mentioning *inter alia* rules of non-discrimination and protection of their cultural features. Part V refers to social security and health as a government responsibility burden and provides for the facilitation of indigenous peoples access to those services. Part VI refers to Education and means of communication. It advocates equality of opportunity of access and recognizes the right of indigenous peoples "to

[64] ILO Convention No. 169, article 4.3.
[65] Ibid.
[66] ILO Convention No.169, article 3.1.
[67] Ibid., at article 5.
[68] Ibid.,at article 8.1.
[69] Ibid., at article 8.2.
[70] Ibid., at article 9.1.
[71] Ibid., at article 10.
[72] ILO Convention No.169, article 13.2.
[73] Ibid., article 14.

establish their own educational institutions and facilities, provided that such institutions meet minimum standards established by the competent authority in consultation with these peoples."[74]

Part VII refers to contacts and cooperation across borders affirming that "[g]overnments shall take appropriate measures, including...international agreements, to facilitate contacts and co-operation between indigenous and tribal peoples across borders, including activities in the economic, social, cultural, spiritual and environmental fields." [75] Part VIII deals with administrative issues concerning the programmes affecting indigenous peoples and finally, part IX states some general provisions, one of which recognizes that "[t]he application of the provisions of ...[the] Convention shall not adversely affect rights and benefits of the peoples concerned pursuant to other Conventions and Recommendations, international instruments, treaties, or national laws, awards, custom or agreements."[76]

The ILO convention 169 has been ratified by 17 countries up to November 2004, 13 of which belong to the Latin American region: Mexico (1990), Bolivia (1991), Colombia (1991), Costa Rica (1993), Paraguay (1993), Peru (1994), Honduras (1995), Guatemala (1996), Equator (1998), Argentina (2000), Brazil (2002), Dominica (2002) and Venezuela (2002). The other countries that have ratified ILO Convention 169 are: Norway (1990), Denmark (1996), Fiji (1998) and Netherlands (1998).

This convention inaugurated a new stage in the international legal treatment of indigenous peoples' in spite of the criticism of the conception of their legal status as established in article 1.3. The ILO Convention 169 has the virtue of having changed the paradigm of assimilation to national societies to that of multicultural policies within states in respect of indigenous peoples. It has however also been criticised for the ambiguous use of the term 'peoples.' Article 1.3. of the ILO Convention 169 states that "[t]he use of the term *peoples* in this Convention shall not be construed as having any implications as regards the rights which may attach to the term under international law." The formula adopted in article 1.3.of the ILO Convention 169 has important implications. From a semantic point of view, it denotes that "indigenous" are

---

[74] Ibid., article 27.
[75] Ibid., article 32.
[76] Ibid., article 35.

called "peoples" only as a prosaic and stylistic antiphon since use of the term peoples does not have any legal implication at the international level. . From a legal point of view, it implies that indigenous peoples are not imbued with any of the rights ascribed to "all peoples" under international law as in the controversial right to self-determination recognized in common article 1 of the International Covenant on Civil and Political Rights (ICCPR) and the International Covenant on Economic Social and Cultural Rights (ICESCR).

Lex Ferenda

The United Nations Draft Declaration constitutes the most important development in contemporary international law in respect of the recognition and protection of the basic rights and fundamental freedoms of Indigenous Peoples. It was adopted in accordance with the Sub-commission resolution 1994/45 and had direct involvement of indigenous peoples themselves. It was also heavily influenced by the substantive contributions of government representatives, specialized agencies and non-governmental organizations that participated in the annual sessions of the Working Group on indigenous populations.

The Draft Declaration contains a preamble and 45 articles and has been divided into nine main parts. The preamble contains 19 paragraphs with a number of important general principles. It affirms, *inter alia*, equality in dignity and rights of indigenous peoples with all other peoples while recognizing the right of all peoples to be different. It recognises the urgent need to respect and promote the inherent rights and characteristics of indigenous peoples; it also reaffirms the importance of the recognition of the right of self-determination for all peoples. It emphasizes the important role of the United Nations for the promotion and protection of the rights of indigenous peoples[77] as well as it encourages States to comply with, and effectively implement, all international instruments, in particular those related to human rights, as they apply to indigenous peoples, in consultation and cooperation with them.[78]

Part I refers to the fundamental principles of equality and non-discrimination regarding indigenous peoples collectively as peoples and individually as

[77] See: UN Draft Declaration, preamble at paragraph 17.
[78] *Ibidem* at paragraph 16.

human persons. The Draft Declaration specifically refers to self-determination as a right of all peoples. It also recognizes the right of indigenous peoples to a nationality, to maintain and strengthen their distinct characteristics and legal systems while retaining their right to participate fully, if they so choose, in the political, economic, social and cultural life of the State.

Part II recognizes the rights of indigenous peoples to their physical existence and cultural identity. It explicitly rejects the four principal threats: forced relocation; forced assimilation; militarisation of their territories; official denial of indigenous identity. It also recognizes the right of indigenous peoples to special protection and security in time of armed conflict.

Parts III, IV and V focus on issues of special concern to indigenous peoples in the exercise of their right to equality, self-determination and collective identity. They refer to the need to strengthen the distinctiveness of indigenous societies within states, and address issues concerning religious, spiritual, cultural and linguistic freedom, and the renewal of indigenous institutions in the field of education, health, the economy and communications. They also refer to the equality of, and non-discrimination against, indigenous peoples in respect of the full enjoyment of all rights established under international labour law and national labour legislation. There is also reference to the right of indigenous peoples to maintain and develop indigenous decision-making institutions and systems in the social political and economic fields.

Part VI deals with land, natural resources, cultural and intellectual property and other economic rights. It also focuses on the protection of the environment and ecological security. Part VII offers general guidelines for those situations in which indigenous peoples exercise their political rights through forms of autonomy or internal self-government within States. It reaffirms that indigenous peoples' institutions have the responsibility to respect internationally recognized human rights' standards and establishes that "conflicts and disputes which cannot otherwise be settled should be submitted to competent international bodies agreed to by all parties concerned".[79]

Part VIII addresses the specific responsibilities of States with regard to indigenous peoples and the international community role in ensuring recognition of and respect for the rights of indigenous peoples and the

[79] *Ibidem*, article 36.

implementation of the provisions of the Draft Declaration. One of the most important innovations of the Draft Declaration is article 41 relating to the creation by the United Nations of a body at the highest level, with special competence in the field of implementation of the Draft Declaration with the direct participation of indigenous peoples. Finally, part IX clarifies some general principles of interpretation and application of the Draft Declaration.

The rights recognized in the Draft Declaration are considered minimum standards for the survival, dignity and well being of the indigenous peoples of the World. If approved it will clarify the status of indigenous peoples under contemporary international law, particularly their status as peoples holders of the rights recognized to all peoples at the international level.

Past Trends in Decision at the Domestic Level

Policies towards indigenous peoples at the domestic level vary from place to place and alternate between the denial of recognition, and the recognition of their existence; between the recognition of certain "special" individual rights, and the recognition of certain collective rights. Rights to autonomy and self-determination also vary.

The denial of the recognition of indigenous peoples is an unfortunate pattern in some regions of the world. In 1993 within the framework of the International Year of the World's Indigenous Peoples, the former UN Centre for Human Rights published a map[80] locating, in a non-exhaustive manner, the regions of the world where indigenous peoples live. The list of the indigenous peoples of the world identified on the map was based on information from States available to the United Nations.[81] The list underlined that all regions of the world have to be concerned about indigenous peoples. The distribution of this map had to be suspended. Asian states considered that neither the mandate of the UN – nor the mandate of any other intergovernmental organization-

[80] United Nations, "Where Indigenous Peoples live", DPI/1316-93295-Nov.1992-9M. A similar map locating in a non-exhaustive way the regions of the world where indigenous peoples inhabit may be found in Ethel (Wara) Alderete (comp.), *The Health of Indigenous Peoples* (1999) published by the World Health Organization, available at:<www.ku.edu/~insp/referencesite.html. [Web site visited in January, 2003.]

[81] UN Doc. No. E/CN.4/Sub.2/1986/7/Add.4, page 5 at paragraph 19.

authorized the UN to identify indigenous peoples within their territories.[82] They considered this identification process as a threat to sovereignty, territorial integrity and unity among the member states.[83]

Nowadays, only a few countries do not recognize indigenous peoples within their territories. In this regard France is an example in respect of French Guyana and New Caledonia. In the countries where indigenous peoples are recognized, the distinction between the indigenous individual and the indigenous-group plays an important role in the determination of their legal Status at the domestic level. Indigenous individuals are, more likely to be able to enjoy, without discrimination, the rights recognized to all citizens of a particular state as well as to assume the obligations that citizenship implies. It might even be possible to suggest that nowadays the legal status of the indigenous individual is undisputed at the domestic level. The status or nature of these individuals is usually accommodated within domestic law in one of two ways. Firstly by being recognized as an individual entitled to the set of rights all individuals are entitled to. Secondly by being considered for legal purposes, as a member of a linguistic, ethnic or religious minority, and therefore, entitled to the special protection and individual rights recognized in article 27 of the ICCPR.

Assimilationist policies towards indigenous peoples still persist in some countries. It is important to mention that the ILO Convention 107, is still in effect in 17 countries: Angola, Belgium, Cuba, Egypt, Ghana, Iraq, Pakistan, Portugal, Tunisia, Bangladesh, Brazil, Dominican Republic, El Salvador,

---

[82] The map did not mention the countries where indigenous peoples inhabit but located and named the indigenous groups. The Countries of the world which –in the view of the UN- were involved with indigenous peoples are: Africa: cap-Green, Central Africa, Kenya, Mali, Namibia, Uganda, Rwanda, Sudan, Tanzania and Zaire. The Americas: Argentina, Belize, Bolivia, Brazil, Canada, Chili, Colombia, Costa Rica, Dominica, El Salvador, Ecuador, Guatemala, Guyana, Honduras, Mexico, Nicaragua, Panama, Paraguay, Peru, Surinam, United States of America and Venezuela; Asia: Bangladesh, Cambodia, China, India, Indonesia, Japan, Laos, Malaysia, Myanmar, Nepal, Pakistan, Papua-New Guinea, Philippines, Sri Lanka, Taiwan and Thailand; Europe: Denmark (Greenland only), Finland, France, Norway, Russia and Sweden; Oceania: Australia, New Zealand and Vanuatu. See: Norbert Rouland (dir), Stéphane Pierré-Caps and Jacques Poumarède, *Droit des minorités et des peuples autochtones,* [Law of Minorities and Indigenous Peoples],PUF, 1996, 581p, *Chapter 3, footnote 4,* at pages 440-441.

[83] UN. Doc. No. E/C.4/1994/36/Add.1

Guinea Bissau, India, Malawi, Panama and the Syrian Arab Republic. [84] In addition, policies towards the recognition and/or promotion of multiculturalism may vary from country to country.

It is important to note that even the 17 countries that have ratified ILO Convention 169 do not have uniform policies towards indigenous peoples although some regions of the world show common patterns. For instance, Norway and Finland may be classified as countries that recognize indigenous peoples, as holders of individual and certain collective rights and which grant to them a moderate degree of autonomy. However, Denmark in respect of Greenland and the Faeroe Islands recognizes a high degree of autonomy to indigenous groups but autonomy is not recognized on the basis of ethnicity but on the basis of residence since the Inuit are clearly a majority in Greenland. [85]

V. EMERGING TRENDS IN THE AMERICAS

The American continent is one of the most poly-ethnic and multicultural regions of the world and contains numbers of indigenous individuals, groups and peoples within its population. It has been estimated that there are more than 40 million indigenous individuals in the American continent and no less than 400 identifiable ethnic and indigenous groups and peoples. [86] The working paper of the 2001 Summit of the Americas mentions that there are more than 1.5 million indigenous people in North America, 13 millions in Mexico and Central America and 18.5 million in South America.

Emerging trends in the Americas in respect of indigenous peoples' rights should be considered at both continental and the Latin American levels. At the continental level, there is a trend toward the recognition of indigenous peoples' individual and collective rights. This trend is reflected in quasi-judicial and judicial decisions of the inter-American bodies in charge of human rights' protection. At the Latin American level, two trends may be identified. The first

[84] The following countries had ratified the ILO Convention 107 but denounced it as a result of the ratification of the Convention 169: Argentina, Colombia, Ecuador, Paraguay, Bolivia, Costa Rica, Mexico and Peru. The Status of Ratification of all ILO Conventions up to the year 2002 is available at: http://www.ilo.org/public/english/standards/relm/ilc/ilc90/pdf/rep-iii-2.pdf.

[85] Martin Scheinin, *Interview*, Miami, FL (USA), February, 2003.

[86] Organization of American States, « The Human Rights situation of the Indigenous Peoples in the Americas », document *OEA/Ser.L/V/II.1.08*, october 20th, 2000 at the introduction.

one is characterized by the constitutionalization of indigenous peoples' rights. The second one concerns the recognition of legal pluralism in some countries of the region.

Indigenous Peoples' Rights and Protection at the Inter-American Level

The Inter-American System for the Protection of Human Rights is composed of the Inter-American Commission of Human Rights (IACHR) and the Inter-American Court of Human Rights, which are the human rights bodies of the Organization of American States (OAS). At the inter-American level, indigenous peoples' rights are tenuous and there is no a continental legal instrument recognizing them specifically. Indigenous peoples' protection in the inter-american system arises from the American Declaration of the Rights and Duties of Man and the American Convention on Human Rights under the right to equality, within the provisions barring discrimination on grounds of, *inter alia,* race, colour, language, religion and social status.[87] This approach to the indigenous questions via the concept of minorities or the prohibition of discrimination has been criticized as being incomplete, reductionist and inadequate. Accordingly, the Inter-American Commission on Human Rights approved in 1997 a text of a proposed American Declaration on indigenous populations expected to be adopted in the coming years.

The Inter-American Commission of Human Rights has already decided several cases concerning indigenous-individuals and has recognized their rights to life, personal liberty and humane treatment, their right to property, the rights of the family and their right to judicial protection. It has also condemned the discriminatory military recruitment of indigenous men as a violation of the rights to personal liberty, protection of human dignity and freedom of movement.[88] In its practice, it has also accepted and recognized the concept of *collective rights* in the sense of rights to which groups or organizations of people are entitled. For example, in case 1690 from 1970 and concerning the Guahibo population of Colombia, the Commission referred to the rights of these indigenous communities alleged to have been violated by the incursions of settlers and armed military operations into indigenous ancestral lands. In 1973, the Commission accepted the case 1802 concerning the Aché people of

[87] Article II of the Declaration and Article 1 of the Convention.

[88] See: Doctrine and Jurisprudence of the IACHR on Indigenous Rights (1970-1999), available at: http://www.cidh.org/indigenas/chap.3.htm.

Paraguay, allegedly suffering attacks, practices of forced malnutrition, attempts to enslave and threatens with extinction. The report of the Special Rapporteur of the Commission not only referred to infringements of the rights of the individual Aché i.e. the right to life and humane treatment, but also included an analysis of rights of collective nature: alleged genocide, refusal to recognize collectively owned lands, and eradication of language, traditional music and religious practices. Likewise, in 1985 the Commission recognized the right of the Yanomami people from Brazil to the limitation and demarcation of the Yanomami territory and recommended the Brazilian State to take steps to implement Yanomami land rights.

In contrast, the Inter-American Court of Human Rights has only decided two cases concerning indigenous peoples' rights. In 1993, pursuant to an application by the Commission, the Inter-American Court of Human Rights dealt with *Aloeboetoe v. Suriname,*[89] in which it recognized the lawfulness of reparations based on indigenous customary family law, including polygamy as practiced by that community, in the context of a massacre of members of an indigenous group. In 2001, in a judgment of August 31, the Inter-American Court [hereinafter "the Court"] dealt with *Mayagna (Sumo) Awas Tingni v. Nicaragua*[90] in which it found Nicaragua in violation of articles 25 (judicial protection), article 1(1) (obligation to respect rights), 21 (right to property) in relation to articles 1(1) and 2 (domestic legal effects) of the American Convention on Human Rights to the detriment of the Mayagna Community. Accordingly, the Court decided that Nicaragua should adopt all domestic measures necessary to create an effective mechanism for delimitation, demarcation and titling of indigenous communities' property,

> in accordance with their customary law, values, customs and mores…

The Court also concluded that the judgment in law constituted *per se* a form of reparation for the Mayagna (Sumo) Awas Tingni Community and in equity

---

[89] Inter-American Court of Human Rights, *Case of Aloeboetoe et al. Vs. Suriname*, Series C No.11, Judgment of December 4, 1991 and, Inter-American Court of Human Rights, *Case of Aloeboetoe et al. Vs. Suriname. Reparations*, Series C No.15, Judgment of September 10, 1993.

[90] Inter-American Court of Human Rights, *Case of the Mayagna (Sumo) Awas Tingni Vs. Nicaragua*, Series C No.79, Judgment of August 31, 2001.

> that the State must invest, as reparation for immaterial damages, in the course of 12 months, the total sum of US$ 50,000... in works or services of collective interest for the benefit of the Mayagna (Sumo) Awas Tingni Community...

and that

> the State must pay the members of the Mayagna (Sumo) Awas Tingni Community, through the Inter-American Commission of Human Rights, the total sum of US$ 30,000... for expenses and costs incurred by the members of that Community and their representatives, both those caused in domestic proceedings and in the international proceedings before the inter-American system of protection....[91]

These two decisions are excellent examples of the potential effectiveness of both human rights law and indigenous peoples' rights. They show how governments may become accountable for indigenous peoples rights' violations and for the lack of recognition of indigenous peoples' laws. These decisions certainly constitute a major breakthrough in the recognition of legal pluralism in the region as well as in the protection of individual and collective indigenous peoples' rights. Currently the Court is studying a new lawsuit against Nicaragua in respect of a violation of the political rights of some indigenous political parties.

Indigenous Peoples' Rights and Protection in the Latin American Region

Countries within the American continent share histories rooted in colonialism characterized by the dispossession and genocide of native inhabitants. Nevertheless the relationships between governments and the indigenous groups and peoples are not all the same as it was not so between the colonizers and the people they colonised. Treaties between the Indians and the colonizers and after decolonisation, between the Indians and the sovereign governments are not a common feature in all countries of the region. This is one of the reasons why public policies towards indigenous groups and peoples' as well as their legal treatment over the continent as a whole is somewhat mixed. There are though some common features. The Latin American region is exemplary. It is not only the region where most countries have ratified ILO Convention 169, but it is also the only region of the world where a legal indigenous jurisdiction

---

[91] Inter-American Court of Human Rights, Mayagna (Sumo) Awas Tingni Community v. Nicaragua, judgment of August 31,2001, available in English at: http://www.utulsa.edu/law/classes/rice/INTERAMER_CT_HUMAN_RTS_Mayagna.htm.

to administer justice in compliance with indigenous laws has been recognized making clearly a difference in respect of the cases of Nunavut (Canada) and Greenland (Denmark)) where the indigenous jurisdiction refers only to political autonomy.

I shall briefly describe the recognition of indigenous peoples rights some of the Latin American constitutions and secondly describe a new trend that seems to be leading to the consolidation of legal pluralism in the region.

The Constitutional Recognition of Indigenous Peoples in Latin America

The recognition of cultural and ethnical diversity as a constitutional principle is one of the fundamental changes that most Latin American states experienced in the last decades. The recognition of the multicultural nature of States including indigenous peoples entitled to specific rights may also be considered a trend in Latin America. These features characterized the wave of constitutional changes and amendments which began in the 1970s with Ecuador and continued to 2002 and which includes, Argentina,[92] Bolivia,[93] Brazil, [94] Colombia, [95] Ecuador, [96] Guatemala, [97] Mexico, [98] Nicaragua, [99] Panama, [100] Paraguay, [101] Peru, [102] Venezuela. [103] Chile [104] and Uruguay are however exceptions.

---

[92] See article 75.17 of the Argentinean constitution available in Spanish at: http://www.georgetown.edu/pdba/Constitutions/Argentina/argen94.html, and in English at: http://www.oefre.unibe.ch/law/icl/ar00000_.html.

[93] See articles 1 and 171 of the Bolivian Constitution available in Spanish at: http://www.georgetown.edu/pdba/Constitutions/Bolivia/consboliv1615.html.

[94] See articles 22, 231 and 232 of the 1988 Constitution of Brazil, available in Portuguese at: http://www.senado.gov.br/bdtextual/const88/const88i.pdf

[95] See articles 7, 10, 68,72, 176-177, 246 and 329-330 of the 1991 Constitution of Colombia, available in Spanish at: http://www.georgetown.edu/pdba/Constitutions/Colombia/col91.html.

[96] See articles 1, 3, 62, 66, 69, 83-84 of the 1994 Constitution of Ecuador available in Spanish at: http://www.georgetown.edu/pdba/Constitutions/Ecuador/ecuador98.html.

[97] See articles 66-70 of the 1985 Constitution of Guatemala amended in 1993, available in Spanish at: http://www.georgetown.edu/pdba/Constitutions/Guate/guate93.html.

[98] See articles 2 and 27.VII of the 1917 Constitution of Mexico as amended in 2001, available in Spanish at: http://www.georgetown.edu/pdba/Constitutions/Mexico/mexico2001.html.

[99] See articles 8 and 89-91 of the 1987 Constitution of Nicaragua as amended in 1995, available in Spanish at: http://www.georgetown.edu/pdba/Constitutions/Nica/nica95.html.

[100] See articles 84, 120 and 121 of the 1972 Constitution of Panama amended in 1994, available in Spanish at: http://www.georgetown.edu/pdba/Constitutions/Panama/panama1994.html.

The rights recognized for the benefit of indigenous peoples differ from country to country. For example, Brazil has into effect both ILO Convention 107 and ILO Convention 169. The Brazilian constitution of 1988 amended in 1994 and 1996 recognizes the authority of the legislator over the indigenous question (article 22), protects and recognizes the indigenous forms of social organizations, their ancestral territories and their intellectual property rights (article 231) as well as their legal personality to bring a lawsuit to defend their rights and interests (article 232). The Constitution of Argentina, however, only recognizes that Congress is empowered to: "recognize the ethnic and cultural pre-existence of indigenous peoples of Argentina; to guarantee respect for the identity and the right to bilingual and intercultural education; to recognize the legal capacity of their communities, and the community possession and ownership of the lands they traditionally occupy; and to regulate the granting of other lands adequate and sufficient for human development; ....To guarantee their participation in issues related to their natural resources and in other topics affecting them..." (article 75.17).

A New Trend Leading Toward the Consolidation of Legal Pluralism in Latin America?

One of the emerging trends in the Latin American region is the recognition of indigenous peoples laws and legal systems. This trend may be found in the form of the so-called "special indigenous jurisdiction" in the 1991 Constitution of Colombia (article 246), the 1993 Constitution of Peru (article 149), the 1994 Constitution of Bolivia (article 171), the 1998 Constitution of Equador (article 191), the 1999 Constitution of Venezuela (article 260), the 2000 Constitution of Paraguay (article 63) and the 1917 Constitution of Mexico as amended in 2001 (article 2.A.II).

[101] See article 62-66, 77 and 104 of the 1992 Consitituion of Paraguay, available in Spanish at: http://www.georgetown.edu/pdba/Constitutions/Paraguay/para1992.html.

[102] See articles 48, 88 and 89 of the 1993 Constitution of Peru available in Spanish at: http://www.georgetown.edu/pdba/Constitutions/Peru/per93.html.

[103] See articles 119-126 and 260 in the 1999 Constitution of Venezuela, available in Spanish at: http://www.georgetown.edu/pdba/Constitutions/Venezuela/ven1999.html.

[104] The 1980 Constitution of Chile was amended in the year 2000 but do not make specific reference to indigenous peoples or ethnic groups within its territory and do not recognized the multiculturalism as a component of the Chilean Society. The Constitution of Chile is available in Spanish at: http://www.georgetown.edu/pdba/Constitutions/constudies.html.

These articles enshrined in seven constitutions of the region express four common features. Firstly, indigenous peoples are recognized as legal entities and their authorities are recognized as having judicial functions. Secondly, indigenous peoples' authorities should exercise judicial functions within the indigenous territories in compliance with their own norms and procedures. Thirdly, indigenous norms and procedures should be respected as such when they are in compliance with the constitutions and the laws in force in the states. Finally, law should establish the method of coordination between the special indigenous jurisdiction and the national judicial system.

The seven Latin American countries, whose constitutions show this pattern, have ratified ILO Convention 169. Accordingly, the special indigenous jurisdiction may be considered a domestic implementation of this legal instrument. In fact, the provision of article 8.2 recognizes the right of indigenous peoples "to retain their own customs and institutions, where these are not incompatible with fundamental rights defined by the national legal systems and with internationally recognized human rights" as well as it highlights that "[p]rocedures shall be established, whenever necessary, to resolve conflicts which may arise in the application of this principle". Likewise, article 5 states that "the social, cultural, religious and spiritual values and practices of these peoples shall be recognised and protected, and due account shall be taken of the nature of the problems which face them both as groups and as individuals".

VI. RECOGNIZING LEGAL PLURALISM IN PRACTICE: THE COLOMBIAN CASE

Colombia is a developing country located in the northwestern corner of South America. As a multicultural and poly-ethnic State,[105] Colombia has identified 84 indigenous groups with different socio-cultural characteristics within its current population. Indigenous peoples speak 64 different tongues belonging to 13 linguistic families.[106] They are located in all regions of the country,

[105] The 1991 Colombian Constitution distinguishes three categories of ethnics groups as special holders of rights: indigenous peoples, afro-colombian communities and native communities from St. Andrés, Providence and St. Catalina. A fourth category, the "Roma people" or "gypsies" has been added recently in the realm of public policies.

[106] See: UN. Doc. E/1994/104/Add.2. *Aplicación del pacto Internacional de Derechos Económicos, Sociales y Culturales*, ECOSOC, United Nations, 1995, p. 3.

excepting some islands located at the northwest.[107] Currently, they constitute approximately the 3% of the national population.[108]

Two long established institutions form part of the internal organisation of the Colombian indigenous peoples: the *Cabildos* and the *Resguardos*. The *Cabildos* are the political bodies of indigenous peoples. Their legal existence stems from article 3 of the law 89 (1890), which established that "in every place where there is a settlement of indigenous groups, it shall be a little *cabildo* whose members will be elected in compliance with the indigenous customs." This law also added that the "indigenous groups already governed by *cabildos* may continue to function in the way prescribed by the indigenous groups." Nowadays, the *cabildos* are also considered public entities[109] and may be grouped in associations.[110] The *Resguardos*, are a legal and socio-political institution of special character composed by either one or a number of indigenous communities possessing a collective title of property over a territory and who are governed by their own normative system and protected by the "indigenous privilege".[111] Up to December 2000,[112] the Colombian government had recognized 545 indigenous *resguardos*.[113]

The development of the legal status of indigenous peoples has evolved notoriously during the last decades. Assimilationist public policies and discriminatory legislation characterized the legal treatment of indigenous

[107] The Colombian Islands where indigenous peoples do not inhabit are the islands of St. Andres, Providence and St. Catalina).

[108] The last oficial census by the National Statistics Department [Departamento Administrativo Nacional de Estadísticas -DANE-] shows a percentage of 1.61 indigenous within the Colombian territory. See: *XVI Censo Nacional de población y V de vivienda*, 1993, available at: http://www.dane.co. However, the statistical data available in 1994 in the Data Bank of the Inter-American Indian Institute shows a percentage of 2% of indigenous in Colombia. See: *Revista América Indígena*, Volumen LV, No.3, July-September 1995, p. 51.

[109] See: Colombian Constitutional Court, Decision T-001 (1994) and Republic of Colombia, Decree 2001 (1988), available in Spanish at: www.banrep.gov.co.

[110] See: Republic of Colombia, Decree 1088 (1993), available in Spanish at: www.banrep.gov.co

[111] See: Republic of Colombia, Decree 2164, 1995, article 21.7.

[112] Information collected in the former Direction of Indigenous Affairs of the Colombian Ministry of internal affairs, December 2000.

[113] Regarding the recognition of "Resguardos" in Colombia, see: Colombian Constitutional Court, decisions T-567 (1992) and T-188 (1993). Regarding the collective property of *resguardos*, see: Colombian Constitutional Court, decision T-253 (1993). The decisions of the Colombian Constitutional Court are available in Spanish at: www.ramajudicial.gov.co.

peoples until the beginning of the 1980s.[114] It is important to mention that Colombia has been an independent country since 1810 and since 1890, indigenous peoples were governed by the law 89[115] that regarded them as "wild", consigned their government to the ecclesiastical authorities and limited their legal personality through capacity restrictions.[116]

This situation has radically changed in the 1990s. In 1991, a new constitution set up the protection of cultural and ethnic diversity as a fundamental principle of the state (article 7) and recognized several rights to indigenous peoples[117] (articles 10, 68, 72, 176, 177, 329 and 330) as well as the judicial powers of their traditional authorities (article 246).

---

[114] It is important to mention that the changes concerning the policy oriented toward indigenous peoples began in the 1960s. In fact, the Congress passed a law on the agrarian reform that favoured the creation of indigenous reserves in 1961. In the 1970s policies of biculturalism and bilingual education are introduced within the Colombian legal system and, in the 1980s, the ex-president Virgilio Barco Vargas (1986-1990) revisited the "indigenous question" and promote the legal protection of indigenous peoples in Colombia. See: Presidencia de la República, *Fuero Indígena Colombiano*, [Colombian Indigenous Privilege], Imprenta Nacional, Bogota, 1990.

[115] Ley 89 del 25 de noviembre de 1890 "Por la cual se determina la manera como deben ser gobernados los salvajes que vayan reduciéndose a la vida civilizada".[Law 89, November 25, 1890 "determining the way as should be governed the savages who are becoming civilized"]

[116] See: Republic of Colombia, Law 89, 1890, article 40.

[117] The rights ascribed to the indigenous peoples in Colombia include at least four different categories. The first category is the set of universal human rights to which every one is entitled. This set of rights are found in the 1991 Constitution in terms similar to those used by the Universal Declaration of Human Rights, and by the two international Covenants of 1966 ratified by Colombia in 1969. The second category of rights is the set of specific rights recognized to the persons belonging to the ethnic, linguistic or religious minorities as set up in article 27 of the ICCPR, which states: "[I]n those States in which ethnic, religious or linguistic minorities exist, persons belonging to such minorities shall not be denied the right, in community with the other members of their group, to enjoy their own culture, to profess and practice their own religion, or to use their own language." It is important to notice that the freedom of religion is a right recognized to all Colombians in article 19 of the 1991 Constitution. However, indigenous peoples are recognized as holders of specific linguistic rights (article 10) and are also explicitly entitled to the right to enjoy their own culture through an education system that respects their cultural identity (article 86). The third category is the set of special rights of indigenous peoples and of indigenous individuals, as set up in the ILO Convention No.169 incorporated into the Colombian legislation through the law 21 of March 4, 1991. This last category is complemented, by a fourth set of rights under the Colombian constitution and laws recognizing indigenous peoples as special beneficiaries. The Special Indigenous Jurisdiction belongs to the latter category.

Indigenous peoples' legal autonomy has been recognized in Colombia under the form of the so-called Special Indigenous Jurisdiction (The SIJ) set up in article 246 of the 1991 Political Constitution, in the following terms:

> The authorities of the indigenous peoples may exercise judicial functions within their territories according to their own norms and procedures, provided that they are not contrary to the Constitution and the laws of the Republic. The law shall establish the forms of coordination of this special jurisdiction with the national judicial system. (Translation by the author)

This provision not only recognized that indigenous authorities may administer justice within their territories but also delegated to them legislative power to conduct and resolve the potential tension between national sovereignty and indigenous autonomy; there is however still a legislative lacuna in this respect.

The unfinished work of the SIJ has had three main consequences in the Colombian legal system. First, conflicts regarding the status, scope and limits of the SIJ arose soon after the 1991 Constitution entered into effect. Secondly, the judicial system faced a number of conflicts of jurisdictional competence between national judicial and indigenous authorities. Thirdly, judicial decisions on a case-by-case basis were favoured given the absence of a law of "coordination" and the necessity to establish rules applicable to the factual functioning of the SIJ.

The quest for the pacific coexistence of a plurality of legal regimes has been achieved in Colombia through judicial decisions. However, the process of implementation of the SIJ has been complex. It has encountered a number of difficulties and has raised important issues concerning the interpretation of human rights. I shall next consider some problems inherent in the SIJ and some of the legal precedents set up in the settlement of disputes involving what I have called inter-systemic and intra-systemic conflicts concerning the SIJ.

SOME PROBLEMS INHERENT IN THE IMPLEMENTATION OF A SPECIAL INDIGENOUS JURISDICTION

The relation between the State and the indigenous peoples is inherently a tense one. On the one hand the State holds the monopoly on normative production and implementation of Law. On the other hand, the indigenous forms of legal, political, and social regulation persist within indigenous groups that insist on their validity and application within their territories that are located within the geopolitical space administered by the State.

In the case of the SIJ there is an unequal competition between legal orders. The competition is between the "national judicial system" and the "special indigenous jurisdiction". This competition is between a legal jurisdiction of national application and a legal jurisdiction of restricted character, since it is only competent in matters involving indigenous peoples within indigenous territories.

In cases of conflict, the national judicial system is imposed on the indigenous judicial systems. Nevertheless it is important to note that "the State recognizes and protects the cultural and ethnic diversity of the Colombian nation" and consequently, the State is obliged to respect the indigenous legal systems even if their scope is narrower.

This issue becomes further complicated by virtue of the fact that indigenous legal systems and western legal systems may have important differences in relation to their nature, norms, prescribed crimes, punishment and gender-based policies.

A first set of differences may be found in the nature of indigenous and western legal systems. While State laws and legal systems of western countries are usually written, codified and/or based on precedents, most of the indigenous rules are unwritten, flexible and dynamic and based on oral traditions. Several authors have criticized the western demand for indigenous peoples to have written laws. Van Cott, for instance, points out that "codification by indigenous peoples may reflect an attempt to "sanitize" indigenous law for Western consumption". She supports her assertion with a case in Lowland Bolivia where the Guarani Communities of Alto and Bajo Izozog wrote their laws down after they burned to death a suspected witch, and the State authorities tried to punish those responsible. The Written version of their laws did not include the burning sanction, although some authors have observed that the practice continues.[118]

A second set of differences lies in the nature of some norms of the indigenous communities. For instance, Rodolfo Stavenhagen points out that indigenous

[118] Van Cott, 2003, *op. cit.*, p. 26.

and western systems of justice may compete because they are based upon different sets of cultural values.[119] A belief in respect of twins in some pre-Columbian indigenous communities from Colombia may illustrate this assumption. Thus according to a local pre-Columbian tradition within the Muisca-Guanes communities, the second of newborn twins represents evidence of infidelity and/or excessive lustful passion of the woman. Accordingly, members of the tribes punished her or mock her publicly.[120] A similar custom in the U'Wa Communities that inhabit a part of the eastern and northeastern Colombian territory raised important issues and drawn public attention some years ago.

A third set of differences lies in the nature of what is considered a crime in indigenous and non-indigenous legal systems. Some crimes in western legal systems may not be considered crimes in indigenous legal systems i.e. bloodthirsty revenge. Conversely, some crimes in indigenous legal systems may not be considered as crimes in western legal systems such as witchcraft and gossip.[121]

A fourth set of issues arising in the implementation of legal pluralism refers to the different nature of punishment imposed by indigenous and non-indigenous legal systems. Stavenhagen illustrates this difficulty with an example from Oaxaca, Mexico, where a man who killed another in a drunken brawl was ordered to marry the victim's widow and take care of her and her children. Although the Mexican State tried to interfere, the community and the individuals involved rejected this interference and the sentence was honoured.[122]

A fifth set of issues revolves around gender-based policies. As mentioned by Van Cott, the vast majority of indigenous authorities consist of men. Women have a subordinate political and social role in most indigenous communities although indigenous women have begun to question indigenous traditional rules that perpetuate this discrimination.[123]

---

[119] See, inter alia: Stavenhagen, 1988, *op. cit.*, and Iturralde, 1990, *op.cit.*

[120] Ardila *Díaz, El pueblo de los Guanes, raíz gloriosa de Santander*, [The Guanes people, glorious root of Santander],Sena editions, Bogota, 1970.

[121] See: Van Cott, 2003, *op.cit.*, pp 27-8.

[122] Stavenhagen, 1988, *op. cit* as quoted by Van Cott, 2003, *op. cit.*, p. 29.

[123] Van Cott, 2003, *op. cit.*, p.27.

Considering the differences one is confronted with a Janus[124] like picture. Fortunately, we are not dealing with irreconcilable legal orders. Indigenous and western legal systems may have functional and structural logics that may be radically different but not necessarily opposite. All these issues may however have important implications concerning human rights. There are a number of cases in which there is an apparent clash between indigenous peoples norms, customs and punishments and the traditional interpretation of international human rights' standards for example as in the case of punishment by whipping. Conversely, western practices such as oil exploitation may in some cases threaten indigenous peoples with extinction and therefore, be considered by them as an act of genocide. In order to achieve a better understanding, it will be useful to present the typology of conflicts related to the SIJ and then, some of the precedents established by the Colombian Courts.

THE CONFLICTS DERIVED FROM THE RECOGNITION OF THE SIJ IN COLOMBIA

Conflict stemming from the recognition of the SIJ in Colombia are captured in the classic division between judicial and extra-judicial conflicts, and, between conflicts of interest and conflicts of Law. The latter frequently overlap in practice and conflicts inherent in the SIJ have not been an exception. In fact, conflicts of interests usually accentuate disagreements between parties and frequently necessitate resort to judicial intervention. Thus, the opposition of an indigenous community to the extraction of petroleum by a multinational enterprise in a territorial area that according to its common traditions is considered sacred, becomes a legal conflict when the native community insists on the protection of cultural and ethnic diversity. The initial conflict of interests is transposed to the legal world where it is frequently translated in terms of resolution of normative antinomies.[125] The judicial function is then

[124] Janus is the ancient Roman God of beginnings and activities related to beginnings. The god Janus has a distinctive appearance in art, as he is often depicted with two faces looking in opposite directions. Nevertheless, in early statues he has been depicted with four faces. Historians have said that Janus was represented in this peculiar fashion due to the notion that doors and gates look in two directions. Accordingly, one of the God's faces could look forward, while the other looked backward. Janus did not have a couterpart in Greek mythology.

[125] Legal rules are considered antinomies where they are in conflict when applied to a concrete case. Antinomics arc usually identified as legal norms mutually exclusive but aplicable to the resolution of a particular case. See: BOBBIO Norberto, 1998, "Des critères pour résoudre les

called on to weigh the legal principles at stake: the general interest of the State[126] on the one hand, and the protection and respect of cultural and ethnic diversity on the other hand, and then decide which of them should prevail. Accordingly, I shall depart from the premise that conflicts of interests are distinct from the category of the conflicts of Law, and I will use the term 'conflict' in its broadest meaning.

In the Colombian context there are, basically, two the types of conflicts stemming from the recognition of indigenous judicial authorities: conflicts between legal systems and conflicts between judicial authorities.

The Conflicts Between Legal Systems

The first type of conflicts can be described as a collision among the conceptions and bases of "indigenous law" and those of the national legal system. In this type of conflict there is a competition as to whether the indigenous customs, norms and procedures are adapted to fit within the parameters established by the Colombian legal system. The question the judges are called to resolve is whether the indigenous authorities in the exercise of their judicial functions surpassed the limits imposed on the holders of judicial power in Colombia. This might be the case where an indigenous individual who, considering inadequate the mechanisms used by the indigenous judicial authorities to judge him, decides to present a complaint to the judicial organs of the State requesting the protection of his/her right to due process of law. The judicial organs of the State are then called on to intervene directly within the indigenous community to demand that the indigenous judicial authority revise or modify its decision in order to render it in compliance with the core of non-derogable human rights recognized within Colombian territory. From a legal standpoint, the State's intervention may be considered as an imposition of a second review unforeseen by the indigenous systems.

This type of conflict I call "inter-systemic" since at a theoretical level, this type of conflict is between two systems: the national legal system and the

antinomies", *Essais de théorie du droit (recueil de textes)*[Essays of Legal Theory (digest of textes)], translated to French by Michel guéret, LGDJ, Paris, pages 89-103, p. 89.

[126] The principle of prevalence of the general interest of the State is grounded in the right of Sovereignty. It is important to remark that under a number of UN Resolutions as well as in the Charter of Economic Rights and Duties of States and in the Stockholm Declaration on the Human Environment, states are declared to have absolute sovereignty over the use of natural resources within their territorial boundaries.

indigenous legal system. I would like to emphasize that the conflict is between two systems and not between two jurisdictions since article 246 does allude to the necessary coordination among "the national judicial system" and "the special indigenous jurisdiction" - whose objective is the application of the judicial indigenous systems. Inter-systemic conflicts are, by nature, unequal. In fact, these conflicts are between a system and a subsystem since indigenous legal systems are conceived of as a part of the Colombian legal system.

Conflicts Between Judicial Authorities

The second type of conflict may be described as a collision between judicial authorities involving the adjudication of cases involving indigenous peoples. The main legal issue here is to determine the relative seniority and authority as between judicial authorities.

At first sight, it could be argued that these types of conflict are not important since their resolution may be reduced to the systematic application of predefined elements to settle disputes between judicial authorities. However, as of November 2002 the Colombian legal system did not address the minimum required to establish indigenous jurisdiction. Moreover, it was only in 2001 that some norms of criminal law establishing the so-called "exception of inimputability by ethno-cultural diversity" and some special measures of security for indigenous individuals accused of criminal offences entered into force.[127]

I call this type of conflict 'intra-systemic' since the conflict is between judicial authorities legally recognized as on the same hierarchical level within, and under the rules of, a single legal system, the national one. It should be emphasised that the resolution of this type of conflict is not found in the existence of a plurality of legal systems but in the existence of a plurality of judicial authorities one of them being indigenous. In this type of conflict the point at issue is whether an indigenous or a non-indigenous judicial authority may decide the case.

[127] See articles 73 and 368 of the law 599 of July 24, 2000 and article 479 of the law 600 of July 24, 2000 corresponding respectively, to the new Penal Code and Code of Criminal Procedure into effect from July 24, 2001.

THE RESOLUTION OF INTER-SYSTEMIC CONFLICTS IN COLOMBIA

The "acción de tutela" (writ of injunction) is the most common legal remedy used by indigenous peoples and/or their representatives to demand the resolution of inter-systemic conflicts. By virtue of the "acción de tutela" every person in Colombia, including children and foreigners may claim before the judges, orally, or by a written statement the protection of his/her fundamental human rights and even without mentioning them technically.

The efficacy of this remedy rests in its speed and in the control that the Constitutional Court exercises over it. The judge at first instance must make a decision during the 10 days that follows the lodging in court of the complaint and, in the second instance, the Court of appeal must decide within a period of twenty days. In spite of the preferential and summary nature of this remedy, it is a remedy of last resort since it only operates in the absence of other judicial remedies or to prevent the imminent violation of a fundamental constitutional right.

All judges may decide cases involving the SIJ through the writ of injunction. All decisions concerning this writ are automatically referred to the Constitutional Court as the guardian of the Colombian Constitution. The Court has discretion to choose what decisions are to be reviewed and in practice, it has considered as a priority to study both "hard cases" and cases of particular importance for the protection of human rights or having social and/or political impact. Repeatedly, the Court has reviewed judicial decisions dealing with the SIJ.

The decisions of the Constitutional Court in its review of the judgments delivered on the writ of injunction are the cornerstone of the implementation of the SIJ in Colombia.[128] It was in 1994, in decision T-254, that the Court made clear that the exercise of judicial functions by indigenous authorities was not dependent on the existence of a law coordinating the relationship between the "national judicial system" and the "special indigenous jurisdiction". It also highlights the four elements of the SIJ as set out in article 246: first, indigenous peoples may have judicial authorities; secondly, the judicial

[128] See, inter alia, the decisions: T-254 (1994), T-349 (1996), T-496 (1996), T-523 (1997), T-344 (1998), T-667A (1998) and T-266 (1999).

authorities of indigenous peoples may establish their own norms and proceedings; thirdly, indigenous norms and proceedings must be in compliance with the constitution and the laws of the republic; fourthly, the legislative branch should pass a law defining the nature of the relationship between the special indigenous jurisdiction and the national judicial system.

In decision T-496 (1996) the court recognizes the great effort involved in the achievement of intercultural understanding, reaffirmed the State's obligation to promote the pacific coexistence between individuals, groups and peoples and began to set standards for implementing the SIJ. It first pointed out that the recognition of the SIJ implies the right of indigenous peoples to be judged by their own authorities, norms and proceedings and within their territorial areas. The Court named this right *fuero indígena* [indigenous privilege] and characterized it with personal and territorial elements. By virtue of the personal element, indigenous authorities may judge indigenous individuals. By virtue of the territorial element, indigenous authorities only have jurisdiction within indigenous territorial areas legally recognized as such.

However, the Court concluded that the elements of the "indigenous privilege" must be established simultaneously since the SIJ has limits that must be determined under case-by-case basis. Thus, some of the elements that must be analysed in practice are: the place where the facts occurred, the particular cultural features of the indigenous people involved in the case, the degree of isolation or integration of the indigenous individual in respect of the majority culture, and the possible effects that the anticipated punishment may have on the indigenous individual. The Court also stated that the adjudication of a criminal case involving an indigenous individual who committed a crime against a non-indigenous individual and outside the territorial jurisdiction of his/her community must be decided by the national judicial system. Moreover the settlement of disputes involving indigenous individuals who commit crime outside the territory of their communities, and which affect non-indigenous individuals must be adjudicated to the national judicial authorities. When the accused is an indigenous individual, the judge should determine whether that individual is entitled to the "indigenous privilege". Then, the judge should "determine whether the author of the crime understood the illicit character of the act s/he perpetrated.' If the "indigenous privilege" is recognized, the judicial authority should transfer the indigenous individual to its cultural environment «for the sake of preserving indigenous peoples' special ethnic conscience».

The Court affirmed that the special indigenous jurisdiction is subject to limits to be determined on a case-by-case basis. However, the Court introduced rules of interpretation applicable to resolve conceptual differences and conflicting values in the practical application of a diversity of legal systems. In the Court's view, these rules of interpretation are the following:

(1) Autonomy is granted to indigenous groups and peoples in proportion to the extent that they have preserved their norms and customs. Accordingly and as further developed in decision T-349 (1996), the basic rule of interpretation is the maximisation of the indigenous peoples autonomy and the minimisation of restrictions to autonomy either to those necessary to safeguard interest of the upper hierarchy i.e. national security, or to those less detrimental for the protection of indigenous peoples' cultural values.

(2) The core of non-derogable human rights is a precondition to achieve the pacific co-existence between culturally diverse peoples.

(3) Indigenous customary law prevails over ordinary civil laws in case the latter conflict with cultural norms

(4) Imperative norms (norms of public order) prevail over indigenous norms and customs whenever they are intended to protect a constitutional value or principle of a higher hierarchy than the protection of cultural and ethnic diversity.

These rules of interpretation raise the question about the criteria to resolve tension between on the one hand the protection of cultural and ethnic diversity, with on the other hand, other constitutional principles. In its consideration the Court is likely to be influenced by liberal theory relating to human rights and the precondition for pacific coexistence between cultures, namely that individual rights have priority over collective rights. Applying this test, the right to life, the prohibition of slavery, exile, cruel, inhuman and degrading treatment and punishment as well as the respect of the due process of law, and the legality of crimes and punishments are considered constitutional principles of an upper hierarchical value.

The most interesting developments in relation to the implementation of the SIJ revolve around the interpretation of human rights in cases of potential clashes with western conceptions. In decision T-523 (1997) the Court dealt with a case in which an indigenous individual brought a judicial action under the form of a writ of injunction against the governor of his *Cabildo* and the Chief of the Association of Indigenous *Cabildos* of his region. He alleged, *inter alia*, the violation of his right to the due process of law and the lack of jurisdiction of the indigenous judicial authorities to judge the crime of homicide. In this case, the mayor of a municipality located in an indigenous territory was murdered. Two days later, the governors of several *cabildos* established a commission whose objective was to investigate and punish the crime. The first measure was to detain six indigenous individuals with suspected involvement in the crime. These suspicions were based on an earlier incident where the detainees defamed and slandered the victim. One of them was accused of having alleged publicly that the victim was organizing a community group to maintain the local security and to combat the insurgent groups and that he had squandered public funds. This last accused was also suspected of spreading rumours by informing the members of an insurgent group that the victim was a member of a contra-insurgent armed group. The commission of investigation collected the testimony of the accused that requested to be defended by a lawyer. The commission responded by saying that access to assistance by a lawyer was related to group membership and knowledge of the particular indigenous norms, customs and procedures. When the investigation finished the Commission organized an assembly of *Cabildos* to present its conclusions. The day after the announcement of the assembly, the defendant decided to present a writ of injunction against the governor of the *Cabildo* and the Chief of the Association of indigenous *Cabildos* of that region. The defendant alleged violation of the due process of law and the lack of jurisdiction of the indigenous authorities to judge a case of murder. Five days later, with the decision still awaited, the Assembly of indigenous "cabildos" took place. The members of the "resguardos" deliberated and found the accused guilty. He was condemned to 60 blows of the "fuete"[129] to be applied in a rate of two by "resguardo", the loss of the right to take part in elections and be elected in his community and banishment.

The judge at first instance decided the writ of injunction in favor of the claimant, and, the judge at second instance confirmed the decision. Nevertheless, the Constitutional Court in its review of the case revoked these decisions.

[129] A "fuete" is the name for a primitive instrument used to punish; it is like a whip.

How did the Colombian Constitutional Court arrive at such a decision? In this case, an indigenous individual was involved and the crime was committed inside the indigenous territory. However, the accused was not assisted by an attorney during the proceedings.[130] Likewise, corporal punishment, and all those acts that may be count as cruel inhuman or degrading treatment,[131] as well as exile[132] are proscribed by the Colombian Constitution.. [supress This could be described as one of Dworkin's[133] "hard cases". In these judges usually face antinomies and/or legal lacunas.[134] Judges may also face "hard cases" even if there is certainty on the *lex specialis*. For example, when it contains vague linguistic expressions or when the existing legal precedents have become anachronistic or inadequate in changing societies.[135]

In this case, the Colombian Constitutional Court undertook the resolution of antinomies when the constitutional principle of protection and respect to cultural and ethnic diversity was in collision with other constitutional principles. In the view of the Court, the basic rule was "maximize indigenous autonomy and reduce its restrictions only to those necessary to protect interests of an upper hierarchy".

To decide this case, the Constitutional Court called for expert evidence on the nature of the *fuete* as a punitive sanction within the indigenous community and its relationship with torture. Inspired by the precedents of the European Court of Human Rights, the Colombian Constitutional Court stated that a punitive sanction is to be considered torture if it produces *intense and cruel physical and/or mental suffering*. The expert evidence showed that punishment with

[130] One of the legal guarantees under the Colombian criminal judicial system is the right to be represented by an attorney. See: Republic of Colombia, Political Constitution, 1991, article 29.

[131] See: Republic of Colombia, Political Constitution, 1991, article 12.

[132] See: Republic of Colombia, Political Constitution, 1991, article 34.

[133] Dworkin, R, "Hard Cases", *Harvard Law Review* No.*88*, 1975.

[134] A legal lacuna denotes a lack or legal deficiency affecting the resolution of a particular legal conflict. In the terms of Jean-André Arnaud, a legal lacuna indicates that the legal system "ne contient pas de propositions définissant le statut déontique d'un cas déterminé". Accordingly, The recognition of a lacuna "implique toujours un jugement de valeur sur l'incomplétude du système normatif". Arnaud, 1993, *op. cit. p.* 335. The most frequent legal formula used to resolve cases involving legal lacunas is the analogy.

[135] Under this circumstance, the judges are usually authorized to decide "in equity" which is considered as a secondary criteria to light the legal interpretation as set up in article 230 of the Colombian Constitution.

fuete took place within a ritual intended to recover the equilibrium between offender and the environment. Based on this evidence, the Constitutional Court concluded that the *fuete* was a common punitive sanction with symbolic significance within the particular indigenous community involved in the case. In the Court's view this type of punishment could not be considered as torture or as cruel, inhuman or degrading treatment or punishment given the particular context of the case.

In respect of the due process of law, the Constitutional Court criticised the first and second instance decisions concerning the right of an indigenous individual to be represented by an attorney. It considered that such a requirement was not in compliance with the principle of cultural and ethnic diversity since it is a western concept alien to the indigenous community.

Finally, in respect of banishment as a punishment, the view of the Court was that the sanctions imposed by the indigenous authorities were to be considered as applicable only within the indigenous territory. Therefore, the indigenous community did not violate the proscription of banishment set out in the Colombian Constitution.

In decision T-349 (1996) the Court reviewed a judicial decision on a writ of injunction brought by an indigenous individual condemned of murder within his community. The defendant avoided the indigenous judicial authorities and went voluntarily to the government attorney's office [Fiscalía] where he was detained. After some months, the *Cabildo* of the detainee's region made public its decision to sentence him to eight years prison. The government attorney's office stopped the investigation of the case, but, at a latter date, the General Assembly of the Indigenous community decided to increase the punishment to 20 years prison. In the Constitutional Court's view, the indigenous community violated the detainee's right to the due process of law. Based on expert evidence, the Court concluded that the punishment imposed by the community on the defendant was completely alien to the indigenous legal order since the punishment traditionally imposed in similar cases was three years of forced labour and the *cepo*.[136] Accordingly, the Constitutional Court decided to consult the indigenous community about the possibility of either re-sentencing the defendant in accordance with their traditional practices or, considering the transfer of the case to the national judicial authorities.

[136] The cepo is similar to whip but less harmful.

More recently the Court tackled again the issue of harmonizing cultural practices with human rights standards. A couple of year ago, some Colombian indigenous communities were the subject of public and international attention when the parents of a couple of twins abandoned them in a forested area because twins were considered as bringers of bad news and representatives of *sisrama* (the devil) by the U'Wa community. The writ of injunction in favour of the children was brought by the Colombian Institute of Family Welfare [ICBF] to request the protection of the children, their health and their right to have a family through a declaration of abandonment in order to facilitate adoption. The Court taking into consideration the opposition of the indigenous parent of the Children supported a process of consultation and internal reflection promoted by community members inside the indigenous community. It concluded that the parents' decision to abandon the children rested upon their fear of a possible rejection of them and the children by their community because of an ancient belief. It also considered however, that the process promoted inside the community and their request to return the children to it was sufficient proof of the indigenous will to re-evaluate the cultural practice of rejection that was unacceptable within the framework of human rights. In decision T-030 (2000), the Court expressed the view that the most sensible means of guaranteeing the immediate protection of the rights of the children was by overseeing their return to the indigenous community. The SIJ could thereby promote traditional practice and continue their process of consultation in order to guarantee the Children protection in conformity with the standards establish in the Colombian Constitution.

THE RESOLUTION OF INTRA-SYSTEMIC CONFLICTS IN COLOMBIA

The competent organ to settle disputes between judicial authorities in Colombia is the "Consejo Superior de la Judicatura"[137] through its Disciplinary Jurisdictional Room. [138] The decisions of the Jurisdictional Disciplinary Room

[137] I shall not used an English translation of the "Consejo Superior de la Judicatura" because of its hybrid nature. Its functions square with two French organs: "Le Conseil Supérieur de la Magistrature" and the "Tribunal des Conflits".

[138] The "Consejo Superior de la Judicatura" is divided into two rooms, one administrative, [Sala Administrativa] the other, disciplinary jurisdictional [Sala Jurisdiccional Disciplinaria]. The first one is composed of six members and the second one of seven. One of the functions of the Disciplinary Jurisdictional Room is to settle the conflicts between judicial authorities as well as

(JDR) in cases involving the SIJ have focused on criminal law cases. Although influenced by the precedents set up by the Constitutional Court, the criteria set up by the "Consejo Superior de la Judicatura"[139] for adjudicating cases within the SIJ are far more demanding. The JDR usually considers five criteria to settle disputes involving indigenous judicial authorities:

1) The legal recognition of an indigenous *cabildo*.
2) The membership of the indigenous accused to a *cabildo*.
3) The perpetration of the crime within a *resguardo*. (Territorial element of the "indigenous privilege" set up by the Constitutional Court)[140]
4) The membership of the indigenous accused to an indigenous community (personal element of the "indigenous privilege" set up by the Constitutional Court)[141]
5) The membership of the victim to an indigenous community or the fact that the object with which the crime was perpetrated belongs to an indigenous community. (Objective element)

The judicial decisions of the JDR show a rapid evolution in the interpretation of these five elements. In a decision of April 8, 1999, the fact an indigenous individual studied in a university was considered a proof of significant acculturation. In a decision of June 24, 1999 however «the interchange, communication and relations between majority and minority cultures does not lead us to infer that the latter lost their identity or that they do not have the aspiration to preserve their traditions, or that they do not intend to settle their own conflicts according to their rules».[142]

The interpretation of the objective element of the "indigenous privilege" has also rapidly changed. In general terms, the DJR has required that the crime belongs "naturally" to, or directly affects, an indigenous community. Thus, even if indigenous individuals have perpetrated the crimes within indigenous

between administrative authorities with judicial functions attributed by the laws. See: Republic of Colombia, Political Constitution, 1991, articles 254-257.

139 See, inter alia: Consejo Superior de la Judicatura, decisions of February 18, 1999; April 8, 1999; May 13, 1999; June 24, 1999; July 8, 1999; Julio 15, 1999; July 29, 1999; August 19, 1999 and September 16, 1999.

140 See *supra* The resolution of Inter-systemic conflicts in Colombia

141 Ibidem.

142 Consejo Superior de la Judicatura, Decision of Abril 8, 1999, Magistrate Rapporteur: Edgardo José Maya Villazón. In this case the dispute deals with a criminal process against an indigenous accused of murdering his indigenous wife adjudicated to the national judicial authorities. See also: sentencia de Julio 15 de 1999 and sentencia de Septiembre 16 de 1999.

territorial areas, as a general rule, the JDR does not adjudicate within the SIJ cases concerning homicide,[143] illegal carrying of weapons,[144] and rape.[145] However, in a decision of June 24, 1999, cases concerning intended murder and illegal carrying of personal weapons were adjudicated to the SIJ. Likewise, the crime of drugs trafficking has been object of a plurality of interpretations in a number of cases. For example, whereas in a decision of September 24, 1998 a case on this matter was adjudicated within the SIJ, in a decision of February 18 1999, a similar case was adjudicated to a non-indigenous judicial authority arguing - at the request of the indigenous community – that the nature of the crime was alien to indigenous cultural values of the community to which the accused belonged.

VII. APPRAISSAL AND RECOMMENDATIONS

The relationship between indigenous peoples, States, international organizations and the international community have been gaining importance during the last three decades. In spite of, or possibly because of, the complexity of these relationships, there is a need for a policy-oriented perspective grounded in an understanding of conflicting claims. There is a need to explore constructive procedures and models for dealing with potential and ongoing conflicts. This process should be influenced by social research and should also empower indigenous peoples in the sense of offering them the possibility to present their own proposals. Even if conflicts and disputes in which indigenous peoples are involved do not become intractable conflicts or threats to peace or regional stability, pro-active measures rather than reactive responses to disputes is, without any doubt the better option. The permanent Forum of Indigenous Peoples could be a major actor in this process at the

[143] See: Consejo Superior de la Judicatura, decisions of April 8, 1999; July 15, 1999 and September 16, 1999.

[144] See Decision of July 29, 1999 dealing with the adjudication of a case against two indigenous one accused of murder and other accused of illegal carrying of fire weapons of personal defence. Even if the facts took place within the territory legally recognized to the indigenous community the case was adjudicated to the national judicial authorities.

[145] See: Decision of May 13, 1999. This case deals with the adjudication of a dispute on a criminal process against an indigenous accused of perpetrating a rape against an indigenous child within the territory legally recognized to an indigenous community. It was adjudicated to the national judicial authorities. A similar case can be found in a decision of July 8, 1999.

international level and the implementation of legal pluralism is certainly a plausible option at the domestic level.

From a practical point of view, the recognition of legal pluralism brings challenging solutions within the framework of human rights to the numerous problems encountered in the achievement of pacific coexistence between distinct normative systems in multi-ethnic societies. The recognition of indigenous judicial authorities and the implementation of legal pluralism constitute not only an example for the American continent but also for the rest of the world with regard to the efforts to grant a high degree of legal autonomy to indigenous peoples. The establishment of a special indigenous jurisdiction constitutes a major breakthrough in the implementation of the right of indigenous peoples to preserve their own forms of legal organization.

The implementation of legal pluralism through judicial decisions in Colombia should result but in a positive balance between the respect of indigenous peoples' laws and the interpretation of international human rights standards. However, the assessment of the Colombian case should not be limited to the formal function of Law. [146] Through judicial decisions, the discourse on indigenous judicial authorities, the cosmological values of indigenous peoples, the cultural and legal pluralism of Colombian society, the need to respect ethnic and cultural diversity as a cornerstone principle of the State has been established. The Colombian society has accepted this discourse as valid. In fact, the changes introduced by the 1991 Constitution concerning indigenous peoples and its further implementation did not imply only a variation in the normative orientation toward indigenous peoples. They also implied the (re) construction of social imagery. Indigenous peoples have fortified their ethnic identity, and, a positive change in the perception of indigenous peoples has been introduced in Colombia. The democratic election of the "taita"[147] Floro

[146] It is important to recall, as Danièle Loschak, that Law has a double dimension as a prescriptive instrument and a descriptive discourse. It is this double dimension which grants its efficacy as factor of standardization of behaviours and forms of thought; as a vector of inculcation of the dominant values in the society and finally, as a factor of normalization.See: Daniele Loschak, "Droit, normalité et normalisation"[Law, Normality and Normalization], in *Le Droit en Procès* [Law in Action], PUF, Paris, 1983, p 54.

[147] ..."A los primeros gobernadores, los guambianos los llamaron tata, el papá de la comunidad..." [The "guambianos" called their first governant "tata", the father of the community.."] See: "Conceptos Básicos de la Cosmovisión Guambiana en relación con sus procesos de lucha" [Basic Concepts on the Cosmovision of the Guambianos in relation to their fighting processes],Bogotá, 1997, available at:

Tunubalá as governor of the department of the Cauca, in southwestern Colombia, was an edifying example welcomed by Colombian society and extensively covered by the Colombian media.

The process of implementation of legal pluralism in Colombia illustrates achievement of the principle of protection of cultural and ethnic diversity and cross-cultural respect that should prevail in multicultural societies. The Colombian example also highlights the need to educate civil societies, judges and attorneys, governments, human rights activists and defendants as well as members of human rights' governmental and non-governmental organizations concerned with indigenous peoples' rights, about indigenous peoples' cosmo-visions, legal norms and practices. An uninformed reader could be worried or even scared when reading some appeals by huge international NGOs to prevent indigenous people from practicing torture or other inhuman, cruel and degrading treatment and punishment within their communities. A better approach is to try to understand indigenous peoples cosmo-vision, and, then, conclude whether they are violating human rights As Mary Robinson stated some years ago, human rights should not be another form of colonialism.

Cultural and religious practices are one of the most complex issues to analyze in light of human rights. Sometimes these practices violate human rights and sometimes they only affect their full enjoyment. Dealing with situations of tension in multicultural societies may imply the tolerance and/or acceptance of practices that actually do not comply with human rights standards. Accordingly, a distinction must be drawn between practices which interfere with the enjoyment of human rights and that happen to be acceptable and those that are not. Accordingly, there is also a need to promote processes of reflection inside the indigenous communities in order to revaluate those practices that are unacceptable within the framework of international human rights law. As shown in the Colombian case concerning the abandoned twins, indigenous peoples are also able to initiate processes to respect and protect core human rights as the common ground to achieve cross-cultural understanding.

I am not advocating the rejection of human rights. Indigenous peoples' desire to be treated with respect for their culture, to participate within the state and fashion their own future. Modern democracies conducted with due regard for the rule of Law require common ground based on non-derogable human rights

http://www.colciencias.gov.co/seiaal/documentos/lgvu19.htm.

as a precondition for cross-cultural understanding. This aspiration may be achieved in multi-cultural and multiethnic States through legal pluralism.

CONCLUSION

Legal pluralism is a credible method of achieving the coexistence of distinct legal systems in multicultural societies. It must be based on the recognition of conflicting claims. It implies the acceptance of the necessity for effort to achieve the pacific and harmonic interaction between international human rights law and indigenous peoples' law. The process should be guided by intercultural respect as well as respect for human dignity and the promotion of social justice.

The recognition of indigenous peoples' norms and legal systems implies the recognition of their cultural, social and legal practices. It is based on indigenous peoples' right to practice, develop and preserve their culture and includes the recognition of their right to social, political and legal autonomy. As mentioned however in article 8.2 of ILO Convention 169, conflicts may arise in the application of this principle and in guaranteeing the rights inherent in it. These conflicts are related to a number of complex issues, which may complicate the implementation of legal pluralism within state boundaries. Accordingly, there is a need to achieve common ground, which should be based on both the existence of international and domestic laws protecting individual and collective rights, and the respect and protection of the core of non-derogable human rights. The requirement to achieve such coexistence is to educate western societies and indigenous peoples, the former in indigenous peoples' customs and legal practices, the latter in international standards of human rights. Thus, legal pluralism may facilitate true cross-cultural understanding creating dialogue and comprehension among peoples.

BIBLIOGRAPHY

Alderete, Ethel (Wara) (comp.), 1998.*The Health of Indigenous Peoples* , The World Health Organization, www.ku.edu/~insp/referencesite.html

Arnaud, Jean-André,

1998. *Introduction à l'Analyse Sociologique des Systèmes Juridiques* [Introduction to the Legal Systems' Sociological Analysis], Bruyllant, Brussels

1993. *Dictionnaire encyclopédique de théorie et de sociologie du droit* [Encyclopaedic Dictionnary of Legal Theory and Sociology], second edition, LGDJ, Paris

Bobbio, Norberto, 1998, "Des critères pour résoudre les antinomies", *Essais de théorie du droit (recueil de textes)*[Essays of Legal Theory (digest of textes)], translated to French by Michel guéret, LGDJ, Paris

Buergenthal, Thomas , David P. Steward, Dinah Shelton, 2002. *International Human Rights in a Nutshell,* Nutshell Series, third edition

Carbonnier, Jean, 1978. *Sociologie Juridique* [Sociology of Law], PUF.

Cassese, Antonio,1995. *Self-determination of peoples. A legal reappraisal*, Cambridge University Press

Loschak, Danièle 1983. "Droit, normalité et normalisation"[Law, Normality and Normalization], in *Le Droit en Procès* [Law in Action], PUF, Paris

Díaz, Ardila, 1970. *El pueblo de los Guanes, raíz gloriosa de Santander*, [The Guanes people, glorious root of Santander],Sena editions, Bogota
Dworkin, R, 1975. "Hard Cases", *Harvard Law Review No. 88*

Flood, Patrick James, 1998. The Effectiveness of UN Human Rights Institutions", Praeger Publishers

Fuller, Chris "Legal Anthropology, Legal Pluralism and Legal Though" in *Anthropology Today*, Vol.10, No.3, June 1994

García, Fernando et al., 2000. *De la Exclusion a la Participación: Pueblos Indigenas y sus Derechos Colectivos en el Ecuador* [From Exclusion to Participation: Indigenous Peoples and their Collective Rights in Equator], Quito

Gurvitch, Georges, 1935. *L'Expérience Juridique et la Philosophie Pluraliste du Droit* [The Legal Experience and the Pluralistic Philosophy of Law] Paris

Peña Guzmán, Mireya Maritza, 1996. "The Emerging System of International protection of Indigenous Peoples' Rights", in *St. Thomas Law Review,* Vol.9

Helander, Elina. *Les Sami de Norvège* [The Sami of Norway], Ministry of Foreign Affairs, the Information document UDA309FRA

Hudson, Manley O.,

World Court Reports, 1922-1942: Permanent Court of International Justice, Oceana Publications, 1969.

World Court, 1922-1929: A Handbook of the Permanent Court of International Justice, Gaunt Incorporated, 2001.

Kymlicka, Will (ed.), 1996. *The Rights of Minority Cultures*, Oxford University Press

Lijphart, Arend. *Democracy in Plural Societies. A comparative Exploration,* London, 1977, at page 53 and "Typologies of Democratic Systems" in *Comparative Political Studies 1*, April 1968, pages 3-44.

Lustick, Ian "Stability in Deeply Divided Societies: Consociationalism versus Control", in *World Politics,* No.31, 325-344

Merry, S.E. "Legal Pluralism", *Law and Society Review 22:* 869-96

Orakhelashvili, Alexander, 2001. "The Position of the Individual in International Law", in *California Western International Law Journal*, Vol . 9,

Patel, Bimal N., 2002. *The World Court Reference Guide Judgment, Advisory Opinions and Order of the Permanent Court of International Justice and the International Court of Justice*, 1922-2000, Kluwer Law International

Pellet, Allan "*State Sovereignty and the protection of fundamental human rights: an international law perspective*", http://www.pugwash.org/reports/rc/pellet.htm

Peterlini, Oskar, 1997. *Autonomy and the protection of ethnic minorities in trentino-South Tyrol. An overview of the history, law and politics,* Collection Ethnos 48, Braumuller editors

Rouland, Norbert (dir), Stéphane Pierré-Caps and Jacques Poumarède, 1996. *Droit des minorités et des peuples autochtones,* [Law of Minorities and Indigenous Peoples],PUF

Sieder, Rachel (ed.), 2003.*Guatemala After the Peace Accords*, Institute of Latin American Studies, London

Sillanpää, Lennard, 1994. *Political and Administrative responses to Sami Self-determination. A comparative Study of Public Administration in Fennoscandia on the Issue of Sami Land Title as an aboriginal Right*, Societas Scientiarum Fennica [The Finish Society of Sciences and Letters]

Sonders, Yvonne M., 2002. *Towards a Right to Cultural Identity*, School of Human rights Research Series, Volume 15, Maastricht

Starn, Orin, 1991. *Con los llanques todo barro: reflexiones sobre rondas campesinas, protesta rural y nuevos movimientos sociales* [Reflexions on *the Rondas Campesinas*, rural protest and new social movements], Lima, Peru

Stavenhagen, Rodolfo "Indigenous Organizations: rising actors in Latin America", *Cepal Review* No.62, August 1997, pages 63-75.

Stavenhagen, Rodolfo and Diego Iturralde (eds.), 1990. *Entre la ley y la costumbre. El derecho consuetudianrio indígena en América Latina* [Between Law and Custom. Indigenous Customary Law in Latin-America], Mexico

Van Cott, Donna Lee, 2000. "A political Analysis of Legal Pluralism in Bolivia and Colombia", *Journal of Latin American Studies,* No. 32, Cambridge University Press, 2000, pp 207-234, at page 209.

Van Cott, Donna Lee, 2003. "Legal Pluralism and Informal Community Justice Administration in Latin America", Conference on informal Institutions and politics in Latin America sponsored by the Harvard University and the Kellog Institute.

Woodman G.R., 1993. "The Idea of legal pluralism", *Legal Pluralism in the Arab*, Kluwer Law International, 1999: 3-19

Other sources:

"Conceptos Básicos de la Cosmovisión Guambiana en relación con sus procesos de lucha" [Basic Concepts on the Cosmovision of the Guambianos in relation to their fighting processes],Bogotá, 1997, available at: http://www.colciencias.gov.co/seiaal/documentos/lgvu19.htm.

Daes, Erica-Irene *Interview*, Miami, FL (USA), September, 2002

PCIJ, Advisory Opinion, *Nationality Decrees Issued in Tunis and Morocco*, Series B, Nº 4, p. 24.

Scheinin, Martin *Interview*, Miami, FL (USA), February, 2003.

United Nations:

Study of the Problem of Discrimination against Indigenous Populations", presented to the UN Sub-Commission on the Prevention of Discrimination of Minorities, 1986, in UN Doc. E/CN.4/Sub.2/1986/7/Add.4, United Nations Publication,

"*Where Indigenous Peoples live*", Cobo, José Martínez (Special Rapporteur), DPI/1316-93295-Nov.1992-9M

Aplicación del pacto Internacional de Derechos Económicos, Sociales y Culturales, ECOSOC, United Nations, 1995, UN. Doc. E/1994/104/Add.2.

Commission on Human Rights, Sub-Commission on Prevention of Discrimination and Protection of Minorities, Working Group on

Indigenous Populations, 14th Session July-August 1996, UN Doc. E/CN.4/Sub.2/AC.4/1996/2

Organization of American States, October 20th, 2000, *The Human Rights Situation of the Indigenous Peoples in the Americas, OEA/Ser.L/V/II.1.08*

Inter-American Court of Human Rights

Aloeboetoe et al. Vs. Suriname, Series C No.11, Judgment of December 4, 1991

Aloeboetoe et al. Vs. Suriname. Reparations, Series C No.15, Judgment of September 10, 1993.

The Mayagna (Sumo) Awas Tingni Vs. Nicaragua, Series C No.79, Judgment of August 31, 2001.

XVI Censo Nacional de población y V de vivienda, 1993, Revista América Indígena, Volumen LV, No.3, July-September 1995, p. 51.available at: http://www.dane.co

Republic of Colombia (http:// www.banrep.gov.co)

Consejo Superior de la Judicatura, Decisions:
April 8, 1999
February 18, 1999
April 8, 1999
May 13, 1999
June 24, 1999
July 8, 1999
July 15, 1999
July 29, 1999
August 19, 1999
September 16, 1999.

Constitucional Court Decisions (http:// www.ramajudicial.gov.co)
T-567 (1992)
T-188 (1993)
T-253 (1993)

T-001 (1994)
T-254 (1994)
T-349 (1996)
T-496 (1996)
T-523 (1997)
T-344 (1998)
T-667A (1998)
T-266 (1999).

Decree 2001,1988
Decree 1088, 1993
Decree 2164, 1995

Presidencia de la República, *Fuero Indígena Colombiano*, [Colombian Indigenous Privilege], Imprenta Nacional, Bogota, 1990.

Websites:

http://ww.africa-union.org
http://www.archives.govt.nz/holdings/treaty_frame.html
http://www.cidh.org
http://www.departments.bucknell.edu
http://www.europa.eu.int
http://www.georgestown.edu
http://www.ilo.org
http://www.inic.utexas.edu
http://www.johannesburgsummit.org/html/documents/summit_docs/1009wssd_pol_declaration.doc>.
http://www.oas.org
http://www.odin.dep.no
http://www.senado.gov.br
http://www.solon.org
http://www.summit-americas.org/Quebec-Indigenous/indigenous-archives-eng.htm
http://www.un.org
http://www.unhchr.ch
http://www.uni-wuerzburg.de/law
http://www.usask.ca/nativelaw/ddirplain.html
http://www.193.194.138.190/html/racism/minorpam14.doc

Traditional (in)Justice: Honour killings in Pakistan

Are Knudsen

INTRODUCTION[1]

Honour killing is an imprecise term for murder precipitated by the aggressor's loss of "honour" and can provisionally be defined as a "ritualised form of violence ,usually with male perpetrators and often, but not always, female victims".[2] This extra-judicial punishment is meted out by private actors according to customary law, and there is usually no way to repeal the sentence. The offender is typically killed by close family members, most often a brother, father or husband, on their own accord. Honour killings form part of what has been termed "traditional justice" or "tribal justice", a contested form of private retribution that many find unwarranted and illegitimate.[3] For the purpose of this paper, traditional justice denotes: "extra-judicial retribution by private actors legitimised with reference to a common (but often contested) moral and behavioural code enshrined in non-written form as a local 'tradition' or 'customary law'".

Worldwide honour killings claim the lives of at least 5,000 women although the true figure is probably much higher.[4] There are no official countrywide statistics for honour killings in Pakistan. The current estimate is 1,000 victims although the true figure is probably much higher.[5] If this figure is corroborated, Pakistan probably has the highest per capita incidence of honour killings in the world. What is the reason, or reasons that promotes honour killings in Pakistan? In 1999 Amnesty International published a detailed report on honour killings in Pakistan.[6] The report was based on field visits by Amnesty's local staff, who recorded testimonials from victims and their relatives. The report provided

---

[1] *Acknowledgements*: I am indebted to Mohammad Manzar Zarin, who assisted in collecting and translating the case material used in this paper. I owe special thanks to the Kohistani men who were interviewed for this paper and disclosed details of painful memories and traumatic events. The paper has benefited from comments by Karin Ask, Ivar Kolstad and Farhat Taj. None of them are responsible for the views expressed here, which, along with any mistakes, are solely my own.

[2] Cees Maris and Sawtiri Saharso, "Honour Killing: A Reflection on Gender, Culture and Violence" in *Netherland's Journal of Social Sciences*, Vol. 37, No. 1, 2001.

[3] Nancy V. Baker, Peter A. Gregware and Margery A. Cassidy, "Family Killing Fields: Honor Rationales in the Murder of Women," in *Violence Against Women*, Vol. 5, No. 2, 1991.

[4] UNPA (United Nations Population Fund), *Lives Together, Worlds Apart: Men and Women in a Time of Change*, New York, 2000.

[5] HRCP (Human Rights Commission of Pakistan), *State of Human Rights in Pakistan 2001*. Lahore, 2002.

[6] AI (Amnesty International), *Pakistan: Violence against Women in the Name of Honour*. New York, 1999 (www.amnestyusa.org/countries/pakistan/reports/honour/)

graphic details both of women and men brutally killed for a range of offensive acts such as defying arranged marriages, marrying a man of their own choice, seeking divorce, being raped as well as fake honour killings, that is, homicide under the pretext of honour loss. The report concluded that in most of these cases there was no conviction and a concomitant recourse to tribal justice.

In many countries in the Middle East, adultery is not only a breach of sexual morale but also a criminal offence that carries the death penalty. This is either because they have inscribed Quranic punishments for adultery in the civil penal code or, as in some Gulf-states, fully implemented Islamic law (*Sharia*). In both cases homicide is excused if adultery is proved.[7] In the case of honour killings, there is hence a convergence between jural laws and customary or "traditional justice" which sanctions homicide according to particularistic notions of honour and revenge.[8] In order to examine the relation between jural laws and traditional justice in Pakistan, the paper begins with a brief account of the social significance of honour, and then gives an overview of the jural laws governing the prosecution of honour killings. Following an assessment of the scanty national data on honour killings, I examine first-hand accounts of honour killings in the North-West Frontier Province where aggregate data on honour killings are missing. This allows me to investigate details of traditional justice that have received scant attention in the literature on the subject.[9]

INTERPRETING HONOUR KILLINGS

In general, attempts to circumscribe honour killings by attributing them to particular geographical regions ("Middle East"), cultures ("Kurdish" or "Pakistani" culture), faiths ("Islam"), or societies ("tribal", "Islamic") have failed because honour killings transcend such one-dimensional attributes. In order to understand why honour killings occur, we need to move beyond

---

[7] Abdel Salam Sidahmed, "Problems in Contemporary Applications of Islamic Criminal Sanctions: The Penalty for Adultery in Relation to Women", in *British Journal of Middle Eastern Studies*, Vol. 28, No. 2, 2001.

[8] Maris and Saharso, 2001, *op. cit.*

[9] CIMEL (Centre for Islamic and Middle Eastern Law) and INTERIGHTS (International Centre for the Legal Protection of Human Rights), *Preliminary Bibliography: "Crimes of Honour"*, (www.soas.ac.uk/honourcrimes/Bibliography.pdf); see also, Unni Wikan, *For Ærens Skyld: Fadime Til Ettertanke,* [For the Sake of Honour. Reflections on Fadime], Oslo, Universitetsforlaget, 2003.

simple descriptive labels. As the term "honour killings" implies, most academic research, media coverage, and news bulletins assume that homicide is provoked by the perpetrator's "loss of honour" and a key question is therefore what honour is. In Pakistan honour is a multidimensional term that includes familial respect (*izzat*) and social prestige (*ghairat*). Honour can be described as a relation between a person's own feelings of self-worth and that of the peer-group ("honour group") to which he belongs. Because honour bestowed socially, it is ephemeral and can be lost.[10] Losing honour invites ridicule and disgrace and subjects the family to "shame". Honour cannot only be lost, however, but also regained by returning the offensive act. A wide range of acts are considered shameful, but none more than those that compromise female chastity. Adultery, romance, and even flirting invites shame on the offender and his/her family. In honour-bound societies, female chastity represents the family's "symbolic capital".[11] To protect it, the offending woman must be killed rather than divorced or excommunicated, an act which in itself is considered shameful.[12] Killing her removes the offensive act, redeems family honour, and resurrects its prestige.[13] The murder is therefore a means to an end and used instrumentally to "restore honour" and "remove shame". Nonetheless, the killing of a spouse or a sister is an extremely traumatic event and therefore not possible without psychological distancing that weakens the social bonds between the victim and the aggressor. A striking feature of "typical" honour killings is that the victim's family does not publicly express regret over the murder nor is there any open expression of grief. Instead, close family members condemn her for betraying family loyalty for personal gratification. This reversal of injury turns male aggressors into victims and female victims into culprits.

The most common cause of honour killings is accusations of female adultery. To understand why, it is not enough to consider the role of honour but also the

[10] Frank Henderson Stewart, *Honor*, Chicago, University of Chicago Press, 1994.

[11] Pierre Bourdieu, *Outline of a Theory of Practice,* Cambridge, Cambridge University Press, 1977.

[12] Richard Tapper, and Nancy Tapper, "Marriage, Honour and Responsibility: Islamic and Local Models in the Mediterranean and the Middle East", in *Cambridge Anthropology*, Vol. 16, No. 2, 1992.

[13] It is important to warn against the impression that women accused of adultery are always killed, see, Unni Wikan, "Shame and Honour: A Contestable Pair", in *Man*, Vol. 19, 1984. In the Middle East there are institutions that can disprove accusations of infidelity, see Joseph Ginat, *Blood Revenge: Family Honor, Mediation and Outcasting*, Portland, Or., Sussex Academic, 1997.

structural opposition between romantic love and marriage must be taken into account.[14] In Muslim societies, marriage, in which romance has no place, upholds social structure and the alliance between families, lineages and clans, and the reproduction and creation of offspring. Hence, marriage is instrumental, a means to an end. Romance, on the other hand, is the structural anti-thesis concerned with personal gratification, always in secret and in contravention of official morals. This structural opposition helps explain why all forms of illicit romance provoke condemnation, ostracism, and frequently the killing of those involved: it is not only a threat to "personal honour", but also to that of the "honour group" who subscribe to the same honour code.[15] This explains why neighbours and unrelated co-villagers often laud honour killings.

In Pakistan and a number of other countries the Middle East, homicide in the case of adultery is excused because men are considered victims of circumstance and pardoned because the murder is impulsive and passionate. This gendered explanation locates the propensity for violence not in males in general, but in culturally constituted ways of "being a man" which links masculinity and aggression.[16] In societies where honour killings are prevalent, we commonly find that masculine virtues include complete control of the women in the family, causing honour killing to be blamed on patriarchy.[17]

Honour killings can be considered a typical example of traditional justice, but it is important not to infer that they only take place in "traditional" or "pre-modern" societies.[18] In recent years, honour killings have found their way into modern societies and challenged legal institutions such as the law and the judiciary.[19] In parts of the Middle East honour killings are no longer only a rural phenomenon, but also common in urban and peri-urban settings. There are indications that urbanisation spurs honour killings because it offers more opportunities for male-female socialization, less scope for enforcing rigid

[14] Charles Lindholm, "Love and Structure", in *Theory, Culture and Society*, Vol. 15, No. 3-4, 1998.

[15] Stewart, 1994, *op. cit.*

[16] Matthew C. Gutmann, "Trafficking in Men: The Anthropology of Masculinity", in *Annual Review of Anthropology*, Vol. 26, 1997.

[17] Mikael Kurkiala, "Interpreting Honour Killings: The Story of Fadime Sahindal (1975–2002) in the Swedish Press", in *Anthropology Today*, Vol. 19, No. 1, 2002.

[18] Thor Aase (ed.), *Tournaments of Power: Honor and Revenge in the Contemporary World*, Aldershot, Ashgate, 2002.

[19] Maris and Saharso, 2001, *op. cit.*; Wikan, 2003, *op. cit.*

social segregation of women (*purdah*), and increased peer-group pressure to defend personal honour. In addition, urban settings provide new avenues for social mobility and increased competition for social status and esteem, which in turn promote honour killings.[20]

The argument has also been made that religion itself is the cause of honour killings. This is because religion is the ultimate arbiter of sexual chastity and prescribes harsh punishments for those who compromise it. In Pakistan, the state-sponsored islamisation programme that began under Zia-ul-Haq's regime (1979–88) promoted Islamic orthodoxy and made adultery a criminal offence by turning sections of Islamic law (the *Sharia*) into statutory law. The growing orthodoxy made the protection of honour not only a social but a religious duty, thereby spurring homicide of men and women.[21] In sum, this means that honour killings cannot be attributed only to "honour", one must also consider the complex cultural, social and political context in which honour is embedded as well as the jural laws which are meant to discourage homicide and punish offenders.

PROSECUTING HONOUR KILLINGS

In 1996 Pakistan ratified the U.N. Convention on the Elimination of All Forms of Discrimination against Women (CEDAW). Under CEDAW, Pakistan assumed the obligation to protect women from sexual and other forms of gender-based violence perpetrated by state agents and private actors alike.[22] The current president, Pervez Musharraf, has condemned honour killings, instructed courts to investigate incidents as premeditated murder, and promised to punish offenders. Work is under way to review the criminal legislation concerning women, but nothing has yet been done to overhaul Pakistan's legislation concerning women's rights and repeal jural laws and regulations that discriminate against women. Instead, amendments to the criminal legislation during the past decade have disadvantaged women's legal status

---

[20] Gideon M. Kressel, "Sororicide/Filiacide: Homicide for Family Honour", in *Current Anthropology*, Vol. 22, No. 2, 1981.

[21] Lincoln Keiser, *Friend by Day, Enemy by Night: Organized Vengeance in a Kohistani Community*, Fort Worth, Holt, Rinehart and Winston, 1991.

[22] HRW (Human Rights Watch), "Crime or Custom? Violence against Women in Pakistan", 1999 (*www.hrw.org/reports/1999/pakistan*)

and incorporated elements of traditional justice into statutory law, thereby reducing the likelihood of punishing offenders.

Pakistani criminal law, the Pakistan Penal Code of 1860 (PPC), was originally a British imposition. As part of the islamisation of the penal code, the sections dealing with physical injury, manslaughter, and murder were revised in 1990 with the promulgation of the "Qisas and Diyat Ordinance" subsequently passed by parliament in 1997 as the "Qisas and Diyat Act" ("Retribution and Compensation Act").[23] The amendment had far-reaching consequences for the legal prosecution of homicide in general and honour killings in particular. The law privatises justice by shifting the emphasis from homicide as a crime against the state to a private offence against the victim. This allows the victim's legal heir (*wali*) the power to close the criminal investigation, accept monetary compensation (*diyat*), and to pardon the accused at any stage of the prosecution as well as to commute the death sentence. The death penalty (*qisas*, i.e. "death for a death") can only be imposed if very strict evidentiary requirements are fulfilled. If there is insufficient evidence to pass a death sentence, (or: to impose the death penalty)or the victim's legal heir (*wali*) is the direct descendant of the offender, the death penalty is commuted and the maximum sentence reduced to fourteen years imprisonment. Thus, a man who kills his wife on adultery charges is pardoned by her family and escapes legal prosecution. The Qisas and Diyat Act repealed the old penal code provision (Section 300-1) that pardoned homicide due to "grave and sudden provocation", in which case the murder charge was reduced to manslaughter.[24] Nonetheless, provocation is still invoked by courts as a mitigating cause and used in order to pardon male offenders or impose discretionary punishment (*tazir*), usually monetary compensation (*diyat*).

The Qisas and Diyat Act elevates elements of traditional justice to statutory law and encourages out-of-court settlements in accordance with local customs, often involving compensation payment and exchange of marriageable girls.[25] The result has been that honour killings seldom lead to conviction, and this

---

[23] AI, 1999, *op. cit.*

[24] "Culpable homicide is not murder if the offender, whilst deprived of the power of self-control by grave and sudden provocation, causes the death of the person who gave the provocation", *Ibid.*

[25] The penal code (section 310) states that giving a woman in compensation is not a valid form of negotiated compensation (*badal-i-sulh*) but it does not prohibit the practice, see AI, 1999, *op. cit.*

could be an important reason for the subsequent rise in honour killings since the promulgation of the Qisas and Diyat Ordinance in 1990.[26]

In addition to the imposition of the Qisas and Dyat Act, women's legal rights were further reduced when the Hudood Ordinance were passed in 1979 introducing Quranic punishment for adultery (*zina*) The Hudood ("Zina") Ordinance made fornication and rape criminal offences and punishable by stoning or public flogging if certain evidentiary requirements are fulfilled.[27] The Hudood Ordinance does not strictly differentiate between rape (*zina-bil-jabr*) and fornication (*zina*), consequently a rape victim who cannot prove that she did not consent to intercourse risks being charged with fornication and punished accordingly.[28] This anomaly is a major reason for using rape to defame the victim, her family and relatives.[29] Due to the Law of Evidence, introduced in 1984, a woman's testimony is not equal to that of a man's, a gender bias that further disadvantages women and reduces their chances of being acquitted.

In 1978 Pakistan instituted a parallel system of justice with the introduction of "Sharia Courts". Their initial purpose was to review whether the existing laws were contrary to the Sharia, the Holy Law of Islam. The Sharia Courts were organised as a parallel judicial system with Sharia Benches located in all the four provinces and the Supreme Court in Islamabad. In 1983 local level courts were introduced, led by an Islamic cleric acting as a religious judge (*Qazi*).

---

[26] Between 1985 and 1994 there was a 55 per cent increase in the number of reported homicides in Pakistan. The homicide rate peaked in 1990 with close to eight deaths per 100,000, see A. Ghaffar, A. A. Hyder, M. I. Mastoor, and I. Shaikh, "Injuries in Pakistan: Directions for Future Health Policy", in *Health Policy and Planning*, Vol. 14, No. 1, 1999.

[27] The penalty can only be applied if the accused confesses to the crime, or if there are four pious adult Muslim male eye-witnesses to the actual act of penetration. It is important to note that there is no example yet of women being stoned to death in Pakistan. Women convicted of adultery and sentenced to stoning by lower courts have always had their verdict overturned in higher courts. An example is the case of Zafran Bibi, a woman from Kohat in the NWFP who was charged with fornication after registering a rape case. She was subsequently sentenced to stoning under the Hudood Provisions by a lower court, but later acquitted of the charge by the Federal Sharia Court in Islamabad, see BBC News Online, "Pakistan Stoning Sentence Overturned", 6 June 2002,
(*http://news.bbc.co.uk/2/hi/south_asia/2029020.stm*)

[28] Sidahmed, 2001, *op. cit.*

[29] Shahla Haeri, "The Politics of Dishonour: Rape and Power in Pakistan", in Mahnaz Afkhami (ed.), *Faith and Freedom: Women's Human Rights in the Muslim World*, London, Tauris, 1995.

Qazi Courts hear cases concerned with Islamic law at the local level.[30] While the Sharia Benches have eight-members, which include five former justices as well as three higher ranking Islamic scholars, the Qazi Courts are presided over by a low-ranked cleric who has been educated in a religious seminary. The Qazi Courts frequently reach verdicts that punish women while men are absolved.

Not only the legal system is an obstacle to prosecuting honour killings, so are the police in charge of recording the crimes and investigating them. Understaffed, the policemen spend little time and effort in investigating honour crimes, and being underpaid they demand bribes to register an offence, known as a First Inquiry Report (FIR). If an investigation is carried out, the policemen routinely manhandle suspects during interrogation to force a confession.[31] They also beat up men and rape women who file charges. For these reasons, honour crimes are seldom registered with the police and the victim's family is left with the option to punish the culprit themselves according to traditional justice or suffer the dishonour of leaving the offence unavenged.[32]

MEASURING HONOUR KILLINGS

Pakistani authorities do not provide official statistics of the number of honour killings. This task has been left to the non-governmental Human Rights Commission of Pakistan (HRCP), which collects data on honour killings in two of Pakistan's four provinces. The HRCP's surveys are based on cases reported by the press or registered with the police. This means that cases neither picked up by the press nor registered with the police go unnoticed. The true figures of honour killings could therefore be considerably higher than current statistics indicate. In addition, there is an increasing number of fake honour killings used to cover up other offences as well as homicide under the pretext of honour which further distort the number of offences and makes true estimates difficult.

[30] John L. Esposito, "Islam: Ideology and Politics in Pakistan", in Ali Banuazizi and Myron Weiner (eds.), *State, Religion, and Ethnic Politics: Pakistan Iran, and Afghanistan*, Lahore, Vanguard Books, 1987.

[31] AI, 1999, *op. cit.*

[32] In order to encourage women to press charges, Women Police Stations have been instituted in two cities in the NWFP (Peshawar and Abbottabad). Despite having an all-female staff, very few women report offences at these stations (Farhat Taj, pers. comm.).

The most detailed statistics of honour killings are from the southern Sindh province. There the HRCP's survey found that honour killings averaged 412 victims per year during the five-year period 1998–2002.[33] The number of victims fluctuates from one year to the next, which may reflect inadequate reporting rather than proofs of a "rise or fall" in honour killings. The gender ratio of victims, however, shows little variation throughout this period. About 60 per cent of the victims were women, and only about half of the incidents were reported to the police (226 cases).[34] There is no information of how many were acquitted of the charge. Most probably the majority of the accused were acquitted due to missing evidence or defective investigation. In the Punjab province, there is even less information about honour killings. In 2001 honour killings numbered 227 women (22 men), compared to 315 women (35 men) the previous year.[35] Only in a fraction of the reported cases was the charge of adultery based on eye-witness accounts and adultery suspected rather than proved. This is testimony to the fact that protecting honour has become more important and punishing offenders has therefore become more brutal and widespread.

The HRCP survey shows that there is considerable variation in the magnitude, type, and frequency of honour killings in Sindh and Punjab, the two most populous provinces.[36] There is no comparable information from the North-West Frontier Province (NWFP) where, allegedly, honour killings first originated as a tribal custom.[37] Nonetheless, it is often inferred that due to the patriarchal nature of society in the NWFP, the limited state presence in rural areas in combination with the strict honour code which prevails there such as the Pashtun code of honour (*Pashtunwali*), honour killings are more common

---

[33] Year (victims): 1998 (341), 1999 (452), 2000 (457), 2001 (434), 2002 (376). The figures have been compiled from HRCP (Human Rights Commission of Pakistan), *State of Human Rights in Pakistan 2001*, Lahore 2002 and HRCP, *State of Human Rights in Pakistan 2002*, Lahore 2003.

[34] The main reason for the many male victims in Sindh is the prevalence of *karo-kari* killings. The offenders are referred to as "black", a black man (*karo*), a black woman (*kari*), and the murders therefore referred to as *karo-kari* killings. The colour symbolism underlines the gravity of the offence and explains why the victims' bodies are desecrated and disposed of without proper burial, see, Nafisa Shah, *A Story in Black: Karo-Kari Killings in Upper Sindh*, Oxford, Reuters Foundation Paper, No. 100, 1998.

[35] HRCP, 2002, *op. cit.*

[36] *Ibid.*

[37] AI, 1999, *op. cit.*

and more brutal than in the rest of the country. The police records from the province for the period 1990–2002 estimate that about 1,844 women have been killed in the name of honour, the large majority of them (1,383) in the so-called "tribal areas" where powerful ethnic groups enjoy a measure of political autonomy. [38] There is reason to believe that the actual numbers are considerably higher, because of underreporting and the prevalence of traditional ("tribal") justice in the NWFP.

This means that there is scanty knowledge of honour killings in Pakistan in general, and the NWFP especially, where traditional justice is particularly stern. The reports on honour killings are either based on secondary sources or interviews with the victim's family or relatives. There are neither first-person accounts with the perpetrator/s nor any first-hand information about the legal prosecution of honour killings. Instead, the incidents are sourced from meagre news reports or gleaned from defective police records. Thus, we lack detailed background information about individual cases of honour killings that can help us understand not only their instrumental function but also their cultural meaning.[39]

TRADITIONAL JUSTICE

In order to fill this lacuna, this section is based on taped interviews with male perpetrators of honour killings collected during ethnographic fieldwork in District Kohistan.[40] District Kohistan, which is located in a remote north corner of the NWFP, is a tribal area under provincial administration. It scores low on all development criteria and suffers from poor infrastructure and government neglect. The ethnic Kohistani villagers are for the most part poor and illiterate and there are frequent conflicts over land, property, and women. Here male aggression is an accepted fact and homicide among men common. Any offence that is deemed to involve loss of honour can give rise to lethal conflict (*kané*). The conduct of lethal conflicts conforms to customary law (*dastoor*) stipulating when force can legitimately be applied and revenge

[38] HRCP, 2003, *op. cit.*

[39] It is important to stress that understanding honour killing is not condoning it, but a key to prevention, see Pieter Spierenburg, "Faces of Violence: Homicide Trends and Cultural Meanings: Amsterdam, 1431-1816", in *Journal of Social History*, Vol. 27, No. 4, 1994.

[40] Are Knudsen, *Violent Belonging: Land, Love and Lethal Conflict in a Kohistani Community, Pakistan,* Bergen, book manuscript under review for publication, 2003

exacted. Most conflict resolution is local with minimal involvement of the police and the judiciary. In recent years the spread of automatic arms such as the ubiquitous AK-47 has increased the number and ferocity of lethal conflicts which claim the lives of men of all ages and, more recently, young women. A strongly patriarchal society where boys and girls are engaged at a young age, may be the explaination of the high frequency of extra-marital love affairs, which, if they become public knowledge, are punishable by death for both offenders. In the case of adultery allegations, the male offender is considered a "thief of honour" (*choor*) and can legitimately be killed along with the offending woman. Once adultery accusations become public, they cannot be retracted and the aggrieved party will be under pressure to substantiate the allegations by killing the offending woman and her paramour. If both are killed, no further proof of illicit relations is needed. In a number of cases, however, the male offender is informed about the threat to his life and helped to escape. Resettling somewhere in the down-country gives only temporary relief, and he is often tracked down and killed months or years later by the female victim's family or in-laws. The killing of both offenders can prevent further bloodshed, but if the murders are considered unjustified, it will trigger new enmity. To prevent this outcome, local mediators try to convince the parties to settle their differences by payment of money and exchange of marriageable girls. Should the parties to the conflict reject the mediators' offer, more pressure is applied from local consensual assemblies (*jirga*). If mediation fails, the ensuing vendetta can claim a number of male victims. For protection, the men party to the conflict wear magical amulets for protection and seek house confinement that in some cases lasts for years. In the end the weaker party is usually forced to leave or is killed in an ambush. Homicides of men are sometimes registered with the local police to prevent the culprit from escaping and resettling somewhere where killing him is more difficult. The murder of women is never reported because disclosing the reasons for her murder would be dishonourable and could incriminate male family members or in-laws.

Among the migrants who for personal reasons have been forced to leave District Kohistan and resettle in urban and peri-urban parts of the NWFP, adultery allegations also lead to homicide. However, in "settled areas" police inquiry into murder is routine and private justice is not commonly accepted. This increases the risk of being apprehended by the police and prosecuted by the courts. Nonetheless, they still commit murder when their honour is at stake. Homicide of men is often registered with the police, but the killing of women is usually covered up, and the victims are buried without notifying the police.

When honour killings of men are referred to courts, they seldom lead to conviction. Analysing case studies show that the suspects confess to the crime under the threat of being beaten or manhandled by the police. They are offered to escape torture by paying bribes and told that large sums of money can help them escape prosecution. To prevent this outcome, the plaintiffs likewise bribe the police to admit fake evidence which incriminates the suspect. In the courtroom, the defendants retract their confession and plead not guilty. To obstruct justice, the defendants or their relatives threaten witnesses to their life so that they fail to appear in court. For lack of evidence to prove the murder charge, the judge is left with the option of sentencing the defendant for manslaughter. To prevent this outcome, the defendants try to make the plaintiffs agree to an out-of-court settlement that includes paying compensation. The Qisas and Diyat Act instructs the court to heed out-of-court settlements, and consequently the court invokes the *diyat* ("blood money") provision laid down in the penal code and rules that the defendant pay the agreed monetary compensation to the victim's family (i.e., the legal heir, *wali*). In some cases, the defendant tries to avoid paying compensation because it contradicts local honour codes. Instead of paying, forged acknowledgement of the payment is put before the court. Should the judge, members of the jury, the plaintiffs, or their lawyer raise objections, threats to their lives will make them change their mind. After years of wrangling in court, the legal prosecution is closed and the suspect released. Bringing a killing to court is locally construed as dishonourable and a breach of tradition. For this reason, co-villagers often laud the defendant while rebuking the plaintiff, who as a consequence stands dishonoured.

Closing the legal case does not end the conflict, which is often followed by attacks on the defendant by the plaintiff and his family. In recent years also women have become targets of revenge killings although customarily, women could not be killed in revenge for the murder of a man. Because of the threats to their lives, the men frequently seek help from religious specialists to identify their adversaries and gain protection from bodily harm. The former involves reciting passages from the Quran and the latter elaborate rituals to invoke divine protection. Nonetheless, many of them are killed in treacherous revenge killings, which transform the original honour killing into a vendetta.

TRADITIONAL JUSTICE AND FORMAL LAW

Comparing the details of honour killings in "settled" and "tribal" parts of the NWFP illustrates the complex intertwining of jural law and traditional justice in Pakistan. In a tribal setting, jural law is secondary to traditional justice and police presence is minimal, hence homicide is seldom registered with the police, and consequently the perpetrators are not prosecuted in court. Instead, the aggrieved party seeks out and kills the murderer. In settled areas, honour killings more often end up in court, partly because private justice carries a higher personal risk of being apprehended by the police, and legal institutions are readily available in the form of local courts. Nonetheless, legal prosecution is usually rendered ineffective because of the many ways defendants can obstruct it. Even if the court is able to pass a verdict, this does not prevent the aggrieved party from seeking personal revenge. The reason is that the legal system is unable to provide justice for the loss incurred: only traditional justice can do this. This applies not only to revenging a woman or man's death but also the loss of honour produced by adultery allegations. The loss of honour cannot be redeemed by a jury or judge, nor reinstated through punishment or fines. Civil courts can make the parties agree to a formal settlement, but this is not equivalent to local concepts of justice. In the case of homicide justice cannot be rendered by the court, it can only be achieved through adhering to local notions of honour and revenge.

It is often claimed that in Pakistan "honour killings mostly go unreported and almost all go unpunished".[41] The examples provided here substantiate the first claim, but not the latter. Only the murder of Kohistani men is reported to the police and the offender brought to trial by the victim's family. The murder of women remains unrecorded.[42] This substantiates that honour killings of women are underreported and much more prevalent that current figures indicate.[43] Murderers either escape legal prosecution or receive lenient sentences. At least some of them are killed in revenge by relatives of the victim according to traditional justice. The juror's verdict closes the lengthy legal case, but does not foreclose the revenge killings that follow in its wake.

[41] AI, 1999, *op. cit.*

[42] If the murder were registered with the police, the family members would incriminate themselves.

[43] HRCP, 2002, *op. cit.*

This explains why honour killings of women often provoke an inter-family vendetta.[44]

Despite being a signatory to CEDAW, the killing of Pakistani women and men goes unpunished. The criminal legislation does not deter would-be aggressors, and being acquitted of murder charges is feasible through bribes, death threats and token monetary compensation. The Qisas and Diyat Act has "tribalised" the Pakistani Penal Code and made it subservient to traditional justice. This significantly reduces the courts' powers and promotes out-of-court settlements that absolve homicide against token monetary compensation. The lenient sentences that are meted out mean that the perpetrators do not fear being apprehended by the policy and prosecuted in court. Moreover, the policemen can be bribed to ignore the offence or, conversely, produce fake evidence, which incriminates the suspect. In either case, it is money and not misdeeds which decides the suspect's fate. This also explains why the aggrieved party, who commonly finds that justice is not served through the judicial system, refrains from registering the offence with the police and seeks personal revenge instead.

In Pakistan, the jural system and traditional justice tend to reinforce rather than counteract each other. Traditional justice sanctions homicide of men and women in the case of adultery. Although the burden of proof is greater, the Hudood Ordinance likewise prescribes death as punishment for an adulteress. Similarly, traditional justice sanctions revenge killings, a principle that under certain conditions is also sanctioned in the Qisas and Diyat Act's notion of "just retribution" (*qisas*, "death for a death"). If the evidence for passing *qisas* is insufficient, the aggrieved party is awarded monetary compensation (*diyat*). Monetary compensation ("blood money") is also part of traditional justice, but accepting it is construed as a sign of weakness, and as a rule the aggrieved party seeks revenge because only this can fully restore honour.

Despite areas of convergence between jural laws and traditional justice, there are still important differences that make tribesmen in the NWFP resort to the latter rather than the former. One reason is that traditional justice is personalised, unlike the impersonal punishment integral to statutory law where justice is rendered by a third party. Moreover, legal justice is slow, costly and often ineffectual, meaning that only by taking the law into their own hands are

[44] Knudsen, 2003, *op. cit.*

people assured that justice is served and the dead avenged. Revenge is locally construed as a "right" (*haq*), which the aggrieved party can legitimately exact from the perpetrator (or close male relatives) at any time. A key to the local code of honour is therefore retaliation, which is different from monetary compensation, which is interpreted as a sign of weakness and can therefore invite future attacks and incursions. Customarily, the parties to a conflict will only accept arbitration when there is parity in death or injury. At this stage of the conflict, local mediators plead with the parties to end hostilities. The transfer of money and exchange of marriageable girls between the parties will formally conclude the enmity. While the exchange of girls is crucial to making peace according to traditional justice, it is not a valid form of negotiated compensation according to the Pakistani Penal Code. This means that statutory law lacks culturally acceptable means for ending enmities and reconciling former adversaries.

CONCLUSION

This paper has examined first-hand accounts of honour killings that provide new insights into the nature of traditional justice among tribesmen in the NWFP. Before discussing their general validity, let me briefly summarise the main findings. First, it shows the strong preference for local conflict resolution based on traditional justice, which prescribes homicide in the case of adultery and extra-marital infidelity. There is a strong peer-group pressure to kill adulterers as well as refraining from bringing homicide cases before civil courts. In those rare cases where homicide is tried in court, the penal code's criminalisation of adultery (Hudood Ordinance) and sanctioning of extra-judicial retribution (Qisas and Diyat Act) in accordance with "customary law" make conviction unlikely. Adding to this, the courts, jurors and jury tend to admit fake evidence either due to faulty investigation by corrupt police officers or under threat from the defendants who also commit perjury to secure an acquittal. In sum, this means that customary law takes precedence over jural law, encouraging the offended party to seek private justice. To what degree are these findings applicable to Pakistan as a whole? In my opinion, they point to general failings of Pakistan's legal system that serve to promote honour killings. The "tribalisation" and "islamisation" of the penal code have made prosecuting honour killings ineffectual and provided legal sanction for traditional justice. The legal system is further undermined by weak courts, a corrupt police force, and a widening scope for settling conflicts in accordance with traditional justice. Taken together, this encourages private retribution and allows honour killings to flourish.

However, as this paper has shown, most honour killings do not, as is often claimed, "go unpunished". Murderers frequently escape legal prosecution, but they often become targets of revenge killings that may claim their own life and those of their family and relatives. In most cases of revenge killings, the perpetrator's identity remains unknown. They therefore differ from "typical" honour killings where the murderer publicly admits responsibility for the misdeed and thereby redeems both his own and his family's honour . If revenge rather than honour is the primary motive, this suggests that more strident? prosecution of honour killings by the state would satisfy the plaintiffs demand for justice and discourage taking the law into one's own hand.

In the NWFP, both women and men are murdered in honour killings, and most of them are killed simply on suspicion of illicit relations. Still, existing research on the subject tends to focus narrowly on the plight of women and disregards the gendered dimension of honour killings. Both women and men are victims of honour killings consequently an examination of honour crimes cannot focus selectively on the homicide of women, or "femicide" as it has also been labelled .[45] Instead, honour killings need to be seen in a gendered perspective that includes both aggressor and victim and the importance of taking revenge, which may turn the male aggressor into the next victim. Thus, there is a need to question the dichotomy between "honour killings" of women and "vendetta" affecting men. In addition, there is a need to consider the indigenous aspects of homicide, which are often passed over or disregarded in the discussion of honour killings. The honour killings examined here are integrated with religious practices and indigenous beliefs. In a society where treacherous murders are common, divine protection provides the parties to a conflict a symbolic insurance against death and injury. This finding may have wider applicability for our understanding of honour killings in the Middle East and South Asia and therefore also how to prevent them.

In his magisterial work, *The Civilizing Process*, the German sociologist Norbert Elias argued that interpersonal violence and homicide rates all over Europe gradually declined from the late medieval times because of an increase

[45] Fadia Faqir, "Intrafamily Femicide in Defence of Honour: The Case of Jordan", in *Third World Quarterly*, Vol. 22, No. 1, 2001.

in emotional control and state monopoly on the use of force.[46] Applied to Pakistan, Elias' theory suggests that the combination of weak law enforcement and low emotional control promote homicide. The victims of honour killing are murdered according to a preconceived plan and not in a state of shock and affect. The fact that the murder is premeditated suggests that weak law enforcement, rather than low emotional control, promotes homicide in Pakistan. Stricter penal laws and more forceful prosecution of offenders could therefore significantly reduce the honour killing problem.[47] Instead, the imposition of the Hudood Ordinance and passing of the Qisas and Diyat Act have added tribal characteristics to the Pakistan Penal Code. The first step in preventing honour killings is a legal reform that revokes the Qisas and Diyat Act. A second priority should be implementing CEDAW fully and repeal the Hudood Ordinance that provides judicial sanction for Quranic punishments of women charged with adultery. At present, only a minority of the honour killing incidents are reported to the police or picked up by the press. A third step should therefore be instituting a national database on honour killings and gendered-based violence that could determine the magnitude of the problem and make combating it a political priority.

BIBLIOGRAPHY

Aase, Thor (ed.), 2002. *Tournaments of Power: Honor and Revenge in the Contemporary World*, Aldershot, Ashgate

Baker, Nancy V., Peter A. Gregware and Margery A. Cassidy. "Family Killing Fields: Honor Rationales in the Murder of Women," in *Violence Against Women*, Vol. 5, No. 2, 1991.

Bourdieu, Pierre, 1977. *Outline of a Theory of Practice,* Cambridge, Cambridge University Press

[46] Norbert Elias, *The Civilizing Process,* Oxford, Blackwell, 1994.

[47] A legal reform alone will not be enough to put an end to honour killings in Pakistan. Better economic policies and political governance could also lower the homicide rate, as suggested by a recent study of cross-national panel of homicide rates, see, Eric Neumeyer, "Good Policy Can Lower Violent Crime: Evidence from a Cross-National Panel of Homicide Rates, 1980-97", in *Journal of Peace Research*, Vol. 40, No. 6, 2003.

Esposito, John L, 1987. "Islam: Ideology and Politics in Pakistan", in Ali Banuazizi and Myron Weiner (eds.), *State, Religion, and Ethnic Politics: Pakistan Iran, and Afghanistan*, Lahore, Vanguard Books.

Elias, Norbert, 1994. *The Civilizing Process,* Oxford, Blackwell

Faqir, Fadia. "Intrafamily Femicide in Defence of Honour: The Case of Jordan", in *Third World Quarterly*, Vol. 22, No. 1, 2001.

Ghaffar, A., A. A. Hyder, M. I. Mastoor, and I. Shaikh. "Injuries in Pakistan: Directions for Future Health Policy", in *Health Policy and Planning*, Vol. 14, No. 1, 1999.

Ginat, Joseph, 1997. *Blood Revenge: Family Honor, Mediation and Outcasting*, Portland, Or., Sussex Academic, 1997.

Gutmann, Matthew C., "Trafficking in Men: The Anthropology of Masculinity", in *Annual Review of Anthropology*, Vol. 26, 1997.

Haeri, Shahla, "The Politics of Dishonour: Rape and Power in Pakistan", in Mahnaz Afkhami (ed.), *Faith and Freedom: Women's Human Rights in the Muslim World*, London, Tauris, 1995

Keiser, Lincoln, *Friend by Day, Enemy by Night: Organized Vengeance in a Kohistani Community*, Fort Worth, Holt, Rinehart and Winston, 1991.

Knudsen, Are, forthcoming. *Violence and Belonging: Land, Love and Lethal Conflict in a Kohistani Community, Pakistan,* NIAS Press, Copenhagen.

Kressel, Gideon M., "Sororicide/Filiacide: Homicide for Family Honour", in *Current Anthropology*, Vol. 22, No. 2, 1981.

Kurkiala, Mikael, "Interpreting Honour Killings: The Story of Fadime Sahindal (1975–2002) in the Swedish Press", in *Anthropology Today*, Vol. 19, No. 1, 2002

Lindholm, Charles, "Love and Structure", in *Theory, Culture and Society*, Vol. 15, No. 3-4, 1998

Maris, Cees and Sawtiri Saharso, "Honour Killing: A Reflection on Gender, Culture and Violence" in *Netherland's Journal of Social Sciences*, Vol. 37, No. 1, 2001.

Neumeyer, Eric, "Good Policy Can Lower Violent Crime: Evidence from a Cross-National Panel of Homicide Rates, 1980-97", in *Journal of Peace Research*, Vol. 40, No. 6, 2003

Shah, Nafisa, 1998, *A Story in Black: Karo-Kari Killings in Upper Sindh*, Oxford, Reuters Foundation Paper, No. 100

Sidahmed, Abdel Salam ,"Problems in Contemporary Applications of Islamic Criminal Sanctions: The Penalty for Adultery in Relation to Women", in *British Journal of Middle Eastern Studies*, Vol. 28, No. 2, 2001.

Spierenburg, Pieter, "Faces of Violence: Homicide Trends and Cultural Meanings: Amsterdam, 1431-1816", in *Journal of Social History*, Vol. 27, No. 4, 1994.

Stewart, Frank Henderson, 1994. *Honor*, Chicago, University of Chicago Press

Tapper, Richard and Nancy Tapper, "Marriage, Honour and Responsibility: Islamic and Local Models in the Mediterranean and the Middle East", in *Cambridge Anthropology*, Vol. 16, No. 2, 1992.

Wikan, Unni:

"Shame and Honour: A Contestable Pair", in *Man*, Vol. 19, 1984.

For *Ærens Skyld: Fadime Til Ettertanke,* [For the Sake of Honour. Reflections on Fadime], Oslo, Universitetsforlaget, 2003

Other sources:

AI (Amnesty International), 1999. *Pakistan: Violence against Women in the Name of Honour*. New York, www.amnestyusa.org/countries/pakistan/reports/honour/

BBC News Online, 6 June 2002, *Pakistan Stoning Sentence Overturned,* http://news.bbc.co.uk/2/hi/south_asia/2029020.stm

CIMEL (Centre for Islamic and Middle Eastern Law) and INTERIGHTS (International Centre for the Legal Protection of Human Rights), *Preliminary Bibliography: "Crimes of Honour"*, http://www.iwhc.org/docUploads/HonorCrimesBiblio.PDF

HRCP (Human Rights Commission of Pakistan), Lahore
2002, *State of Human Rights in Pakistan 2001*
2003, *State of Human Rights in Pakistan 2002*

HRW (Human Rights Watch), 1999, *Crime or Custom? Violence against Women in Pakistan* (*www.hrw.org/reports/1999/pakistan*)

UNPA (United Nations Population Fund), New York, 2000, *Lives Together, Worlds Apart: Men and Women in a Time of Change*

Indigenous Law and the Protection of Indigenous Peoples' Rights in Ecuador

Tiina Saaresranta

INTRODUCTION[1]

Indigenous peoples' own practices of law in relation to their increasing demands for justice within national societies is a topical issue in the Andean region. Indigenous organizations are in the process of formulating and experimenting with different legal and political strategies aimed at the realization of their rights, which over centuries have been violated due to colonialism and structures that followed it. Promotion of the recognition and implementation of indigenous law is part of the general context of indigenous peoples' political and legal strategies, where elements such as greater participation in national society and internal self-determination are being put forward.[2]

The significance of indigenous law can be looked at from different perspectives. On one view, it can be connected with the very existence of indigenous peoples as separate *cultures and peoples*. The maintenance of a group different from others depends on the success it has in the transfer of its cultural values and the adaptation of its identity in relation to societal change. This process depends on the effectiveness of the group's socialization strategies and on the effectiveness of its social control,[3] both of which are related to indigenous organization and law. In legal discourse this approach takes the form of the drive towards the protection of indigenous peoples' cultural rights. As stated by the UN Special Rapporteur Stavenhagen: "Indigenous community life, and therefore the viability of indigenous culture, depend upon the vitality of the group's social organization and, in many instances, the active implementation of local customary law ... The non-recognition of *local social organization and customary law* by the state legal system and the public administration also contributes to the weakening and

[1] Access to sources concerning the Andean region was gained during the author's stay in Ecuador from December 2000 to September 2002, and would not have been possible without the guidance and contacts provided by the Fundación de Culturas Indígenas Kawsay in Quito, Ecuador.

[2] In Ecuador since 1996 indigenous organizations have fielded their own candidates in the elections for the national parliament and municipalities. Political movements that are directly identified with certain indigenous organizations have been created.

[3] Esther Sánchez Botero and Isabel Cristina Jaramillo Sierra, *La Jurisdicción Especial Indígena* [The Special Indigenous Jurisdiction], Santa Fé de Bogotá, Procuraduría General de la Nación and Instituto de Estudios del Ministerio Público, 2000, p. 122.

eventual disappearance of indigenous cultures."[4] In Ecuador indigenous peoples currently find themselves in this situation; legal processes fail to respect or take into account indigenous legal systems and traditions.[5] Lawyers and judges do not receive training in indigenous law and cultural diversity, and the issue in general is left without much attention by the state. The Committee on the Elimination of all Forms of Racial Discrimination has noted the incapacity of the Ecuadorian state to provide information on indigenous judicial systems.[6]

From another view, the discussion of indigenous law is influenced by a critique aimed at the corrupted and inefficient nature of national systems of justice. In countries such as Ecuador the national legal system faces serious limitations, including corruption. Further problems arise from the fact that the functions and services of the state do not efficiently reach the countryside or poor sectors of urban areas, where the majority of indigenous peoples live.[7] Also racism as well as cultural and linguistic barriers weaken the access to justice of indigenous persons within the state law. According to an OAS[8] report, frequent complaints are received concerning the treatment of indigenous persons within the judicial system in Ecuador. The implementation of indigenous peoples' linguistic rights also remains weak within the judicial system. Legal processes where indigenous persons are involved are conducted in Spanish and translations are not provided for those who understand only their native language.[9]

To facilitate the understanding of the context of indigenous law in Ecuador, the point of departure chosen for this article is a description of the basic character

---

[4] Rodolfo Stavenhagen, *Indigenous Peoples as Emerging Actors in Mexico and Latin America*, Paper presented at the Woodrow Wilson Center in Washington DC, 1994, p.15. (http://www.nyu.edu/classes/Yudice/Democrat/staven.htm). Author's own emphasis.

[5] OEA, *Report on the Situation of Human Rights in Ecuador*, OEA/Ser.L/V/II.96 Doc. 10 Rev. 1, 24 April 1997, Chapter IX, p. 2. This report is from the year 1997, however no significant changes have taken place in the judicial practice after the constitutional reform of 1998.

[6] Committee on the Elimination of Racial Discrimination, *Concluding Observations: Ecuador*, CERD/C/62/CO/2 of 21 March 2003, para 19, Unedited version.

[7] According to the Committee on the Elimination of Racial Discrimination disproportionately high percentage of indigenous people, Afro-Ecuadorians and members of other minorities live in conditions of poverty. *Op. cit.*, para 13.

[8] Organization of American States.

[9] OEA, *Report on the Situation of Human Rights in Ecuador*, OEA/Ser.L/V/II.96 Doc. 10 Rev. 1, 24 April 1997, Chapter IX, p. 2. Another factor is that due to cultural reasons it may be more difficult for indigenous persons than non-indigenous persons to understand the logic of legal reasoning and concepts of justice within the national system.

of indigenous law. Thereafter, the scope of recognition of indigenous law, such as provided by the *ILO Convention No. 169 Concerning Indigenous and Tribal Peoples in Independent Countries*, the UN and OAS drafting processes on indigenous peoples' rights, and the Ecuadorian Constitution, is studied. For the solution of possible conflicts of competencies between national and indigenous authorities, and to define the relationship between indigenous law and human rights law an intercultural dialogue is suggested and discussed in the following section. Thereafter two cases, where the practises of indigenous law in Ecuador in relation to international human rights standards require discussion and clarification, are presented, namely the rights of indigenous women, and the prohibition of torture, cruel and inhuman treatment.

In Ecuador the indigenous movement has initiated a discussion on the need to study, strengthen and develop indigenous legal systems, however little systematized and published research exists on this topic.[10] Indigenous legal practices are dynamic and vary from region to region, therefore this article does not aim at presenting generalisations that would be valid in all these different contexts. However, the cornerstones of indigenous law are based on some common elements of indigenous *cosmovisions* that will be described in the section below.[11]

In this paper the term *indigenous law*[12] will be used instead of *indigenous customary law*, since in the Latin American context the latter term has acquired a negative connotation, that is, understood to describe a system of inferior value, a system that is static, inflexible and with limited possibilities of development.[13] This use of concepts also corresponds to the preferences of indigenous organizations of the Andean region.[14]

---

[10] See for example the CONAIE proposal for the constitucional reform of 1998: CONAIE, *Las nacionalidades indígenas y el estado plurinacional* [The Indigenous Nationalities and the Plurinational State], Quito, CONAIE, 1997.

[11] Indigenous worldview based on the understanding of human beings as a part of the cosmos and in communication with all of its elements.

[12] In Spanish: *derecho indígena.*

[13] To better understand these interpretations, see e.g. Esther Sánchez Botero and Isabel Cristina Jaramillo Sierra, 2000, *op. cit.*, p. 58; or Raquel Yrigoyen Fajardo, *Pautas de Coordinación entre el Derecho Indígena y el Derecho Estata*l [Guidelines of Coordination between Indigenous Law and State Law], Ciudad de Guatemala, Fundación Myrna Mack, 1999, pp. 11-20.

[14] Also other terms are used, such as *indigenous legal systems* or *own law* (*derecho propio*).

CHARACTER OF INDIGENOUS LAW

For indigenous organizations in Ecuador the vindication of their own systems of law as *law* is part of the ongoing process of decolonialization and strengthening of their identity and own institutions.[15] The organizations aim at the recognition of indigenous law as a "complete and valid system of law" that should not be reduced to "customs" or "alternative mechanisms of conflict resolution", which are the descriptions often used of indigenous law, but give a limited scope of application, which is not satisfactory from the point of view of indigenous organizations.[16] CONAIE,[17] the most influential indigenous umbrella organization in Ecuador has defined indigenous law in the following way:

> It is a set of norms and laws of indigenous peoples and nationalities to defend and administrate our lands and territories to maintain peace and order in our communities and peoples.[18]

According to Trujillo,[19] indigenous law is a

> ...set of norms produced by indigenous persons through their institutions, to which they have trusted the task of establishing the obligatory norms of conduct that everybody shall obey. Some rules are established because they guarantee the

---

[15] This view is supported by many scholars. See e.g: Raquel Yrigoyen, "The Constitutional Recognition of Indigenous Law in the Andean Countries" in Willem Assies, Gemma van der Haar and André J. Hoekema (eds.), *The Challenge of Diversity: Indigenous Peoples and Reform of the State in Latin America*, Amsterdam, Thela Thesis, Thela Thesis Latin American Series, 2000, pp. 197-222, at p. 202; Julio César Trujillo "Introducción al Derecho Indígena" [Introduction to Indigenous Law] in Julio CésarTrujillo, Agustín Grijalva and Ximena Endara, *Justicia Indígena en el Ecuador* [Indigenous Justice in Ecuador], Quito, Universidad Andina Simón Bolívar, Sede Ecuador, 2001, pp. 9-18; and in Ximena Endara, "El derecho indígena en el Ecuador" [Indigenous Law in Ecuador] in Julio César Trujillo, Agustín Grijalva and Ximena Endara, 2001, *op. cit.* pp. 59-81.

[16] This is the language used e.g. in the Constitution of Bolivia, in article 171(III).

[17] Confederation of Indigenous Peoples and Nationalities of Ecuador.

[18] CONAIE, *Conceptos Básicos de un Estado Plurinacional* [The basic Concepts of a Plurinational State], Primer Congreso de los Pueblos y Nacionalidades del Ecuador, Quito, 8 al 12 de octubre de 2001, (http://www.llacta.org/organiz/coms/com62.htm), p. 2. Own translation from the Spanish original.

[19] Ecuadorian lawyer with widely recognized experience and knowledge in questions related to indigenous law.

> peaceful coexistence of the community members, and others because they preserve the identity of the community...[20]

According to the Committee of Indigenous Issues and Other Ethnic Groups of the National Parliament, indigenous law is a

> set of traditional norms and laws that regulate the social development of indigenous peoples and nationalities. It is based on the ancestral practices of exercise of authority and administration of justice in a way that is fair, transparent and direct, always aiming at educating and raising the awareness of the individual. All conflicts are resolved collectively, orally, in manner that is just, rapid, appropriate and dynamic.[21]

These definitions reflect the ideals of indigenous law, and as in any system of law, in their practice the ideals may be challenged. The strength of indigenous law is however, that it is considered as something created by the community through direct participation of its members and based on values and principles that originate from ancestral practices, which by each generation are adapted to the changes in society. Therefore, indigenous law is normally perceived to be highly legitimate by its users. This is reflected in the results of a study made in Guatemala, where the interviewees were asked why they used they used the Maya legal system instead of the national system. A series of interesting answers were provided, such as:

- the problems are solved more rapidly
- it is not so expensive
- you do not have to pay bribes
- you are treated well
- the processes are in your own language
- you do not have to be afraid to talk
- the same cultural and linguistic codes are used
- the solutions are fair and legitimate

---

[20] Julio César Trujillo, "Administración de justicia indígena" [Administration of Indigenous Justice] in Judith Salgado (ed.), *Justicia Indígena: Aportes para un debate* [Indigenous Justice: Contributions for a Debate], Quito, Ediciones Abya-Yala and Universidad Andina Simón Bolívar, 2002, pp. 91-104 at p. 101.

[21] Comisión de Asuntos Indígenas y Otras Etnias del Honorable Congreso Nacional et al, *Anteproyecto de Ley de Administración de Justicia Indígena* [Draft Law on Indigenous Administration of Justice], Quito, 2002, p. 3.

- you can freely participate in the process
- a dialogue and reflection concerning the facts is made
- future problems are avoided since none of the parts involved is favoured
- advice on how to live in the future are provided
- the problems are solved in the same community, any day and time
- the implementation is done according to our cultural values
- there is no punishment[22]
- at the end the damages are repaired[23]

These answers may partly present an idealistic picture of indigenous legal systems, as a result of the process of the revival and strengthening of indigenous organization and identity. Simultaneously they provide a critical analysis of the way the national legal system functions in the indigenous context. The national system of law is often perceived as something external, illogical, imposed and dysfunctional.[24] In Ecuador this situation has been noted by the UN Committee on the Elimination of Racial Discrimination, which has expressed a concern about the "lack of confidence on the part of members of ethnic minorities in the Ecuadorian judicial system", and has requested the State party to report on its causes.[25]

The philosophical bases of indigenous law are based on indigenous worldview, where life and society are normally perceived holistically. This *cosmovision* is based on the constant search to maintain well-being and internal as well as external equilibrium of the community or group. In Kichwa this is called

---

[22] In indigenous law the sanctions decided by the community are often accepted as acts of rehabilitation and not punishment.

[23] In Defensoría Maya, *SUK'B'ANIK Administración de Justicia Maya/Experiencias de Defensoría Maya* [Maya Administration of Justice/Experiences of Defensoría Maya], Guatemala, 2001, p. 30.

[24] See for example the interviews of César Umaginga (member of the Kichwa indigenous people and the Prefect of the Cotopaxi Province) and Jaime Cuchiparte Toaza (Chairperson of the local Kichwa organization of La Cocha, Cotopaxi). El Comercio, viernes 10 de mayo del 2002.

[25] Committee on the Elimination of Racial Discrimination: Concluding Observations: Ecuador. CERD/C/62/CO/2 of 21 March 2003. Unedited versión, para 17. See also Ximena Ortíz Crespo, "Presentación" [Presentation] in Judith Salgado, (ed.) *Justicia Indígena: Aportes para un debate* [Indigenous Justice: Contributions for a Debate]. Ediciones Abya-Yala and Universidad Andina Simón Bolívar, Quito, 2002, pp. 7-14, at p. 8.

sumak kawsay, the "excellent" life in harmony and respectful to the value system and teachings of the ancestors.[26] Santillán, a member of the Otavalo Kichwa people has described in the following way how the Kichwa worldview is reflected in the legal understanding of his community, and how this is related to spiritual life as an inseparable dimension of the normative system:

> The *approach* of Western rights is material and aimed at profit. Where I come from, there are other aspects considered important that are born in the heart, this is what the others call spirituality. There is something superior to us, towards which we are accountable, the nature. Reciprocity exists in this relation also. The issue is more spiritual, harmonic. Not only the superficial counts, but there are also internal things that are useful. What has to be analyzed is the relation between the material and the spiritual organization when speaking about law in our culture.[27]

Since world order is interpreted in holistic and reciprocal[28] terms, it is not considered essential or possible to clearly distinguish the concepts of *rights* and *duties*, it is understood that there is a reciprocal relation between these two concepts. The indigenous legal system is part of the general organizational structure of the community, and therefore the same authority has the faculty to create, implement and reform the law. The concept of separation of powers does not exist in the sense it is understood in the Western tradition. Here it is important to remember that no indigenous authority has the power to arbitrarily and individually impose norms or sanctions. Indigenous jurisdictions are local systems with normally strict mechanisms of social control, where the authorities are held responsible for their actions towards the

[26] A parallel can be drawn to the Mayas. According to Defensoría Maya, 2001, *op. cit.*, p. 88, Maya law is composed of theoretical and philosophical elements that are based on the worldview of the Mayas and whose exercise permits the construction of unity, balance and harmony, not only in human relations within a specific territory, but also in the relationship of humans via Mother Nature.

[27] Oscar Santillán's intervention at a workshop to discuss the indigenous concepts of law. He is member of the Otavalo Kichwa people and knowledgeable in issues concerning the spirituality of his people. In Fundación de Culturas Indígenas Kawsay, *Memoria del taller para la definición de las bases teóricas y conceptuales de la Universidad Intercultural Tinku* [Workshop for the Definition of the Theoretical and Conceptual Bases of the Intercultural Tinku University], Quito, 25 February 2002, p. 2. As stated above, indigenous peoples views of the national legal systems are often very critical and based on experiences they have had with the national courts and practitioners of law, which very often have been riddled with racism, inequality and corruption.

[28] Reciprocity is a central concept for the social, economic and legal dimensions of Andean indigenous cultures. Society is organized around complicated forms of reciprocity which community members fulfill in different situations and phases of their lives.

whole community. Solutions and sanctions are sought collectively, in consensus within the community, including the participation of family members of the affected parties. It is common in indigenous legal processes that lawmaking consists of a series of dialogues and negotiations to reach common ground, not by declaring winners and losers.[29] For example, in indigenous penal law,[30] the aim is to change the attitude of the person who has acted against the norms, and reintegrate him/her back to the community as its full member, with all corresponding rights and responsibilities. The solution of the problem is also expected to serve as an example for the rest of the community. Indigenous law is mainly oral, even though some of its sources include also written materials, such as, minutes of community meetings and internal statutes of the community.

In the indigenous way of organising society and law, the individual is not at the centre, instead the emphasis is put on the group. However, in the majority of cases, collective and individual rights are not contradictory but complementary to each other. In the indigenous interpretation of law the combination of the best interests of the community and the individual or the family are highlighted, whereas the rights of the individual are much more highlighted in the national/international system.[31] The individual identifies him/herself first as part of the group and, secondly, as an individual. This collective approach to life is reflected in various ways in indigenous law, where the whole community may participate in legal processes, not only the interested parties and the community authorities. The community participates e.g. in the determination of the type of behaviour considered harmful, in the hearings, as well as in the definition and implementation of sanctions or rehabilitation mechanisms. In some cases of indigenous law the family members may also be held responsible of the wrongdoings committed by their relatives. When indigenous law enters into contact with the national law, conflicts may occur. If the rights of the individual prevail in a case resolved by

[29] Raquel Yrigoyen "The Constitutional Recognition of Indigenous Law in the Andean Countries" in Willem Assies; Gemma van der Haar; André J. Hoekema (eds.), 2000, *op. cit.*, pp. 197-222, at p. 205.

[30] It should be noted that in indigenous law such a distinction between different areas of law is not made. Here the term "penal law" is used to facilitate comprehension.

[31] These points were vividly discussed and analyzed in a workshop organized by the Fundación de Culturas Indígenas Kawsay in Quito, Ecuador on February 25th in 2002, *op. cit*. The participants were indigenous leaders and academics who with their interventions contributed to the opinions presented here,

the national system, this presents a demand to the indigenous group to adopt values and views that are different to their *cosmovision.* If the group rights prevail when the case is dealt within the indigenous system this might imply that the individual is left without a protection that would be provided in a similar situation within the national system.[32]

The administration of indigenous law takes place in different spheres within the community: first the extended family, secondly the authorities, or leaders of the community, and thirdly the community assembly. Depending on the type and severity of the problem, the persons responsible for the guidance of other community members, know which forum or approach has the competence to resolve the problem. Generally, in the first sphere the persons to resolve conflicts are close relatives, grand parents and neighbours, in the second sphere they are community leaders, and in the third sphere the whole group of the indigenous community lead by their authorities. In some grave cases, the community may decide not to resolve the problems internally, but present them to the leaders of the provincial indigenous organizations, who offer guidance in these situations. This modality however does not have the function of revision of decisions made in the community level similar to the hierarchical order between the different legal instances in the national system. The decisions are of a definitive character, the cases are closed after the corresponding authority has taken its decision.

In Ecuador a process of revitalizing the use of indigenous law has been experienced in the past few years. This is partly explained by the fact that indigenous peoples perceive the national legal system as increasingly corrupt, expensive and inefficient, and therefore seek alternative remedies from local systems of justice. Another reason is that indigenous organizations have gradually become stronger and more aware of their rights, and therefore are more openly exercising their rights. This development is also supported by the constitutional recognition of indigenous law, which will be analysed below. During the past decade some indigenous organizations have taken a stronger position in relation to the strengthening of their own legal systems. There are even examples of organizations, which in their statutes have included

[32] See also in Esther Sánchez Botero and Isabel Jaramillo Sierra, 2000, *op. cit.*, p. 108.

prohibitions on their members using the national legal system without the permission of the community authorities.[33]

RECOGNITION OF INDIGENOUS LAW

ILO Convention No. 169 and other Emerging Norms

In international human rights law, the only binding instrument that explicitly refers to the existence and recognition of indigenous legal practices is the ILO Convention 169.[34] For the purpose of this article, a brief analysis of the convention concerning the recognition it gives to indigenous customary law is pertinent, since Ecuador ratified the Convention in 1998, and the text of the convention inspired the constitutional reform of the same year. Other human rights instruments do not directly touch upon the issue of indigenous law, but can be of relevance due to their functions in the protection of the right to culture. These instruments include the International Covenant on Civil and Political Rights. In the implementation of article 27 of the Covenant, which protects minorities' right to cultural life, the Human Rights Committee has given a wide interpretation to culture,[35] and the article has on many occasions been invoked by indigenous peoples, not only by minorities.[36] Also relevant are two draft declarations on indigenous rights, namely the UN Draft Declaration on the Rights of Indigenous Peoples (UN Draft Declaration)[37] and the American Declaration on the Rights of Indigenous Peoples (American Draft Declaration).[38] Even though the drafting of these two instruments has not yet been concluded, they provide interesting material due to the fact that indigenous organisations and experts on indigenous rights have had an

[33] See discussion in Fernando García, *Formas indígenas de administrar justicia* [Indigenous Forms to Administer Justice], Quito, FLACSO Sede Ecuador, 2002, specifically on the prohibition to seek remedy from the national judicial authorities, p. 42.

[34] Also the ILO Convention 107 Concerning the Protection and Integration of Indigenous and Other Tribal and Semi-Tribal Populations in Independent Countries from the year 1957 is still in force in some countries. Articles 7 and 8 concern of the ILO Convention 107 concern indigenous customary law, this convention is however not analyzed here, since its norms are in general outdated and Ecuador has already ratified Convention 169.

[35] See General Comment 23. U.N. Doc. HRI/GEN/1/Rev.1 at 38 (1994).

[36] Due to limited space, other instruments will not be further analyzed.

[37] E/CN.4/Sub.2/1994/2/Add.1 (1994).

[38] *Consolidated text of the Draft Declaration Prepared by the Chair of the Working Group*, June 2003, OEA/SER.K/XVIGT/DADIN/Doc.139/0317.

important contribution to their contents. This is especially the case for the UN Draft Declaration, which more than other sources of international law reflects the visions and priorities of indigenous peoples themselves.

The terms used in the ILO Convention 169 to define indigenous law, as found in articles 8 and 9, are: *customs, customary law* and *customarily practiced methods for dealing with offenses*. The Convention protects the following rights that have relevance to the recognition, exercise and development of indigenous law:

a) The right to preserve indigenous customs and institutions

According to article 8(2) of the ILO Convention 169 indigenous peoples shall have "...the right to retain their own customs and institutions, where these are not incompatible with fundamental rights defined by the national legal system and with internationally recognized human rights". Here limited protection is given to indigenous law as a part of indigenous customs, as well as to the institutions that develop and implement indigenous law.

In the drafting process of the international declarations on indigenous peoples' rights, the recognition of indigenous customs and institutions has been one of the points of analysis. The American Draft Declaration in its articles Articles VI(2) and XIX(1) recognizes indigenous peoples' right to their social, political and economic organization, "without interference and in accordance with their values, usages, customs, ancestral traditions, beliefs and spirituality". The UN Draft Declaration, articles 4 and 21, recognizes indigenous peoples' right to maintain and develop their distinct political, economic and social systems as well as cultural characteristics, including their legal systems".

b) The right to the exercise of indigenous law among indigenous peoples

The ILO Convention 169 in article 9(1) provides that: "to the extent compatible with the national legal system and internationally recognized human rights, the methods customarily practiced by the peoples concerned for dealing with offenses committed by their members shall be respected". By this provision the Convention recognizes indigenous law in cases where it does not enter into conflict with the national legal system and human rights. These limits will be discussed below.

In the American Draft Declaration of its present form, article XXI is dedicated to "Indigenous Law and Jurisdiction". The Draft in article XXI(2) recognizes explicitly the right of indigenous peoples to maintain and strengthen their legal systems. The Draft, article XXI(1), makes a connection between indigenous law and development by declaring that: "Indigenous law shall be recognized as part of the legal system and of the States' framework for social and economic development." Further in article XXI(2) the scope of indigenous law is defined to comprise internal matters of indigenous communities, applying their own rules and procedures, including matters related to the resolution of conflicts within and between indigenous peoples, and to the preservation of peace and harmony. The UN Draft Declaration dedicates article 33 for the recognition of indigenous law, according to which indigenous peoples have the right to "promote, develop and maintain their institutional structures and their distinctive juridical customs, traditions, procedures and practices, in accordance with internationally recognized human rights standards". In article 34 the Draft reinforces these rights by highlighting indigenous peoples' collective right to determine the responsibilities of individuals in relation to their communities.

c) Indigenous law and land rights

Indigenous law in relation to land rights is specifically taken into account in these human rights instruments. The ILO Convention 169 in its article 14(1) requires state parties to recognize "the rights of ownership and possession of the peoples concerned over the lands which they traditionally occupy". The convention does not explicitly mention the source of law to identify the lands traditionally occupied by indigenous peoples, however it is logical that indigenous law and relevant historic and current documents would constitute adequate sources.

The American Draft Declaration in article XXIV recognizes indigenous peoples' "property and ownership rights with respect to the lands are territories they historically occupy",[39] as well the right to "attribute ownership within the community in accordance with the values, usages, and customs of each peoples".[40] It is interesting that the current version of the American Draft

[39] Article XXIV on Traditional Forms of Property and Cultural Survival. Right to Land, Territory and Resources, para. 1.

[40] Article XXIV(5).

Declaration in article XXIV(1) mentions indigenous rights in relation to their territories, however limiting this right "by the principles of the legal system of each state". In practice this means that non-renewable natural resources in most states belong to the domain of the state, thus limiting indigenous peoples' rights to the use of natural resources over their territories.[41] The proposed version of the UN Draft Declaration in article 26 makes a clear connection between indigenous peoples' land rights and indigenous law by recognizing their right to own, develop, control and use the lands and territories, without any reference to state legal systems, including the right "to the full recognition of their laws, traditions and customs, land-tenure systems and institutions for the development and management of resources".

d) The obligation of states to take into account indigenous law when applying national law on indigenous peoples and individuals

According to article 8(1) of the ILO Convention 169, when states are applying national laws and regulations to indigenous peoples, "due regard shall be had to their customs or customary laws". The Convention therefore recognizes that differentiated treatment in the application of national law towards indigenous peoples is motivated due to the existence of indigenous peoples' own legal systems and concepts. This implies that indigenous law does not have relevance only as a system and source of law applied by indigenous authorities, but also state authorities have to take it into account when considering cases in which indigenous peoples are involved. This article may be used to support an interpretation, where indigenous law concerning e.g. the use of natural resources and territorial limits shall be taken into account by the state in favor of indigenous peoples.[42]

A similar provision is found in article XXI(4) of the American Draft Declaration, where states are required to take measures "to ensure that the judiciary is knowledgeable of and applies indigenous law and custom, and to ensure that it is taught in law schools". The Draft takes explicitly into account the training of lawyers in indigenous law, a measure of great importance, since

[41] In the ILO Convention 169 indigenous peoples' territorial rights are also mentioned, however not in connection with article 14, which concerns the issues of ownership. The convention defines the concept of territory to cover "the total environment of the areas which the peoples concerned occupy or otherwise use" (article 13(2)).

[42] The limits set in article 8(2) for indigenous customs and institutions, i.e. fundamental and human rights, are applicable also here.

currently lawyers in Latin America in general have little knowledge in this field, and may be influenced by prejudice.

The Convention in article 9(2) notes especially that differences may exist between indigenous and non-indigenous penal systems by stating that "the customs of these peoples in regard to penal matters shall be taken into consideration by authorities and courts dealing with such cases." This open formulation of the article may leave a lot of room for interpretation as to how to take into account indigenous customs in situations, where e.g. some action maybe punishable in indigenous law but not in the national system or vice versa, or when the forms of punishment are very different between the two systems. In these cases the national authorities are obliged at least to take into account indigenous norms and procedures.

e) The right to receive state support in the development of indigenous institutions and initiatives

In applying the provisions of the ILO Convention 169, according to article 6(1)(c) governments shall "establish means for the full development of these peoples' own institutions and initiatives, and in appropriate cases provide the resources necessary for this purpose". This implies a responsibility to establish means that make possible the development of indigenous institutions, including those that are in charge of indigenous law, such as indigenous forms of authority and organization.

The American Draft Declaration in article XXI(4) highlights explicitly the need to strengthen indigenous legal institutions and to establish mechanisms of coordination with national law, by requiring the states to "take measures to reinforce the judicial capacity of the indigenous peoples, to establish their jurisdiction, and to coordinate it with all other national jurisdictions, as appropriate."

f) The right to be consulted when the state is planning legislative or administrative measures that may affect the exercise of indigenous law

The ILO Convention 169, article 6(1)(a) requires states to consult indigenous peoples when planning legislative or administrative measures which may have direct impact on indigenous peoples. Indigenous peoples' right to be consulted covers legislative and administrative measures that may affect indigenous law, e.g. the establishment of mechanisms of coordination between indigenous authorities and state judicial authorities or when the mandate of indigenous authorities or scope of indigenous law would be subject to these measures.

g) *Indigenous peoples' special characteristics shall be taken into account when imposing penalties of the state penal system on indigenous persons*

The ILO Convention 169, according to article 10(1) urges the state parties to take into account indigenous peoples' economic, social and cultural characteristics when imposing penalties on indigenous individuals. According to this Convention, article 10(2). When defining the type of punishment the state authorities shall give preference to non-custodial methods of punishment. These provisions of article 10 of the ILO Convention 169 do not directly relate to the recognition of indigenous systems of law, but refer to the protection of indigenous individuals within the state system of law. This requires the states to take into account indigenous cultural and other characteristics, including their legal tradition, specifically in relation to the type of punishments, which in indigenous cultures in general do not consist of imprisonment.

It can be concluded that the recognition of indigenous law in human rights law is two-fold: first by the *internal* recognition of the exercise of this right within indigenous communities, and, secondly by *external* recognition formulated by the obligation of state authorities to take into account indigenous customary law when applying national legislation in respect of indigenous peoples.

The ILO Convention 169 aims at providing equal rights for men and women, as stated in article 3(1), whereas any specific rights of indigenous women or an additional protection of the rights of women as an especially vulnerable group among indigenous peoples is not considered. In relation to the protection of the rights of indigenous women within systems of indigenous law, the limitation set in article 8(2) which requires indigenous customs to be compatible with internationally recognised human rights applies also to the international standards that in general protect the human rights of women. Therefore, the convention pays no special attention to the rights of women in relation to indigenous law.

In the analysis of the ILO Convention 169 an issue of interest is the fact that by recognizing indigenous (customary) law and indigenous institutions connected to it, the convention at the same time in articles 8 and 9 defines certain restrictions to them, namely: *international human rights, nationally defined fundamental rights and national legal system*. The wording of the convention reflects the complex situation of indigenous peoples and individuals that form part of modern states, where their rights and responsibilities are regulated by different and competing legal systems. States are bound to respect international human rights law, which is applicable to all citizens of their state, both indigenous and non-indigenous. Indigenous peoples and individuals on the one hand are subjects of national legislation, and on the other hand indigenous persons are part of the normative systems of their own nation or people.

In states where governments over hundreds of years have oppressed indigenous peoples, a clause that maintains indigenous law subordinated under the national legal system gives concern among indigenous organizations. Indigenous peoples that claim self-determination, albeit within their state boundaries, do not see this situation satisfactorily. Indigenous peoples propose legal pluralism that would consist of a dialogue between equals; but how can it be reached, if these limits are already set without the participation of indigenous peoples? The answer proposed by the ILO Convention 169 in article 8(2) is the establishment of procedures to resolve conflicts, which may arise as a result of the recognition of indigenous law and the restrictions set by the convention. The convention does not specify how these procedures should be established. However, they should follow the general spirit of the convention, which is of respect, recognition and protection of the identity, values, cultures and institutions of indigenous peoples; otherwise the recognition of indigenous customary law would be left without any grounds.

Constitution of Ecuador

In Ecuador there are 11 different indigenous peoples that are culturally and linguistically diverse, however no reliable statistics on the number of the indigenous population are available. It has been estimated that between 35 and 45 percent of the national population is indigenous, even though also lower figures have been suggested.[43]

[43] According to CONAIE indigenous peoples represent 45% of the total population (http://conaie.org). The Ecuadorian state has reported (*Informes presentados por los estados partes de conformidad con el articulo 9 de la convención*, CERD/C/384/Add.8 of 9 July 2002, para 31) to the Committee on the Elimination of Racial Discrimination that it has not been able to provide up-to-date information on the number of indigenous persons, a situation that was noted by concern by the Committee (CERD/C/62/CO/2 of 21 March 2003, para 9). The State of Ecuador made reference to a census conducted by the National Institute of Statistics and Censuses in 1990, according to which only 4% of the national population would have been indigenous. The state

In Ecuador indigenous legal systems existed practically clandestine until the 1990´s, when the indigenous movement started gaining more national presence. As a result, indigenous customary law was recognized in the Ecuadorian constitution in 1998, after similar constitutional reforms had already taken place in other countries of the region.[44] The discussion on indigenous customary law in the Ecuadorian society is still at an initial stage, and the topic is considered to be highly sensitive. Only limited work has been done to disseminate and analyze the relationship between indigenous law and national law in the academic world and among legal practitioners. In 1998 Ecuador ratified the ILO Convention 169,[45] and important parts of the convention have been adopted in the reformed constitution[46] of the same year. The new constitution introduces significant reforms in relation to the rights of indigenous peoples in general, and for the first time in the history of Ecuador formally recognizes indigenous law. Ecuador is according to its constitution a pluricultural and multiethnic state.[47] In addition, all Ecuadorian citizens have the duty and responsibility "to advocate unity within diversity, and intercultural relations".[48] In practice, this *responsibility* to respect interculturality is more geared towards indigenous peoples. For example, the system of intercultural and bilingual education is implemented only in indigenous areas.[49] Most of the rights recognized to indigenous peoples and individuals are defined as collective rights in the constitution.[50] Ecuadorian

representative admitted however that there might exist statistical errors, which are due to the "complexity of the technical criteria used to establish precise parameters for determining membership of indigenous groups" (CERD/C/384/Add.8, para 31). The issue is however not purely technical but significantly of political character, since it has been a tendency of the ruling groups to treat indigenous claims for their rights as demands of rebellious minorities that do not represent significant numbers of the population. Ethnicity was also included in the latest national census conducted in November 2001. This latest census presents 8% as the official, but incorrect, amount of indigenous persons. See also OEA, *Report on the Situation of Human Rights in Ecuador*, OEA/Ser.L/V/II.96 Doc. 10 Rev. 1, 24 April 1997, Chapter IX, p. 1.

[44] E.g. Colombia 1991, Peru 1993 and Bolivia 1994.

[45] Registro Oficial No. 304, de 24 de abril de 1998.

[46] Constitución Política de la República del Ecuador.

[47] Article 1 of the constitution. Other adjectives used in article 1 to describe the character of the state are: social state of law, sovereign, unitarian, independent and democratic.

[48] Article 97(12) of the Constitution.

[49] Article 69 of the Constitution. By the definition provided in the Constitution intercultural bilingual education is aimed at indigenous children. In order to reach "unity within diversity" this kind of measures by the state should be directed to the whole population, and not requiring interculturality only from the indigenous population.

[50] A specific chapter of the Constitution is dedicated for collective rights (Chapter 5: "De los Derechos Colectivos"). This chapter consists of three sections, first of them concerns

indigenous peoples define themselves as "indigenous nationalities", this is also respected by the constitution stating that indigenous peoples' own definition is "indigenous nationalities of ancient roots".[51]

The plural character of the state recognised in article 1 of the Constitution is given a concrete content in article 84, which comprises 15 paragraphs concerning the collective rights of indigenous peoples. According to article 84 of the Constitution, the state recognizes and guarantees these rights "in accordance with the Constitution and law, respect to the public order and human rights". Among these rights the ones that are of relevance to the exercise of indigenous law are the collective rights to: "maintain, develop and strengthen their identity and traditions in spiritual, cultural, linguistic, social, political and economic fields"[52] and to "preserve and develop their traditional forms of coexistence and social organization, the establishment and exercise of authority".[53]

The direct recognition of indigenous law is expressed in article 191, which concerns the general principles of the judicial function. The constitutional text recognises indigenous law in the following terms:

> Authorities of indigenous peoples will exercise functions of justice, applying their own norms and procedures in internal conflict solution according to their customs or customary law, in so far as when they are not contrary to the Constitution and the Law. The Law will facilitate these functions within the national legal system.[54]

No direct relationship is drawn here between the exercise of indigenous law and the respect for human rights. The limitations set for indigenous authorities are: 1) they have competence only in *internal* matters, and 2) they may not act contrary to the *constitution and laws*. It is however implicit here that the Ecuadorian constitution and laws promote and protect human rights. Also, as described above, all collective rights recognised in article 84 are to be understood in accordance with the respect for human rights. In addition, ILO Convention No 169, which binds Ecuador, in its articles 8(2) and 9(1) limits indigenous law by 3*) internationally recognised human rights*. The subtext of

"indigenous peoples and the blacks or afroecuadorians", the second one deals with "the environment" and the third one protects the rights of "consumers'".

[51] Article 83. According to the self-definition by indigenous organizations in Ecuador, there are 11 different indigenous *nationalities* in Ecuador.

[52] Article 84(1).

[53] Article 84(7).

[54] Article 191, subsection 4. Author's own translation.

the clauses is the idea that the national state is responsible for and capable of guaranteeing the protection of rights and equality before the law for all its citizens. Ecuadorian citizens who belong to an indigenous people can seek the protection for their rights within their own legal systems as long as these systems do not contradict the national legislation. At the same time the state maintains control over norm violations or abuse of powers, albeit the functions that previously belonged only to the state, now formally will be shared by indigenous authorities.[55]

How to interpret these three parameters that define the competence of indigenous law is still an open question. There are diverse views on e.g. how to define "internal conflicts". It is clear that a too narrow interpretation of article 191 would be contradictory to the pluricultural character of the constitution; instead a balance between different constitutional norms should be the aim.[56] As the Ecuadorian state has proclaimed in article 62 of the Constitution, it will "foster interculturality, its politics will be inspired by, and its institutions formed according to the principles of same value and equality of cultures", evidently these principles are applicable also in the considerations of the relationship to be established between indigenous and national systems of law. The balancing dimension in this point can be found in the commitment of the state expressed in article 3(1) of the Constitution to "strengthen national unity within diversity". The proposal of indigenous organisations for the 1998 constitutional reform included internal self-determination and autonomy, based on a distribution of competencies between indigenous and state authorities.[57] This proposal was however not included in the new constitution. The constitution does not mention indigenous autonomies, but in article 84(1) recognises indigenous peoples right to "preserve and develop their traditional forms of coexistence and social organisation, of establishment and exercise of authority", as well as their *collective right* to "maintain, develop and strengthen their identity and traditions".

The guidance given by the constitution itself in the matter of implementation of the recognition of indigenous law offers two criteria. First,

[55] It is useful to keep in mind that indigenous peoples always have had their own internal systems of control, normally based on direct democracy exercised by the community assemblies where the community members have the right to participate in decision making.

[56] Agustín Grijalva, "La Jurisdicción Indígena: Derecho constitucional, internacional y comparado" [Indigenous Jurisdiction: Constitutional, International and Compared Law] in Julio César Trujillo, Agustín Grijalva, and Ximena Endara, 2001, *op. cit.* pp. 19-57, at pp. 21-23.

[57] CONAIE, 1997, *op. cit.*, pp. 20, 38 and 40.

the rights and guarantees that are determined by the constitution and international instruments that are in force in Ecuador are directly and immediately applicable before any judge, court or authority. Therefore, the recognition of indigenous law provided by article 191 is applicable, even though the specific legislation on coordination between national and indigenous authorities does not yet exist. Secondly, as provided in article 18 of the Constitution, in relation to constitutional rights and guarantees, the interpretation that most favours the effective validity of these rights shall be given priority.

In the experience of the Constitutional Court of Colombia, in situations where the court has considered the relationship and possible conflicts between the fundamental right of indigenous peoples to administer their justice according to their own norms and procedures and another constitutional norm, the court has found that it is not enough to base the analysis on the interpretative rules found in the constitution itself, but that an intercultural appreciation of the facts and rights should take place. According to Trujillo this can be done by examining the facts from each culture's own perspective, taking into account the value given to them in each culture. The aim is to find out the reasons why something that is good or indifferent in one culture may be bad or harmful in other culture. After this analysis the text, ratio and purpose of the norms in conflict must be scrutinised, taking into account the conclusions drawn from the fact analysis. Finally, the norm which would be the most convenient or just to save the values of one culture, at the same time being neutral to or without causing harm to the values of the other will be applied, in other words, a norm that causes least harm will be applied.[58] The experiences of Colombia have offered an interesting point of reference. In Ecuador this model has been considered in the draft law on Administration of Indigenous Justice, which responds to article 191, according to which a law will be created to define the issues of compatibility and limits of indigenous jurisdiction.[59] It proposes that the conflicts of competence between indigenous and state authorities, as well as any claims presented by indigenous persons due to the alleged violations of their fundamental rights or abuse of powers by an indigenous authority shall be resolved by the Constitutional Court.[60]

---

[58] Julio César Trujillo, 2002, *op. cit.*, p. 104.

[59] Elaborated by a group of experts under the academic auspices of the regional university Universidad Andina Simón Bolívar, and politically supported by CONAIE and the Commission for Indigenous Issues and Other Ethnic Groups of the National Parliament.

[60] Article 3, Anteproyecto de Ley de Administración de Justicia Indígena, as of April 2002.

The constitutional recognition of indigenous peoples' right to use their own procedures in the administration of indigenous law is also an issue that is still being discussed. According to this constitutional guarantee, procedures of the national system cannot be imposed on indigenous law, such as the requirement of codification of punishable crimes and their sanctions. If this were required, an important characteristic of indigenous law would be overruled, namely the interpretation made by the community and its authorities.[61] The Constitutional Court of Colombia has interpreted the requirement of due process in indigenous law by stating that demanding the existence of norms and institutions strictly equivalent to the national system would lead to a complete distortion of plurality as a basic principle of the constitution.[62] As stated above, a division of powers or a system of lower and higher instances of courts or legal authorities does not exist among indigenous cultures, a situation which according to some authors is unacceptable. According to these opinions all citizens of Ecuador should have the possibility of taking their cases to forums that can revise the decisions and discover whether there has been any mistake or injustice that has taken place in the decision-making at first instance.[63] Different proposals for these higher forums have been proposed; some would include this in the competence of the constitutional court, others propose that a mixed body of judges and communal authorities could be created.[64]

BETWEEN INDIGENOUS LAW AND HUMAN RIGHTS

Intercultural Dialogue for the Definition of Limits and Competencies

Indigenous law has not existed in isolation , but it has over centuries been influenced by colonial and post-colonial[65] legal systems, which have modified

[61] Esther Sánchez Botero and Isabel Jaramillo Sierra, 2000, *op. cit.*, p. 71.

[62] *Ibid.*, p. 72.

[63] Enrique Ayala Mora, "El derecho ecuatoriano y el aporte indígena" [Ecuadorian Law and the Indigenous Constribution] in Judith Salgado (ed.), 2002, *op. cit.* , pp. 105-123, at p. 109.

[64] *Ibid.*, p. 117-118.

[65] The concept of post-colonialism is very controversial. Even though the colonial powers formally left Ecuador in 1830, the independence did not lead to the constitution of a new order of society. The state administration and legal system still respond to the models implemented during the colonial time. Indigenous and Afro-Ecuadorian movements claim for the re-definition of the state in order to reflect the special characters and history of Ecuador.

indigenous forms of organisation and authority, resulting e.g. in imported forms of punishment.[66] As stated above, in the ILO Convention169 possible conflicts of competence and challenges in the definition of limits of both systems of law are foreseen, and as a solution the states are urged to establish mechanisms to resolve these situations. The Ecuadorian Constitution in its turn defines that a law will be created for this purpose. To date, this law has not been passed in the Ecuadorian parliament. Therefore, the implementation of another mechanism, the one of intercultural dialogue is suggested here. It is based on the plurality of the state recognised by its Constitution, as well as interculturality, the same value and equality of cultures, which all are defined as responsibilities of the state. Intercultural dialogue as a possible tool for coordination between indigenous law and national law is discussed in this section. Thereafter the specific cases of prohibition of torture and women's human rights will be considered.

Human rights and the equality of rights should be implemented with respect for the identity of all persons, which implies the right to be different.[67] This approach can be grounded in the principle of indivisibility and interdependence of human rights. A human right cannot be fully enjoyed, if at the same time other rights are violated, such as the right to the exercise of ones culture.[68] If a conflict exists, the implementation of human rights can be done

---

[66] For example whipping and pillory (in Spanish: cepo) now commonly used forms of sanction among indigenous peoples of the Andean region were introduced by the Spaniards. See e.g. in Willem Assies, *Indian Justice in the Andes: Re-Rooting or Re-Routing?,* (http://www.geocities.com/alertanet2/F2b-Wassies-en.htm). The article was posted in the Alertanet – Portal on Law and Society pages in June 2001; or Emiliano Borja Jiménez, *Introducción a los fundamentos del derecho penal indígena* [Introduction to the Foundations of Indigenous Penal Law], Valencia, Tirant lo Blanch, 2001, p. 151.

[67] Hector Gros Espiell, *Universalidad de los derechos humanos y diversidades culturales* [Universality of Human Rights and Cultural Diversities]. http://www.unesco.org/issj/rics158/grosespiellspa.html.

[68] As expressed by Nina Pacari Vega: "It is not admissible that indigenous administration of justice is analyzed by taking the codes and notions of the dominant culture as the starting point, a culture which believes that everything that is not found within its format and conception is without value or simply does not exist." Nina Pacari Vega, "Pluralidad juridical: una realidad constitucionalmente reconocida" [Legal Pluralism: A Constitutionally Recognized Reality] in Judith Salgado, 2002, *op. cit.*, pp. 83-89, at p. 87. Own translation from the Spanish original. Nina Pacari Vega is Kichwa, lawyer and former parliamentarian. From January to August 2003 she was the Minister of Foreign of Affairs of Ecuador, being the first woman and the first indigenous person in this post.

through an *intercultural*[69] *dialogue or interpretation* of these rights. Another possibility proposed by some authors is to seek solutions from *interlegality* to establish, how legal norms of different systems and cultural conceptions can be inserted into a common system.[70] When establishing the compatibility between indigenous and state law the Ecuadorian draft law on the administration of indigenous justice proposes the use of intercultural interpretation of the facts and the law, without affecting the dignity of a person. The draft does not define what is understood with intercultural interpretation.[71]

Sousa Santos points out that it is important to be aware of the power relations that exist between cultural groups representing different legal systems within one state, when considering the possibility of a dialogue. In Latin America the long history of inequality has resulted in three consequences for indigenous peoples: the undervaluing of their own culture by indigenous peoples themselves and by the others, uncontrolled contamination by the other culture as a strategy of invasion or survival, and the production of silence by force. When thinking about a dialogue to be created between indigenous and non-indigenous concepts of law and justice, these products of inequality are often forgotten, especially that possible contributions by indigenous peoples to this dialogue have been erased from their collective memory through the production of silence. According to Sousa Santos, due to these factors, it is highly probable that dialogue would result in fraud, misunderstanding or a more subtle form of cultural destruction. Therefore, a dialogue between cultures of unequal power relations is legitimate only when it contributes to diminishing this inequality. This can be reached by establishing three conditions: First, the dialogue in itself has to be conducted in multi or intercultural conditions, its aim is not to consult, or to give information, but to

[69] Catherine Walsh, "Interculturalidad, reformas constitucionales y pluralismo jurídico" [Interculturality, Constitutional Reforms and Legal Pluralism] in Judith Salgado (ed.), 2002, *op. cit.*, p. 24. Walsh uses the following definition of interculturality: "based in the necessity of constructing relations *between* groups, as well as *between* practices, logics and different knowledge, with the urge of confronting and transforming the power relations (including the structures and institutions of the society) that have naturalized the social asymmetries". She uses also another definition, namely the *pluricultural* interpretation of laws "the recognition of different functions, contexts and social goals of different legal norms" This adds the indigenous system to the formal legal system, based in the recognition and inclusion, without significantly transforming the formal system, without rethinking the totality (p. 31). (Author's translations from Spanish, italics as in the original text).

[70] As in Enrique Ayala Mora, 2002, *op. cit.*, pp. 108-109. According to him interculturality corresponds only to cultural phenomena, which are separate from legal issues.

[71] Anteproyecto de Ley de Administración de Justicia Indígena, *op. cit.*, Article 18.

be a process of reaching an agreement, on the basis of autonomous proposals by the different groups that take part in this dialogue. Secondly, indigenous communities should be able to decide when they are ready for the dialogue. Thirdly, indigenous communities may refuse the dialogue or to decide on which issues they are ready to establish the dialogue.[72]

According to Sánchez Botero multidisciplinary approaches need to be developed, in order to construct *structured logical systems* that allow for an adequate understanding of different aspects of indigenous legal orders. These systems allow the appraisal of indigenous concepts and arguments with adequate analytical instruments and their proper contextualization. The imposition of a particular worldview has to be avoided since this would be contrary to principles of legal plurality and equality of cultures.[73]

Borja Jiménez proposes a minimum consensus on the validity of human rights in all cultures and traditions, even though this consensus would be strictly limited and with different interpretations. In the indigenous context this requires the interpretation of individual guarantees within a more collective and social focus, with a supraindividual dimension (the community) that is different from the vision of Western cultures. The preconditions for a conciliatory solution for this conflict are: the coexistence of different cultures in equality, with a minimum consensus of the universal validity of certain human rights, and an acceptance that a distinct interpretation of these rights is possible according to the cultural point of view in question. To define these commonly agreed human rights Borja Jiménez suggests that account should be taken of the principle of free development of the personality, right to life, physical integrity, freedom of expression, freedom of association and right to security.[74] A view similar to this has been taken by the Constitutional Court of Colombia, which in the interpretation of cases has concluded that the establishment of some minimum standards of tolerance that respect the

---

[72] Boaventura de Sousa Santos, "Pluralismo jurídico y jurisdicción especial indígena" [Legal Pluralism and Indigenous Special Jurisdiction] in Dirección General de Asuntos Indígenas del Ministerio de Interior and Ministerio de Justicia y del Derecho, *Del Olvido surgimos para traer nuevas esperanzas: La jurisdicción especial indígena* [From the Forgotten We Emerge to Bring New Hope: The Indigenous Special Jurisdiction], Santa Fé de Bogotá, 1997, pp. 201-211, at pp. 201-202, 206-211.

[73] Esther Sánchez Botero, "The *Tutela*-system as a Means of Transforming the Relations between the State and the Indigenous Peoples of Colombia" in Assies et al. (eds.), 2000, *op. cit.*, pp. 223-241, at pp. 225-228.

[74] Emiliano Borja Jiménez, 2001, *op. cit.*, pp. 177-182.

different value systems is necessary. A consensus on minimum common standards is needed for the coexistence of different cultures, without requiring that any of them has to renounce the premises that are characteristic for their identity.[75] Grijalva has stated that the pluricultural and multiethnic character of the state as defined in the Ecuadorian Constitution, implies the recognition of indigenous peoples as possessors of rights, and the exercise of their rights includes the recognition of the existence of diverse normative systems. Therefore, it is unavoidable to consider fundamental rights in their particular cultural contexts, applying moderate relativism.[76]

Encouraging examples of how to put into practice an intercultural dialogue of rights concepts and practices and their compatibility with human rights standards, can be found in sentences of the Constitutional Court of Colombia. The court has started developing a framework for peaceful coexistence, co-ordination and mutual respect between the national legal system and indigenous legal systems. Rich case law that is unique in Latin America has been developed around the interpretation of constitutional provisions in line with the ILO standards that recognise indigenous law in Colombia. The Colombian constitutional article 246 is substantially equivalent to article 191(4) of the Ecuadorian constitution.[77]

The court has interpreted the constitutional *principle of protection of ethnic and cultural diversity*[78] in relation to fundamental human rights in cases where it has considered the constitutionality of decisions made by indigenous authorities. When weighing conflicting situations between indigenous and national norms, the court has taken the standpoint that the aim of the principle of the protection of ethnic and cultural diversity is the cultural survival of indigenous peoples, which is possible only when the state can guarantee these peoples a high degree of autonomy. Therefore, the court has developed a rule of interpretation of the *maximisation of the autonomy of indigenous communities and minimisation of its restriction.*[79] According to this rule of

---

[75] Corte Constitucional de Colombia: Sentencia T-523/97, Chapter II: Consideraciones de fondo.

[76] Agustín Grijalva, 2001, *op. cit.*, pp. 34-36.

[77] According to article 246 of the Constitution of Colombia "The authorities of indigenous peoples may exercise jurisdictional functions within their territory, according to their own norms and procedures, always when not contrary to the constitution or the laws of the republic. The law will establish the forms of coordination between this special jurisdiction and the national system." (Author's translation)

[78] Protected by the Colombian Constitution in its articles 10, 70, 171, 176, 246 and 286.

[79] According to the court, there are different grades of implementation of this principle; this protection is strongest when the case is internal (in all its elements) to an indigenous

interpretation, restrictions on the jurisdictional autonomy of indigenous communities are acceptable only when they are indispensable to safeguard interests of a superior hierarchy. When deciding on a restriction, the measure to be chosen should be the least grave possible to indigenous autonomy. According to a court decision from 1996, the *only* interests of superior hierarchy that set limits to indigenous law are: 1) right to life; 2) prohibition of slavery and torture; and 3) requirement of the legality of procedures, and in penal matters, the legality of crimes and penalties.[80] The court has motivated this conclusion by explaining that these are the only standards, where: a) true intercultural consensus can be reached, and b) they are intangible human rights that cannot be suspended in any circumstances.[81]

Case 1: Prohibition of Torture

Differences between indigenous law and national law in Ecuador are especially visible in the types of punishments that are considered appropriate. For example, from the point of view of state law, the existence of corporal punishment in indigenous communities is unacceptable, whereas expulsion from the community, which is considered as a very serious punishment among indigenous peoples, in some cases can be seen as a too mild punishment in relation to the crimes committed. On the other hand, in the indigenous view imprisonment is often seen as very harmful and a disproportionately cruel form of punishment, which isolates the convicted person totally from his community, and therefore hinders the process of rehabilitation that in indigenous law takes place within the community. These differences can be at least partly explained due to values strongly connected to the individual in national society and the collective values of indigenous community life.[82] In general, among the indigenous cultures of Ecuador sanctions that separate the individual from his community are imposed only for the most serious crimes, and are implemented only when no other method has been effective. An individual without his

community, since all persons involved share the same legal tradition. Constitutional Court of Colombia, Sentence No. T-349/96: La interpretación del artículo 246 de la Constitución Política.

[80] The court has clarified this last requirement by stating that: "It is obvious that the requirement in this case cannot go beyond what is necessary to guarantee the foreseeability in the conduct of authorities; in other case this requirement would lead to a complete ignorance of own forms of norm production and autochthonous rituals of judging, which is precisely what is pretended to preserve." (own translation) Sentence No. T-349/96: 2.3. La interpretación del artículo 246 de la Constitución Política.

[81] Constitutional Court of Colombia, Sentence No. T-349/96: 2.3. La interpretación del artículo 246 de la Constitución Política. See also Sentence No. T-254/94.

[82] Emilio Borja Jiménez, 2001, *op. cit.*, pp. 158-161.

natural social context practically fails almost to exist and loses the sense of being. In the ILO Convention 169, article 10, this view is taken into account by recognising that imprisonment is not recommendable among indigenous peoples

One of the most controversial aspects of indigenous forms of punishment in Ecuador are the commonly used practices of whipping, bathing in cold water, or in water mixed with nettle leaves, and their possible incompatibility with human rights.[83] The possible relationship between these practises and the prohibition of torture will be briefly discussed here. International human rights law prohibits torture and other cruel, inhuman or degrading treatment or punishment in article 7 of the International Covenant on Civil and Political Rights (ICCPR)[84] and in article 5 of the Universal Declaration of Human Rights. The state obligation to prevent acts of torture and other cruel, inhuman or degrading treatment or punishment are elaborated in the Convention against Torture and Other Cruel, Inhuman or Degrading Treatment or Punishment (CAT).[85] In Ecuador, the constitutional article 23(2) prohibits cruel penalties, torture, all inhuman or degrading procedures, or procedures that imply physical, psychological or sexual violence or moral coercion.

CAT defines torture as "any act by which severe pain or suffering, whether physical or mental is intentionally inflicted on a person", when "such pain or suffering is inflicted by or at the instigation of or with the consent or acquiescence of a public official or other person acting in an official capacity". Torture, according to article 1(1), does not include "pain or suffering arising

[83] Whether the death penalty exists in indigenous law is also a very debated issue in Ecuador. E.g. according to García, the death penalty is not part of indigenous law, cases of capital punishment in the rural areas of Ecuador fall outside of the exercise of indigenous law as such. Fernando García, *Formas indígenas de administrar justicia* [Indigenous Forms to Administer Justice], Quito, FLACSO Sede Ecuador, 2002, pp. 39-40. On the other hand some authors state that death penalty also exists in the communities. See e.g. Xiména Ortiz Crespo, 2002, op. cit., p. 11. The Ecuadorian Constitution (article 23(1)) prohibits the use of capital punishment. Among the Kichwa of the Amazonia, shamans who are accused of causing the death of a community member by abusing their spiritual powers may be killed by a community member to prevent the death of several persons. To differentiate a killing of a shaman from the exercise of indigenous laaw as such, García has characterized the former one as "social death", the provocation of the death of another person to avoid other deaths in the community. García, pp. 39-40. Due to the extension of the discussion on death penalty, it will not be dealt with in this article.

[84] Ratified by Ecuador on March 2nd, 1976.

[85] Ratified by Ecuador on April 29, 1988.

only from, inherent in or incidental to lawful sanctions" CAT does not define cruel, inhuman or degrading treatment or punishment, it only mentions (in article 16) that they may comprise acts that do not amount to torture. ICCPR does not provide any definitions of the concepts used in article 7. The Human Rights Committee has come to the conclusion that it is neither necessary to draw up a list of prohibited acts nor to establish sharp distinctions between different kinds of punishment or treatment. According to the Committee these distinctions depend on the nature, purpose and severity of the treatment applied.[86]

According to the Human Rights Committee, the aim of article 7 is to protect both the *dignity* and physical and mental *integrity of the individual*, inflicted by persons in their official capacity, outside their official capacity or in a private capacity.[87] According to the Committee, the article must extend to corporal punishment, including excessive chastisement ordered as a punishment or as an educative or disciplinary measure.[88] In the case George Osbourne v. Jamaica,[89] where the state party imposed a punishment of whipping with the tamarind switch on the claimant, the Human Rights Committee decided that *corporal punishment* constitutes cruel, inhuman and degrading treatment or punishment that is contrary to article 7.[90]

Indigenous peoples strongly defend their traditional practices that they perceive efficient both in preventive and rehabilitative sense. Sanctions that a community imposes on its members are not aimed at exposing the offender to embarrassment or causing excessive suffering and pain, but at the provision of a process where the offender can reflect on his wrong doings, and acquire the possibility of receiving forgiveness from the community and reintegration to it as a full member. Often the ritual elements of these sanctions are emphasised. For example bathing in nettle water is not contrary to dignity and physical and mental integrity of the individual, but a form of purification, where a person with high moral authority in the community gives the symbolic bathing to the

---

[86] Human Rights Committee: General Comment 20, Replaces general comment 7 concerning prohibition of torture and cruel treatment or punishment (art.7). 10/03/92, para 4.

[87] *Ibid.* , para 2.

[88] *Ibid.*, para 5.

[89] Communication No. 759/1997.

[90] Communication No. 759/1997, para 9.1.

offender.[91] Whipping in indigenous communities seeks similar aims, and therefore cannot be compared with practices of some states, where the objective is to humiliate and cause suffering to the convicted, such as the situation referred to in the case of George Osbourne v. Jamaica. The above mentioned types of punishment, which are common among indigenous cultures of Ecuador, do not constitute corporal punishment, but are characterised by their ritual contents and healing effects.

The Constitutional Court of Colombia, has analysed in detail indigenous forms of punishment in the light of human rights protection, and especially in relation to the recognition of jurisdictional autonomy of indigenous communities as an essential tool to protect their cultural survival. In a case, where the Court analysed the constitutionality of whipping imposed as a punishment by indigenous authorities on one of the community members, the court pointed out that in the non-indigenous society of Colombia corporal punishment is rejected for being contrary to human dignity, however in indigenous societies punishments such as whipping are considered purifying and necessary for the rehabilitation process of the convicted.[92] After an analysis of the CAT[93] and with reference to the criteria used by the European Court of Human Rights, the Constitutional Court of Colombia concluded that even though whipping causes grief, its purpose is not to cause excessive suffering, but represents an element that seeks to purify the individual.[94] According to the Court, the whip fulfils a ritual purpose, and is used in order to censure the individual and at the same time contribute to the return of harmony to the community. The court pointed out that even though the ritual aspects would not be considered, the suffering caused in the practice of the Páez indigenous people does not amount to torture, neither can it be considered as degrading punishment, since it is a practice that does not intend to "give a lesson" in public, but to help the wrongdoer to regain his/her place in the community.[95]

---

[91] In this form of punishment the person/s chosen to give the bath give/s advice and counseling to the offender – and at the same time become/s exposed to the burning effect of the nettle leaves. See e.g. the study of Emilio Borja Jiménez, 2001, *op. cit.*

[92] Sentencia No. T-523/97, Expediente T-124907, Santa Fé de Bogotá, 15 de octubre 1997. Chapter 3.3.3 La legalidad de las penas: a) El fuete.

[93] In force in Colombia through Law No. 78, 15 of December of 1986.

[94] In the world view of the indigenous people concerned in this sentence (the Páez), the whip is associated with the lightning.

[95] Sentencia No. T-523/97, *op. cit.*

Case 2: Human Rights of Women

The general protection of women's human rights remains weak in Ecuador; society still maintains structures and attitudes that discriminate against women. This has been observed e.g. by the Committee on the Elimination of Discrimination Against Women by stating that "the Government was not giving serious consideration to the advancement of women. There was a *de jure* and *de facto* gap in the attainment of women's equality"[96] The Human Rights Committee has expressed its concern that it is difficult for women to obtain remedies regarding crimes committed against them due to the reluctance of the authorities to act in these cases: "... the many instances of violence against women and the very few judicial decisions thereon. The Committee stresses that all reported acts of violence against women should be investigated and appropriate judicial proceedings instituted."[97] In the case of indigenous women this situation is even more serious, since they suffer multiple discrimination: they are *indigenous*, they are *women*, and they (usually) belong to a social class with very *limited economic resources*. These individual groups suffer discrimination in general in society and are also in a disadvantageous position in relation to the legal system.[98] In addition, many indigenous women do not have sufficient skills in Spanish in order to be aware of their rights and present their claims. The Ecuadorian legislation does not consider any specific measures for the protection of the rights of indigenous women.

Problems concerning the protection of women's rights may be identified also in indigenous communities and their implementation in indigenous law. Since indigenous law does not consist of codified norms, the sources of law are to be found in analyses of indigenous *cosmovision* and the customary law. No systematic empirical research is available on possible patterns of discrimination or the probability that women may be discriminated against

---

[96] Concluding observations of the Committee on the Elimination of Discrimination Against Women: Ecuador 12/04/94, A/49/38, para. 510.

[97] Concluding observations of the Human Rights Committee: Ecuador 18/08/98, CCPR/C/79/Add.92, para. 10.

[98] The Committee on the Elimination of all Forms of Racial Discrimination has expressed its concern on the persisting pattern of discrimination against indigenous and Afro-Ecuadorian population, despite of the constitutional and legal guarantees, and especially against women belonging to these groups. Committee on the Elimination of Racial Discrimination: Concluding Observations: Ecuador. CERD/C/62/CO/2 of 21 March 2003, paras. 11 and 15.

within indigenous legal systems in Ecuador. This type of research would appear to be necessary because there seems to be a gap between on the one hand the *cosmovision*-based discourse of complementarity and the same value and dignity between men and women (the theory of indigenous law), and on the other hand the implementation of indigenous law, whereby many indigenous women suffer domestic violence and do not have equal access to education or leadership positions.[99]

It is commonly accepted that according to the *cosmovision* of the majority of indigenous peoples in the Americas, gender relations are based on complementary duality. [100] Complementarity in gender relations can be constructed in a way where the two genders are needed to realise a common task,[101] or in a substitutive way,[102] where under certain circumstances a person can substitute the activities normally done by the opposite sex. [103] In the Andean cultures complementarity may be characterised as a search for equilibrium. It is very common that the man represents the family in public, however women have their areas of responsibility that give them a stable position within the family and in the community structure; their access to formal or public authority is more restricted however. Gender relations in one

---

[99] E.g. Lourdes Tibán has affirmed that "the discourse of gender and equality within the indigenous movement in relation to its practise is a contradiction". Lourdes Tibán, *Género y sustentabilidad: nuevos conceptos para el movimiento indígena* [Gender and Sustainability: New Concepts for the Indigenous Movement], Boletín ICCI-Rimai Publicación mensual del Instituto Científico de Culturas Indígenas, Año 3, No. 29, Quito, agosto del 2001, p. 5. (Electronic version of the bulletin is found in: http:// icci.nativeweb.org/boletin/29/tiban.html),

[100] See e.g. Center of Studies and Information of the Multiethnic Woman, CEIMM of the University of the Autonomous Regions of the Caribbean Nicaraguan Coast, URACCAN, *Background Paper on Gender from the Indigenous Women's Perspective*, First Indigenous Women Summit of the Americas, Oaxaca, December 4th, 2002. http://www.mujeresindigenas.net/documentos_de_discusion/ingles/genero-desde-la-vision-de-las-mujeres-indigenas-ingles.doc. In Ecuador complementary duality is a view presented by the national indigenous organizations such as the CONAIE.

[101] For example in *ayllu* (a traditional Andean form of organization) type of organization of the society, where only a couple can perform leadership functions. Both man and woman have their specific tasks as leaders, but none of them can alone become a leader.

[102] E.g. in agriculture men and women have their defined tasks that vary between different cultures.

[103] On the different types of complementarity see: Perrin, M. Y Perruchon, M. , (coord.), *Complementariedad entre hombre y mujer: Relaciones de género desde la perspectiva amerindia* [Complementarity between Men and Women: Gender Relations from American Indian Perspective], Biblioteca Abya-Yala No. 43, Quito, Ediciones Abya-Yala, 1997, p. 14.

culture are normally not of one type only, but vary on contextual interaction, e.g. the socio-economic position and age of the person concerned.

Different explanations may be given as to why the theory of equilibrium in the relations between men and women is not always successfully implemented in practice, for example:

a) Deepened poverty and other changes that are the result of external influence in indigenous communities have increased conflicts and violence. This has affected community and family structures, and has had the tendency of weakening the position of women.[104] Other changes can be related to attitudes and values that are a product of e.g. the school system.
b) Due to a long history of political and spiritual colonisation, indigenous organisations and mechanisms of control have been weakened to such a degree that it is no longer possible to live up to the ideals of indigenous law in practice.[105]
c) The defence of the rights of indigenous peoples as a group in relation to the state has been considered as the priority of indigenous movement. Not enough time and resources have been allocated to address possible internal inconsistency, such as the situation of women. This may also have strategic political reasons, as rehearsing internal problems could diminish the credibility of indigenous movements claiming a just society.[106]
d) The gender vision in indigenous cultures is often sustained by references made to the historical development of gender roles in indigenous cultures and how they were perceived before the conquest. It is a commonly held view that the current injustices or inequities are the outcome of "cultural corruption" produced by a clash between indigenous cultures and the European influence.[107] There is also a strong need among indigenous cultures of the Andes to reconstruct their own history, which until now has been told from the

[104] UNIFEM, *Voces de los Andes: Testimonios de mujeres indígenas y campesinas* [Voices from the Andes: Wittnesses of Indigenous and Peasant Women], Quito, 1998, pp. 29-31.

[105] On the effects of colonization on indigenous women, see e.g. Center of Studies and Information of the Multiethnic Woman, CEIMM of the University of the Autonomous Regions of the Caribbean Nicaraguan Coast, URACCAN, 2003, *op. cit.*

[106] See on different positions taken within indigenous movement in relation to this topic. *Ibid.*, p. 5, 8-9.

[107] *Ibid.*, p. 2.

conquistador point of view. To clarify these arguments, more detailed research in gender aspects is still required.

Indigenous women and their organisations are in the process of defining their own gender concepts and ways of promoting gender equity. Indigenous women's gender discourse is often centered towards the promotion of *equidad* (equity) instead of *igualdad* (equality). With this distinction indigenous women activists and leaders want to emphasise their coherence with their *cosmovision* of complementarity and equilibrium. Western proposals for gender equality are often rejected by indigenous women's organisations.[108] According to a definition elaborated at the First Indigenous Women Summit of the Americas; "...gender perspective for indigenous women refers to the power differential between women and men, a perspective that provides an equilibrium between women and men that ensures equality amongst indigenous peoples, an inclusive attitude, a pluricultural and diverse view, and the exercise of our individual and collective rights."[109] It is commonly seen that indigenous women defend the gender views of their cultures, stating that the gender views of their cultures are different, but functional within their societies. Therefore their gender perceptions should not be condemned from outside, but be respected in states such as Ecuador that are founded on the legal principle of diversity.[110] At the same time, the discourse of indigenous women leaders speak for change in society in order to reach equity within their cultures. This position taken by indigenous women is to support their struggle for self-determination as peoples, seeing women's human rights in a wider context. The approach of indigenous women's organisations is normally not centred on gender issues only, but declarations, agendas and statements by national women's organisations or international gatherings that take up a variety of issues that concern the well being of indigenous peoples – women, men and children. This is visible for example in the Beijing Declaration of

[108] See e.g. the Declaration of the First Indigenous Women's Summit of the Americas: "Recognizing that the gains in international instruments have not resulted in the improvement of the lives of indigenous women in their communities, because the policies have been written from a Western perspective." Declaration on the Occasion of the First Indigenous Women's Summit of the Americas. Oaxaca, December 4th, 2002, (http://www.mujeresindigenas.net/documentos_de_discusion/declaracion_mujeres_english.htm).

[109] *Ibid.* Declaration and Platform of Action.

[110] See e.g. Lourdes Tibán, 2001, *op. cit.*, pp. 5-6. Lourdes Tibán is young Kichwa woman, who has held important leadership positions both within the state administration and indigenous organizations.

Indigenous Women, where indigenous women present a critical view on the draft Platform for Action. According to the representatives of the indigenous women's organisations, who had signed the indigenous women's declaration, the proposed objectives and actions of the Beijing Declaration"... are hollow and meaningless if the inequality between nations, races, classes, and genders, are not challenged at the same time... the Platform's overemphasis of gender discrimination and gender equality depoliticises the issues confronting indigenous women".[111]

In the administration of justice in an indigenous community in most cultures, both men and women have the possibilities to express their views and give their proposals. The role of women is significant in the legal process, however, greater recognition and encouragement of women's participation is needed. Women's opinions are possibly not as easily heard as men's, as most of the community leaders are men. The leadership of women is often hard to discern and may be indirect. The reasons for this depend partly on the tradition, where only men have been prepared for public office, and partly due to women's lower schooling rates. Attitudes are slowly changing, and it is more common to find indigenous women in leadership positions in the community, municipalities or in the national politics.[112] Cultures are in a constant process of change, where the roles of men and women are slowly changing. It is not desirable that these changes should be the result of an external imposition, but the cultures should internally evaluate their needs for change, according to their evolutionary needs.[113] These slow changes of attitudes might become visible in the indigenous legal systems. According to García, new types of gender related cases are emerging within indigenous law, such as claims concerning the marginalisation of women in decision-making and their access to leadership positions.[114]

---

[111] Beijing Declaration of Indigenous Women, NGO Forum, UN Fourth World Conference on Women. Approved and signed on 7 September 1995 at the Indigenous Women's Tent, Huairou, Beijing, China. http://www.tebtebba.org/tebtebba_files/gender/beijing.html, para. 16.

[112] See Fernando García, 2002, op. cit., pp. 40, 49-50, and Lucila Lema, "Aportes a la discusión" [Contributions to the Discussion] in Fernando García, (coordinator), *Las sociedades interculturales un desafío para el Siglo XXI* "Aportes a la discusión" [Intercultural Societies, a Challenge for the 21st Century], Quito, Flacso, 2000, pp. 99-104, at p. 102.

[113] Lourdes Tibán, 2001, *op. cit.*, p. 6.

[114] Fernando García, 2002, *op. cit.*, p. 30.

Indigenous organisations in Ecuador have started to adopt the rights of indigenous women as part of their agendas. In the ECUARUNARI[115] proposal for the constitutional reform of 1998 the perspective of gender equity and the promotion and valuing of the democratic participation of women in all areas of the national life was defined as an action to be mainstreamed throughout the constitutional reform.[116] Some of the most significant indigenous organisations of Ecuador are also providing courses of leadership training for indigenous women.[117]

Some initiatives have been taken, to analyse, whether indigenous law could provide mechanisms to combat discrimination against indigenous women, and thereby, promote the fulfilment of their rights. For example, the procedures of the national system in cases of violence against women can be very traumatic, and seldom lead to any concrete remedy, in a society, where *machismo* is accepted and is reflected also in the behaviour of the state authorities. In the national legal system indigenous women can seldom receive professional support in their own language, by a person who understands their culture, and with whom they can have a confidential relationship. Indigenous law, however, could have possibilities to act rapidly and efficiently. In international indigenous women's forums the relation between indigenous law and the protection of women's rights has also been considered. In the Beijing Declaration of Indigenous Women the following statement was made: "That Indigenous customary laws and justice systems which are supportive of women victims of violence be recognised and reinforced. That indigenous laws, customs, and traditions which are discriminatory to women be eradicated."[118] In the Plan of Action of the First Indigenous Women Summit of the Americas the indigenous women established a demand that their states recognise, respect and promote the application of indigenous law in all its aspects, civil, penal,

---

[115] The biggest of the regional indigenous organizations in Ecuador. Forms part of CONAIE and represents indigenous organizations of the Ecuadorian highlands.

[116] ECUARUNARI, Derechos de los pueblos indígenas y propuesta política de la nacionalidad y los pueblos quichuas de Ecuador: Síntesis de los talleres sobre derechos de los pueblos indígenas [Indigenous Peoples' Rights and the Political Proposal of the Quichua Nationality and Peoples: Summary of the Workshops on Indigenous Peoples Rights] ,Documento de base No. 1, Quito, 4,5,6 de marzo de 1998, pp. 18-19.

[117] Of the representative indigenous organizations at least CONAIE and ECUARUNARI have ongoing programs on women's leadership training.

[118] Beijing Declaration of Indigenous Women, 1995, *op. cit.*, para. 36.

commercial and international, and adopt state politics and legislation to indigenous law.[119]

CLOSING REMARKS

Through the legal recognition of indigenous law its existence has been brought to national attention, which may lead to a situation, in which decisions taken by indigenous authorities will be scrutinised to a greater extent than before, both externally by the national legal system, and internally within their own systems. This tendency has been visible in Colombia, the only country in the Andean region, where rich case law exists on the relationship between indigenous law and state law. The constitutional recognition and interpretations made by the Constitutional Court have in some cases changed and influenced the decisions of indigenous authorities, particularly in cases concerning the relationship between indigenous law and human rights. For example in cultures, where the abuse of spiritual power has been considered as a crime to be punished with the death penalty, there are now new cases where this crime is punished with other, milder forms of penalties in order to avoid conflicts with the national authorities.[120] According to Assies, the recognition of indigenous law, the public debate and the case law of Colombia have influenced indigenous organisations that are seeking to strengthen their own justice systems. They have started to create mechanisms to review cases that are controversial from human rights points of view without resorting to non-indigenous courts, thus maintaining their autonomy. References of human rights have been included in the decisions made by indigenous authorities. Some indigenous representatives consider this development as interference in indigenous internal affairs, and some see it as positive development of indigenous justice.[121]

The exercise of indigenous law is a legitimate claim of indigenous peoples. The right to have access to justice that is not only respectful to their cultures, but is based on the needs and principles that have been developed during thousands of years within their own cultural context. Indigenous

[119] Plan de Acción. Primera Cumbre de Mujeres Indígenas de las Américas, 2002, *op. cit.*, chapter "Derechos Humanos y Derechos Indígenas", para 4.

[120] In Esther Sánchez Botero and Isabel Jaramillo Sierra, 2000, *op. cit.*, p. 74. The original source to which reference was made is: Jurisprudencia Paez, recopilada en terreno por Oswaldo Gonzálex, ICBF, Cauca, 1999.

[121] Willem Assies, 2001, op. cit., pp. 9-10.

authorities should have the right, as recognised in the Constitution of Ecuador and in the ILO Convention 169, to develop and administer their justice without the fear of being sanctioned by national authorities who administer another system of law. The creation of a forum to co-ordinate and interpret constitutional principles and to create an intercultural dialogue in the field of justice is necessary. One of the tasks of this instance would be to discuss the relationship between indigenous law and human rights law. The task of this instance would be to create a reciprocal legal dialogue, where the activities of both national and indigenous legal authorities would be discussed, in the spirit of the ILO Convention 169 as analysed above.

The public discussion on indigenous legal systems in the Andean region has had the tendency to focus on human rights violations that might occur, when indigenous authorities are given "free hands to judge". Indigenous visions of justice and its implementation are often different from state law, however among indigenous communities their own legal systems are considered highly legitimate, efficient and fair. It has not been proven that incompatibility with human rights is a bigger problem in indigenous than in non-indigenous legal systems. Problems of satisfactory implementation of human rights exist in both indigenous and non-indigenous systems. In some cases indigenous law may provide more efficient human rights protection than the national law. This is due to its characteristics analysed above, such as, its accessibility (in time, space and economic terms), cultural closeness (indigenous persons identify closely with its principles and forms of implementation, and are knowledgeable of its contents), and because it is administered in the local communities thereby diminishing the probability of corruption, so that community members feel capable of participating in the legal process.

BIBLIOGRAPHY

Assies, W., 2001. *Indian Justice in the Andes: Re-Rooting or Re-Routing?* http://www.geocities.com/alertanet2/F2b-Wassies-en.htm. (The article was posted in the Alertanet – Portal on Law and Society pages in June 2001.)

Ayala Mora, E., 2002. "El derecho ecuatoriano y el aporte indígena" in Salgado, J. (ed.) *Justicia Indígena: Aportes para un debate.* Ediciones Abya-Yala and Universidad Andina Simón Bolívar, Quito, pp. 105-123.

Beijing Declaration of Indigenous Women. NGO Forum, UN Fourth World Conference on Women. Approved and signed on 7 September 1995 at the Indigenous Women's Tent, Huairou, Beijing, China. http://www.tebtebba.org/tebtebba_files/gender/beijing.html.

Borja Jiménez, E., 2001. *Introducción a los fundamentos del derecho penal indígena*, Tirant lo Blanch, Valencia.

Center of Studies and Information of the Multiethnic Woman, CEIMM of the University of the Autonomous Regions of the Caribbean Nicaraguan Coast, URACCAN, 2003. *Background Paper on Gender from the Indigenous Women's Perspective.* First Indigenous Women Summit of the Americas. Oaxaca, December 4th, 2002.
http://www.mujeresindigenas.net/documentos_de_discusion/ingles/genero-desde-la-vision-de-las-mujeres-indigenas-ingles.doc.

El Comercio, Viernes 10 de mayo del 2002 (newspaper articles) "La Cocha quiere aumentar el castigo en caso de muerte" and "No hay confianza en la ley (interview of César Umaginga, Prefecto de Cotopaxi)".

Comisión de Asuntos Indígenas y Otras Etnias del Honorable Congreso Nacional et al, 2002. *Anteproyecto de Ley de Administración de Justicia Indígena*, Quito.

Committee on the Elimination of Racial Discrimination: General Recommendation 23: Indigenous Peoples 18/08/97. A/52/18, annex V.

Committee on the Elimination of Racial Discrimination: Concluding Observations: Ecuador. CERD/C/62/CO/2 of 21 March 2003. Unedited version.

CONAIE, 2001. Conceptos Básicos de un Estado Plurinacional. Primer Congreso de los Pueblos y Nacionalidades del Ecuador, Quito, 8 al 12 de octubre de 2001. http://www.llacta.org/organiz/coms/com62.htm.

CONAIE, 1997. Las nacionalidades indígenas y el estado plurinacional. Quito.

Concluding observations of the Committee on the Elimination of Discrimination Against Women: Ecuador 12/04/94. A/49/38.

Concluding observations of the Human Rights Committee: Ecuador 18/08/98. CCPR/C/79/Add.92.

Constitución Política de la República del Ecuador. Registro Oficial No.1, de 11 de agosto de 1998.

Corte Constitucional de Colombia.

Sentencia número T-349/96. Magistrado ponente Carlos Gaviria Díaz. Santafé de Bogotá, 8.8.1996.

Sentencia No. T-523/97, Magistrado ponente Carlos Gaviria Díaz. Expediente T-124907, Santa Fé de Bogotá, 15 de octubre 1997

Declaration on the occasion of the First Indigenous Women's Summit of the Americas. Oaxaca, December 4th, 2002. http://www.mujeresindigenas.net/documentos_de_discusion/declaracion_mujeres_english.htm.

Defensoría Maya, 2001. *SUK'B'ANIK Administración de Justicia Maya/Experiencias de Defensoría Maya,* Guatemala.

Dirección General de Asuntos Indígenas et al, 1997. Del olvido surgimos para traer nuevas esperanzas: La jurisdicción especial indígena, Santa Fe de Bogotá.

ECUARUNARI, 1998. Derechos de los pueblos indígenas y propuesta política de la nacionalidad y los pueblos quichuas de Ecuador: Síntesis de los talleres sobre derechos de los pueblos indígenas. Documento de base No. 1, Quito, 4,5,6 de marzo de 1998.

Endara, X., 2001. "El derecho indígena en el Ecuador" in Trujillo, J. C., Grijalva, A. and Endara, X. *Justicia Indígena en el Ecuador*. Universidad Andina Simón Bolívar, Sede Ecuador, Quito, pp. 59-81.

Fundación de Culturas Indígenas Kawsay, 2002. Memoria del taller para la definición de las bases teóricas y conceptuales de la Universidad Intercultural Tinku, Quito, 25 February 2002.

García, F., 2002. *Formas indígenas de administrar justicia*, FLACSO Sede Ecuador, Quito.

Grijalva, A., 2001. ”La Jurisdicción Indígena: Derecho constitucional, internacional y comparado” in Trujillo, J. C., Grijalva, A. and Endara, X. *Justicia Indígena en el Ecuador*. Universidad Andina Simón Bolívar, Sede Ecuador, Quito, pp. 19-57.

Gros Espiell, H., 2002. *Universalidad de los derechos humanos y diversidades culturales.* http://www.unesco.org/issj/rics158/grosespiellspa.html.

Human Rights Comité,

General Commment 23. U.N.Doc. HRI/GEN/1/Rev.1 at 38, 1994.

General Commment 20. Replaces general comment 7 concerning prohibition of torture and cruel treatment or punishment (art.7). 10/03/92.

Communication No. 759/1997, George Osbourne v. Jamaica.

Lema, L., 2000. “Aportes a la discusión” in García, F. (coordinador) *Las sociedades interculturales un desafío para el Siglo XXI*, Flacso, Quito, pp. 99-104.

OEA, 1997. *Report on the Situation of Human Rights in Ecuador.* OEA/Ser.L/V/II.96 Doc. 10 Rev. 1, 24 April 1997.

Ortiz Crespo, X., 2002. “Presentación” in Salgado, J. (ed.) *Justicia Indígena: Aportes para un debate.* Ediciones Abya-Yala and Universidad Andina Simón Bolívar, Quito, pp. 7-14.

Pacari, N., 2002. “Pluralidad juridical: una realidad constitucionalmente reconocida” in Salgado, J. (ed.) *Justicia Indígena: Aportes para un debate.* Ediciones Abya-Yala and Universidad Andina Simón Bolívar, Quito, pp. 83-89.

Plan de Acción. Primera Cumbre de Mujeres Indígenas de las Américas. Oaxaca, December 4th, 2002.
http://www.mujeresindigenas.net/documentos_de_discusion/plan_accion.htm.

Perrin, M. Y Perruchon, M. (Coord.), 1997. *Complementariedad entre hombre y mujer: Relaciones de género desde la perspectiva amerindia.* Biblioteca Abya-Yala No. 43, Ediciones Abya-Yala, Quito.

Reports submitted by States parties under article 9 of the Convention. Sixteenth periodic reports of States parties due in 2001. Addendum. Ecuador. CERD/C/384/Add.8. 1 October 2002.

Sánchez Botero, E., 2000. "The *tutela*-system as a means of transforming the relations between the State and the indigenous peoples of Colombia" in Assies, W.; van der Haar, G.; Hoekema, A. (eds.) *The Challenge of Diversity: Indigenous Peoples and Reform of the State in Latin America.* Thela Thesis Latin American Series, Thela Thesis, Amsterdam, pp. 223-241.

Sánchez Botero, E. and Jaramillo Sierra I., 2000. *La jurisdicción especial indígena.* Procuraduría General de la Nación, Instituto de Estudios del Ministerio Público. Santa Fé de Bogotá.

Soussa Santos, B., 1997. "Pluralismo jurídico y jurisdicción especial indígena" in Dirección General de Asuntos Indígenas del Ministerio de Interior and Ministerio de Justicia y del Derecho: *Del Olvido surgimos para traer nuevas esperanzas: La jurisdicción especial indígena"*, Santa Fé de Bogotá, pp. 201-211.

Stavenhagen, R., 1994. *Indigenous Peoples as Emerging Actors in Mexico and Latin America.* Paper presented at the Woodrow Wilson Center in Washington DC. http://www.nyu.edu/classes/Yudice/Democrat/staven.htm.

Tibán, L., 2001. *Género y sustentabilidad: nuevos conceptos para el movimiento indígena.* Boletín ICCI-Rimai. Publicación mensual del Instituto Científico de Culturas Indígenas. Año 3, No. 29, agosto del 2001. Electronic version of the bulletin is found in:
http:// icci.nativeweb.org/boletin/29/tiban.html.

Trujillo, J. C.,

2002. "Administración de justicia indígena" in Salgado, J. (ed.) *Justicia Indígena: Aportes para un debate.* Ediciones Abya-Yala and Universidad Andina Simón Bolívar, Quito, pp. 91-104.

2001. "Introducción al Derecho Indígena" in Trujillo, J. C., Grijalva, A. and Endara, X. *Justicia Indígena en el Ecuador*. Universidad Andina Simón Bolívar, Sede Ecuador, Quito, pp. 9-18.

UNIFEM, 1998. *Voces de los Andes. Testimonios de mujeres indígenas y campesinas*. Quito.

Walsh, C., 2002. "Interculturalidad, reformas constitucionales y pluralismo jurídico" in Salgado, J. (ed.) *Justicia Indígena: Aportes para un debate.* Ediciones Abya-Yala and Universidad Andina Simón Bolívar, Quito, pp. 23-35.

Yrigoyen, R., 2000. "The Constitutional Recognition of Indigenous Law in the Andean Countries" in Assies, W.; van der Haar, G.; Hoekema, A. (eds.) *The Challenge of Diversity: Indigenous Peoples and Reform of the State in Latin America.* Thela Thesis Latin American Series, Thela Thesis, Amsterdam, pp. 197-222.

Yrigoyen, R., 1999. *Pautas de Coordinación entre el Derecho Indígena y el Derecho Estatal*. Fundación Myrna Mack, Ciudad de Guatemala.

"San Bushmen Are Not Forever": Human Rights Perspective of Land Access Issues of Hunter-Gatherer Societies in Southern Africa

Boipuso Nkwae

1. INTRODUCTION

Although most of southern Africa is populated mainly by Bantu-speaking peoples, it has to be acknowledged that the most indigenous inhabitants of the region are the San or Basarwa,[1] commonly known as the Bushmen in the western literature. The San are the most marginalized ethnic groups in southern Africa because of their unique and distinct way of life. There has been a lot of concern about the indigenous hunter-gatherer communities in southern Africa and around the world. The plight of the San hunter-gatherers has been raised in various forums such as seminars, conferences and other international gatherings.

In some of these meetings, the San's access to land has been mentioned as critical to their socio-economic well-being. Recent global activism by civil society in Europe, North America and Australia has highlighted the issue of aboriginal land rights. At the same time, the debates about indigenous land rights in southern Africa have also gained momentum especially after independence. Such debates have been fueled by the ignorance of the indigenous land rights such as exhibited by the litigant consultant for the Attorney Generals Chambers in Botswana:

> As far as I have been able to ascertain the Masarwa (sic) have always been true nomads, owing no allegiance to any chief or tribe, but have ranged far and wide for a very long time over large areas of the Kalahari in which they have always had unlimited hunting rights, which they enjoy even today despite the Fauna and Conservation Act. The right of the Masarwa to hunt is, of course, very important and valuable as hunting is their main source of sustenance. ...Without much clearer information it is impossible to give a confirmed opinion about the

[1] Hunter-gatherers in southern Africa are referred to as San, Khoisan, Bushmen, Batwa, and Basarwa depending on the country of residence. The use of the term Bushmen has always been controversial, as it sounds discriminatory, sexist and politically incorrect. The term 'Bushmen' is still used because that is the term western people are most familiar with. In Botswana, the hunter-gatherer societies are referred to as Basarwa, and the origin of the word is still unknown. Taylor, I. and G. Mokhawa (2003. "Not forever: Botswana, conflict diamonds and the Bushmen". *Africa Affairs*, 102:261-283) suggest the word means 'people who do not rear cattle' whilst Hitchcock and Biesele ((n.d.) "San, Khwe, Basarwa, or Bushmen?: terminology, identity, and empowerment in Southern Africa'. Accessed on August 2003, http://www.kalaharipeoples.org/documents/San-term.htm) think the word signifies 'people of the south'. It seems the preferred term by most of the hunter-gatherer groups in southern Africa is the Nama word 'San'. However, the use of the term does not imply that the San are a homogenous group. In fact, in Botswana alone, more than twenty linguistic groups have been identified (*ibid*).

> Masarwa. Tentatively, however, it appears to me that the true nomad Masarwa can have no rights of any kind except rights to hunting.[2]

Many social scientists have been appalled by this display of ignorance by the Attorney General regarding the organization of San territoriality even though this opinion did not become an official indication of the status of San land tenure. Several researchers have proved that the San have well defined spatial boundaries and ownership rights vested among band members. The identification and description of San land tenure have been pursued by some researchers to the point where they have concluded that San land tenure is similar to that of other indigenous African groups. For instance, Wilmsen contends that:

> The only conclusion that can be reached is that San tenure has been, and continues to attempt to be, generally stable and sanctioned by traditional native rules that are congruent with other southern African systems.[3]

Several authorities,[4] have recognized the problem of "jamming" western property concepts into indigenous tenure systems as this has resulted in confusion and misconceptions over traditional land tenure concepts. Forcing the comparison of San land tenure to the Bantu forms of tenure by authors like Wilmsen (after recognizing the problems) has not helped the San hunter-gatherers in protecting and reclaiming their land rights. Since governments in the region have chosen to ignore the unique and distinctive features of San land tenure, their land rights and way of life is going to disappear without any compensation. In justifying the dispossession of the hunter-gatherers of their indigenous land rights,[5] pointed out "government officials in Botswana invoke published works of anthropologists in support of their particular positions during debates over land allocation".

---

[2] Quoted in Hitchcock, R. K 1980. "Tradition, Social Justice, and Land Reform in Central Botswana." *Journal of African Law*, 24(1): 1 -34.

[3] Wilmsen, E.N., 1989. "Those who have each other: San relations to land" In Edwin N. Wilmsen, *We Are Here: Politics of Aboriginal Land Tenure*, Berkeley: University of California Press, p.65

[4] Bohannan, P., 1963. "'Land', 'tenure' and land-tenure", In Daniel Biebuyck, *African Agrarian Systems*. London: Oxford University Press; von Benda-Beckmann, 1995, Wilmsen, 1989

[5] Hitchcock, R. K. 1982. *Tribal Grazing Land Policy, 1981 Programme Review*. (TGLP Monitoring) Ministry of Agriculture, Gaborone

This paper will discuss the historical developments that led to the marginalization of the San land rights and aspects of San territoriality. It will also analyze the human rights perspectives of San Bushmen access to land together with the debates surrounding their land dispossession. It will finally analyze various strategies that can be followed to secure the San Bushmen using Botswana as a case study.

2. HISTORICAL BACKGROUND

The first European settlers, in 1688, in southern Africa met with the San and the Khoikhoi. The San led a much more nomadic life of hunting and gathering than the Khoikhoi, who were both hunter-gatherers and pastoralist. Some of the earliest conflicts over land and natural resources between Europeans and Africans (San) were due to scarce wildlife resources. As the Dutch took to hunting wild animals as a means of livelihood, "slaughtering an immense number, as well as driving the rest away"[6] from the familiar hunting grounds of the San, "the latter took to looting the herds and flocks of the Colonists". The result was the first fight between the Dutch and the San over cattle. Although similar altercations did occur between the San and other African groups such as the Bantu and the Khoikhoi, the various African groups had learnt to co-exist with each other. The San also experienced what other ethnic minorities went through in places like Canada and the United States of America, where the First Nations People were hunted down and shot. For instance, in southern Africa,

> Regular commandos were formed to hunt them down. The men were shot down as wild beasts, and the women and children carried off as slaves. ...This went on until the game was practically exterminated in the Union of South Africa. And so the struggle between the colonists and Bushmen went on until the latter, like the herds of game, practically ceased to exist, at any rate as a menace to the white man.[7]

---

[6] Dornan, S.S., 1975. *Pygmies & Bushmen of the Kalahari*. Cape Town: C. Struik (Pty) Ltd. 2nd Edition., p.44

[7] Ibid.

3. NATURE OF PROPERTY RIGHTS AMONG THE HUNTER-GATHERER SOCIETIES

According to MacPherson,[8] property is a set of enforceable rights, held by individuals to the use or benefit of some object. Property as an institution comprises a set of established legal and social relationships among people that govern their behavior with respect to the resources they control as a group. A group may include a clan, band, tribe village, cooperative or government. In the case of the San:

> Whatever was killed by one was the common property of the family or clan, and all made haste to the feast.[9]

Further, Dornan states:

> The clans were small, and each kept to its own hunting grounds. The intrusion of neighbouring clans was fiercely resented, although there were no definite tribal districts. As the Bushmen lived by the chase alone, and never cultivated the soil, they wandered over large tracts of the country, following the game from place to place in its annual migrations.[10]

Barnard and Woodburn[11] define property rights as the relations between people in respect of "things" and these relations "exist, of course in all societies, although in no society is everything owned". They identify five distinct property rights in hunter-gatherer societies:[12]

- *rights over land, water resources (water-filled pans and wells), ritual sites, dwelling sites, prepared hunting sites, dams, weirs, pit traps, etc.;*
- *rights over movable property – tools and weapons, clothing, cooking pots and containers, beads and other ornaments;*

[8] MacPherson, C. B., 1978. "The meaning of property", Chapter 1 in *Property in the Mainstream and Critical Positions*, C.B. MacPherson, ed. Toronto: University of Toronto Press

[9] Dornan, 1975, p.52

[10] Ibid.

[11] Barnard, A. and J. Woodburn, 1988. "Property, power and ideology in hunter-gathering societies: an introduction". In Ingold, T., Riches, D. and Woodburn (eds). *Hunters and Gatherers Vol. II*. New York: Martin's Press.

[12] Ibid., p.14

- *rights over game meat, harvested vegetable foods and other garnered food and raw materials;*
- *rights over certain capacities of specific people – over their hunting labour, over their sexual capacity, over their reproductive capacity;*
- *rights over knowledge and intellectual property – over songs, over sacred knowledge, over ritual designs, etc.*

Although the list is not exhaustive, it does point to the most important property rights recognized by hunter-gatherer communities. However, the property rights of hunter-gatherer societies are not always easy to define clearly because there are areas of ambiguity. There has been much debate on whether the San (Bushmen) have any concept of individual property. But the fact that there is widespread gift-giving among the hunter-gatherers is evidence of individual property rights. Lowie states:

> There was … a pronounced tendency to make presents, whether of food, necklaces, slings, spears or other implements; and the acceptance involved the obligation of making a suitable return gift. The very fact of this institution constitutes proof of individual property rights.[13]

Even though it is common practice for a hunter of a large carcass to share it equally amongst all members of the group, there is still evidence of individual property rights as "the individual ownership actually entitles the owner [hunter] to distribute the meat and to gain prestige from doing so".[14] However, Barnard warns:

> Hunter-gatherer territories are not 'property' in quite the same sense as property is defined in Western legal systems, but such territories do possess some of the characteristics of 'property' as the term is conventionally employed in anthropological monographs.[15]

Barnard further clarifies that:

> In most hunter-gatherer societies we find no ownership in resources that can be gathered or hunted; but once they are collected, they become the property of the

[13] Cited in Barnard and Woodburn, 1988, p.26

[14] Barnard and Woodburn, 1998, p.26

[15] Barnard, A., 1992. "Social and spatial boundary maintenance among Southern African hunter-gatherers" In M. J. Casimir and A. Rao, *Mobility and Territoriality: social and spatial boundaries among the foragers, fishers, pastoralists and peripatetics*. New York: Berg, p.146

> person who has put labour (sic), even if he or she is afterwards obliged to share these items.

Hitchcock has noted:

> Ownership of land among the [Basarwa] is by territory owner on behalf of a band, and groups have access rights to specific localities according to their consanguineal or affinal ties to those people who are considered to be "owners" of the areas.[16]

4. ASPECTS OF SAN TERRITORIALITY

The San territoriality can be viewed as lying in a continuum between two opposite ends of a spectrum, at one 'common property' and at the other 'individual private property'. Depending on whether the resource is of low abundance and high risk or high abundance and low risk, various groups are known to react differently to newcomers. Some hunter-gatherer groups are known to exhibit increasing territorial behaviors when the natural resources are of high abundance, and other groups have been more territorial in areas of resource scarcity probably because the resources were not worth defending (see Figure 1). The understanding of human territoriality in mobile societies is essential to our understanding of access to natural resources in hunter-gatherer communities. Casimir defines human territoriality as:

> Human territorial behaviour is a cognitive and behaviourally flexible system which aims at optimising the individual's and hence often also a group's access to temporarily or permanently localized resources, which satisfy either basic and universal or culture-specific needs and wants, or both, while simultaneously minimising the probability of conflicts over them.[17]

---

[16] Hitchcock, 1980

[17] Casimir, M.J., 1992. "The dimensions of territoriality: an introduction". In M. J. Casimir and A. Rao, *Mobility and Territoriality: social and spatial boundaries among the foragers, fishers, pastoralists and peripatetics*. New York: Berg., p.20

FIGURE 1: The two perspectives of the San territoriality

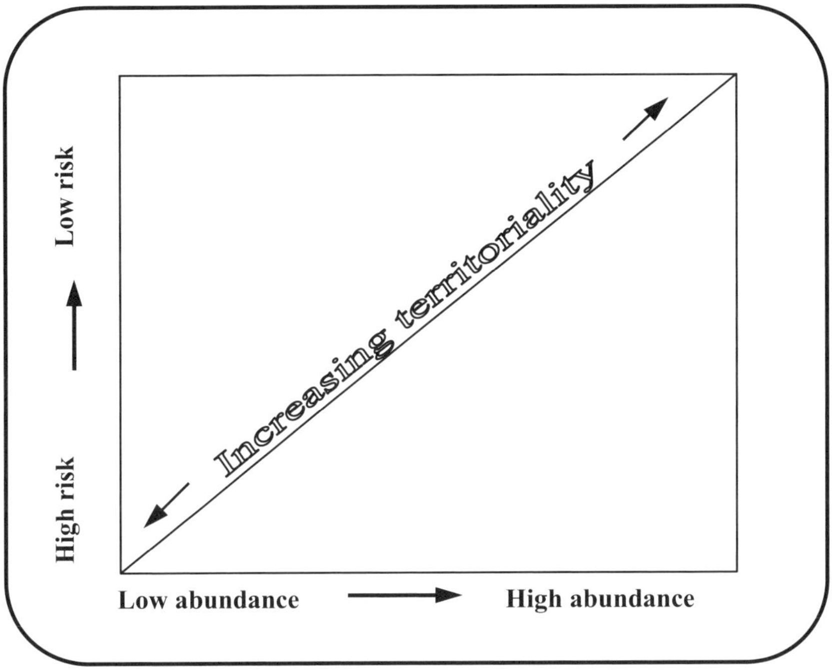

The debate by anthropologists over the existence of territoriality among the hunter-gatherers have contributed to the attitude of some government officials and expatriates who insist that the Basarwa do not exercise claims over defined areas of land.[18] The government's argument went: because the San/Basarwa lack territories, it therefore follows that they have no land rights. This government thinking is in contrast with Tswana tribal chiefs, who have always recognized the customary land claims of the hunter-gatherers. In allocating cattle posts and sites for drilling boreholes, land overseers and headmen always took into consideration the pre-existing local land tenure patterns in order to avoid conflicts.[19]

[18] Hitchcock, 1980
[19] Ibid.

In Botswana's hunter-gatherer populations:

> Territoriality, in the sense of defence of resources and spatial boundary maintenance, functions primarily in relation to like populations. When herders move into hunter-gatherer territories there is no conflict, though there would be if other Bushmen were to move in and take over. [20]

The above quotation from Barnard cannot be said to be universally true because the San have lived for centuries providing cheap labor for Bantu pastoralists and white commercial ranches. In the western and eastern areas of Botswana today it is common for the San and non-San territories to overlap. Barnard argues that this is possible because the pastoralists and commercial ranchers and hunter-gatherers 'exploit different ecological niches'.[21] The white commercial farms are owned under western freehold ownership, but explains this situation by saying:

> The fact that in Botswana law a particular ranch is owned by one cattle herder to the exclusion of all others does not necessarily exclude hunter-gatherers from using it or from continuing to define their own territories, irrespective of **legal title** or wire fences.[22]

In southern Africa the current disruption of the San Bushmen way of life has been worsened by the forcible removal of the San from their ancestral lands into government resettlement camps to live a more sedentary type of life (a process seen by many commentators as acculturation). The forcible resettlement of the San in the region is a highly charged political issue with both government and the San groups fighting each other to the tooth. The arguments for the forced removals are very controversial:

- The government argues that it is too expensive to provide services to nomadic people;
- Animal populations have been depleted so the San can longer sustain their way of life;
- In terms of the Central Kalahari Game Reserve, the government says it is for wildlife only and not for human habitation.

---

[20] Barnard 1992, p.145

[21] Barnard, 1992

[22] Ibid., p.145, emphasis added.

- The government wants to counter the racism of anthro-tourism, i.e. the desire of international NGOs to see the San frozen in time so that they can study them and make money from movies, an example of which is the movie entitled the "The Gods Must be Crazy" which became the biggest foreign box-office hit ever released in the United States of America. It sees resettlement and farming as an alternative means of Bushmen's social and economic survival.
- On the other hand, the San groups and the international non-governmental organizations argue against the forced removals by saying:
    - The main reason why the government is forcibly resettling the hunter-gatherer communities is to pave way for mineral prospecting, especially diamonds.
    - Other reasons cited are that the government wants to clear the area for tourism and cattle ranching.

5. DEFINING INDIGENOUS RIGHTS UNDER INTERNATIONAL LAW

The term *indigenous* is derived from the Latin *indigena*, meaning "born in a country," or "native". The Oxford English Dictionary defines indigenous as people or products "born or produced naturally in a land or region; native or belonging naturally to the soil, region, etc".[23] However, Hodgson states:

> Its current social, political, and legal definitions, however, are much more ambiguous and even controversial, especially as the term has been taken up by a range of disenfranchised groups.[24]

As pointed out by Renee Sylvain:

> Currently, the only definition of indigenous that is legally binding for signatory states is the one proposed by the International Labour Organisation (ILO) Convention 169 (1989).[25]

---

[23] The Oxford English Dictionary, 2003

[24] Hodgson, D.L., 2002. "Introduction: comparative perspectives on the indigenous rights movement in Africa and the Americas". *American Anthropologist*, 104(4), p.1038

[25] Sylvain, 2002, p.1075

According to Article 1 of the ILO Convention,[26] indigenous peoples are:

- *tribal peoples in independent countries whose social, cultural and economic conditions distinguish them from other sections of the national community, and whose status is regulated wholly or partially by their own customs or traditions or by special laws or regulations;*
- *peoples in independent countries who are regarded as indigenous on account of their descent from populations which inhabited the country, or a geographical region to which the country belongs, at the time of conquest or colonization or establishment of present state boundaries and who, irrespective of their legal status, retain some or all of their own social, economic, cultural and political institutions*

Another definition of indigenous is one adopted by the United Nations proposed by Cobo that states:

> Indigenous communities, peoples and nations are those which have a historical continuity with pre-invasion and pre-colonial societies that developed on their territories, consider themselves distinct from other sectors of society now prevailing in those territories, or parts of them. They form at present non-dominant sectors of society and are determined to preserve, develop, and transmit to future generations their ancestral territories, and their ethnic identity, as the basis for their continued existence as peoples, in accordance with their cultural patterns, social institutions and legal systems.[27]

The Cobo-UN definition is not legally binding and has been criticized by Dorothy Hodgson for being a "fairly narrow, inflexible definition of indigenous that may not reflect the present (or future) realities of some indigenous livelihoods and lifestyles".[28] There are important differences in the context, meaning and use of the concept of indigenous in North America and Africa, and these differences have had significant bearing on the indigenous rights movement in southern Africa and elsewhere. When asked to sign the ILO Convention 107 on indigenous peoples, the government of Botswana

[26] 1989: Article 1.1 cited in Sylvain, R., 2002. "Land, Water, and Truth": San Identity and Global Indigenism. *American Anthropologist*, 104(4): 1074 – 1085.

[27] 1989 quoted in Hodgson, 2002, p. 1039

[28] Ibid.

refused to sign claiming that everybody is indigenous. The definition of indigenous entails being in close relationship with the land, having distinct language and cultural identity, attachment to ancestral lands, etc. In the southern African context, the above definitions of indigenous have serious limitations in terms of advancing the San land claims, but this is not to undermine the fact that international laws and conventions have played an important role in the debate on the rights of ethnic minorities in the sub-continent.

The struggle of indigenous rights around the world has been fought at two levels: indigenous people's demand for the recognition of their collective rights in national and international law, (e.g. Canada and Australia); as well as the demand to exercise their right to self-determination, i.e. to govern themselves according to their own traditional laws and customs independent of the national legal norms. However, many nation states would be uncomfortable with the latter demand, which challenges national sovereignty. Shalini Randeria observed that the demand for self-determination has only been conceded in only a few countries.[29] Randeira further pointed out that many states would prefer the use of the term "*minorities*" in place of "*indigenous people*" as being recognized as "*indigenous*" under national and international law carries several advantages such as:

- *In the UN Declaration on Minorities neither the right of self-determination nor collective rights are mentioned whereas under the UN Draft Declaration on the Rights of Indigenous People the two rights are explicitly stated.*
- *Indigenous people have a special status within the broad category of minorities and this is legitimated by their history as victims under colonization.*
- *Indigenous people have been defined as having a spiritual relationship to land and this has placed them strategically to assert their land and resource rights.*

[29] Randeria, S., 2003. "Protecting the rights of indigenous communities in the new architecture of global governance: the interplay of international institutions and post-colonial states. In Pradhan Rajendra (ed.) *Legal Pluralism and Unofficial Law in Social, Economic and Political Development*. Papers of the XIIIth International Congress, 7-10 April 2002, Chiang Mai, Thailand. Vol 3, Kathmandu: ICNEC.

- *The Rio Declaration on Environment and Development defines indigenous people as guardians of nature; bearers of important ecological knowledge, which helps to protect bio-diversity.*

Since indigenous people are victims of colonization, they should then be restored their right to self-determination. It is probably this latter right, which prompts nation states like Botswana to declare that everybody is indigenous.

> Other tribes, especially the Basarwa/San peoples, are reported to suffer from cultural, social, economic and political exclusion, do not enjoy group rights to land, and do not participate in the House of Chiefs.[30]

Further

> The Committee expresses concern that the ongoing dispossession of Basarwa/San people from their land and about reports stating that their resettlement outside the Central Kalahari Game Reserve does not respect their political, economic, social and cultural rights.[31]

6. OPTIONS FOR SECURING SAN LAND RIGHTS: BOTSWANA EXAMPLE

> We shall never achieve harmony with the land, any more than we shall achieve justice or liberty for people. In these higher aspirations, the important thing is not to achieve, but to thrive.[32]

a. Acquisition of Freehold Land

This category of land constitutes 5% of the land area in Botswana. Although freehold is exclusive and absolute, lesser interests such as easements, permits or licenses can be accommodated under this tenure regime. Freehold farms were carved out the San territory with total disregard of the pre-existing indigenous rights. The result of this approach was outright land dispossession of the San as evidenced by the landless San groups in northwestern Botswana.

---

[30] Hitchcock, 1980, p.27

[31] Ibid., p.27

[32] Leopold, A., 1949. *A Sand County almanac and sketches here and there*. New York: Oxford University Press.

The irony is that some San communities have now ended up in an unenviable position of being described as "squatters" in the land they used to own.

To redress the past injustices, one possible strategy for the San to reclaim their lost land is through adverse possession. According to the *Prescriptions Act* of Botswana, one can only claim a right of ownership if land has been in continuous occupation for a period of 30 years. The requirements of adverse possession will be difficult to fulfill legally unless the landowner, e.g. cattle rancher, is very slack and careless, which might be very rare for someone owning a piece of land with very high economic potential. The other difficulty is with regard to Botswana law not recognizing hunting and gathering as effective occupation of the land. There is need therefore to revise the definition of what constitutes effective occupation in the context of the hunter-gatherers.

Another way to restore the indigenous land rights of the San is through compulsory purchase of the freehold farms. This would be a very expensive solution for the government because of the constitutional requirements of "prompt payment and adequate compensation".[33] It is therefore highly unlikely that the government would go down this route.

b. Acquisition of State Land

State land is what used to be Crown land during the colonial period. It constitutes 25% of the total land area. According to Section 14(3) of the *Prescriptions Act*, rights on State Land can never be claimed through adverse possession. Ng'ong'la claims this is because of government policy to choose to ignore "illegality" of any occupation of State Land.[34] This has also been the practice when the colonial administration appropriated Crown lands. The State can choose to legitimize the occupation of State Land by indigenous populations by converting it into tribal land. This had indeed happened after a decade of independence in order to alleviate the land shortage in the northeast and southeast of Botswana. Ng'ong'la regards this as a more effective strategy that can be used in securing the San land rights as opposed to solely relying on the constitutional protection of the freedom of movement which states:

---

[33] Botswana Government, 1966. *Constitution of Botswana Act*. Gaborone: Government Printer.

[34] Ng'ong'ola, C., 1997. "Land rights for marginalized ethnic groups in Botswana, with special reference to the Basarwa". *The Journal of African Law*, 41:1-26.

> No person shall be deprived of his freedom of movement … the said freedom means the right to move freely throughout Botswana, the right to reside in any part of Botswana, the right to enter Botswana and immunity from expulsion from Botswana.

And further,

> Nothing contained in or done under … any law shall be held to be inconsistent … for the imposition of restrictions on the entry into or residence within the defined areas of Botswana of persons who are not Bushmen to the extent that such restrictions are reasonably required for the protection or well-being of Bushmen.[35]

However, this might not be a viable option for restoring land to the San since all State Land has now been turned into national parks, game reserves and leases for the tourist industry.

c. Acquisition of Customary Land

The first two options seem to offer limited prospects in terms of securing the San land rights, but there is a third option, namely customary land, the biggest land category in the country, constituting 70% of the land surface. When discussing the plight of the marginalized land rights of minority ethnic populations, Ng'ong'ola identifies three types of San populations as:

- those that live in tribal territories dominated by Tswana tribes;
- those that live in tribal areas where they dominate other ethnic groups; and
- those that are being displaced from their ancestral lands by government policies such as the Tribal Grazing Land Policy (1975) and the Agricultural Fencing Policy (1991).

Despite the problems facing customary land administration in Botswana, the government has shown no intention of replacing customary tenure with another tenure regime. It has to be noted that only a tiny percentage of the present San population still lead a complete hunter-gatherer type of life.

---

[35] *Constitution of Botswana Act*, S.14

The first group used to be denied access to land on the basis of ethnicity. The national Land Boards were only empowered to allocate land to Botswana citizens, who were tribesmen of a particular tribal territory, but the *Tribal Land Act* has only been amended in 1993 and the word 'tribesman' has been replaced by the word 'citizen'. Having been accepted as 'full members,' they can now acquire land in these tribal territories dominated by the Tswana tribes. But land in these tribal territories can only be allocated according to the Tswana customary tenure model, which does not always fit with the San land tenure model. The *Tribal Land Act* should be amended so that it accommodates those tenure regimes that do not fit the current model. This has been done before when common law leases were introduced in customary land administration. The composition of the Land Boards should include ethnic minorities so that their interests could also be accommodated. There is also a need to sensitize the Land Boards on the rights of ethnic minorities.

Although the second group might be said to be in a far much better position, their land rights are also under threat from other ethnic groups. Ng'ong'ola suggests a legislative reform to favor the marginalized groups and award them exclusive land allocations in certain areas as this will not be contrary to the Constitution, probably similar to the reserve situations in North America. It is difficult to contemplate the Botswana government taking this route because of the history of apartheid in the region. The current government's position is:

- All Batswana are citizens of Botswana irrespective of their ethnic background hence in promoting its non-racial policy; the government argues that there are no distinct or separate tribes in Botswana.
- The San are discouraged from identifying themselves as indigenous people or to make claims to land.
- Setting aside separate land or reserves would be tantamount to segregation and the government gains its support from the anti-apartheid lobby in southern Africa.[36]

The third group is targeted for commercial ranches under the Tribal Grazing Land Policy leases and the Agricultural Fencing Policy. Allocations of ranches have continued in total disregard of existing San land rights. Land reform

[36] Ng'ong'ola, 1997

planners, especially those of the Tribal Grazing Land Policy, "assumed that there were vast resources of uninhabited pasture land into which ranches could expand";[37] even maps produced by the government showed vast portions of the Kalahari as "unused". The myth about the emptiness of the Kalahari was perpetuated despite the evidence of "anthropological reports, showing that many of these so-called unused portions of the Kalahari actually contained hunting and gathering populations". These "were apparently ignored by those who drafted the land use maps".[38] The Kalahari was considered "empty" because hunting and gathering appears not to have been considered a valid form of land use by the planners. As Hitchcock pointed out:

> The long standing tradition of serfdom in Botswana has contributed to the attitude currently held by some, which maintains that a segment of Botswana society lacks rights to land and property.[39]

The ruling elites are composed of cattle barons, and it would be hard to convince them of the rights of the hunter-gatherers. Any litigation on the San land rights would be blocked both politically and legally.

In fact, Mmegi has recently argued that there are various power blocs or stakeholders (see Table 1)[40] that can be identified as contributing to the San Bushmen land rights problem. These players are the politicians, bureaucrats, academics and the international non-governmental organizations.

Mmegi [2003a] has argued for the empowerment of the San when saying:

> Wittingly or unwittingly, the Basarwa [San] issue has become a convenient platform where various stakeholders express, exercise, demonstrate and showcase their power, influence and control. The Basarwa then become a turf for power games and ego aggrandizement for various stakeholders and not targets for genuine empowerment.

---

[37] Ibid.

[38] Hitchcock 1980, p.13

[39] Ibid.

[40] Mmegi, 2003a. "Basarwa are pawns in a political game – Lucas", 19-25 September 2003. Accessed from World Wide Web on September 2003. http://www.mmegi.bw/2003/September/Friday19/408334805271.html

d. Using international experience of aboriginal rights

Various jurisdictions such as Brazil, the United States of America, Canada, New Zealand and Australia have been grappling with the problem of aboriginal rights for many years. There have been some notable developments in Canada since the 1970's state recognition of aboriginal title. For example, the Inuit in Nunavut have achieved semi-autonomous self-determination; the aboriginal self-determination and the settlement of aboriginal land claims have

Figure 2: Matrix of the Power Struggle over the San/Bushmen Land Rights

	Politicians	**International NGOs**	**Bureaucrats**	**Academics**
Politicians	formulating policies favoring the cattle industry and multi-national corporations	showcase of power; dislike NGOs setting the agenda	partnerships to advance their own political objectives	partnership to enhance their own agenda
International NGOs	showcase of power in terms of financial resources	setting the agenda for San/Bushmen empowerment	critical of bureaucrats' efforts in handling San/Bushmen issues	partnership to enhance their own agenda
Bureaucrats	partnerships in terms of implementing policies and programmes	frustrating NGO efforts e.g. the Remote Area Dweller Program sponsored by NORAD	formulating and implementing government policies and programmes	partnership to enhance their own agenda
Academics	financial resources for research	financial resources for research	financial resources for research	yearn for recognition and self-satisfaction

"resulted in some of the largest land redistribution in the World".[41] Although Canadian aboriginal peoples have been gaining victories over the years, there are still some groups and individuals who are still fighting for recognition of their status as indigenous. Legal battles are far from over in Canada, and in 1999 the Supreme Court decision in *R v. Marshall,* ruled that aboriginal peoples have a treaty right to catch and sell fish within the ancestral territory group. This was after Donald Marshall, a Mi'kmaq Indian, was charged with fishing and selling eels without a license during a closed season. His defense was that he possesses a treaty right to catch and sell fish under the 1760-61 treaties between the British and the Mi'kmaq Indians.

Commenting on the *Marshall* decision, Ken Coates states:

> First Nations advocates of sovereignty see Marshall as a relatively minor success – it recognizes limited treaty rights to commercial harvesting rights, not an inherent indigenous right to commercial resources – and intend to push for much greater authority.[42]

Ken Coates further argues:

> Gaining access to resources in the early twenty-first century is also something of a phyrric victory. Aboriginal treaty rights have been secured in declining economic sectors. The regional logging industry has been far from prosperous in recent years, and the resources for ocean and river harvesting have been uncertain at best.[43]In Australia, the 1992 High Court decision in *Mabo v. The State of Queensland* (known as "the Mabo Case"), overturned the *terra nullius* doctrine and has had far-reaching implications in the Australian land tenure system. The case was centered on the Murray Islands in the eastern part of the Torres Strait Islands. The Meriam people led by Eddie Koiko Mabo took the legal action to overturn the doctrine of *terra nullius* – land belonging to no-one, thus avoiding recognizing the rights of pre-existing right holders. This culminated in the establishment of 1993 *Native Title Act* that sanctioned the court's ruling and established processes for settling native land claims.

In Africa, "many countries have long recognized certain communal rights over certain areas; more frequently than not, however, the legal status of those

---

[41] Nichols, S. and M. Rakai, 2001. "Canadian land reform: an overview of Aboriginal rights and land claims settlements". Accessed from World Wide Web on November 2003, http://www.fao.org/DOCREP/003/Y0434T/Y0434t08.htm

[42] Coates, 2000. *The Marshall Decision and Native Rights*. Montreal: McGill-Queens's University Press., p.188

[43] Ibid., p.193

rights and of the groups that purportedly hold them has been only weakly and ambiguously defined in national laws".[44] In southern Africa like in North America and Australia, the indigenous peoples are expected either to evolve in the face of the dominant culture or become extinct. Further, what many governments fail to recognize is that:

> The survival of indigenous peoples and their cultures contributes to a richer cultural diversity, from which the whole world community can benefit. The current trend in international treaties and conventions is towards the recognition of indigenous rights of hunter-gatherer societies to enjoy their own cultures, and participate in the management of their resources, and they can contribute to the sustainable use of the world's biological diversity.[45]

In Botswana, the government has been removing the San/Bushmen from their ancestral lands under its "villagization programs". Because the Bushmen are too weak to resist and inarticulate to fight for their land rights, there is need for the government to acknowledge their rights to their lands and ways of life. Unlike in North America, where formal treaties and Royal Proclamations protect the aboriginal rights, in southern Africa, the battle is going to be harder. In Africa and many Asian countries, when the question of who is indigenous is asked, the governments say everybody is indigenous, thus avoiding the question of aboriginal rights completely. But other governments such as the Philippines have taken a more enlightened approach by issuing "certificates of ancestral domain title", thus protecting the property rights of its indigenous populations.

In the wake of recent legal developments in Canada, Australia and New Zealand, the question asked is whether southern Africa can learn from aboriginal rights issues in these jurisdictions. Can we use priority of existence to assert the San land rights? The paper will not dwell into the doctrine of aboriginal title but it will suffice to highlight the limitations of applying the Canadian and Australian experience in southern Africa. Some of the limitations are:

- Much of southern Africa has a Roman-Dutch law heritage whereas in Australia, Canada, New Zealand, and the United

---

[44] Fingleton, J.S., 1998. *Legal recognition of indigenous groups*. Accessed from World Wide Web on August 2003. http://www.fao.org/legal/prs-ol/paper-e.htm, p.11

[45] Ibid., p.9

States, the doctrine of aboriginal title has been developed under English common law.

- Apart from South Africa that was a settled colony, most of the African countries were protectorates and the doctrine of aboriginal title was developed in line with the English common law of settled colonies.
- In many of the North American and Australian colonies, royal proclamations, treaty provisions, formal agreements and late legislations has reinforced the demands for the recognition and protection of aboriginal rights. In contrast, the indigenous hunter-gatherer societies in southern Africa have not been accorded such political recognition during and after the colonial period. The various European powers only signed treaties and formal agreements with the dominant 'tribes'.
- Customary tenure systems of San-speaking peoples are not recognized within the region; consequently this makes it difficult to bring forward land claims.
- The various country constitutions protect property rights of 'any description'; consequently it would be difficult to attack the respective constitutions on the basis of minority rights.

Even if the doctrine of aboriginal title were accepted as part of the Roman-Dutch law in southern Africa, there would be other constraints such as:

- passage of time would make it difficult to prove native title; and
- deliberate acts of the State in the exercise of sovereign power would have extinguished any surviving titles such as the allocation of Crown land under freehold, leasehold and quit rent.

But where the land is still held under State (Crown) land, especially the national parks and game reserves, the doctrine of aboriginal title might be useful in terms of recognizing the hunter-gatherer rights. However, Clement Ng'ong'ola concludes:

> The doctrine of aboriginal title would otherwise be of little use in the correction of past injustices and reclamation of original Basarwa rights or titles lost to the freehold or state land sectors.[46]

[46] Ng'ong'ola, 1997, p.26

e. Designing a new land administration system

The government of Botswana is consulting the nation on its new land policy recommendations, aimed at addressing current land use conflicts brought about by the introduction of new concepts and systems of land administration resulting from social and economic progress.[47] Among the recommendations of the new land policy is the proposal to set aside separate land for exclusive use by the rural dwellers (San). This proposal is similar to the native reserve situations in North America, Australia and New Zealand.

As part of Botswana's democratic process, in mid-2003, the Minister of Lands and Housing engaged on a nationwide tour consulting the nation on several issues raised by the new land policy. Whilst the general public was in agreement with most of the recommendations in the new land policy, they were strongly opposed to the idea of setting up reserves for the San/Bushmen. Some of the arguments raised by the public can be summarized as:

- The public generally disagreed with the recommendation and preferred a situation whereby the San were developed, "but not as isolated, as separate treatment would be discriminatory".[48]
- Since the San are citizens of Botswana, they are entitled to be allocated land anywhere in the country.
- The reserve system would encourage tribalism, tension and conflicts between the San and other citizens.

Although the argument that the San are entitled to land anywhere in the country may be valid, "full open access has yet to be realized in practice" in Botswana.[49]

The proposed land reforms also concerned the administration of customary land. Whilst Botswana's customary land administration has been hailed as the

---

[47] Daily News, 2003a. "Don't give Basarwa preferential treatment on land", 18 August. Accessed August 2003. http://www.gov.bw/cgi-bin/news.cgi?d=20030818

[48] Ibid.

[49] Werbner, 2002. "Introduction: challenging minorities, difference and tribal citizenship in Botswana". *Journal of Southern African Studies*, 28(4): 671-684.

best model so far,[50] it is not fully participatory as the San are generally excluded from any level of land control. Therefore, there is a need to design or revise the current land administration system in order to incorporate the San land rights. In designing a new land administration model, there will be a need for certain issues to be clarified and that can be done through relevant research. The research into new land administration models should address the following questions:

- What do the San really want?
- What are their needs?
- What are the constraints?
- What are the opportunities?
- What are the priorities?
- What are the available land administration options?

Until the needs of the San are clearly articulated, it will be difficult to resolve the San land issues equitably, reasonably and effectively.

7. ACCESS TO LAND BY SAN BUSHMEN: A HUMAN RIGHTS ISSUE?

There is no doubt that the problem of access to land by the hunter-gatherers has now become a human rights problem. Land policy can play a central role in addressing the San/Bushmen's access to land and poverty reduction. For instance, there is a need to review the previous land reform policies and related acts such as the *Tribal Land Act*, Botswana Settlement Policy, Rural Area Dwellers Development Programme, Tribal Grazing Land Policy, and the Agricultural Fencing Policy. These policies have not played a positive role in the access to land by the marginalized groups, and there is also a general consensus that they did not close the gap between the rich and the poor as earlier envisaged. Botswana has one of the highest income disparity represented by a Gini-coefficient of 0.54.[51] A Gini-coefficient is a number

---

[50] Quan, 2000. "Land Board as a mechanism for the management land rights in southern Africa". Chapter 10 in *Evolving Land Rights, Policy and Tenure in Africa*, C. Toulmin and J. Quan, eds. London: DFID/IIED/NRI

[51] BIDPA, 1998. "Summary of the 1997 Botswana Human Development Report". Accessed December 2003, http://www.bidpa.bw/undp.htm

between zero and one and it is an economic measure of inequality. Therefore Gini-coefficient of 0 implies absolute equality, and a coefficient greater than 0.5 implies a very high concentration of income. The above policies and instruments failed to reduce the gap between the rich and the poor. The rural poverty is represented by:

- Serious lack of competence for reducing poverty and sustainable rural development strategies;
- Serious deficiencies of post settlement support services;
- Lack of monitoring and evaluation of resettlement schemes;
- Lack of technical assistance and marketing of goods; and
- Policies that favour commercial ranches, establishment of cattle posts, tourist ventures and mineral prospecting licenses.

Why is access to land by hunter-gatherers a human rights issue? The reality in Botswana is that "the critical issue of land rights has not received attention in and of itself for the simple reason that the Sarwa are as much citizens as anyone else born in Botswana and are therefore guaranteed rights to property".[52] Hitchcock reports that in 1977 in Kgatleng District, southeast Botswana, the San/Basarwa were denied access to land on the basis that they "were not 'tribesmen' and therefore did not have land rights under customary law".[53] The above argument has a historical basis:

> In 1899, when the tribal reserves were originally defined, there was no land set aside specifically for the [Ba]Sarwa, nor were any areas defined for them subsequently. By recognising the tribal areas as "reserves", the Protectorate Administration and later the Government of Botswana were in effect stabilising and legitimising tribal territories which were the result of expansionist and incorporation processes that were tied to land use practices involving **pastolarism and arable agriculture**. **Hunting and gathering**, although practiced in Tswana and other tribes in Botswana, **was not viewed as a legitimate form of land use in and of itself**. The people living in the remote parts of the Kalahari, far from cattle posts and arable land areas, did not have officially sanctioned title to the areas they occupied.[54]

Hunter-gatherers, as already pointed out, have a very strong spiritual attachment to land. In southern Africa, the hunter-gatherers are already at the

[52] Hitchcock, 1980, p.21

[53] Ibid.

[54] Ibid., emphasis added.

bottom of the ladder in terms of poverty - they are the poorest of the poor. Their poverty and social marginalization is worsened when access to natural resources, especially land is denied. Although the hunter-gatherer economy is made more precarious by natural disasters such as drought, their poverty becomes more magnified when access to productive resources such as land is denied. Part of the role of government is to combat hunger and poverty, and this should be seen as more than a good government program; it is a human right obligation that every national government should endeavor to undertake. The Universal Declaration of Human Rights of 1948 Article 25, states:

> Everyone has the right to a standard of living adequate for the health and well-being of himself and his family, including food, clothing, housing, and medical care.

According Suarez (n.d.), the right to adequate food, just as any other human right, imposes three levels of State obligations:

- *Every State is obliged to* ***respect*** *the right to adequate food of everyone under its jurisdiction and in all circumstances. This means that States may not take any measure that result in the destruction of the existent access of vulnerable groups to sources of food. Forceful displacement or seizure of land without adequate compensation by the State is a violation of the right to feed oneself because the victims depend on their land for subsistence.*
- *Additionally, the States Parties have the obligation* ***to protect*** *everyone under their jurisdiction from third parties who may threaten their access to food. If, for example, peasant or indigenous communities are evicted with violence by landowners or enterprises from their land, the State has the obligation to protect the communities by preventing that land is seized and thus that they remain without access to food.*
- *Should an individual or group lack access to adequate food, the States Parties have the obligation to* ***fulfill*** *this access. To this end, the States Parties are required to open up to the restoration of rights of marginalized groups, allowing them to participate in the monitoring of their situation. The States Parties are also required to offer vulnerable groups, effective strategies and programmes that lead to secure the long-term development of their competence and resources to feed themselves.*

In order to avoid future land use conflicts there is need for the States to recognize the existing property rights of the hunter-gatherers. Denying hunter-gatherers access to land and natural resources can further perpetuate the already worse situation of the San poverty.

8. IMPLICATIONS FOR RURAL DEVELOPMENT POLICY AND ACCESS TO LAND RIGHTS

Current thinking in the southern African region among government officials is that the San Bushmen should be encouraged to discard their 'primitive' nomadic way of life of hunting and gathering and lead a normal life like everybody else. Survival International, an NGO which has been fighting for the rights of the San/Bushmen in Central Kalahari Game Reserve views this position by the national governments as 'extremely backward' and not in line with current international thinking. The Minister of Lands and Housing, Dr Margaret Nasha, disagrees and says since everybody is equal in Botswana there should be equal treatment of everybody; and further states: "Basarwa should be treated like any other citizen of the country" [Daily News 2003b]. Instead of talking of equal treatment, the Minister should be talking of equity in terms of allocation of natural resources instead of equality.

Under the Botswana Constitution sub-section 14(3) (c) every citizen including San Bushmen is entitled to a piece of land but in reality only a few do have access to land. The Local Land Boards can only allocate individual land rights, but nowhere in the *Tribal Land Act* is there mention of communal land rights of hunter-gatherers.

When the Kalahari hunter-gatherers subsistence and settlements systems were modelled, Hitchcock and Ebert revealed that their resettlement would be detrimental to their way of life. [55] They questioned the "villagization programme", which was being and is still being pursued by the government, as unviable and having a number of undesirable side effects. On the contrary, one might argue that any resettlement scheme is bound to have social and

[55] Hitchcock, R.K. and J.I. Ebert, 1989. "Modeling Kalahari hunter-gatherer subsistence and settlement systems: implications for development policy and land use planning in Botswana". *Anthropos*, 84:47-62

economic hardships. But if one weighs the costs and benefits of this government policy, it seems there are more social costs and fewer benefits. A number of the social costs may include:

- the increasing conflict over scarce resources;
- boredom in the resettlement camps leading to excessive drinking;
- high prevalence of communicable diseases such as tuberculosis;
- breakdown of the San/Bushmen social networks;
- high population increase;
- economic and social differentiation; and
- decline in nutritional status due to changes in diet.

Given these social problems, is the government policy of "villagization" of the San Bushmen really appropriate? The answer is unconditional **No**. The problem is that the "villagization programme" is not based on a sound understanding of the social problems associated with resettlement. There should be adequate provision of infrastructure and services. With the removal of humans from national parks and game reserves, introduction of commercial ranches and cattle posts, issuing of mineral prospecting licenses in the San/Bushmen territory, there is need to set aside blocks of land where people can live and have access to social services. These areas need to be adequately planned so that the San/Bushmen can gradually develop sustainable and viable livelihoods. The current practice whereby people are simply given a small plot for arable agriculture and livestock is not sufficient in terms of ensuring that they are adequately compensated or that they have an opportunity to develop alternative lifestyles. The resettlement of the San must not be seen in terms of only providing social services like schools, health posts, and water; but there must be land set aside for "Hunting and Gathering Areas" not very far from these settlements. This can be achieved in terms of Wildlife Management Areas to support hunter-gatherer activities.

Various strategies are required such as providing the post settlement support services for arable agriculture and animal husbandry, provision of loan-schemes, and training in eco-tourism. Other strategies may include technical assistance in manufacturing items such as baskets, mats, arts and crafts, or skins, and in establishing a marketing system where people can sell their products.[56] The reality in southern Africa is that governments tend to do a poor job when it comes to post settlement support, implementation, monitoring and evaluation of resettlement schemes (e.g. Botswana, Namibia, South Africa, and Zimbabwe). Land tenure is often not very secure, the settlements are too small to meet their needs, and the post settlement support services provided are unreliable and inadequate.

9. CONCLUDING REMARKS

This paper concludes by outlining further issues which needs to be addressed and they may include the following:

- *The definition of indigenous rights.* Although the definition of indigenous rights is highly contested in Africa, the marginalized groups can still argue that they share a similar structural position vis-à-vis their nation-states as indigenous peoples in the Americas and Australia: cultural distinctiveness; experience of subjugation, marginalization, and land dispossession by both the colonial and the post-colonial states.[57] In fact, the developments in North America regarding aboriginal title have encouraged indigenous groups in southern Africa to push for their land claims, and the recent successes in South Africa bear testimony to that effect: the return of traditional land around the Kalahari Gemsbok National Park; [58] and the recent ruling in the High Court of the Richtersveld Community.[59] These two cases have set precedents for other countries in the region that operate under the Roman-Dutch legal system, which includes Botswana, Namibia, and Zimbabwe.

- *The processes established to resolve land claims.* Canada and Australia have put in place complex legal principles and land settlement processes to resolve land claims issues. These processes involve for example, procedures for establishing what evidence to be heard, how evidence is gathered, and how overlapping land claims between groups are to be

[56] Ibid.
[57] Hodgson, 2002
[58] Sylvain, 2002
[59] Mmegi, 2003b. "SA ruling has effect on Botswana", 17-23 October 2003. Accessed on October 2003,

addressed.[60] Including traditional ecological knowledge as a valid form of evidence can further widen these procedures and Geographic Information Systems can be used to document such evidence.

- *The policy of assimilation*. The fundamental feature of nation-states is the need to assert homogeneity of its citizens, and this tendency has been criticized as "fundamentally against pluralism".[61] Since the policy has not born the desired results, maybe Botswana and other countries in the region should take the lead and follow other jurisdictions like Canada and embrace the concept of multi-culturalism.

How the southern Africa region adjusts the interests of hunter-gatherers, pastoralists, commercial ranchers, conservationists, tourism and mining conglomerates will deeply affect the kind of states that these countries will become. As these countries are very young parliamentary democracies compared to other countries in the world, the region must be seen to be upholding the human rights of all its citizens especially the land rights of the marginalized hunter-gatherer societies. The national governments of countries such as Botswana have always maintained social justice and upheld democratic principles when making major decisions concerning its citizens. The social implications of forced resettlement of the hunter-gatherers are tremendously important; far more so than the economic and ecological goals; we cannot deny people access to land on the basis of ethnic affiliation.

BIBLIOGRAPHY

Barnard, A. and J. Woodburn, 1988. "Property, power and ideology in hunter-gathering societies: an introduction". In Ingold, T., Riches, D. and Woodburn (eds). *Hunters and Gatherers Vol. II*. New York: Martin's Press.

Barnard, A., 1992. "Social and spatial boundary maintenance among Southern African hunter-gatherers" In M. J. Casimir and A. Rao, *Mobility and Territoriality: social and spatial boundaries among the foragers, fishers, pastoralists and peripatetics*. New York: Berg.

[60] Nichols and Rakai, 2001
[61] Werbner, 2002

Benda-Beckmann von, F., 1995. "Anthropological Approaches to Property and Economics". *European Journal of Law and Economics*, 2: 309-336.

BIDPA, 1998. "Summary of the 1997 Botswana Human Development Report". Accessed December 2003 http://www.bidpa.bw/undp.htm

Bishop, K., 1998. Squatters on their own land: San territoriality in Western Botswana. Accessed on July 2003,
http://www.gtz.de/orboden/capetown/cape07.htm

Bohannan, P. (1963). "'Land', 'tenure' and land-tenure", In Daniel Biebuyck, *African Agrarian Systems*. London: Oxford University Press, pp. 101-115.

Botswana Government,

1959. *Prescriptions Act, Chapter 13:01*. Gaborone: Government Printer

1966. *Constitution of Botswana Act*. Gaborone: Government Printer.

1970. *Tribal Land Act, Chapter 32:02*. Gaborone: Government Printer

Casimir, M.J., 1992. "The dimensions of territoriality: an introduction". In M. J. Casimir and A. Rao, *Mobility and Territoriality: social and spatial boundaries among the foragers, fishers, pastoralists and peripatetics*. New York: Berg. pp.1-26.

Coates, K., 2000. *The Marshall Decision and Native Rights*. Montreal: McGill-Queens's University Press.

Daily News,

2003a. "Don't give Basarwa preferential treatment on land", 18 August. Accessed August 2003.
http://www.gov.bw/cgi-bin/news.cgi?d=20030818

2003b. Don't reserve land specifically for Basarwa", 1 September. Accessed September 2003.
http://www.gov.bw/cgi-bin/news.cgi?d=20030901

Dornan, S.S., 1975. *Pygmies & Bushmen of the Kalahari*. Cape Town: C. Struik (Pty) Ltd. 2nd Edition.

Fingleton, J.S., 1998. *Legal recognition of indigenous groups*. Accessed from World Wide Web on August 2003. http://www.fao.org/legal/prs-ol/paper-e.htm

Hitchcock, R. K 1980. "Tradition, Social Justice, and Land Reform in Central Botswana." *Journal of African Law*, 24(1): 1 -34.

Hitchcock, R. K. 1982. *Tribal Grazing Land Policy, 1981 Programme Review*. (TGLP Monitoring) Ministry of Agriculture, Gaborone

Hitchcock, R.K. and M. Biesele (n.d.) "San, Khwe, Basarwa, or Bushmen?: terminology, identity, and empowerment in Southern Africa". Accessed on August 2003, http://www.kalaharipeoples.org/documents/San-term.htm

Hitchcock, R.K. and J.I. Ebert, 1989. "Modeling Kalahari hunter-gatherer subsistence and settlement systems: implications for development policy and land use planning in Botswana". *Anthropos*, 84:47-62.

Hodgson, D.L., 2002. "Introduction: comparative perspectives on the indigenous rights movement in Africa and the Americas". *American Anthropologist*, 104(4): 1037 – 1049.

Leopold, A., 1949. *A Sand County almanac and sketches here and there*. New York: Oxford University Press.

MacPherson, C. B., 1978. "The meaning of property", Chapter 1 in *Property in the Mainstream and Critical Positions*, C.B. MacPherson, ed. Toronto: University of Toronto Press, pp. 1-13.

Mmegi,

2003a. "Basarwa are pawns in a political game – Lucas", 19-25 September 2003. Accessed from World Wide Web on September 2003. http://www.mmegi.bw/2003/September/Friday19/408334805271.html

2003b. "SA ruling has effect on Botswana", 17-23 October 2003. Accessed on October 2003, http://www.mmegi.bw/2003/October/Friday17/7187410931715.html

Nichols, S. and M. Rakai, 2001. "Canadian land reform: an overview of Aboriginal rights and land claims settlements". Accessed from World Wide Web on November 2003, http://www.fao.org/DOCREP/003/Y0434T/Y0434t08.htm

Ng'ong'ola, C., 1997. "Land rights for marginalized ethnic groups in Botswana, with special reference to the Basarwa". *The Journal of African Law*, 41:1-26.

Oxford English Dictionary, 2003. Accessed on December 2003 from the World Wide Web http://dictionary.oed.com

Quan, J., 2000. "Land Board as a mechanism for the management land rights in southern Africa". Chapter 10 in *Evolving Land Rights, Policy and Tenure in Africa*, C. Toulmin and J. Quan, eds. London: DFID/IIED/NRI

Randeria, S., 2003. "Protecting the rights of indigenous communities in the new architecture of global governance: the interplay of international institutions and post-colonial states. In Pradhan Rajendra (ed.) *Legal Pluralism and Unofficial Law in Social, Economic and Political Development*. Papers of the XIIIth International Congress, 7-10 April 2002, Chiang Mai, Thailand. Vol 3, Kathmandu: ICNEC.

Suarez, S.M. (n.d.). *Access to land: a human rights obligation*. Accessed from the World Wide Web on 6th August 2003. http://www.monolayout.de/dateien/Monsalve.pdf

Seligman, C.G., 1957. *Races of Africa*, 3rd edition. London: Oxford University Press.

Sylvain, R., 2002. "Land, Water, and Truth": San Identity and Global Indigenism. *American Anthropologist*, 104(4): 1074 – 1085.

Taylor, I. and G. Mokhawa, 2003. "Not forever: Botswana, conflict diamonds and the Bushmen". *Africa Affairs*, 102:261-283.

United Nations High Commissioner for Human Rights, 2002."Concluding Observations of the Committee on the Elimination of Racial Discrimination: Botswana. 01/11/2002". Accessed from World Wide Web on August 20003. http://193.194.138.190/tbs/doc.nsf/(Symbol)/A.57.18,paras.292-314.En?OpenDocument

United Nations, 1949. *Universal Declaration of Human Rights [adopted and proclaimed by the General Assembly of the United Nations on the tenth day December 1948]*. New York: United Nations Department of Public Information.

Werbner, R., 2002. "Introduction: challenging minorities, difference and tribal citizenship in Botswana". *Journal of Southern African Studies*, 28(4): 671-684.

Wilmsen, E.N., 1989. "Those who have each other: San relations to land" In Edwin N. Wilmsen, *We Are Here: Politics of Aboriginal Land Tenure*, Berkeley: University of California Press, pp. 43-67.

Dilemmas Connected to Recognising Customary Law and Courts in South Africa

Ragnhild L. Muriaas

INTRODUCTION[1]

Contrary to what many believed in the heydays of decolonisation and democratisation, traditional courts are still a significant judicial authority in Africa. Customary law does in different ways coexist with state law in many societies, something that can be quite a dilemma since its procedures are embedded in distinct moralities and are connected to additional spheres of authority.[2] With the preamble "one law for one nation" the South African Constitution of 1996 offers an extensive legal protection of individual rights. At the same time, it also puts forward a constitutional recognition of customary law and the judicial authority of traditional leaders. From a liberal point of view this have caused an apparent dilemma: How is it possible to balance policies aimed to protect the constitutional rights of all citizens to be "equal before the law" with policies designed to accommodate a customary system of law where for instance women are regarded as minors under the guardian of their father or a husband, have no locus standi, no right to inherit or own property, or to sign any legal contracts at all?

By employing a political perspective, the intention with this article is to analyse this and other dilemmas that the South African governments have encountered in their efforts to balance policies designed to accommodate customary law and traditional courts with policies aimed to protect universal human rights. By doing this, an explanation is offered as to why these dilemmas have created an incoherent policy towards traditional authorities, and subsequently, disclose some consequences that this inconsistent reform process has had on the complex judicial system in rural areas.

PART 1: DILEMMAS CONNECTED TO LEGAL PLURALISM

Before I turn to examine the dilemmas that ANC governments have encountered in their process of balancing policies aimed to accommodate the judicial function of traditional authorities with policies aimed to protect human

[1] The author would like to thank the Chr. Michelsen Institute - Development Studies and Human Rights, Bergen, in general and Hugo Stokke in particular for help with achieving financial support for writing this article. The author is also grateful to Dr. Sten Schamburg-Müller from Aarhus University for his insightful and valuable comments on the first draft of this article. I would also like to thank Dr. Siri Gloppen for her support in the early stages of this process.

[2] See Richard A. Wilson, "Reconciliation and Revenge in Post-Apartheid South Africa: Rethinking Legal Pluralism and Human Rights", *Current Anthropology*, Vol. 41, 2000, 76.

rights, I will in the following part of the article discuss some theoretical considerations regarding whether states *do* in fact or *ought to* have a monopoly of law enforcement in society. Particularly within the field of legal pluralism, it has been common to argue that the state does not have a monopoly of law enforcement within its territory. From a political point of view, a key question related to this is whether the government tries to find strategies to reduce discrepancies between formal law and how legal behaviour is observed in the society, or whether the government accepts and formally recognises that such discrepancies between the state and certain groups exist. Formal recognitions like these are frequently formulated as part of a strategy to recognise the cultural rights and legal traditions of a minority culture within the boarder of the state. However, as I will argue in the next pages, such recognitions do indeed bring on certain ethical dilemmas.

Do states have a monopoly of law?

Sheleff has remarked that although the main characteristic of a state is its power to make laws, rules of an obligatory nature are created without the formal procedures of parliaments, courts, and other constituted bodies of the state. [3] This and similar anthropological approaches towards law, which emphasises how legal, illegal and non-legal norms all intermesh in one social field, [4] are known as legal pluralism. Wilson defines legal pluralism as a descriptive term and an analytical concept "which attempts to address the existence of more than one legal system in a single political unit", and subsequently, the crucial phenomenon under enquiry for legal pluralists is "the relationship between state law and informal moralities and mechanisms of adjudication".[5]

Moore presented the rationale of legal pluralism in *Law as Process* in 1978. Her argument is that though formal legal institutions may enjoy a monopoly on the legitimate use of force, they cannot be said to have a monopoly on other forms of effective coercion or effective inducement. The reason for this is that between the "body politic and the individual there are interposed various smaller organised social fields to which the individual

[3] Leon Sheleff, The Future of Tradition: Customary law, common law and legal pluralism, London, Frank Cass, 2000, p. 1.

[4] Sally Falk Moore, *Law as Process*, London, Routledge & Kegan Paul, 1978, p. 59.

[5] Wilson, 2000, *op.cit.*, p. 76.

'belong'".[6] Consequently, if centralised governments try to invade these social fields by force of legislation, the intended purposes will not be achieved. Her explanation to this assumption is that "new laws are thrust upon going social arrangements in which there are complexes of binding obligations already in existence".[7] This does not mean that government legislation never have an impact on norms operating in semi-autonomous social fields, it just indicates that legislation often have unplanned and unexpected consequences.[8]

While Moore is reluctant to argue that norms in semi-autonomous social fields can be understood as law, Ehrlich has argued that these norms are to be interpreted as living law. State law is even subordinate to the living law,[9] and accordingly, formal law plays only a part and sometimes no part at all, even in areas where it purports to regulate.[10] In relation to this, Sheleff has argued that people seem to carve out their own rules, and these rules "are deeply embedded in the very fibre of their community life, attuned to its possibility and responsive to their needs".[11]

Though few will question the existence of non-legal norms that bind people's behaviour, there are vast academic discussions regarding whether one can interpret this as 'informal or living laws' that coexist with state law. Schaumburg-Müller calls attention to the dilemma that, by making use of the concept "law", legal pluralists equate law with reality. He agrees with legal pluralists that it is interesting to investigate empirically the discrepancies between what the law prescribes and what people do, but it is not necessary to categorise the practices of people as law in order to make those practices relevant.[12] If one equates law with reality, one ends up with the assumption that "what people do in practice (…) is law, because this is what people do".[13] Law is not intended to describe what people do, but prescribes what people ought to do ideally based on careful considerations about principles of justice. The question of how to interpret discrepancies between what formal law prescribes and how people do in fact behave have important ethical

[6] Moore, 1978, *op.cit.*, p. 56.

[7] *Ibid.*, p. 58.

[8] *Ibid.*

[9] See discussion on Ehrlich in Peter Fitzpatrick, "Law and Societies", *Osgoode Hall Journal*, Vol. 22, 1984, p. 116.

[10] Graham Huges, "Concept of Law" in Philip P. Wiener (ed.) *The Dictionary of the History of Ideas*, Vol. 3., New York, Charles Scribner's Sons, 2003, p. 3.

[11] Sheleff, 1999, *op.cit.*, p. 3.

[12] Sten Schaumburg-Müller, "Pursuing Theory on the Ground", in *Retfærd* no 99, 2002, p. 40.

[13] *Ibid.*, p. 37.

consequences. Because ignoring the position of legal centralism might lead to an acceptance of whatever norms are prevalent, "acceptance not only in the sense of realising that they exists, but in the sense of accepting any prevalent norms as (good as) law".[14]

Should the state have a monopoly of law?

The next question is thus how does the government deal with the discrepancies between what formal law prescribes and how people in fact behave, in a situation where people's behaviour supplants formal law but simultaneously is considered an important expression of a particular group's culture. The government in a liberal democracy is obliged to protect the fundamental right to equal justice for all. All citizens in a liberal democracy are to be regarded as equals and share a set of universal rights entrenched in a comprehensive constitution; consequently a liberal government cannot easily dismiss the position of legal centralism. The idea of a universal law that regulates the relationship between state and society in a just and equal manner is influenced by the writings of Kant. Kant stresses that all men are equally endowed with the capacity to reason, and this capacity is identical in all men.[15] It is this universal human potential as rational agents, rather than anything a person may have made out of it, that entitles all people to be treated as equals.[16] Accordingly, in a liberal democracy, individuals are to be recognised simply because they are, not for who they are. Equal rights must therefore be prior to perceptions of good and the protection of cultural particularities. A liberal society must refrain from deciding what the good life is and restrict it self to ensure that, however differently they see things, the citizens ought to deal fairly with each other, and the state ought to deal equally with all.[17]

However, there are also normative reasons for a government to protect particular cultures and their practises. Different cultural groups have gained support for their challenge of the universalistic liberal notion of the relationship between individuals and states. These groups have argued that, in certain circumstances, it is significant to recognise the individuals' interests as

---

[14] *Ibid.*, p. 42.

[15] Andrea T. Baumeister, *Liberalism and the Politics of Difference*, Edinburgh, Edinburgh University Press, 2000, p. 7.

[16] Charles Taylor, "The Politics of Recognition" in Amy Gutman *Multiculturalism*, New Jersey, Princeton University Press, Princeton, 1994, p. 41.

[17] *Ibid.*, p. 57.

members of a cultural group.[18] From a liberal point of view, such perspectives are regarded as problematic: how is it possible to strike a balance between the accommodation of minority groups' traditions and within-group protection of an individual's citizenship rights? [19] When theoretical thinkers such as Kymlicka speaks in favor of cultural groups' legal right to practice certain customs in order to help them "express their cultural particularity and pride within the economic and political institutions of the dominant society,"[20] law might be subjugated to power relations and suppressive mechanisms in local communities.

According to Shachar, a liberal government can protect particular cultures with illiberal features if neither group nor state claims all-inclusive power over a concrete territory. Both should rather strive to develop flexible, accountable and broadly applicable solutions for the division of authority because it enhances the possibility of self-legislation, although neither group nor state should have autonomous power.[21] If different authorities interact in order to find mutually acceptable solutions to how justice shall be administered in a society, various methods to re-allocate power between the state and cultural groups may thus be agreed upon.[22]

Like Moore, Shachar also stresses that some persons belong to more than one political community, and consequently, have rights and obligations that derive from more than one source of legal authority. The individuals must therefore be granted the right to choose which sets of law to live by and the right to have their cases tried in a traditional court. To achieve certainty in the administration of justice, a dialogue between different non-monopolist power centres must be encourage since neither an "all-knowing" state nor a group should impose their particular vision of law upon individuals.[23] The next parts of this article will examine whether it is reasonable to assume that such individual choices really can be made in a society where different sets of normative moralities exist, and how the African National Congress (ANC) governments have tried to balance their policies aimed to accommodate the

---

[18] *Ibid.*, p. 29.

[19] Ayelet Shachar, *Multicultural Jurisdictions – Cultural Differences and Women's Rights*, Cambridge, Cambridge University press, 2001, p. 1.

[20] Will Kymlicka, "Three forms of Group-Differentiated Citizenship in Canada" in Benhabib (ed.), *Democracy and Difference, Contesting the Boundaries of the political*, New Jersey, Princeton University Press, 1996, p. 154.

[21] Shachar, 2001, *op.cit.*, pp. 91-92.

[22] *Ibid.*, p. 90.

[23] *Ibid.*, p. 88.

judicial function of traditional authorities with the right to equality after the 1996 Constitution.

PART 2: THREE EMPIRICAL DILEMMAS

In this part of the article, three dilemmas, which are supposed to affect the process of balancing the accommodation of customary law and the judicial function of traditional leaders with fundamental human rights, will be examined empirically. The first dilemma is the capacity dilemma, the second is the ethical dilemma and the third is the strategic dilemma. The intention of this part of the article is to reveal how a compound of these dilemmas has caused an incoherent process, which has not managed to transform the complex legal system in local communities to a sufficient degree.

1) The capacity dilemma

The question of accommodating traditional authorities was one of the most controversial in the negotiations prior to the drafting of the South African Constitution of 1996. Many South Africans lived in rural areas governed by traditional authorities and customary law.[24] One of the first challenges for the new ANC led government was to find a way to balance policies aimed to accommodate the judicial function of traditional authorities with universal human rights entrenched in the constitution. This part of the article addresses a capacity dilemma regarding observable discrepancies between formal law and observed legal behaviour in regard to customary law, which the government had to relate to. To understand the current situation, it is however important to elaborate briefly on how customary law developed in South Africa.

The development of customary law in South Africa

The codification of customary law was a colonial attempt to systematise customary rights by seeking to provide a legal definition of the rules applied in traditional courts. The administrators who codified customary law were influenced by legal positivism, and in their opinion legal practitioners should

[24] Richard Spitz and Matthew Chaskalson, The Politics of Transition – a hidden history of South Africa's negotiated settlement, Oxford, Hart Publishing, 2000, p. 379.

have a systematic code of rules to draw their decisions on.[25] The aim was to integrate the customary system into formal law and make it an official sub-category of a formal plural legal system. In South Africa the Native Administration Act 38 of 1927 authorised the application of customary law in a constituted hierarchy of courts. In socio-legal studies, colonial and apartheid legislation, it was common to argue that different laws ought to apply to different people due to their cultural differences. Africans were divided on ethnic or tribal lines, and as Bennett has argued "each tribe was studied as if it was, and ought to remain, free from the subversive influences of European culture. It followed that change was socially harmful and that when two cultures were brought into contact with one another, there was bound to be a conflict".[26] This understanding operated also politically as a functionalist "value-free" justification for segregation, by stressing that differing cultural groups naturally have and require different laws.[27]

However, in reality the codified customary law was a product of legislation that reflected the apartheid administration's view of acceptable aspects of customary law as it operated in 1927, with modifications to suit government policy.[28] Formally, the codification turned customary law into a very static justice system, where traditional believes regarding relations between generations and genders were written down as unquestionable facts about power relations in African societies. Studies made by Chanock reveal that these "facts" were not neutral, but often provided by elderly males, who had interests of depicting their traditional law according to their own needs.[29] The process of codifying customary law thus ran counter to what has been considered the essence of customary law, which is "the law customarily observed by the community, acceptable to it and flexible enough to change with changing circumstance".[30] In day-to-day practicing of customary law this living version continued to exist despite the colonisers' efforts to codify and formalise customary law. Customary law continued to vary from community to

[25] T. W. Bennett, A Sourcebook of African Customary Law for Southern Africa, Cape Town, Juta & Co, Ltd, 1991, p. 1.

[26] Bennett, 1991, *op.cit.*, pp. 16-17.

[27] *Ibid.*, p. 55.

[28] Sandra B. Burman, "The Interaction of Legislation relating to Urban Africans and the Laws Regulating Family Relationships" in T. W. Bennett et al *Urban Black Law*, Cape Town, JUTA & Co, Ltd, 1984, p. 90.

[29] Martin Chanock, Law, *Custom and Social Order. The colonial experience in Malawi and Zambia,* Cambridge, Cambridge University Press, 1985, p. 16.

[30] Burman, 1884, *op.cit.*, p. 90.

community, and it remained more flexible and liable to constant and imperceptible change than what the codified version reflected.

The dual legal system, initiated by the central colonial governments, evolved into a complex system of law. The codification of customary law had made a sever impact on decisions made in traditional courts. Still, norms and customs continued to change in accordance with the society, and decisions made in traditional courts did not only draw from the codified official customary law. These non-official rules where in 1997 interpreted as 'living' laws by the South African Law Commission (SALC), who referred to them as "how laws were actually observed in African communities".[31] The ANC government had to relate to this discrepancy between official customary law and how legal behaviour actually was observed in local communities. If the ANC wanted its legislation to have at least some substantial effect, it would require extensive resources, supported by efficient political will to enforce these laws.

How to address the capacity dilemma in a new constitutional order?

Problems connected to the government's capacity to enforce law were apparent. In rural areas access to formal state justice was extremely limited, and litigants in rural areas had to pay the costs of travelling to the nearest town to get their case tried in a formal state court. Magistrate courts in South Africa operated with an extremely limited infrastructure and did not always have the capacity to deal with minor disputes. Many proceedings were subject to considerable delays at all stages, mainly as a result of the sheer number of cases to be processed in a limited number of courts.[32] For the ANC led government, any attempt to address the problems of access to justice associated with the formal state system immediately encountered the fact that the cost of bringing the formal state system to ordinary people would be immense. Penal Reform International has argued that to reduce the distances and delays associated with an already congested state system, a massive expansion of that system would be required. Only few states in Africa have been in a position to provide either the number of courts at the local level or the additional legal aid and interpretation resources that are required. An

---

[31] South African Law Commission, *Customary Marriages*, Discussion paper 74, Project 90, 1997, p. 6.

[32] Penal Reform International, Access to justice in sub-Saharan Africa: The role of traditional and informal justice systems, London, Astron Printers, 2000, p. 6.

estimate anticipates that in South Africa it would require up to 3 000 new courts if all people living in rural areas were to have equal access to the formal state system of justice.[33]

The most important task, however, was not to make customary law superfluous, but to make it compatible with the Constitution. In order to make the South African legal system more just in the eyes of the people, Mbatha, at the Centre for Applied Legal Studies, stressed the importance of making laws in accordance with how people practise their culture: "It is very important that the law should draw from what people are doing in practice. In practice people are complaining about marriage in accordance to both customary and western law. And why do they complain? Because neither is based on their culture as they know it."[34] Though most would agree on the necessity of observing how customary law in fact operated in society, there where discussions on how much the customary law system had to be transformed in order to be compatible with the constitutional principles. The ANC acknowledged the fact that they did not have the capacity to alter the legal system in South Africa. Still, they saw the need for vast judicial reconstructions. To achieve this, a process of reforming customary law had to start by enacting central legislation. As Schaumburg-Müller warned, one could not equate law with reality, and accept how it at present operated in traditional courts in South Africa.

2) The ethical dilemma

It is important to emphasise that the constitutional recognition of customary law does not grant complete immunity to traditional legal practices, as specific applications of customary law are limited by both national legislation and the Bill of Rights: "The courts must apply customary law when that law is applicable, subject to the Constitution and any legislation that specifically deals with customary law".[35] This denotes that though customary law and traditional courts are recognised in the Constitution, both were conditioned by national legislation and political will to enforce constitutional obligations. The ANC was eager to transform society in order to achieve justice for all, but how was it possible to find a strategy for balancing policies aimed at recognising

---

[33] *Ibid.*, p. 7.

[34] Likahapa Mbatha, Centre for Applied Legal Studies, University of Witwatersrand, Johannesburg the 2nd of July 1999.

[35] Constitution of the Republic of South Africa, Act 108 of 1996.

traditional courts and customary law with policies aimed to protect the universal right to equality?

The right to culture vs. the right to equality

The conditioned recognition of customary law and traditional authorities did, in accordance with Shachar's strategy, encourage a process of dialogue between the new ANC government and traditional authorities. The core intention with the reform was to reach mutual acceptable ways to reconcile constitutional tensions between cultural recognition and all citizens' right to equality before the law. Two features were soon identified as particularly problematic from a human rights perspective. First, women's position as minors in customary law rendered many laws and practices incompatible with the constitution. Second, it was far from clear when customary law was applicable. A clear and explicit choice of laws rules had to be enforced to protect the right to certainty in the administration of justice.[36]

Though there were deep divisions within the ANC regarding the position of traditional authorities, the main direction of legal change after 1994 was towards greater centralisation as state officials attempted to "restore the legitimacy of state legal institutions".[37] Consequently, a project affirming the authority of traditional legal systems ran counter to the centralising trend within the government. The ANC was more determined to eliminate discriminating features of customary law than to clarify the position of traditional authorities. In their 1997 resolutions, customary law was only mentioned in relation to the importance of protecting women's right to equality: "Women in traditional communities and under customary and religious law do not enjoy equal rights in areas such as community decision-making, marriage, divorce, inheritance and land allocation". As a consequence of this the ANC have to "campaign for the review of all laws, customs, traditions and any other discriminatory and oppressive practices which are totally against the equality clause in the Constitution".[38]

Apparently, if the ANC government was to share judicial power with traditional authorities and justify a dual legal system, a customary law that did

[36] South African Law Commission, *Conflicts of Law*, Discussion paper 76, Project 90, 1998, p. 2.

[37] Wilson, 2000, *op.cit.*, p. 78.

[38] African National Congress, 50th National Conference Resolutions, Post-Conference Documents, *Customary law*, Mafikeng, 16-20 December 1997.

not discriminate against anyone had to be applied in traditional courts. The position of traditional leaders was, however, strengthened by the support of prominent figures within the ANC, such as Mandela. In his address to the ANC youth in 1990, Mandela emphasised the need to respect traditional leaders:

> I have touched on the question of homeland leaders and traditional chiefs. It is not the policy of the ANC to condemn the chiefs as such. These are our traditional leaders, some of whom have an impressive record in the fight against apartheid. We say we must give them the respect that they deserve as traditional leaders.[39]

This quotation illustrates an observation made by Thornton, that all battles over chieftainships, including that leading up to the constitution, "are fought in terms of ideology rather than with reference to knowledge of how (and if) the institution really exists on the ground, or works as claimed".[40] He further states that even though many summoned respect of traditional leaders, this was based on ideological considerations about "the golden and good about pre-colonial age of African innocence", rather than based on knowledge about traditional institutions.[41]

Still, it is possible to make arguments in favor of customary law that are based on more substance than merely referring to a golden past. As for instance, the Penal Reform International emphasises that the justice offered by formal courts may be inappropriate for the resolution of disputes between "people living in rural villages or urban settlements where the breaking of individual social relationships can cause conflict within the community and affect economic co-operation on which the community depends".[42] Further, it is also argued that traditional and informal justice systems aim at restoring social cohesion within the community by promoting reconciliation between disputing parties, while formal state systems by contrast is characterised by its adversarial style and emphasis on retribution.[43]

---

[39] Nelson Mandela, *Address to the youth*, Official Statement, KaNyamazane, 13 April 1990.

[40] Robert Thornton, "Chiefs: Power in a Political Wilderness" in I. Ray and P.S. Reddy (eds.) *Grassroots Governance? Chiefs in Africa and the Afro-Caribbean*, Calgary, University of Calgary Press, 2003, p. 139.

[41] *Ibid.*, p. 139.

[42] Penal Reform International, 2000, *op.cit.*, p. 9.

[43] *Ibid.*

Features speaking in favour of traditional justice systems are that they are easily accessible, few costs are involved, they are informal, they use the same language as the disputants, and their proceedings are reasonable. Conversely, the disadvantages with the traditional courts is not only that they regard women as minors, but proceedings of traditional courts are in conflict with common universal rights such as "to choose and be represented by a legal practitioner" and "the right to silence".[44] An additional problematic feature concerns the composition of courts. For instance, traditional leaders are *primae facie* proficient in customary law, but does that automatically make them qualified to preside over a court of law?[45]

Reforming customary law in line with the liberal constitution

A reform process with the object of balancing policies aimed to recognise customary law and traditional courts with fundamental rights entrenched in the constitution commenced in 1996 when the ANC government initiated a new project directed by The South African Law Commission (SALC): "Project 90: The harmonisation of the common law and the indigenous law".[46] The predominant focus of legislation was a legal reform of customary law. Three reforms were initiated. These were: a project regarding recognition of customary marriages, a project concerning conflicting personal laws, and in 1998 a project regarding succession in customary law. Simultaneously, different projects regarding communal land reform were also discussed in various departments and councils.[47]

Consultation with the people was the key strategy molding this process of legal reform. Professor Nhlapo, the former leader of SALCs harmonisation process, emphasised the importance of popular consultation in an interview in 1999: "...because if you are going to make laws, you have to make them with the people, not just for the people".[48] Several workshops were arranged all

---

[44] South African Law Commission, *Traditional courts and the judicial function of traditional leaders*, Discussion paper 82, Project 90, 1999, p. 3.

[45] *Ibid.*, p. 4.

[46] South African Law Commission, "Harmonisation of common law and Indigenous law", *Annual Report*, Project 90, 1996.

[47] For thorough discussions of the question on Communal Land Rights see Lungisile Ntsebeza, "Traditional Authorities, Local Government and Land Rights in I. Ray and P.S. Reddy (eds.) *Grassroots Governance? Chiefs in Africa and the Afro-Caribbean*, Calgary, University of Calgary Press, 2003, p. 220.

[48] Thandabantu Nhlapo, South African Law Commission, Pretoria, 17th of June 1999.

around South Africa, both in traditional communities and with key NGOs. The intention was not only to ask people for advises on how customary law *ought* to function, but efforts where also made to investigate de facto legal behaviour. Yet, another intention with the deliberations was of an educational character; i.e. to teach traditional leaders liberal ideas.

In 1998 the "Recognition of Customary Marriages Act" was passed by the parliament.[49] The main purpose of the act was to lay down rules for a valid customary marriage and to regulate the registration of customary marriages, and hereby recognise customary marriages (including polygamous marriages) as legal. Additionally, the act also regulates the proprietary consequences of customary marriages and determines the contractual capacity of spouses to litigate and dissolve marriages, with the intention to improve women's position in customary marriages.[50] The current Deputy Minister for Justice and Constitutional Development, Cheryl Gillwald, has thus argued that the act is supposed to operate on two distinct levels: engender respect for the African legal tradition as well as elevate the status of women and children in customary marriages "by improving their position in line with the constitutionally entrenched notion of equality".[51]

However, it is apparent that with this act an attempt was made at riding two horses at the same time, i.e. to try to accommodate both the perspectives of legal centralists and perspectives of legal pluralists. The act refers to customary law as a living law by defining it: "...the customs and usages traditionally observed among the indigenous African peoples of South Africa and which form part of the culture of those peoples". This denotes that it is the law and custom as it is practised on a daily basis that is recognised as customary law. On the other hand, Himonga has called attention to a contravening feature of the law, namely that to achieve the "noble goal" of protecting women's position as equals in customary marriages, the legislator's method was to "substitute customary law with the common law".[52] She argues

[49] Though it did not come into effect before November 2000.

[50] For a more thorough analysis of this Act see for instance: Victoria Bronstein, *Confronting Custom in the New South African State: An Analysis of the Recognition of Customary Marriages Act* in South Africa Journal of Human Rights 2000, Vol 16 Part 3, p. 558.

[51] Cheryl Gillwald, Address to workshop on customary marriages, in 2002, http://www.doj.gov.za/speech/21june2002.htm, p 2.

[52] Chuma Himonga, "Legislative and judicial approaches to the reform of the customary law of marriage and succession in South Africa: Implications for the advancement of women's rights", paper presented at the conference on Advancing Women's Rights' hosted by the women's Legal Centre 30th - 31st October, Cape Town, p. 17.

further that the present customary marriage law is regulated in several important respects by the common law, something which may render this law a "mere paper law and of no use to the people [the women] they are intended to benefit".[53] Apparently, to both respect customary law as it is practised and at the same time make customary law compatible with a scheme of formal rights, is an ethical dilemma that is hard to solve.

Almost ten years into the process, this is the only legal reform of customary law that has been passed by the parliament. Though the process of harmonising customary marriages with the constitution can be perceived as an ideal opportunity to strengthen Shachar's strategy of constructive dialogues between the state and cultural groups, the further process collapsed. Tensions regarding succession, inheritance, property, communal land and women's administrative position in customary courts were not that easily settled.

As the process moved on, it became apparent that not only the problem of two conflicting normative principles and the question of the enforcement capacity influenced the process, there were additional considerations too. Leading figures within the ANC had been determined to enforce the rule of law in South Africa when they came into power. Despite these efforts, the process of making customary courts and customary law compatible with the constitution ran into delays and indecisiveness. To explain this, it is important to look at the third dilemma regarding the process – the strategic dilemma.

3) The strategic dilemma

In Nelson Mandela's speech to the ANC youth in 1990, he employed a strategic argument for making political alliances with traditional leaders in the future democratic South Africa:

> You must remember that it is going to be difficult for our organisation to take root and be strong in the countryside unless we are able to work together with them [traditional leaders] in their respective areas. And those who feel that we have nothing to do with the chiefs do not know the policy of the ANC and have no idea how to strengthen the organisation in the countryside. In fact, the National Party detected this weakness on our part, of not having strong organisation in the countryside. That is how they succeeded in forcing the homeland policy on the masses of our people...[54]

---

[53] *Ibid.*, p.2.
[54] Mandela, *op.cit.*, 1990.

This part of the article intends to reveal that difficulties due to balancing the accommodation of traditional courts and customary law with universal human rights became even more difficult because the ANC had to balance this process with its interests in maintaining its strategic alliance with traditional leaders.

The strategic alliance between the ANC and traditional leaders

ANC's alliance with traditional leaders started in 1988, the year after "progressive chiefs" had formed the self-declared ANC-aligned organisation, the Congress of Traditional Leaders (Contralesa). In a democratic society the ANC needed as much support as possible, and traditional leaders argued that they possessed powers to mobilise votes for ANC.[55] The idea of a "block vote" was put forward in 1990 by Zulu chief, Mhlabunzima Maphumulo: "Once a chief has identified himself with us, then we know that the whole tribe or the majority of the people in that area are now with the progressive forces."[56] Contralesa became an important rural partner in ANC's extensive strategy to isolate the New National Party (NNP) and the Inkatha Freedoms Party's (IFP) support base. Simultaneously, many chiefs started to view Contralesa as the best forum to safeguard their interests under a future ANC led government.

Accordingly, it is interesting to analyse the developments of the process in light of different elections. The alliance between the ANC and Contralesa was in its initial stage prior to the national elections in 1994. In Northern Province, Contralesa managed to recruit quite a considerate number of chiefs. In the elections the ANC won 92 percent of the total vote in this province. Though this result did not verify the theory that traditional leaders could deliver a block vote, the theory was strengthened. Despite this, when the ANC came into power it was, as a radical freedom movement, more interested in transforming the society, than clarifying the role and functions of traditional leaders. Consequently, the ANC paid more attention to reforming customary law, than to clarify what the political function of traditional leaders should be in the future.

---

[55] For further discussion on this subject see Ineke van Kessel and Barbara Oomen, "'One Chief, One vote': The Revival of Traditional Authorities in post-apartheid South Africa", *African Affairs*, Vol. 96, 1997.

[56] Catherine Payze, "The elimination of political opponents: the Maphumulo assination" in Minnaar et al. *Patterns of violence: Case studies of conflicts in Natal*, Pretoria, Human Science Research Council, 1992, p. 247 –258.

The collapse in 1998 of the process of balancing the recognition of customary law with human rights should not be interpreted as a decline in traditional authorities' position in society. It is rather to be understood as a sign of revitalisation. A watershed in the relationship between the ANC and the traditional leaders came with the withdrawing of the Succession Bill from parliament in 1998. In an interview Nhlapo argued that the government rushed this bill since it was "very keen to enact as much fundamental and radical legislation as possible before the elections."[57] The Bill raised sensitive issues, but did not achieve support because it was not properly consulted. As Nhlapo remarked:

> Many chiefs were not opposed to the principles of the Succession Bill. They said; 'The last time we saw that project was when the Law Commission asked for our views on it.' Open-ended questions in the Issue Paper. 'We have just started to take these questions and recommendations to our people, and now all of a sudden we see the discussions have reached the parliament. We do not like that!' So it was withdrawn.[58]

Other political actors had at this point become aware of the tensions between traditional leaders and the ANC. When the United Democratic Party (UDM) was formed in late 1997, it aimed at challenging ANC's alliance by wooing the chiefs. UDM started to talk directly to traditional leaders in their speeches, and pointed at the importance of traditional leaders' involvement in politics. The leader of Contralesa, who also was an ANC Member of Parliament, Patekile Holomisa, announced in Mail & Guardian in October 1997 that he planned to cut ties with the ANC and join the UDM. His organisation "felt betrayed by the ANC government" and now had to consider seeking new political alliances.[59] To save its political alliance with traditional leaders, the ANC had to change its strategy and focus on reforms clarifying the future role and function of traditional leaders.

Clarifying the function of traditional courts

Just in time for the elections in 1999, the government initiated a reform process called "Traditional courts and the judicial function of traditional leaders". The purpose of the reform was to specify the judicial function of

[57] Nhlapo in an interview 1999.
[58] *Ibid.*
[59] Wally Mbhele, *Betrayed chiefs cut ANC ties*, Mail & Guradian, 3rd of October, 1997.

traditional leaders by focusing on practical recommendations, and avoid "too much academic speculation and analysis".[60] For the first time, after three years of reforming customary law, the government discussed the institutional framework in which customary law was going to operate. The government initiated the process of clarifying the function of traditional courts, and workshops were arranged all over the country. Still, after the elections, the processes slowed down. In a media statement by the South African Law Commission (SALC) in January 2003, the government explained that the process was first delayed because the first round of workshop did not include the views of women to a sufficient degree. [61]

The government was still reluctant to give in to traditional leaders claim for power, but prior to the local elections in 2000 a tremendous clash between the government and traditional leaders changed the government's policies again. In the process of drawing municipal boundaries, traditional leaders were bypassed, and many of the new municipality boundaries crossed the boundaries of traditional communities. To settle the dispute, the government tried to include the functions and roles of traditional leaders in a new bill on municipal structures. This created only greater discrepancies since the government, at that time, wanted to keep the formal political and administrative powers of traditional authorities at a minimum by arguing that the role and function of traditional leaders ought to consist of tasks like "facilitate the gathering of firewood" and "coordinate rainmaking ceremonies".[62] Suffice it to say, the traditional leaders did not support this new piece of legislation, and it was withdrawn.

Recent initiated legislation

In 2003, four years after this reform was initiated prior to the national elections in 1999, SALC presented a new report on Traditional Courts and the Judicial Function of Traditional Leaders. The report recommends that customary courts should have full powers of hearing and determining cases in both criminal and civil matters subject to the prescribed limitations. The report suggests that some areas of jurisdiction should be excluded to conform to the Constitution. The exclusions regarding civil cases are related to maintenance, dissolution of

---

[60] South Africa Law Commission, 1999, p. xi.

[61] South Africa Law Commission, "Media statement on its investigation into traditional courts and the Judicial Function of Traditional Leaders (Project 90), 2003, p. 2.

[62] Local government: Municipal Structures Second Amendment Bill 2000.

marriage, interpretation of wills and determination of guardianship over minors. Regarding criminal cases, the report still does not give any clear answers to whether customary courts should have criminal jurisdiction at all. Accordingly, there are still many vacillating questions regarding the jurisdiction of customary courts.

In December 2003 the first act specifying the function and role of traditional authorities was enacted, the Traditional Leadership and Local Governance Framework Act, No. 41 of 2003. In this act traditional councils are granted a far more extensive role than what have been suggested in earlier policy drafts regarding traditional authorities. Traditional authorities are to perform important judicial, developmental and political functions in rural areas. Traditional councils are for instance to participate "in the development of policy and legislation at local level", promote the "ideals of cooperative governance, integrated development planning, sustainable development and service delivery" and "exercise and perform those powers and functions conferred by customary law".[63] The new act implies that the government is prepared to grant the traditional councils legal power to partake in the governance of several functions in the local communities, including judicial, executive and legislative functions.

Rather than being relics of the past, traditional authorities have managed to revitalise their position in South Africa. During the process of balancing policies aimed to accommodate traditional authorities with policies aimed to protect the right to equality for all, traditional leaders have strengthened their internal organisation and voiced their constitutional recognition effectively. Consequently, this article suggests that when analysing people's right to culture, it is always important to emphasise the political games that are played by the different political actors. In South Africa the relationship between traditional leaders and the ANC can be understood as a win-win situation, where the ANC achieves support from local communities, while traditional leaders settle their roles and functions in a democratic society.

[63] Government Gazette, 2003, p. 9.

PART 3: THREE CONSEQUENCES OF THE INCOHERENT PROCESS

The compound of the three dilemmas has made the process of balancing the accommodation of traditional authorities with fundamental human rights very incoherent. It has been a process full of delays and indecisiveness. In this last part of the article I will point out some of consequences this incoherent process has had for how justice operates in local communities in South Africa.

No separation of power

Prior to 1996 different spheres of power were fused into one traditional authority in many rural areas. The authority of traditional leaders was *sui generis*, founded in the land of their forefathers. Traditional leaders were traditional leaders because they were born traditional leaders, and "their powers are deeply rooted in specific cultural landscapes rather than in specific verbal *dicta*, as for instance a constitution".[64] The performance of traditional authorities is a consequence hereof, strongly influenced by the traditional leaders' personal abilities rather than by institutional mechanisms. With the Constitution of 1996, the rule of law was introduced to the South African society. If the rule of law is to function in accordance with its intentions, a separation of power is important. The different branches are then able check each other's powers, in order to prevent the concentration of power in the hands of a few political actors.

Though there have been attempts to eliminate traditional authorities' legislative and executive functions and to minimise and reform their judicial function, they are still involved in all three spheres of power in local communities. In recent draft legislation, limits to traditional authorities' power appear to be diffuse. The power of the traditional leaders is not necessarily all-inclusive, but informally it can still be quite omnipresent. What a traditional leader's role and functions are in a specific community mirrors that leader's personal capacity and the needs of this particular community. Central legislation has not yet managed to transform or clarify the position of traditional leaders. Consequently, illiberal and non-elected traditional leaders are granted a strong position in all spheres of power in some local communities

[64] Thornton, 2003, *op.cit.*, p. 140.

in the South African liberal democracy. Figure 1, below, illustrates the causes and effects of the incoherent process.

No certainty in choice of court

Arguments in favour of acknowledging cultural groups' legal rights are often based on an identity-based perception of jurisdiction, i.e. the idea of coherent communities of people with distinct interests. It is, however, far form clear whether there is a distinct community of people observing customary law in South Africa. Customary law and courts are regarded as preferable for settling some kind of disputes, magistrate courts for others. In a small survey conducted by Barbara Oomen in Sekhukhune Bapedi in 1998-1999, people answered that traditional courts should predominantly concentrate on family matters (71 percent), witchcraft (68 percent), small theft (67 percent), and land issues (62 percent). Only 9 percent stated that traditional courts should try cases of large theft, and 19 percent answered that they should preside over cases regarding maintenance.[65] People are thus not interested in a customary court that provides them justice from the cradle to the grave, but a customary court that settles certain disputes.

A dual law system would in theory be able to provide individuals with an extended access to justice, since it would make it possible to choose between courts. The litigants can take their disputes to the courts in which they feel they have a distinctive advantage, or "come back to the customary courts if they feel that a changed socio-political situation might result in another outcome".[66] Despite the advantages of a dual legal system, dual law systems are vulnerable to local power mechanism and suppressive mechanisms within local communities. Because: who decides which court shall decide the case? If the litigants are to decide, the strongest part will most likely be the one to make the decision, and most certainly not always based on unbiased considerations as to which court it is most likely to ensure that justice prevails.

The most problematic feature, though, is that a choice between courts does not even exist in many communities. Oomen, amongst other, has observed that the magistrate courts frequently send litigants to customary

---

[65] Barbara Oomen, "'Walking in the middle of the road': People's perspectives on the legitimacy of traditional leadership in Sekhukhune", South Africa, paper presented at African Studies Centre, Leiden, 2002, p. 9.

[66] Barbara Oomen, "Legal syncretism in Sekhukhune: Local law and the power of traditional leaders in northern South Africa" in van Binsbergen (ed.) *The Dynamics of power and the rule of law*, African Studies Centre, Leiden, The Netherlands, LIT, 2003, p. 179.

courts, arguing that this is not a case for the magistrate courts. As one magistrate explained to her: "...cases should start at home, then be taken to the chief, and only then to us".[67] If magistrate courts refuse to try certain cases, individuals living in some communities are deprived of their constitutional right to be regarded as equals before the law. In some cases, individuals can not chose to take their case to a state court, which is particularly problematic as often the law applied in customary courts is not in accordance with the fundamental principles entrenched in the constitution.

No certainty in choice of law

As I discussed in the chapter on the ethical dilemma of the process of recognising customary law, customary law does not follow a specified set of codified laws. In a study of local law in Sekhukhune in South Africa, Oomen has explored the relationship between local customary norms and official state legislation.[68] One of her observations is that not just one specific system of law is applied in local courts; the courts draw on a variety of legal and non-legal sources, some refer to state legislation, such as codified customary law, the common law, and the constitution, others to non-legal sources such as common sense, the Bible, development ideology and local tradition. As a consequence, decisions made in some customary courts have elements of negotiation in them; law is made and shaped in the context of local power relations.[69]

Thus power relations are frequently decisive for which opinion will be heard, and decisions often depend on the litigants' position in society. The element of local law creates uncertainty about the application of law in many communities. If decisions are based on whatever source sounds most appealing in the moment, it is impossible to know in advance which set of rules will be applied by the court. The worst-case scenario is therefore that the court's decisions are based on mere whims of traditional leaders. In a system of local law, individuals are not equal before the law, because there is no certainty as to which law will be applied. Figure 1 sums up the causes and the effects of the incoherent process of recognising traditional courts and customary law in South Africa after 1996.

---

[67] *Ibid.*, p. 171.
[68] *Ibid.*, p. 168.
[69] *Ibid.*, p. 177.

Figure 1: Causes and effects of the incoherent process

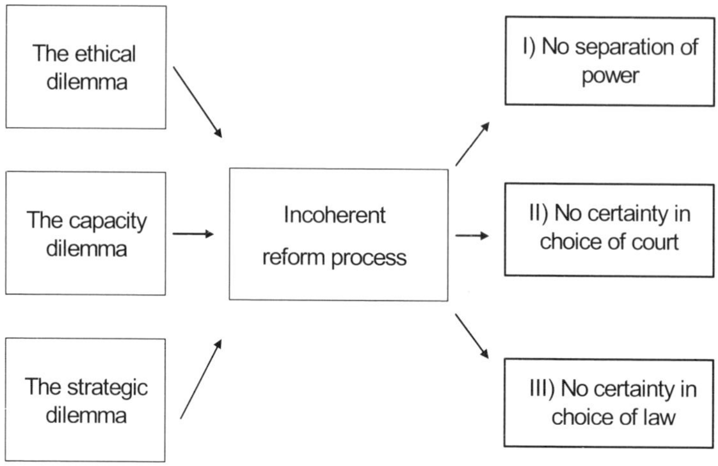

CONCLUSION

In a liberal democracy, equal justice for all is a fundamental right. Accordingly, one should not be surprised that dilemmas arise when a government tries to accommodate the authority of additional legal systems. It has been common to regard the conflict of normative principles, such as the right to equality versus the right to enjoy one's own culture, as insuperable dilemmas. This empirical analysis has revealed that additional dilemmas complicate the process even further. Central governments' lack of capacity to enact national legislation to regulate semi-autonomous fields within their society might create a situation where local law systems are vulnerable to local power relations. As the South African case has shown, governments must be extremely determined if they want to secure the citizens access to equal justice. In order to protect the individuals' constitutional right to be regarded as equals before the law, resources must be made available for the establishment of several state courts in local communities. Additionally, reforms of customary law must be enacted, and traditional courts have to be encouraged to apply these laws in their courts if they want to maintain their status as courts of law.

Such policies require political will. But when the ANC governments have tried to balance their efforts to reconstruct traditional courts and customary law with maintaining their strategic alliance with traditional leaders, they have been hesitant. The governments' attempts to "invade" the existing social fields have thus not achieved the intended purposes, and from a human rights perspective, the outcome is not satisfactory. The incoherent process has not resulted in a clear separation of power in communities were traditional leaders holds a strong position, and certainty in choice of court and choice of law is not existing in many local communities. The idea of allocating judicial power between the state and cultural groups is appealing, but either it must be ensured that the reformed official customary law is applied in these courts, or the right to equal justice will necessitate a double set of legal institutions in all traditional communities. To create this kind of legal system would probably be both too time-consuming and too financial demanding in a society where a judicial reconstruction in rural areas is only a part of the total need for social transformation. Though I am convinced that the ANC has tried to juggle this process with the best intentions, the process illustrates how problematic it is for a government to formally recognise practices that are embedded in different moralities and connected to other spheres of authority than that of the general constitutional imperative.

BIBLIOGRAPHY

African National Congress, 1997. 50th National Conference Resolutions, Post-Conference Documents, *Customary law*, Mafikeng, 16-20 December

Baumeister, Andrea T.,2000. *Liberalism and the Politics of Difference*, Edinburgh, Edinburgh University Press

Bennett, T W,1991. A Sourcebook of African Customary Law for Southern Africa, Cape Town, Juta & Co, Ltd,

Black Administration Act, No 38 of 1927.

Bronstein, Victoria, 2000. "Confronting Custom in the New South African State: An Analysis of the Recognition of Customary Marriages Act" in South African Journal of Human Rights, Vol. 16 Part 3, p. 558.

Burman, Sandra B., 1984. "The Interaction of Legislation relating to Urban Africans and the Laws Regulating Family Relationships" in T. W. Bennett et al., *Urban Black Law*, Cape Town, JUTA & Co, Ltd

Chanock, Martin,

1985. *Law, Custom and Social Order. The colonial experience in Malawi and Zambia*, Cambridge, Cambridge University Press,

1991. "Law, State and Culture: Thinking About Customary Law After Apartheid", South Africa, Acta Juridica

Constitution of the Republic of South Africa, Act 108 of 1996.

Department of Provincial and Local Affairs. A Discussion Document towards a White Paper on Traditional Leadership and Institutions, 11 April 2000.

Electoral Institute of Southern Africa: 1994, 1995/96, 1999 and 2000 election results.

Fitzpatrick, Peter, 1984. "Law and Societies", *Osgoode Hall Journal*, Vol. 22

Gillwald, Cheryl, 2002. Address to workshop on customary marriages, http://www.doj.gov.za/speech/21june2002.htm.

Himonga, Chuma, "Legislative and judicial approaches to the reform of the customary law of marriage and succession in South Africa: Implications for the advancement of women's rights", paper presented at the conference on Advancing Women's Rights' hosted by the women's Legal Centre 30th - 31st October, Cape Town.

Huges, Graham, 2003. "Concept of Law" in Philip P. Wiener (ed.) *The Dictionary of the History of Ideas*, Vol. 3., New York, Charles Scribner's Sons

van Kessel, Ineke and Barbara Oomen, 1997. "'One Chief, One vote': The Revival of Traditional Authorities in post-apartheid South Africa", *African Affairs*, 96

Kymlicka, Will, 1996. "Three forms of Group-Differentiated Citizenship in Canada" in Benhabib (ed.), *Democracy and Difference, Contesting the Boundaries of the political*, New Jersey, Princeton University Press

Local Government: Cross-boundary Municipalities Act No. 29 of 2000.

Mandela, Nelson, 1990. *Address to the youth*, Official Statement, KaNyamazane, 13th April

Mbhele, Wally, 1997. "Betrayed chiefs cut ANC ties", *The Mail & Guardian*, the 3rd of October

Moore, Sally Falk, 1978. *Law as Process*, London, Routledge & Kegan Paul

Ntsebeza, Lungisile, 2003. "Traditional Authorities, Local Government and Land Rights", in I. Ray and P.S. Reddy (eds.) *Grassroots Governance? Chiefs in Africa and the Afro-Caribbean*, Calgary, University of Calgary Press

Oomen, Barbara,

> 2002. "'Walking in the middle of the road': People's perspectives on the legitimacy of traditional leadership in Sekhukhune", South Africa, paper presented at African Studies Centre, Leiden
>
> 2003. "Legal syncretism in Sekhukhune: Local law and the power of traditional leaders in northern South Africa" in van Binsbergen (ed.) *The Dynamics of power and the rule of law*, African Studies Centre, Leiden, The Netherlands, LIT

Payze, Catherine, 1992. "The elimination of political opponents: the Maphumulo assassination" in Minnaar et al., *Patterns of violence: case studies of conflicts in Natal*, Pretoria, Human Science Research Council

Penal Reform International, 2000. *Access to justice in sub-Saharan Africa: The role of traditional and informal justice systems*, London, Astron Printers

Reiss, H. (ed.), 1970. *Kant's Political Writings*, Cambridge, Cambridge University Press

Republic of South Africa, 2003. *Traditional leadership and governance framework Bill,* Government Gazette

Republic of South Africa, 2003. *Traditional Leadership and Local Governance Framework Act, No. 41 of 2003.*

Sandel, Michael, 1992. "The Procedural Republic", in S. Avinieri & A. de-Shalit (eds.), *Communitarians and Individualism*, Oxford, Oxford University Press

Schaumburg-Müller, Sten, 2002. "Pursuing Theory in Law on Loose Ground", in *Retfærd* no 99

Shachar, Ayelet, *Multicultural Jurisdictions – Cultural Differences and Women's Rights*, Cambridge, Cambridge University press, 2001.

Sheleff, Leon, 2000. *The Future of Tradition: Customary law, common law and legal pluralism,* London, Frank Cass

South African Law Commission,

1997. *Customary Marriages*, Discussion paper 74, Project 90

1998. *Conflicts of Law*, Discussion paper 76, Project 90

1996. "Harmonisation of common law and Indigenous law", *Annual Report*, Project 90

2003. *Media statement on its investigation into traditional courts and the Judicial Function of Traditional Leaders, Project 90*

1999. *Traditional courts and the judicial function of traditional leaders*, Discussion paper 82, Project 90

2003. *Report on traditional courts and the judicial function of traditional leaders*, Project 90

1998. *Succession in Customary Law*, Project 90, Issue Paper 12

Spitz, Richard and Matthew Chaskalson, 2000. The Politics of Transition – a hidden history of South Africa's negotiated settlement, Oxford, Hart Publishing

Taylor, Charles, 1994. "The Politics of Recognition" in Amy Gutman (ed.), *Multiculturalism*, New Jersey, Princeton University Press, Princeton

Thornton, Robert, 2003. "Chiefs: Power in a Political Wilderness" in I. Ray and P.S. Reddy (eds.) *Grassroots Governance? Chiefs in Africa and the Afro-Caribbean*, Calgary, University of Calgary Press

Wilson, Richard A., 2000. "Reconciliation and Revenge in Post-Apartheid South Africa: Rethinking Legal Pluralism and Human Rights", *Current Anthropology*, Vol. 41

Race and Gender Discrimination in a Socio-legal Perspective: the Experience of Chinese Indonesian Women in Indonesia*

Sulistyowati Irianto

* I wish to thank Karenina Susilo, who helped me transform my English into a readable language: I am very grateful.

INTRODUCTION

The goal of this paper is to examine how Indonesian national law addresses humanity, justice and equality in the context of pluralism. It will also examine how Indonesian law addresses these matters in the context of ratified international and national legal instruments. By using critical analysis to confirm normative legal substance and what actually happens I will examine how the law may be observed against its political, economical, cultural, and historical background. This paper focuses on discrimination experienced by the ethnic Chinese in Indonesia as an illustration. The experience of ethnic Chinese women is a portrait of multi-dimensional discrimination based on race, religion and gender. This paper will examine the discourse at both the academic and practical or real levels.

Today, human rights have developed as a main focus of discourse at both an academic level and what I have described as the practical or real level. Human rights have become a significant phenomenon in society in many parts of the world. Ethnic, political economic and religious conflict, is increasing. Violence, inequality and injustice, are still a feature of life all around the world, including in Indonesia. Despite the existence of various international legal instruments, the extensive degradation of human rights continues.

INDONESIAN SOCIETY IN A PLURALISTIC CONTEXT

Indonesia is an excellent example of a complicated pluralistic society. The country is an archipelago that consists of 13.000 islands,[1] 300 ethnic groups, 727 languages, and has a total population of 210 millions. In addition, Indonesians practice several religions[2] and beliefs, as well as living in a broad spectrum of social and economic conditions. The aspiration towards a national

[1] The biggest of the 13.000 islands are Sumatra, Java, Kalimantan, Sulawesi, and Papua.

[2] Formally, there are five religions recongnized by the government: Islam, Catholic, Protestant, Buddhism, and Hindu. Unofficially, there are more minority religions spread all over the country, including Confucianism and animism. Some problems arise from that approach. For example, a marriage of a Confucianist couple may not be registered because of statutory regulations. Normatively, such marriage is considered as unlawful, and children resulting from the marriage are regarded as illegitimate children and are not granted a certificate of birth. Lack of a birth certificate complicates the process of entering school.

spirit was declared by the Youth Congress held in Batavia,[3] October 28th, 1928, long before the independence of Indonesia was actually proclaimed. It was at this congress that groups of young people came from various regions in the archipelago and declared the existence of a single nation, one motherland with one national languange *(bahasa Indonesia)*.

After 350 years of Dutch occupation and 3 years of Japanese occupation, Indonesia declared its dependence on August 17th, 1945. Soekarno and Mohammad Hatta made the declaration of independence. Later, Soekarno became the first President of Indonesia serving until 1965. Mohammad Hatta served as the Vice President until 1956. The Soekarno government was known as 'The Old Order'.

Soekarno was responsible for the Indonesian doctrine, *Bhineka Tunggal Ika,* a Sanskrit motto meaning "Unity in Diversity". Meanwhile, Mohammad Yamin, also considered a founding father,[4] promoted Indonesia's official territory as those regions that the Dutch formerly occupied.

Soekarno and Mohammad Yamin invented *Pancasila* as the philosophy of the state with five basic principles. They are: (1) Belief in One Supreme God Almighty, (2) Justice and civilized humanity, (3) The unity of Indonesia, (4) Democracy led by the wisdom of deliberation among representatives, and (5) Social justice for all. *Pancasila* was established as the basis for the Indonesian way of life. These principles are enshrined in the preamble of our Constitution, known as the 1945 Constitution. *Pancasila* is thus considered as basic law, the highest source of law for any kind of Indonesian laws. The preamble cannot to be amended for any reason. The other part of the Constitution may be amended.[5]

Professor Dr. Harsya Bachtiar once warned that beside a big nation called Indonesia, there were smaller nations called 'old nations'. These old nations were composed of the ethnic groups that were scattered around and formed a

---

[3] Now Jakarta, the capital city of Indonesia.

[4] Persons who are considered as our founding fathers among others are: Soekarno, Mohammad Hatta, Soepomo, Mohammand Yamin. They played very important roles by formulating legal doctrines of Indonesia, *Pancasila, Bhineka Tunggal Ika,* and the 1945 Constitution.

[5] The first amandment of the Indonesian 1945 Constitution was made in the year 2002 – 2003, after the Soeharto's era.

mosaic called Indonesia. Their recognition is central to an understanding of the social legal and historical context of Indonesia.[6]

By establishing the doctrine *Bhineka Tunggal Ika* (Unity in Diversity), the spirit of multiculturalism and diversity was established. This diversity is upheld widely through rights to promote different cultures, including custom (local law, customary law), called *adat*.[7] The doctrine of Unity in Diversity, in accordance with a multiculturalist ideology, conceives and confirms Indonesia as a mosaic.

Multiculturalism itself is an ideology that recognizes and appreciates not only diversity, but also upholds and respects differences in race, religion, ethnic origin, language and political opinion. Multiculturalism, therefore, is closely related to democracy, justice, and equality in the pluralist context. Academic discourse regarding multiculturalism has long existed: one of the pst-structuralists, van Velzen, states that unique differences are normal and not a deviance. It is the rule rather than the exception and should be accepted and respected.[8]

In 1965 the Soekarno government collapsed and Soeharto became the second President of Indonesia. His government was known as The New Order. Most of the 32-year autocratic New Order regime was characterized by on the one hand high economic growth and development and on the other hand by serious corruption at all levels of bureaucracy, together with nepotism and a lack of respect for humanity. To maintain his power, Soeharto and his followers declared the Unity of Indonesia as the highest priority in their policies. This so-called priority, however, went too far. Based on the mantra of a unified Indonesia, the government started to deny the old nations their local rights, including property and human right. Indonesians lived in an artificially imposed unity. The imposition of this imagined community contributed to the decay of human rights as traditional patterns of rights within ethnic groups fell into disuse.

---

[6] Harsya Bachtiar, "Masalah Integrasi Nasional" [Issue on National Integration], Jakarta, Prisma Journal, 8 August, 1976.

[7] *Adat* is a term introduced by Schnouck Hurgronje, meaning customary law in ethnic groups, religion and the recognition of local judge's decisions.

[8] J. van Velzen, "The Extended Case Method and Situational Analysis", in A.L. Epstein (ed.), *The Craft of Social Anthropology*, London, Tavistock, 1967.

The efforts to unite Indonesia were legitimated by the Village Governance Act No. 5/1979. Before the Dutch colonization, local people in the lowest political unit in the village had their own local administration. This lowest administration was closely linked to their cultures, especially their kinship system. The headman or the chief usually administered it. He managed the local administrative system according to *adat* law, a term introduced by the Dutch scholar Schnouck Hurgronye. People consciously observed the *adat* law as guidance for their behaviour. *Adat* mirrored the view of life of indigenous Indonesians, and the content was specifically local. In *adat,* religious values varied by region.[9] Being culturally based, every region had its own unique administration. Generally, native administration also functioned as a dispute-settlement institution.

As soon as the Village Governance Act was enacted, the original local leaderships were dismissed. All local administration in Indonesia was required to be uniform and tended to imitate the Javanese style. Javanese administration is well structured with a village head, secretary, treasurer, and various other individuals with responsibility for specific areas like irrigation, security, social welfare, religious affairs. The biggest ethnic group in Indonesia are Javanese, and Java island is also considered as the centre of civilization, and the land is very productive because of its fertile soil. Since Dutch times, the centre of government has always been located in Java island. However, because of heterogeneity of cultures and disparity in development across the archipelago, Javanese-style governance was often inappropriate for other parts of the country. The Village Governance Act left little or no space for the old nations to exist, let alone a mosaic called Indonesia.

There were many other repressive policies during the time of the Soeharto regime that targeted "unfavourable" groups. These included Indonesian - Chinese. They were not allowed to speak their own language or observe their religion and traditions. They were denied their basic rights as Indonesian

[9] Another Dutch scholar, van Vollenhoven, claims 19 different adat law areas: (1) Aceh, (2) Gayo-Alas and Batak, (3) Nias and Batu, (4) Minangkabau, (6) South Sumatra, (6) Malay, (7) Bangka anda Biliton, (8) Borneo, (9) Minahasa, (10) Gorontalo, (11) Toraja, (12) South Celebes, (13) Ternate archipelago, (14) Ambon and Moluccas, (15) New Guinea, (16) Timor, Bali and Lombok, (17) Central and East Java, (18) Surakarta and Yogyakarta, and (19) West Java. Ihromi, Tapi Omas and Achie Luhulima, "Sociolegal Status of Women in Selected DMC's. Country Study: Indonesia, Final Report", Jakarta, Insan Harapan Sejahtera, Social Science Research and Consultancy, 1997.

citizens. There was however a small group of ethnic Chinese who in exchange for financial favours received unprecedented privilege in the economy and, consequently, enjoyed wealth and luxuries. These privileged Chinese-Indonesian citizens built up and controlled the majority of Indonesia's private sector and industry. Together with the political elite, they became Soeharto's 'cronies.'

Acute corruption during Soeharto's government spun out of control and became the catalyst for his downfall in May 1998. Corruption had led to economic and social disaster increasing the gap between the 'haves' and the 'have nots'. The 'reformation movements' surfaced. These were started by disaffected college students who articulated the dissatisfaction and frustration of Indonesians and finally brought down Soeharto's New Order. Indonesians had apparently developed a taste for freedom after 32 years of Soeharto's iron-fist, autocratic regime.

The reformation movement and post Soeharto era idealized the new Indonesia based on democratic principles and civil society. Unfortunately, successive governments have not acted to eradicate corruption, nepotism, and violence all of which existed during the time of the new governments of Bj. Habibie, Abdurrahman Wahid, and Megawati Soekarnoputri. The path towards a new Indonesia became unclear.

If democracy and civil society are the necessary elements for a new and ideal nation, a break with the current pattern of thinking is required via the dissemination of understanding and the recognition of human rights principles. In a pluralistic society, it is important to recognize multiculturalism not merely as an academic exercise but as a practical every day necessity.

INDONESIAN LEGAL INSTRUMENTS ON HUMAN RIGHTS ISSUES

This section of the paper will address how Indonesian legal instruments regulate human rights issues in the context of the prohibition of discrimination based on race and gender.

A good starting point may be to reflect on the following section from the children's version of the Human Rights Declaration:

> Every one of you should treat the other as sibling, brothers and sisters. It is not what race you come from. It is not whether you are a girl or a boy. It is not what language you speak or what religion you belief in, it is not your political view, what country are you from, or who your family is. It is not from what parts of the world you are from, or whether your country is a Kingdom or a Republic. This right and freedom belong to every one of you.[10]

Since 1948, the Universal Declaration of Human Rights has in effect asked all citizens of the world to reflect on their identities against the background of different ethnicities, races, religions colour and social groups. The social destruction caused by World War II forced nations to acknowledge and respect diversity and differences amongst humans. As the first international instrument of human rights, the declaration has evolved and become the compass to point to equality and justice regardless of the differences between people. The declaration has become a morally binding agreement for every nation and individual to respect and uphold it, and as a member of the United Nations, Indonesia acknowledges the Declaration of Human Rights 1948.

In 1945 the Indonesian Constitution was passed which assures human rights for every citizen. The Constitution provides that every citizen enjoys equal rights and obligations in the fields of education, law, political participation and employment.

Fifty years later, the amendment of the national constitution in 2003 ensures human rights for all. Additionally, Indonesia's own Human Rights Act 39/1999 and Human Rights Judicial Act 26/2000 affirm the state's responsibility to protect the human rights of Indonesian citizens. Both of these Acts were enacted shortly after the departure of Soeharto. His regime was marked by many human rights violation cases, often because he incarcerated his political opponents who also sometimes went 'missing'. It was against this background that the Human Rights Act and Human Rights Judicial Act was enacted.

---

[10] Ruth Totcha and Octavia Roth, Deklarasi Hak-Hak Asasi Manusia Sedunia: Sebuah Adaptasi Untuk Kanak-Kanak [Declaration of Human Rights: An Adaptation for Children], Jakarta, Yayasan Obor, Indonesia, 1995.

THE PROHIBITION OF RACE DISCRIMINATION

The essential international legal instrument of prohibition on race discrimination is the International Convention on the Elimination of all Forms of Racial Discrimination. It was adopted by the United Nation in 1965 and entered into force in 1969.

According to the first article of this convention, race discrimination is defined as:

> any distinction, exclusion, restriction or preference based on race, colour, descent, or national or ethnic origin which has the purpose or effect of nullifying or impairing the recognition, enjoyment or exercise, on an equal footing, of human rights and fundamental freedoms in the political, economic, social, cultural or any other field of public life.

Indonesia ratified this international legal instrument in 2003. The now more than 150 nations that have also ratified it have thus agreed to implement the principles set forth in the convention. For that purpose, they adopt the measures required for the elimination of discrimination in all its forms and manifestations. Chris Sidoti, an Australian human rights expert, states that once a convention is ratified, the state parties commit themselves to make necessary amendments to their national constitutions and to adopt the measures required for the elimination of race discrimination in all its forms and manifestations. It includes sanctions where appropriate to prevent ongoing race discrimination. The state parties also agree to establish legal protections and to ensure through public institutions the effective protection against any act of racial discrimination.[11]

THE PROHIBITION OF GENDER DISCRIMINATION

The main international conventions that prohibit discrimination based on gender include the Convention on Political Rights to Women, ratified by Act

[11] Chris Sidoti, Chris, *Memperkenalkan Empat Buah Dokumen Hak Asasi Manusia Internasional Utama, yang Akan Diratifikasi oleh Pemerintah Republik Indonesia, dalam Komnas HAM, Hak Asasi Manusia, Tanggung Jawab Negara, Peran Institusi Nasional dan Masyarakat*, Jakarta, Komnas HAM, 1999, [Introducing the Four Main International Human Rights Documents Which Will Be Ratified by Indonesian Government. Human Rights, State Responsibility, The Role of National Institution and Society], Jakarta, National Comission on Human Rights, 1999.

no. 68 of 1958, and the Convention on the Elimination of All Forms of Discrimination Against Women (CEDAW), ratified by Act no. 7 of 1984. Reservation was made on article 29 pertaining to any dispute between two or more state parties concerning the interpretation or application of the Convention, which could be referred to the International Court of Justice.

When adopting the conventions, the states are supposed to repeal all national penal provisions, which constitute discrimination against women. They have the obligation to take all appropriate measures, including legislation, to modify or abolish existing laws, regulations, customs and practices that constitute discrimination against women.

The CEDAW, art. 1, defines discrimination as:

> any distinction, exclusion or restriction made on the basis of sex which has the effect or purpose of impairing or nullifying the recognition, enjoyment or exercise by women, irrespective of their marital status, on a basis of equality of men and women, of human rights and fundamental freedoms in the political, economic, social, cultural, civil or any other field.

The ratification of the conventions is a demonstration of the political goodwill of the Indonesian government to realize one of the national objectives set out in paragraph four of the preamble of the 1945 Constitution. The paragraph stipulates that Indonesia takes part in the creation of a World order based on independence, eternal peace and social justice. The ratification of these conventions is also positive proof of international solidarity to eliminate all forms of discrimination against women.[12]

Political will is reflected in the consideration of Act no.7 of 1984 as follows:

a. Every citizen has equal status. Any kind of the discrimination toward women has to be eliminated and is against the ideology of the state, Pancasila and the Constitution.

c. The measurement in the Convention above is in line with the ideology of the state, the Constitution and the national legislation.

---

[12] Ihromi and Luhulima, 1997, *op.cit.*, p 57.

How extensively has legislation in Indonesia adopted the conventions mentioned above? In principle, no provision of Indonesian legislation should conflict with the the conventions.

Long before the CEDAW was ratified, the principle of gender equality was implicitly embodied in Article 27 of the Indonesian 1945 Constitution:

> All citizens have equal status before the law and in government and are obliged to uphold them without exemption;
> Every citizen has the right to employment and conditions of life commensurate with human dignity.

It was re-enacted in the second Amendment of the 2003 National Constitution which states:

> Art. 28a: "Every citizen has the rights to live and has the rights to uphold the living."
>
> Art. 28i: "Every citizen has the rights to free from the discrimination regardless of their status and has the rights to be protected from any discriminatory act ."

In the Indonesian context, a problem arises in implementing international conventions. The problem is this: does ratification have both legal as well as moral effect? Opinions vary. One says that ratification by itself is insufficient to give legal effect without incorporation into national law. Significant numbers of law enforcers agree with this opinion. However, another opinion is that once the convention is ratified, it is legally binding and there is no need for any further formal incorporation. Mulya Lubis, a human rights expert agrees with this opinion. Erna Sofwan Sjukrie, the outgoing Supreme Court Judge, has stated that once the international convention is ratified it becomes immediately applicable and moreover has a higher position in comparison to any other law. As an example, article 11 of the CEDAW relates to discrimination in the workplace and has been utilized in a case where a woman worker was pensioned at the age of 40. According to the Manpower Act no. 14/1969, a worker has right to get pension when he/she is 55 years old. The lawyer refered to article 11 of the CEDAW in her defense, and won the case. So far, this seems to be the only case in which CEDAW has been used in an Indonesian court.

The existence and implementation of various acts and laws in this country indicates that normatively we have substantial legal instruments regarding human rights. These various acts and laws seem to accommodate international conventions, declarations, and agreements. Legal anthropologists view this as a demonstration of legal pluralism. Recent literature defines legal pluralism by reference to interdependency and interelated co-existence among international, national, and local law.[13]

It seems that the legal system in Indonesia, especially the substance of normative law, is already based on the principle of justice and equality. The law prohibits any kind of discrimination. However, in reality discrimination occurs widely. Several legal anthropologists criticize the lack of effectiveness of law in daily life. Law enforcement depends on winning the support and interest of prominent and powerful people who rule the nation. Legislation does not always translate into the creation of justice and equality. This is particularly the case against the background of a lack of accountablilty of government and those involved in the administration of the law, with the result that the supremacy and status of law is diminished.

The failure of the law to be effective may occur for many reasons but one hypothesis is that pluralism has been systematically denied during the New Order Era.[14]

HUMAN RIGHTS AS PRACTICAL ISSUES IN INDONESIA

Millions of Indonesian citizens experience some form of discrimination, including civil, political, economic, social and cultural discrimination. The discrimination can be categorized into three, each addresses specific groups of people: (1) political discrimination caused by political events: the individuals affected tend to be political opponents (mainly communists) of government, (2) discrimination against minorities (for example, the Indonesian-Chinese), (3) discrimination against groups of indigenous people and minority religious groups in society.

---

[13] Kebet von Benda-Beckmann, "The Context of Law," a paper presented to the XIIIth International Congress, Legal Pluralism and Unofficial Law in Social, Economic and Political Development, hosted by the Commission on Folk Law and Legal Pluralism, Chiang Mai, 7-10 April, 2002.

[14]Sukowaluyo Mintoraharjo, "Rekonsiliasi Tanpa Diskriminasi" [Reconciliation Without Discrimination], Newspaper Kompas, 1 December 2003.

The Presidential Instruction issued on January 27th, 1979 is an example of discrimination against minority religious groups. Although a significant number of Indonesian – Chinese practice Confucianism, the Instruction officially declares that Confucianism is not recognized legally as a religion. In Indonesia Confucianism is perceived to be a religion by some groups mainly among the Chinese community. There are cases where Confucian couples have sued because a Marriage Registrar has refused to register their marriages. The Supreme Court [15] has become involved. Usually couples faced with this problem, voluntarily agree to be recognized as Budhist and registered under the Budhism category of people in the Civil Registry rather than having difficulty in registering their marriage.

Discrimination in Indonesia often extends beyond losing civil and political rights, such as loosing the right to vote or the right to hold a public office. Sometimes, it also means losing social status. For example, a person may encounter difficulties in entering the military, public office positions, or certain organizations if someone among his/her family member is considered as a political enemy (mainly Communist) by the authorities. This form of discrimination violates the United Nation Covenant on economic, social, and cultural rights of 1966. Unfortunately, the Indonesian government tolerates such discrimination.

To further demonstrate the discrepancy between theoretical legal rights and their actual implementation, it is revealing to show real examples of multi-dimension discrimination. One of the most obvious examples is discrimination experienced by Chinese-Indonesian women. Their cases reflect discrimination not only based on race, but on religion and gender as well.

ETHNIC CHINESE IN INDONESIA

In 1854, during Dutch colonization in Indonesia, the Dutch Indisch Government introduced a policy that separated the population into three

[15] A case occurred in Surabaya (East Java) when a Confucian couple wanted to marry. The local Civil Registry refused to register their marriage as they insisted that they were Confucian believers. They took their complaint to the Supreme Court. Finally, March 30th, 2000 judges of the Supreme Court declared that they were not in a position to judge whether the Confucianism was a religion or not, but they ordered the local Civil Registry to register the marriage of the couple.

different categories. According to Article 163 of the *Indische Staatsregeling* (IS), the categories were: Europeans, Foreign Orientals, and Natives. The first group comprised of people of Dutch and European origin. Foreign Orientals group were defined by the law as everyone else, except native Indonesians, who were not of Dutch or other European origin. This usually meant Chinese, Arabs, Indians and Pakistanis. The Native group consisted of indigenous Indonesians, except those very few who were able to acquire European status by way of specific and rarely available legal provision.

In 1925, further distinction differentiated Chinese Orientals and non-Chinese Orientals within the Foreign Oriental groups. At certain points, both sub-groups were subject to different regulations. For example, Chinese Orientals were subject to almost the entire Western Civil Code enacted for Europeans. Non-Chinese Orientals were also subject to the Western Civil Law except when it related to Family Law, when they were subject to unwritten Customary Law.[16]

At that time, the ethnic Chinese had a higher rank than the Natives. Their talents in trading and their capacity in economic matters helped their position. The Dutch extended some privileges to them confirming on them citizenship of the scond rank. Enjoying this high status meant that the Chinese were expected to play the important role of mediator or middle man between the Dutch and the Natives. This situation sometimes initiated jealousy among the Natives, and it sparked conflicts and racially motivated incidents.

At the same time, the Dutch profited from the Chinese by way of their aptitude for trading and making money. This caused anger among the Chinese. The economic exploitation of both Chinese and the Natives by the Dutch sometimes created alliances between the two groups. Sometimes they stood up together opposing Dutch treatment and policies. The Dutch sought by their policies to divide the Chinese and the Natives, their tactic was divide and rule.

The following excerpt from a story written by Benny Setiono reflects on the social condition of Chinese in Indonesia during the Colonial period:[17]

---

[16] Ihromi and Luhulima, 1997, *op.cit.*, p. 7.

[17] Benny Setiono, "Kehancuran dan Kebangkitan Martabat/ Jati Diri Etnis Tionghoa ", [Destroying and Ressurection of the Dignity of Ethnic Chinese], a paper presented in the seminar

Batavia was established by Jan Pieterzoon Coen in 1619. He encouraged the Chinese to come to Batavia so they could trade. He insisted that Chinese junks had to sail into atavia instead of Banten. It was said that Dutch sailors often robbed the junks and kidnapped Chinese men, women and children and forcing them to build Batavia. The captives could only win their freedom by hard work in the service of their captors

There was a massacre of Chinese in 1740. The frequent arrivals of Chinese migrants to Batavia scared the Dutch colonial. Governor General Adriaan Valckenier who as a result issued a regulation of "permissiebriefje" authorizing people "to kill or to arrest" the Chinese. Whether or not they had resident permits Chinese could be arrested and exiled to Ceylon or Tanjung Harapan.

Resistance to the Dutch did however occur by an alliance between the Chinese and the *Inlanders* (Natives). They stood together and fought under Paku Buwono II and the King of Java to attack the Dutch in Semarang. In the Diponegoro War (1825-1830) a considerable number of Chinese voluntarily joined the army to defeat the Dutch.

The Dutch tried to implement a policy of divide and rule as between the Chinese and the Natives.This was the start of a segregation policy.. The Chinese were obliged to stay together in a ghetto which later on became known as China Town. A permit was required for a Chinese in order to leave the ghetto. Prominent Chinese were given authority to collect toll, bridges, and markets taxes; they were also given permission to operate gambling and prostitution. The grantingof these favours caused friction and resentment between the Natives and the Chinese who benefited from them.

The Dutch segregation policy reached a culmination point in 1854, with the *Indisch Staatsregeling* which was specifically aimed at controlling the Chinese. When a Chinese faced the criminal law, in minor matters he/she was arraigned before a police court with no right of appeal to a higher court, and before the *landraad* native court for more significant mattersThe Chinese Consul General was prevented from offering assistance with the result that Chinese accused enjoyed very little protection.

---

on "The Role of Ethnic Chinese in the Long of Indonesian's History", hosted by Perhimpunan Inti and Newspaper Suara Pembaharuan, 9th November, 2002.

These events were forerunners of repressive policies towards Chinese-Indonesians. Benny Setiono describes these policies as follows: [18]

> "Restrictions were placed on the Chinese and they suffered extensive discriminationThese affected land, segregation within the Tionghoa Totok (the first generation who migrated to Indonesia) and the Peranakan (the second generation who were born in Indonesia,.Some Chinese were forced to attend Dutch schools thereby creating internal divisions within the Chinese community. This was exacerbated by law which enabled some bu tnot all Chinese to obtain equal status with Europeans: inorder to win this they had to submit to military service and declare themselves no longer members of the Chinese community."

Benny Setiono followed the status of the Chinese-Indonesians during the independence period (around the Soekarno Era). During the revolution, [19] antipathy against the Chinese manifested itself in Java and North Sumatra. Thousands of houses were burnt and hundreds of Chinese were killed. Chinese women were raped in West Java, Middle Java and East Java. The concept "Pejoratif Cina"[20] was developed to insult the Chinese community. However, in 1928 in order to honour Chinese nationalists whose brilliant ideas were adopted by the leaders of the Indonesians, and to show gratitude to the media circle called Melayu-Tionghoa, the concept "Cina" was transformed into "Tionghoa".[21]

However, the restrictions enacted by government to limit Chinese-Indonesians' activities continued. The PP 10 of 1955 (Government Regulation) restricted Chinese-Indonesians involvement economically at the district level. They had no right to become involved in transport, storage, or rice-hulling. However, they were still allowed to maintain their own language and celebrate the Chinese traditions. The relationship between the Chinese and the Natives was relatively harmonious at that time, mainly because the they had relatively equal access to education and economic opportunities.

---

[18] Benny Setiono, *op. cit.,* p. 10.

[19] The end of the Dutch colonial era is called the revolution era, because of the opposition of the Indonesian Movement.

[20] This refers to the term "*Cina Kunciran*". After Manchu conquest of China, the top ranks of Chinese as well as the Chinese in general were ordered to wear an outfit with both ends of cloth embroiderd like a saddle. When they knelt down with their plaited pony tail, they looked exactly like a horse. Benny Setiono, *op. cit.*, p. 13.

[21] *Op. cit .,* p. 18.

The situation, however, took a turn for the worse during the New Order Era under President Soeharto. Racial discrimination became a time bomb that could quickly and easily explode in the context of social disadvantage. The elite maintained a status quo to accommodate their hidden agenda. On the pretext of securing stability and safety Chinese-Indonesians were victimised.

Extermination of those who were suspected of being involved in the Indonesian Communist Party produced thousands of ethnic Chinese victims. They were caught and were killed.[22] Chinese schools were banned and were taken over by the military. Diplomatic ties between China and Indonesia were suspended. There was little protection for those who had Chinese citizenship and were living in Indonesia. An instruction from the Presidium Kabinet Ampera no. 127/U/Kep 12/1966 stated that the Chinese were obliged to change their names to Indonesian ones, and they were also banned from observing Chinese traditions and celebrations.

Limited business activity was all they were allowed to do. They were banned from being involved in politics and in state decision making. The government selected a chosen few Chinese as business partners to accelerate economic growth, but this increased disunity. The Chinese community was often blamed for riots that took place. Relations between Chinese-Indonesians and the native Indonesians were fatally damaged. Riots against Chinese occurred in Medan, Makasar, West Java, and East Java.

During this period, the government emphasized assimilation of Chinese-Indonesians into society. The Decree of the Temporary People's Consultative Assembly[23] no. III/MPRS/1966, article 4, includes the assimilation policy. From an anthropological view, assimilation encourages a certain ethnic group to join a larger community by restricting them from practicing their own culture and forcing them to adopt the values of the larger group. Soeharto's government forbade the Chinese to use their language,[24] religion, and tradition. This policy, however, was not successful.

---

[22] This was at the time of the Cultural Revolution lead by Mao Zedong.

[23] The name of the People's Constultative Assembly at that time was the Temporary People's Consultative Assembly.

[24] They had to use the national language, Indonesian (*bahasa Indonesia*). The Youth Congress held in Batavia, October 28th, 1928 declared the importance of one language: *bahasa Indonesia*.

Although extremely difficult, it was possible for a member of the European or Foreign Oriental group to be declared assimilated into the Native group by the court. The main criteria cited by courts were: conversion to the Islamic faith, long residence in an Indonesian village (at least 5 years), adoption of an Indonesian name, and preference for the use of the national Indonesian language.[25]

THE EXPERIENCE OF ETHNIC CHINESE-INDONESIAN WOMEN

Chinese-Indonesian women often experience the worst discrimination. This seems to flow from a patriarchal concept of society with women regarded as belonging to men and having a subordinate position to that of men who have power. In armed conflicts, one of the strategies to conquer a group (often perceived as men) is to take away or destroy their belongings (their women). This is done to show that they do not have power to protect them. This results in many cases of violence against women in war and in other areas of conflict.

After 32 years of autocratic government, Soeharto resigned immediately following a city-wide riot in Jakarta. During the two-day riot on May 13th and 14th, 1998, not only were shops and buildings severely damaged or destroyed and looted, but also incredibly cruel sexual harassment against Chinese-Indonesian women happened. Race and gender discrimination against Chinese reached a culmination point during the New Order regime. During this period, the Chinese population in Indonesia was 2,8 per cent or less than 6 million people.[26] Interaction between Chinese and Indonesians took place in an atmosphere highly charged with prejudice, stereotypical characterization was common at all levels of society so that Chinese were frequently described as being 'aggressive', 'hard working', 'competitive', 'individualisict', 'animals' and 'superstitious'.

---

[25] Ihromi and Luhulima, 1997, *op.cit.,* p.10.

[26] See Mely G. Tan, "The Social and Cultural Dimension of Gender-based Violence", a paper presented to the International Symposium on "Rebuild the Diversity Indonesia: Step Toward Multiculturalism", hosted by Jurnal Antropologi Indonesia and University of Udayana, Bali, 19-20 July, 2002.

The National Commission on Violence Against Women has data on the Chinese-Indonesian women who were victims in the May riots. The data was collected by the 'Team of Fact Finders'.

Rape and sexual harassment victims in May Riot 1998 in Jakarta and its surroundings:[27]

Date	Rape	Rape and abuse	Rape and burning	Sexual harassment	Total of the victims
13th May	-	2	3 (all dead)	4	9 (3 dead)
14th May	101	17 (7 dead)	6 (all dead)	8 (1 dead)	132 (14 dead)
15th May	-	1 (dead)	-	1	2 (1 dead)
After 15th May until 3 rd July	2 (1 dead)	6 (1 dead)	-	1	9 (2 dead)
Total	103 (1 dead)	26 (9 dead)	9 (all dead)	14 (1 dead)	152 (20 dead)

In addition to Chinese-Indonesian women victims, there were 1,190 ordinary people who died, most of them the urban poor who burned in shopping malls and on the street. The pain and agony of the May 1998 riot in Jakarta remains fresh and unforgettable for many people, especially for Chinese-Indonesians. This riot profoundly disrupted Indonesia's national economic as well as human dignity. Because of their ethnic background and gender, Chinese-Indonesian women suffered the most. There were many reported cases, officially and unofficially, of their abuse and rape by the mobs that systematically swept through almost every part of Jakarta. In the riots women were not only the targets of the gang rape but also of the mutilation of their reproductive organs with sharp or blunt objects.

The lack of action from the authorities caused a huge loss of mutual trust in the society. Despite the fact that the findings and data were collected by reputable

[27] Source: The National Commission of Violence against Women, 2002, p. 231.

institutions such as the National Commission of Violence against Women, the Indonesian Government formally denied that the violence ever occurred! Many women's organizations went to the President,[28] and eventually forced him to offer a apology to the victims and their families. Thus these women activists succeeded in their mission.[29]

These horrible violations show that the state does not intend to protect its citizens and chooses to turn its back on crimes against its own people. This can be considered as state violence. Solomos declares that the state plays a central role in defining the models and the contents of the regulations and the political agenda in controlling the living of their society.[30] Several international and national legal instruments, which should bind a state as well as an individual, fail to be implemented because of the political and economic situation.

While observing the riot as a systematically and well planned incident,[31] some people are of the opinion that it was a device to shift attention from the crisis of Soeharto's government and to blame the Chinese. The May Riot showed that a serious violation against human beings could trigger the collapse of a tyrant, which was unthinkable before.

The May Riot also shows that Indonesians of Chinese descent have not always had an easy time. May 1998's tragedy was only one example of the racial riots that were closely related to the history of the Chinese in Indonesia for centuries, long before the Europeans arrived in Indonesia. Since the Dutch period until the autocratic *New Order* regime, the Chinese minority had a significant economic influence[32] but had been repressed and ill-treated.

---

[28] President Habibie, who formerly played an important role in Soeharto's era, was vice-president at the end of the Soeharto's administration and appointed president as Soeharto stepped down. The presidency of Habibie lasted only 1 year.

[29] This was confirmed by the establishment of the National Commission of Violence Against Women on the President's recommendation. The Commission was headed by Prof. Dr. Saparinah Sadli in 1998.

[30] Solomos, *The Racism Problematic: Contemporary Sociological Debates on Race and Ethnicity*, New York, Edwin Mellen Press, 1996.

[31] It has been found by the Team of Fact Findings under the National Commission of Human Rights. The National Commission of Violence against Women, 2002.

[32] Regarding the involvement of the Chinese-Indonesian in the economy, Gordon Redding describes several views as follows. Firstly, Chinese businessmen were very cautious towards their businesses. Their ability to keep secrets in managing their businesses was inherited by each succeeding generation. This approach developed as a survival strategy in order to maintain their

ROOTS OF DISCRIMINATION AGAINST CHINESE-INDONESIAN WOMEN

There are no records that state precisely when the first Chinese emigrated to the Indonesian archipelago. The Chinese were already living in many parts of Indonesia when the Dutch arrived. The last generation who were born in China and immigrated to Indonesia are still alive in Indonesia today. Generally they are now around 70-80 years old. They are called as the *totok* Chinese, a term referring to a person who was born in China and applies strict Chinese culture in their daily life.

Some of this last generation born in China and migrated to Indonesia became very powerful. They worked very hard and successfully established their own businesses, some of which turned into business empires. Some of these Chinese-Indonesian businesses became conglomerates and were often included in the ranks of the Indonesian bourgeois or middle class.They even counted among the political cronies of the ruling class during the New Order regime.

They established strong influence to pass down to their descendants, and became respected community members. Their descendants who were born in Indonesia became the first generation of Chinese-Indonesian, and no longer called *totok* but *Cina peranakan*. This generation of Chinese-Indonesians still observed their original culture in their daily life such as Confucianism, religious rituals, and sacred days.

Chinese-Indonesian women generally hold a subordinate status in their own community and culture. It relates to the concept of gender (women, wife, man, husband) in Chinese culture. How does Chinese customary law posit women and men in relation to each other? Can this be traced to ancient Chinese culture?

Chinese culture in general is patriarchal culture. Traditionally, women are expected to live by the rules of the men in their lives. They have to obey their fathers when they are still single, their husbands after they are married, and their sons when they are widowed. They have little personal dignity and independence, and often are deprived of the rights to receive high education

business in a very insecure business environment. Secondly, their businesses were scattered around the world. Thirdly, the Chinese always kept a low profile in the business world. The strength of the overseas Chinese was the hidden strength that made them unbeatable. Gordon S. Redding, *The Spirit of Chinese Capitalism*, Hongkong, Walter de Gruyter & Co,, 1994.

and take part in social activities. Chinese women have little voice in determining their own future. They are subjected to physical and mental torture, as well as harassment by polygamy and prostitution. Up to the early 20th century, foot binding was customary to women as sign of social status and sexual pleasure for men. Furthermore it was thought that daughters-in-law ought to devote themselves to their mothers-in-law by doing domestic jobs for the whole family and sometimes by earning money as well. Even after death of their mothers-in-law, daughters-in-law were expected to pay homage to the graves of the deceased and observe rituals at the altar where their ashes rested. This practice often caused conflict and friction within families.

The behaviour of Chinese mothers in law towards their daughters in law can be seen in the context both of age dominance and gender dominance. The mother takes the place of her son representing him in relation to her daughter-in-law. Cultural concepts and values can put husband and wife in an unbalanced power relationshias the following story will reflect.

> A woman is running a shop since her husband lost his business caused by monetary crisis in Indonesia in the year 1998. Prior to the crisis, her husband had a medium scale enterprise which produced "sarong", a kind of textile worn by Indonesian men on many occasions. After failing in finding a job and running another business, the wife becomes the bread winner for the whole family.
>
> She comes from an intellectual family background, which can be seen from her parents who are Dutch speaking Indonesian-Chinese. Considering that, in the colonial period, entering school was a luxury and unaffordable thing for ordinary people, that family must have beeen a special one. She is well educated because her parents sent her to an outstanding school in Bandung, the city where they lived.
>
> She is good in business, her shop is getting bigger and bigger. Her success in doing business does not reduce her domestic role as a house wife and daughter, she is cooking, cleaning the house, rearing her children, preparing food for worship for their ancestor's spirit and there are still many things to do.
>
> Regarding ritual to honour ancestral spirit, according to the Chinese traditon her mother-in-law always tells her firmly that it is her duty to

maintain this ritual. And when her mother-in-law died, she is obliged to honour her ash by having a worship ceremony everyday. She will have to prepare some food and fruit and give prayers to the ashes of the ancestor.

Moreover, her mother-in-law asks her to prepare meals for her husband and the whole family. Everyday she has to cook no less than seven kinds of luxurios Chinese food. Cooking simple food is not allowed, that is only for poor families, her mother- in-law tells her. "We are rich. You should show it by what you serve."

What does she say in response to those obligations for being woman and wife, bound to the Chinese culture? "I am doing everything well, because there is nothing I can do, otherwise my mother-in-law should take me as an unthankful and misbehaving daughter-in-law. I am scared of her and I do not want to have a conflict. But deep in my heart I strongly object to those duties. I am bored doing the same things day after day. Someday, when she dies, there will be no worship for her ashes. I don't want to practice that ritual any longer."

This story shows how the position of women in Chinese culture could be traced from the concepts of man and woman, husband and wife, the so-called " daughter and mother-in law" relationship and other kinship relationships. These concepts are preserved beyond the first generation of Chinese-Indonesians.

The following excerpt indicates the position of Chinese women in their own cultures.

Possessing no political rights, women were completely excluded from social and political life. Economically dependent, women were deprived of property and inheritance rights and possessed no independent source of income.[33]

According to Chinese customary law, a Chinese woman cannot inherit her family's wealth. This remains true for most ethnic Chinese who reside in their adopted countries.

---

[33] The State Council of the People's Republic of China, 1994, p. 1.

Previous research has shown that exploitation of Chinese women was often directed against girls as young as 5 to 6 years old. They were sold as *San Po Tsai, Mui Tsai* and *Pipa Tsai.*[34] *San Po Tsai* were little girls transferred from their birth families to the households of future husbands when they were very young. The wedding did not take place until they were able to consummate the union. The "minor marriage" provided a wife for a son of the receiving family without the normal costly gifts to the bride's family. *Mui Tsai* were child slaves where a daughter from a poor family was sold to a rich household. The girl was adopted by the recipients, who paid the parents often very small sums. In practice, the girls were often treated not as adopted child but as household drudges. Some suffered unbelievable cruelty, including sexual abuse. Some were sold to dealers and changed hands more than once. *Pipa Tsai* were girls who played Pipa, a traditional musical instrument. In theory a pipa tsai was only an entertainer, but opportunities for hiring such girls out to spend the night with clients were eagerly sought by their owners. The owners were often single women who might use a pipa tsai both as a source of income and as an adopted daughter who would care for her soul after her death. The boundaries here between outright exploitation, emotional dependence, servitude, and filial submission were unclear.

Trafficking of women among the Chinese sadly also occurs in Indonesia today. Young women mainly from Singkawang[35] in West Kalimantan (Borneo) are trafficked in the form of mail order brides for Taiwanese customers. Because of poverty and the concept of "*filial piety*"[36] practiced by the community, most parents give permission for their daughters to go to Taiwan. It is not unusual for some money to change hands in these circumstances. After such transactions, many girls go "missing" and disappear without any news. The recruitment process of mail order brides involves many people including the middle men who recruit the girls from their villages, before they are "sold" to the Taiwanese. Soon after their arrival in Taiwan, Taiwanese men marry them;

---

[34] Maria Jashock and Suzanne Miers (eds.), *Women and Chinese Patriarchy. Submission, Servitude and Escape*, London, Zed Books Ltd, 1994.

[35] Singkawang in West Kalimantan is located in a remote area. Most of the population is poor.

[36] The concept of *filial piety* refers to obligation addressed to daughters to adore their parents without question.

most of the girls end up as slaves instead of wives. Some of them are able to go back their village in West Kalimantan as widows with children.[37]

Women trafficking in the form of mail order brides is also associated with *klenteng* or *vihara* (Chinese temples) such as those in Bandung (capital city of the province of West Java). Typically, the keeper of the Chinese temple finds a baby left by her poor mother in front of the door. The keeper raises the baby in the temple. A middle man then asks the keeper to deliver the orphan for some money, then off she then goes to Taiwan and is never heard of again.

This is a story that happened in a Chinese temple located somewhere in Bandung.[38] A couple with five children, three of them girls, gets divorced. The father goes somewhere, and the mother lives alone with her children. Eventually, she gives all of the girls to the keeper of the Chinese temple. The eldest grows up and is very beautiful. One day a middle man comes to the temple to ask the eldest to be married with a Taiwanese. He offers her some money. Usually the keeper agrees to make a deal, but not this time. A lady who lives near the temple warns the keeper not to sell the girl, and she offers to take over the burden. She pays some money to the keeper every month to be used as living cost for that girl, and she makes sure that the beautiful girl stays in the temple peacefully.

Even now, Chinese-Indonesians still practice their customary law. There are of course exceptions, especially for those who went to Dutch schools. The Dutch Government made efforts to advance the status of women by enacting the Civil Code, the *Burgelijk Wet* (BW) from 1848,[39] which helped Chinese-Indonesian women whose status rose as well. The substance of the BW was a source of controversy among the Chinese-Indonesian community at that time.

Sugiastuti Yunita lists five regulations enacted by the Dutch to enhance the status of women: (a) The monogamy principle in marriage; (b) The definition of the husband's roles and responsibilities in marriage; (c) Women's right to appeal for a divorce; (d) A widow no longer belongs to her sons; and (e) Equal

---

[37] Documentary Film on Trafficking of Women, Produced by Jurnal Perempuan, an Indonesian Woman's NGO, 2003.

[38] Data comes from a resource person, Lim Sing Meij, who has significant knowledge about the Chinese temples in Bandung, West Java.

[39] This Code was based on the Code in the Netherlands, and it is still in force in present day Indonesia.

rights between sons and daughters regarding inheritance. Unfortunately, Yunita did not go further to follow up the implementation and effectiveness of the law in daily life. She does mention that after the enactment of the Civil Code, there were decreasing numbers of divorce among the Chinese. This warrants further research to find out the effectiveness of law in daily life.[40]

CONCLUDING REMARKS

There is a dichotomy in Indonesian national law when it comes to human rights. On the one hand it complies with international law via ratification. Human rights are part of the national legal framework, extending to the constitution itself as well as certain specific national acts.

On the other hand one is confronted with regimes that have enacted regulations to prevent Chinese-Indonesians in attaining their rights. The existing law that discriminates against Chinese-Indonesians is an example of how the law treats this ethnic group. This may be seen in the context of a systematic attempt to retain power. The New Order regime used Chinese and communists as scape goats, thus creating a common enemy in society.

This helps to explain how intolerant sentiment against the Chinese has inflamed and caused the violation of human rights, particularly the rights of Chinese women. In a pluralistic society like Indonesia, it is imperative to study the violation of law by taking into account discrimination that takes place in a multidimensional context involving race, religion, and gender. Gender discrimination can be further investigated by observing how cultural values assign roles to men and women in society.

As Indonesia strives towards a civil society and democratic state, its doctrine, Unity in Diversity, is an even more important instrument to achieve this goal. Respecting human rights, multiculturalism, and pluralism is the important first step to prevent racial, religious, and gender discrimination, all of which violate humanity.

---

[40] Sugiastuti Yunita, *Tradisi Hukum Cina: Negara dan Masyarakat: Studi mengenai Peristiwa-Peristiwa Hukum Zaman colonial 1870-1942*, [The Chinese Traditional Law: The State and Society, A study on Legal Cases in the Colonial Period], a dissertation from the Faculty of Law, University of Indonesia, 2002.

BIBLIOGRAPHY

Bachtiar, Harsya, 1976. Masalah Integrasi Nasional [Issue on National Integration], *Prisma Journal*, 8 August

Benda-Beckmann, Keebet von, 2002. "The Context of Law", a paper presented to the XIIIth International Congress, Legal Pluralism and Unofficial Law in Social, Economic and Political Development, hosted by the Commission on Folk Law and Legal Pluralism, Chiang Mai, 7-10 April

Bumiller, Elisabeth, 1992. "Flames: A bride Burning and a Sati", in Elisabeth Bumiller, *May You Be the Mother of A Hundred Sons*, New Delhi, Penguin Books, p 44-74.

Ihromi, Tapi Omas and Achie Luhulima, 1997. "Sociolegal Status of Women in Selected DMC's. Country Study: Indonesia", Insan Harapan Sejahtera, Social Science Research and Consultancy

Jashock, Maria and Suzanne Miers (eds), 1994. *Women and Chinese Patriarchy: Submission, Servitude and Escape*, London, Zed Books Ltd

Jurnal Perempuan (Journal of Women), 2003. Documentair Film on Trafficking of Women, produced by Jurnal Perempuan, an Indonesian Women's NGO

Komnas HAM (The National Commission on Human Rights), 1999. *Hak Asasi Manusia, Tanggung Jawab Negara, Peran Institusi Nasional dan Masyarakat* [Human Rights, State Responsibility, The Role of National Institution and Society], Jakarta: Komnas HAM

Komnas Perempuan (The National Commission of Violence Against Women),

2002. *Peta Kekerasan, Pengalaman Perempuan Indonesia* [Mapping of Violence, The Experience of Indonesian Women], Jakarta, Komnas Perempuan

2003. *Tragedi Mei 1998 dalam Perjalanan Bangsa Disangkal,* [The Denial of May Tragedy in the History of Nation], Jakarta

Mintoraharjo, Sukowaluyo, 2003. "Rekonsiliasi Tanpa Diskriminasi", Reconciliation Without Discrimination, News paper Kompas, 1 December

Redding, S Gordon, 1994. *The Spirit of Chinese Capitalism*, Hong Kong, Walter de Gruyter & Co

Reksodiputro, Mardjono, 1994. *Hak Asasi Manusia dalam Sistem Peradilan Pidana* [Human Rights in the Penal Judiciary], Jakarta, Pusat Pelayanan Keadilan dan Pengabdian Hukum, UI

Setiono, Benny, G, 2002. "Kehancuran dan Kebangkitan Martabat/Jati diri Etnis Tionghoa" [Destroying and Resurrection of the Dignity of Etnic Chinese], a paper presented in the seminar on "the Role of Ethnic Chinese in the Long of Indonesian's History", hosted by Perhimpunan Inti and Newspaper Suara Pembaharuan, 9 November

Sidoti, Chris, 1999. *Memperkenalkan Empat Buah Dokumen Hak Asasi Manusia Internasional Utama, yang Akan Diratifikasi oleh Pemerintah Republik Indonesia, dalam Komnas HAM, Hak Asasi Manusia, Tanggung Jawab Negara, Peran Institusi Nasional dan Masyarakat*, Jakarta, Komnas HAM, 1999, [Introducing the Four Main International Human Rights Documents Which Will Be Ratified by Indonesian Government. Human Rights, State Responsibility, The Role of National Institution and Society], Jakarta, National Comission on Human Rights

Solomos, 1996. *The Racism Problematic: Contemporary Sociological Debates on Race and Ethnicity,* New York, Ontario and England, Edwin Mellen Press

The State Council of the People's Republic of China, Information Office of the State Council of the People's Republic of China, Beijing, 1994.

Tan, Mely G., "The Social and Cultural Dimension of Gender-based Violence in Indonesia: Labeling, Discrimination and Violence", a paper presented to the International Symposium on "Rebuilding Indonesia, a Nation of Unity in Diversity: Towards a Multicultural Society", 16 – 19 Juli 2002, kampus universtias Udayana, Denpasar, Bali.

Totcha, Ruth dan Otavia Roth, 1995. *Deklarasi Hak-Hak Asasi Manusia Sedunia: Sebuah Adaptasi untuk Kanak-Kanak,* [Declaration of Human Rights: An Adaption for Children] Jakarta,Yayasan Obor Indonesia

The United Nations, 1996. *The United Nations and The Advancement of Women 1945-1996*, New York, UN, Department of Public Information

Velzen, J. van, 1967. "The extended Case Method and Situational Analysis" A.L. Epstein (ed), *The Craft of Social Anthropology*. London, Tavistock

Yunita, Sugiastuti, 2002. *Tradisi Hukum Cina: Negara dan Masyarakat: Studi mengenai Peristiwa-Peristiwa Hukum Zaman colonial 1870-1942,* [The Chinese Traditional Law : The State and Society, A study on Legal Cases in the Colonial Period], a dissertation in the Faculty of Law, University of Indonesia

Visions of the Right Order: Contrasts between Mayan Communitarian Law in Guatemala and International Human Rights Law[*]

Stener Ekern

[*] Acknowledgements: The Communal Mayors of the 48 Cantons of Totonicapán in 2000, 2001, 2002, and 2003; The Communal Mayoralties of Chuculjuyup, Paxtocá, and Xolsacmaljá; The Provincial Delegation of the Human Rights Ombudsman in Totonicapán; Santos Norato, Gregorio Tzoc, and the editors of the present volume of the Yearbook on Human Rights.

INTRODUCTION[1]

> Before, everything was well ordered, because there was respect. But now the young ask: Why do we have to perform our [compulsory community] service? Why do we have to carry the staff [of authority]? They are only thinking of personal gain. That is why we established the Rules Committee. What we want to do is to give form to the experience of life (*plasmar la vivencia*) here in Chuculjuyup, and create a set of Internal Rules. We will put the orders by which we rule (*consignas*) into writing, do away with some obsolete things, and adapt to present circumstances. We want to define the norms of living together in this place because our rules are more in line with reality than the Constitution of the Republic.

This is the explanation that I was given by the communal authorities of the rural community of Chuculjuyup when I asked why they had decided to write a constitution for their community. I was visiting as part of larger study of Mayan politics in Guatemala, and also because I knew that the local authorities recently had been in conflict with the provincial office of the national Human Rights Ombudsman. The investigation of this conflict, together with my observations of the process of writing down rules that so far had been transferred only orally, in the form of "orders" (*consignas*), provided me with an excellent opportunity for exploring how Mayas perceive their own community and its ordering. The purpose of the present article is to investigate some of the contrasts between this Mayan communitarian order and the state-based political order that is reflected in international human rights law, and through this approach examine why communal Mayan authorities in Guatemala commonly argue that Guatemalan constitutional law and human rights are out of touch with local realities.

Chuculjuyup is one of the 48 communities or cantons of Totonicapán, a municipality in the Western highlands of Guatemala. With its around 110,000 inhabitants, it is the fifth largest municipality of the country, and it is situated in the historical heartlands of Guatemala's large indigenous population. Mayan Indians make up a solid majority of residents in around 150 of the country's 331 municipalities. The otherwise dominant Spanish-speaking mestizos

[1] The article is based on fieldwork in Totonicapán, Guatemala in 2000 and two-week visits in 1999, 2001, 2002, and 2003. It was originally presented at the 3rd Congress of the Latin American Network of Legal Anthropology (*Red Latinoamericana de Antropología Jurídica*, RELAJU) in Quetzaltenango, Guatemala, on 10 August 2002, and titled *Normatividad y figures sociales. Una exploración de los contrastes entre el derecho comunitario indígena de Totonicapán, Guatemala y los Derechos Humanos.*

(known as *Ladinos* in Guatemala) make up less than 10 % of the population in Totonicapán. Moreover, whereas the Ladinos, who account for just 15 % of the total population, live in compact town centres, the overwhelming majority of Mayas live in rural communities like Chuculjuyup, with populations ranging from 1,500 to 4,000. Thus the ethnic division between Mayas and Ladinos is systematically reinforced by the many social and economic contrasts between urban and rural life, the gap between modernity and tradition, as well as different levels of integration with the Guatemalan nation-state, perhaps particularly as regards the use of the national school system and the system of justice. The rural Mayas of Totonocapán had little access to education and other modern services until the late 1970s, and the state's efforts to integrate them nationally were mostly met with deep scepticism.

From the point of view of the state, a canton is a sub-division of the municipality and the smallest administrative unit of the republic (sometimes accorded official status as *aldea* or village). However, this perspective disregards the ethnic division between Ladinos and Mayas. Starting with the ethnic difference in mind, in Mayan areas a canton is a community of Indians or indigenous people, and historically each canton may trace their origin as a linage-based Mayan social unit far back. As indigenous communities, most cantons enjoy a *de facto* autonomy that nowadays is exercised by a political body popularly known as "the corporation" or "the authorities". In terms of state-derived legality, however, the Mayan community government is no more than an auxiliary mayoralty within the Republic of Guatemala.

While it is true that the peace agreement that formally ended the civil war in 1996 and Guatemala's ratification of the ILO Convention 169/89 on the Rights of Indigenous and Tribal Peoples in 1995 have been instrumental in opening a space for expressing legal and political multiculturalism, at the local level most Mayas continue to regard the state as a kind of "alien authority",[2] just as Ladino authorities persist in viewing Mayan "custom"[3] as backward and substandard when compared with formal legal and administrative requirements.

---

[2] In K'iche', the biggest Mayan language and that which is spoken in Totonicapán, rural people commonly refer to the Government and its many offices in the town centre as *q'atb'al tzij*. Literally, this expression means "imposer of the law", and as this was done by Ladino authorities in town, by extension it means "alien authority" in contrast to the conciliatory justice carried out by the elders in the community.

[3] *Costumbre* or custom is the term commonly used by Ladinos to designate Mayan "pagan" religious activities in particular and by extension all indigenous public activities.

Such images of mutual disapproval are intimately connected with the ongoing construction of the cleavage between Mayas and Ladinos. A deconstruction of this boundary will therefore allow us to examine why and how the introduction of human rights ideas, through institutions like the Human Rights Ombudsman and the UN mission to Guatemala (MINUGUA), by and large has met with more success at the national level than in the Mayan communities.

The Communal Mayoralty—as most Mayan authorities now prefer to style themselves[4]—consists of a series of public duties or "services" (*k'axk'ol*) that are compulsory for all married men of the community. The men that do their services are elected annually at a communal assembly and form a team presided by a Communal Mayor. This latter figure is also known as "auxiliary mayor" in his legally recognised role as the local representative of the municipal mayor. At the municipal level, communal mayors regularly meet with the municipal mayor and generally act as liaisons between Guatemalan officialdom and the indigenous community of the municipality in question. In Totonicapán the group of communal mayors also meet separately, and as such they form an institution called "The Communal Mayors of the 48 Cantons of Totonicapán". This entity is the supreme indigenous authority of the municipality because it continues to perform the functions of its forerunner, the Indigenous Mayoralty (*Alcaldía Indígena*) of Totonicapán.

Previously the Indigenous Mayoralty in Guatemala formally referred to a division of the ordinary municipal administration in charge of indigenous matters, but from an indigenous point of view it has consisted of a number of compulsory duties imposed by the state, analogous to how participation in saint brotherhoods or *cofradías* was required by the Catholic Church. By social scientists, both institutions were commonly called "Mayan hierarchies" as they frequently overlapped and formed a single system of religiously grounded internal rule. In 1927, a long tradition of separate government for Mayas and Ladinos was formally abolished, and since 1944 the Indians have participated as full citizens along with the Ladinos in regularly electing municipal authorities. However, in most highland municipalities a bi-ethnic tradition with separate Mayan communal self-rule has continued to this day, though not without adjustments and innovations. In this way the Mayas of Guatemala live

[4] The new Law on Municipalities from 2002 allows for referring to the vice-mayoralties as "communal" institutions.

under a system of dual government, being both Guatemalan citizens and members of small Mayan polities.

The Indigenous Mayoralty used to be controlled by a selection of elders (*principales)* from the different cantons of the municipality. From the 1970s an onwards, the power of the elders was increasingly weakened partly because their rule was perceived as authoritarian (often they had to serve as military commissioners) and unable to deliver increased welfare in the form of development projects, partly because the municipal authorities at the time actively promoted a reform of what Ladino political leaders considered an obstacle to development.[5] In Totonicapán they were replaced by the figure that up to that point mainly had functioned as the liaison between the elders and the town authorities, i.e. the vice-mayor. By incorporating a range of new services such as the presidencies of the various development committees of the canton, the entire institution has renewed itself and in some cases even proceeded to write constitutions.

But then as now, the Mayan government of Totonicapán - and by this I mean the 48 small communal mayoralties of the cantons as well as The Mayors of the 48 Cantons - is based on a set of norms that are spelt out in a series of "orders" (*consignas*). The sum total of the orders is, in effect, the political constitution of the Mayan community of Totonicapán. Concretely, the orders comprise work manuals for the different services, procedural rules for the functioning of the mayoralty, a socially and morally defined body of knowledge or "wisdom" about how to solve conflicts and order society correctly, and pieces of general advice about current political challenges that face the canton in its dealings with neighbouring cantons and the national authorities. The orders are transferred from the incumbents to the new authorities during a short transition period at the end of the year. Canton autonomy, as it is practiced through the maintenance of a local, Mayan polity can thus be analysed as a customary legislative system, constructed in parallel to the legal system of the state.

[5] The point about the decreasing legitimacy of the elders and the impact of development is argued in my forthcoming doctoral dissertation on the transformation of Mayan politics from a rule of elders to a rule of a younger generation of development-oriented communal mayors in Totonicapán between 1987 and 2000. The point about the municipality acting in favor of the latter group is taken from this work, too, and corroborated by the history of the Indigenous Mayoralty in Guatemala by Lina Barrios: *La Alcaldía Indígena en Guatemala: de 1944 al presente*, IDIES, Universidad Rafaél Landívar, Guatemala, 1998.

METHODOLOGICAL AND THEORETICAL CONSIDERATIONS

The texts that the constitutional committees of Chuculjuyup and other cantons edit (by 2003, at least five cantons had elaborated such documents), the political ideals of which the orders speak, as well as the activities performed by the communal mayoralties, are all closely connected with social norms that govern community life and shape political action in the K'iche'-Mayan communities of Totonicapán. In an anthropological study, analysing such locally constructed texts and participating in e.g. the performance of community services are but two ways of approaching a society, or a set of social processes, in order to understand what is happening. By visiting about half of all the cantons, and by regularly following events in a select group of six or seven, as well as closely following all the activities of "The 48 Cantons" through a whole year and moreover systematically interview a majority of the communal mayors about their work and their political careers, I have been able to construct a detailed understanding of the workings, as well as of recent changes, of the Mayan polities of Guatemala. With these data in mind, and through sustained topical discussions with many informants, I have also been able to appreciate how e.g. ideas about human rights are interpreted and acted upon in Mayan communities.

In this endeavour, analytical concepts like "identity", "person", and "agency" have been particularly helpful. The idea is that by deconstructing the individual and collective identities in which social actors inscribe themselves and their adversaries, as well as local ideas about who and what causes actions and produces effects, it is possible to reconstruct some of the motivation that guide social action. In line with this mode of thinking, community membership can be seen as a way of acquiring a "social body" or "personhood" that communicates certain collective identities held by the individual in question.[6] For instance, in a world of nation-states it has become common practice to categorise individuals in terms of polity of origin and a putative essence of national or ethnic origin flowing from this site. In this way citizenship rights are easily mixed up with other socially based claims and particularly those that

[6] This way of thinking about individuals and communities as sites for the production of meaning owes much to Michel Foucalt (e.g. *Power/Knowledge: Selected Interviews & Other Writings 1972-1977*, New York, Pantheon Books, 1980); see also Thomas Blom Hansen and Finn Stepputat, *States of Imagination. Ethnographic Explorations of the Postcolonial State*, Durham and London, Duke University Press, 2001.

flow from "ethnic" or "cultural" identities. Moreover, as much social and political life is organised around a large state apparatus, people of such societies will imbue large, impersonal institutions with a kind of impartial agency that is difficult to comprehend for someone who grows up in a small, socially autonomous community.

In the introduction I suggested that the division between Mayas and Ladinos in Guatemala is somehow more than an ethnic difference in so far as this particular linguistic dividing line is reinforced by a long series of contrasts in social and economic conditions as well. I chose the term "cleavage" to better catch the multifaceted and divisive qualities of the boundary between the two communities in question, and also to draw attention to how such lines are constructed through social practices in otherwise different fields. Through this article, we will see how a large part of the construction of "the Mayan person" takes place in informal settings (as seen by the state) and by participating in very localised, communitarian activities, and moreover in opposition to a set of other persons (Ladinos) and a state that nevertheless conceives of itself as a political expression common to the two groups in question. As a result of this particular way of constructing a collective identity, Mayas generally do not identify with the Guatemalan nation-state as a "home" the way a citizen of a European country so easily does after having been socialised through the agencies of the many national institutions of her or his "own" country. For most Mayas "home" in this regard is probably a site mostly located in the home community in which she or he acquired the necessary social compatibilities (*etamb'al*)[7] to live a meaningful life. However, also the municipality, the local language group, and even the Republic of Guatemala will be important sites for producing important personal qualities.

Analysed in this manner, a Communal Mayor of a canton in Totonicapán, will act in this way or that because he considers himself to be—as the common expressions go—a "son of the community" and a "respectable" man that "shows respect". Leadership is temporarily bestowed upon him because he has demonstrated the necessary personal qualities, and moreover he has consistently "put the community before his own interest [of personal gain]". His principal task—the first order—is always to "defend the community and

[7] *Etamb'al* is the K'iche' term for experience-based or social intelligence as opposed to *no'j* or the problem-solving aspect of intelligence. Its growth and particularities is intimately connected to socialization in a particular time and place and thus to community membership.

its patrimony" from the various powers that surround it. The political strategies applied by Mayan communal mayors reflect such thinking about actor's identities and agencies and how a right order ought to be sustained.

The next step is to consider the international system of human rights, and the idea of a right order that it propagates, as an analogous case of political thinking. I will argue that this is indeed possible by regarding the two entities as discourses on how to establish a right order, i.e. as "practices that systematically form the objects of which they speak".[8] The international human rights system—understood as a universal declaration embodying a political ideal, a set of international treaties regulating relations between states and individuals, and a set of international and national legal institutions entrusted with the task of assisting states in respecting, protecting and promoting said ideals—was born in the aftermath of a devastating war that engulfed almost the whole world, even if the conflict started among the nation-states of Europe and East Asia. It is therefore tempting to interpret its constitutive documents (the Universal Declaration and the two UN Covenants) as a warning from the elders of the involved nation-states to their own children and the rest of the world: If you wish to avoid repeating past barbarian actions and build a better world, it is necessary to recognise a set of rights as inherent to human beings, irrespective of particular identities, and relentlessly promote their realisation!

The declamatory language of human rights documents has led many observers to qualify human rights as political statements (rather than legally enforceable rules) because, in the words of Marie-Bénédicte Dembour, they "represent the language of not-yet-realised—and ever-to-be re-identified—political claims at the same time as they are phrased in terms of eternal truth".[9] The same author takes this critique a step further by asserting that "the lack of fit between theory and practice … at the core of the human rights concept … depends for its existence and application on a state organisation."[10] Thus Dembour concludes that human rights make the intended sense primarily in social and political contexts organised around a state because the addressee of political

[8] Michel Foucalt, *The Archaeology of Knowledge*, New York, Pantheon Books, 1972, p. 49.

[9] Marie Bénédicte Dembour, "Human rights talk and anthropological ambivalence: the particular context of universal claims", in Olivia Harris (ed.), *Inside and Outside the Law. Anthropological Studies of Authority and Ambiguity*, London, Routledge 1996, p. 20.

[10] *Ibid.*, p. 29.

claims about rights and violations of rights is the state. To this I will add the qualifier *nation-*, for reasons that become clear when we discuss relations between identities and polities in Guatemala. At this point it is interesting to note that in Totonicapán, "politics" is a dirty word because it refers to national society and the actions of the politicians and the political parties that operate there. At the canton level, one never uses the word "politics" about what is happening when people elect their authorities etc., as this would imply a moral condemnation of the action and constitute a grave accusation against the protagonists. Instead these transactions are referred to as "custom" or "our way of life". In this Mayan discourse on the right(s) order we see two different communities juxtaposed and judged.

Before proceeding with the comparison of the two discourses that the article purports to investigate, it will be necessary to present some prominent characteristics of both. First, I will give a brief description of the indigenous authorities of Totonicapán and their recent history. Following this section, I will give an equally brief presentation of the international system of human rights. With selected salient features of two different objects in mind, we will then discuss the work of the Rules Committee of Chuculjuyup and the conflict between the Communal Mayoralty and the provincial delegate of the Human Rights Ombudsman. In conclusion we will demarcate some areas where the two political orders differ and suggest possible ways of closing the gaps.

THE COMMUNAL (AUXILIARY) MAYORALTIES OF TOTONICAPÁN

As a social unit, the canton might be defined as a territory inhabited and worked (developed) by a group of families united through kinship and a duty to safeguard it through time. In 2000, I witnessed a situation where the principal mechanism for achieving this was the continuation of a communal organisation wherein all basic units (today mostly nuclear families, each forming a separate household) are obliged to fulfil a number of conditions. These are: (1) to participate in *faenas* or communal works (e.g. building and maintaining roads), (2) contribute money and manpower for the construction of public infrastructure (bridges, schools, potable water), and (3) carry out a service (*k'axk'ol*) or duty at the Communal Mayoralty at least three times during a married man's lifetime.

Other and more indirect identity-forming mechanisms are compulsory use of traditional dress among women, compulsory use of the Communal Mayor as a first instance judge, use of K'iche' language in everyday speech, as well as constant references to a series of morally grounded differences between "us, the indigenous" and "them, the Ladinos", for instance arguing that Ladinos are less trustworthy because they live "without order" (as the saying goes), but also recognising (and resenting) the superior wealth and power of the Ladinos. In other words, by observing a set of moral conventions, frequently built through contrasting an indigenous "we" to a morally inferior, but also more powerful "other", the K'iche' Mayas of Totonicapán construct a bounded and singular culture. Through the resulting collective identity, achieved by constructing a communal organisation and an ethnic boundary, the indigenous people of Totonicapán confront the world. At the same time it is important to realise that the K'iche's also are subordinated to a nation-state of Iberoamerican heritage whose culture is that of "them, the Ladinos". The K'iche'an community is defined also by this asymmetric relation with the Guatemalan national community.

In former times, the canton may have consisted of two or more clans (patrilineal descent groups) that lived in separate hamlets (*parajes*) and exchanged spouses. Each clan was headed by a *chuchkajaw* (literally: mother-father) who was responsible for maintaining the correct relations with the "lords of the world" (the guardian spirits of the territory they inhabited). This figure was also responsible for the conservation of a sacred order, modelled on the exemplary lives of the ancients. The *chuchkajaw* and other men of age and good repute could become "principals" (*principales, kamal b'e*) who, when acting together, would form a kind of supreme council responsible for defining the political strategies of the clan and of the canton. At the same time, it must be underlined that the importance of the canton also is due to its being used as a unit for tributary and administrative purposes within a larger political unit. The activities that go on in "local" political units in places like Totonicapán are simultaneously taking place within wider political processes of superior polities (at least since the first proto-states formed in the Mesoamerican area some 3,000 years ago).

The above reconstruction of the canton as a local and translocal political unit is based on ethnographic descriptions by Robert Carmack[11] and Ricardo Falla[12] from the neighbouring municipalities of Momostenango and San Antonio Ilotenango. In Totonicapán, there are no longer any *chuchkajaw*[13] and as noted above, the elders lost their power during the 1980s. The cantons still consist of a collection of hamlets, but even if many of them carry patronymic names, today's nuclear families live mixed together, and the young are only dimly aware of the previous order. Neither is canton endogamy absolute as in the past. The young marry those they like whether they come from Totonicapán or not, albeit with the approval of the parents. Only in extremely rare cases do they marry Ladinos. The communal order and its ethnic defence remain the pivots of cantonal politics.

In this way the communal mayoralty is the legitimate heir of the council of principals. Evaluated as a political body, it is more democratic than its predecessor. In a majority of cantons the mayoralty is elected in a secret ballot, after a frank and open discussion about personal qualities and previous merits, at a general assembly where all the "children of the community" participate. Nevertheless, in most cases the candidates are in reality selected by the incumbents before the election, and the foregoing selection process is heavily influenced by a group of elders who are the *de facto* principals of the canton. Women do vote in most cantons, but are seated apart from the men, and it is exceedingly rare that a woman assumes office. The common argument is that "women have other tasks"—a reference to an extremely rigid sexual division of labour that leaves all tasks concerning childcare and food preparation to women.

Also the composition of the mayoralty varies a lot. Typically the assembly names a mayor, a vice-mayor or second mayor, a secretary, two constables (who guard the "documents of the people"—title deeds etc.—that are kept in

---

[11] Robert Carmack, *Rebels of Highland Guatemala. The Quiche-Mayas of Momostenango*, Norman, University of Oklahoma Press, 1995.

[12] Ricardo Falla, *Quiché Rebelde. Estudio de un movimiento de conversión religiosa, rebelde a las creencias regionales, en San Antonio Ilotenango, Quiché (1948-1970)*, Guatemala, Editorial Universitaria, 1995 [1970].

[13] The word also had the meanings of "matchmaker", "witness to marriage" and "in-law" (eventually, all adults in a canton would become *chuchkajaw* to each other; see Falla, *ibid.*). In contemporary Totonicapán, the word is only used in the sense of "master of ceremonies" in a traditional wedding, and then only in some cantons.

the building of The 48 Cantons in the town centre), forest rangers, "plumbers" who guard the water systems, school janitors, "delegates to the baths"—i.e. the men that run the public hot baths in the town centre, a herald, a graveyard custodian, and, in most cases, representatives from the different development project committees that are active in the canton. Thus the corporation exercises the powers of an autonomous government. This state of affairs is well illustrated by the solemnity that surrounds the transfer of power when the group of incumbents and the succeeding authorities together inspect the patrimony of the people (schools, water systems, etc.) and the borders with neighbouring cantons, and pass on the orders. We should also keep in mind that several of the functions of the Mayan authorities are exercised at the municipal level. The mayors are also responsible for the relations with the municipality and other national authorities (including large NGOs etc), and just like the constables, the delegates to the baths, and the representatives of the water committees, they maintain a central organisation that meet every two weeks (or as needs dictate) in the building of The 48 Cantons in town.

RESPECT AS IDEOLOGY

The number of offices in a communal mayoralty may vary from 15 to 60. Consequently in a given year around 2,000 men are performing their services in Totonicapán. No-one has calculated the total quantity of communal works, nor the total amount of contributions to the many community-run development projects, however I am prepared to argue that the aggregate value of communitarian efforts surpasses the total value of government investment in the same area.[14] The capacity for mobilising human resources that these figures speak of gives an indication of the enormous moral strength of the Indigenous Mayoralty of Totonicapán—or to put it differently: the attractiveness of the communal polities among the Mayas of Guatemala.

The salient characteristics of the community that is constructed by the communitarian political practices described above differ from those of the modern nation-state in a number of ways. In the first place, political attention is fundamentally drawn to the figure of the community as such by being conceived of and referred to as a force in its own right. The fundamental

---

[14] The biggest single government undertaking is the school system with 1,500 teachers on the payrolls.

obligation of all canton-citizens is to watch over the well-being of the community, and that is why participation in communal works is mandatory. In fact people will forcefully argue that one cannot acquire the social intelligence (*etamb'al*) necessary to live meaningfully without marrying and performing one's services. The K'iche'an person is thus created communally, or to turn it around: the community lives inside the K'iche'an person, and consequently people's lives depend on how they care for the interests of the community. Such a process of communal personal growth is of course analogous to how a national school system produces national citizens, and indeed K'iche's recognise how different ways of life and systems of learning create different *etamb'al*—the point is that what is taught in Ladino schools is incoherent and morally inferior because it foments what is referred to as "personal interests" (i.e. gain) as opposed to "the good of the community".

Correct morals are derived from how an action or a situation affects the body that is the community. This is illustrated by the regime of sanctions that the authorities apply in case of transgressions of the order, or "failings" (Spanish: *falta*, K'iche': *awas*), and it can be observed in the deliberations the mayors perform when they function as judges (or "fathers") of the community. Those that "fail"—i.e. those that do not work—are thought to "show no respect". Such behaviour is met with public shaming, forced labour, or as a last resort the perpetrators will be cut off from the communal water system. It is also the task of the mayor to mediate in conflicts between spouses, parents and children, as well as neighbours, because the welfare and harmony of the community reside in the responsible behaviour of its children. This balance—or correct way of living together—is kept when the inhabitants submit to a set of prescriptions for good behaviour, defined as "respect".[15] To my mind, no other concept better summarises Mayan morals than this simple word, and it can be said to condense the official ideology of the Mayan polity.

The totality of the authority and the absence of a division of powers also merit attention. It is not uncommon to observe people from the rural cantons visiting all the legal institutions of the town (the tribunals, private lawyers, the prosecutor, the human rights ombudsman) looking for support because they feel offended or victimised by their mayor. Moreover, one perceives a lack of concern for those that in one way or another are different or simply unable to

[15] See Edgar Esquit Choy and Carlos Ochoa García, *Tiqalil q'anej, kunimaaj tziij, niman tzij. El respeto a la palabra. El orden jurídico del pueblo maya*, Guatemala, CECMA, 1995.

comply with the role of a "respectable person". Respect is only gained through correct behaviour, or as the saying goes: "Only those that work have a voice". Paradoxically, the communal construction of the person produces a harsh individualism with little compassion for those that do not succeed in accumulating respect. There are simply no inherent rights. Among the many communal works, social work is absent (though some NGOs and churches have started special programmes for widows and single mothers).

THE ACCOMMODATION OF DEVELOPMENT

These images of a community sustained by communitarian practices and morals may seem eternal and static, and any Mayan ethnography will indeed affirm that the communitarian order was justified by references to the lives of the ancients: As it used to be, so it shall be, because if not, the world will come to an end. However, compared with the civic-religious "Mayan hierarchies" of the ethnographies from the 1940s and 1950s, the cantonal authorities of Totonicapán certainly have demonstrated a lot of capacity for change.

In the first place, one notes the secularism or religious neutrality of contemporary cantonal governments, a state of affairs that stands in sharp contrasts to a past traditionalism that excluded everyone except those who accepted the religious teachings of the elders (called *costumbrismo*).[16] In Totonicapán today, Protestants, Catholics, and the few traditionalists that remain work shoulder by shoulder in the mayoralties and take turns in opening the meetings with the compulsory prayer to God. The causes of this religious tolerance are surely various. For one thing, the almost total victory of Catholic Action against the traditionalists (and the power of the *chuchkajaw*) during the 1950s, and later the stalemate between the Protestants and the Catholics during the 1980s, have created a *de facto* situation of religious pluralism.[17] Moreover, the Indigenous Mayoralty of Totonicapán was always secular and separate

[16] See e.g. Falla, 1995, *op. cit.*, and Douglas Brintnall, *Revolt Against the Dead. The Modernization of a Mayan Community in the Highlands of Guatemala*. New York, Gordon & Breach, 1979.

[17] Cf. Falla, 1995, *op. cit.*, Carmack, 1995, *op. cit.*, and Robert S. Carlsen, *The War for the Heart and Soul of a Highland Maya Town*, Austin, University of Texas Press, 1999. Comparing written material from neighbouring municipalities with what informants remember from the 1950s and 1960s, allows me to conclude that Catholic Action was very powerful and successful in Totonicapán.

from the religious hierarchies of the saint brotherhoods (*cofradías*). Whatever the precedents, nowadays people readily accept that "everyone has his own way to God"—as long as respect is respected.

The other great change is the incorporation of the numerous development committees in the communal authority. Without entering into a detailed account, what seems clear is that one way or another the community had to accommodate the forces of modernisation, or put differently, face an ever growing absorption into regional, national and international economies, and an ever more penetrating Guatemalan state. I will argue that the discourse of development is the decisive factor also here, in so far as the image of a developed canton represents a sharp break with the image of a community ordered in accordance with ancient custom and calls for a reformed leadership too, i.e. that of development-trained mayors as opposed to the elders.

Nevertheless, when contemporary mayors and other authorities justify their actions, references to "our tradition", "our ancestors did it this way", or something in that vein(,) are almost always made. The past, or to be more precise the respect that reigned at the time, is still a positive reference in communitarian politics. Construed as an ideology, it could perhaps be argued that *respect* has survived the destruction of the bonds with the ancients and the guardian spirits and has become connected to the Realm of God as preached by Catholics and Protestants alike. However in daily life, respect above all else is connected with the maintenance of the community and the identities that are thereby created. Respect remains the political discourse of the Mayan community.

THE INTERNATIONAL SYSTEM OF HUMAN RIGHTS

The social norms and political ideals expressed by human rights are concretised in a corpus of international law, i.e. laws that affect states as actors. Legally, human rights are that part of international law and jurisprudence that deals with relations between states and individuals, but socially and politically they are a kind of universal constitution in so far as they provide a blueprint for an orderly and just society. The core human rights documents—the Universal Declaration and the two United Nations Covenants—are premised on a series of fundamental freedoms that are inherent to all individuals, and an obligation for all states to guarantee the same freedoms. Much of this is done by converting the freedoms into a series of legally enforceable rights whose purpose is to protect individuals from any abuse of state authority. The result is that human rights treaties commonly read like catalogues of state obligations limiting the powers of the authorities. Keeping in mind the frequent references to the obligations of individuals to promote human rights values particularly in the preambles to the core documents, such a conclusion is not entirely fair, however, as was pointed out in the introduction, in practice references to human rights easily support(s) political claims against any authority as the obligations are under-communicated.

Human rights are also an international political and administrative system designed to assist, and if necessary force, states to comply with their human rights obligations, primarily through the UN system of collective security and cooperation and the various treaty bodies that oversee the implementation of the conventions. Drawing a parallel to state constitutions, the international human rights system has no standing police force and only a rudimentary court system (except for the recently established International Criminal Court). Enforcement is actually the task of the state. The result is that "shaming"—international condemnation of states that violate human rights — has become a main instrument for upholding human rights law.[18] In this work, a host of international and national NGOs and other pressure groups all over the world has joined forces with the designated UN bodies, and it has also acted to push the whole system towards more decisive and concerted action on the issue. Therefore human rights may be likened to a discourse possessing all the power of "the knowledge of truth"[19] and comparable to the morally grounded practices that maintain Mayan communities as separate polities. Consequently, a modern nation-state is socially as well as legally obliged to institutionalise itself in accordance with a right order—or community blueprint—that includes a division of powers (legislative, executive and judiciary), free elections, Rule of Law and a series of social guarantees, as specified by the core documents of human rights. Even if the texts do not enumerate these institutions, it is difficult to imagine how a polity shall comply with the different treaty articles without organising itself as a modern state.

---

[18] See for instance Tomas Risse, Stephen C. Ropp, and Kathryn Sikkink, *The Power of Human Rights. International Norms and Domestic Change*, Cambridge, Cambridge University Press, 1999.

[19] Michel Foucalt, 1980, *op. cit.*

As was pointed out above, this is the reason why human rights primarily make sense in societies that are already organised in accordance with the democratic ideals. Human rights language is full of references to ideals like equality, solidarity, and progress or development. It functions well for expressing political claims as well as political ambitions directed at the authorities, and precisely the way of referring to such claims as "rights" shows that the authority in question is that of a modern nation-state. It follows that in societies where other collective identities and norms predominate, human rights language will not produce the same resonance. It is worth noting that the Mayan languages lack a word for expressing "right" as something that can be claimed in the abstract without reference to the fulfilment of an obligation. Human rights activists therefore typically resort to the Spanish word *derecho*.

If we position ourselves away from ordinary citizen life in a nation-state(and in circumstances characterised by a plurality of authorities with equal or similar capacity to govern life as that of a state, we might be better placed to reflect upon the particularities of human rights. In the first place, one notes the predominance of the state as an authority. No other institution can command a similar dominion over the public moral order because the state is the guarantor of the freedoms that are necessary to live meaningfully. In the second place, the individual is the protagonist of society. The authorities exist so that these minimal social units can realise their possibilities (and cooperate with others to promote human rights). Thirdly, as shown by the numerous references to progress and development, a scientific *weltanschauung* predominates with its practice of constantly examining alternative solutions for finding a better future. There is no room for spiritual or divine guidance in the realm of politics, and little room for turning the ancestors and the elders into political references. A plurality of ways to God is acknowledged, but no religion and no tradition can exercise a control over society if its practices imply human rights violations.

THE INTERNAL RULES OF CHUCULJUYUP

The "Internal Rules of the Inhabitants of the Village of Chuculjuyup" (*Reglamento Interno de los Habitantes de la Aldea Chuculjuyup*) is an attempt to put in writing the orders of the Communal Mayoralty.[20] The effort may last

[20] The document is on file with the author.

four years, because the Rules Committee can only meet two hours every Sunday night. The committee has no regular contact with the other cantons that have made similar Rules, even though during its three years of existence at least five other cantons have finished similar undertakings.

Briefly told, the Chuculjuyup Internal Rules lay down a series of obligations that rest with the inhabitants by virtue of residing in its territory. Above all else, the people of the canton are obliged to "Recognise and occupy their important place in the authority, at meetings and at assemblies ..." (Art. 1) and "Respect and be respected by any local, national, and international person, authority and entity ..." (Art. 2). The document goes on to specify the numerous obligations of the authorities, for instance, "Carry the staff,[21] button, seal and credential[22] at any event …" (Art. 3), "Inform the residents … through three ordinary general assemblies and extraordinary assemblies according to needs dictated by advances in development ..." (Art. 6), "Oversee and facilitate information from committees and associations …" (Art. 7), "Conserve documents such as title deeds of the community, community buildings, school, baths, communal forest …", and "Receive and file the record books …" (Art. 8).

In this way the document details the responsibilities of the different duties of the Communal Mayoralty. When, during its work sessions, a duty is discussed, the Rules Committee calls on the people that currently perform that duty together with elders and other persons generally considered to be knowledgeable about community matters. The discussions mostly take place in K'iche', however, everything is written down in Spanish. Because 30 % or more of everyday K'iche' vocabulary consists of Spanish words anyway—particularly on topics related with nation-wide institutions—this practice does not cause much problem except when discussing the fine distinctions of good morals and reasonable sanctions. But the legal idiom that is employed in order to achieve the necessary solemnity gives a group of young people much power in the editing process due to their superior fluency in written Spanish.

The articles that deal with the obligation to participate in communal works, take on the various duties, and contribute economically are similar in all the

---

[21] The staff is a two feet long black wooden stick that serves as the symbol of authority of the duty-holders, and is to be carried always when on duty.

[22] The credential is an official document issued by the municipal mayor in order to legally verify that the holder is an auxiliary mayor.

constitutions. All of them specify in great detail the type of sanction to be applied in case of transgressions or "failings" as well as how the use of sanctions must benefit the community. In the case of Chuculjuyup, Art. 30 stipulates that "Income generated by fines shall be used in accordance with the needs of the community. The mayors are obliged to present a report … and the use [of the revenue] shall be overseen by the general assembly." Furthermore, everywhere it is the responsibility of the mayors to "Attend every category of decease …" (Art. 19-23 in Chuculjuyup) and bring this information to the municipal civil register, however, here it should be mentioned that the auxiliary mayors have been given authority to do so through a special arrangement with the municipality.

In the case of Chuculjuyup, certain additional health-related obligations stand out: "Supervise and promote the [work of] the midwives so that they comply with their faculties … (Art. 12), "Oversee, in cooperation with the midwives, persons that get pregnant without anyone taking responsibility in order to avoid a forced abortion …" (Art. 13), and "Supervise and strictly control the pregnancies of singles, widows, and married [women]" (Art 28). Such a preoccupation with the fertility and mortality of the inhabitants of the community is indicative of the continuing force of a patriarchal order among the K'iche's. At a deeper level, it may also bear witness to an intimate relationship between the community and its inhabitants that extends a lot further than is the case of a local community within a nation-state. However, the immediate reason for the inclusion of these articles was the fact that the president of the Rules Committee is a Catholic "pro-life" activist. In other cantons similar proposals were turned down as it was felt that abortion is a family affair, not a mayoralty affair. In any case this detail shows how political and moral debates originating elsewhere are articulated locally.

Restrictive migration rules, too, tell a story of what could be termed "community mystique" in so far as the primary concern is the survival of the community as a distinct social unit. Again the case of Chuculjuyup will serve, but the following list of requirements is common to all the Internal Rules that have been produced so far: "It is the responsibility [of the current auxiliary mayor] to investigate and analyse the causes why person[s] or families that emigrate temporally or definitively, and register [this] in the specific book" (Art. 32). In order to take up residence in the canton, Art. 31 stipulates that "the families or persons should carry the following credentials: (a) certificate of residence (*cédula de vecindad*, Guatemala's most important ID, issued by the municipality), (b) letter of good conduct, signed and sealed by the auxiliary mayor or municipal mayor, … (d) criminal record, … (f) if the conditions are met, he/she may reside in the community and submit to the Rules, … (h) the public service committees will be informed and [the new resident] must present himself at the general assembly, (i) if conditions are not met he/she cannot reside in the community."

The single most pressing reason given for elaborating Internal Rules is the need for constructing order, and to this end a tradition of local autonomy is usually invoked. For instance, the "Internal Rules" of Canton Paxtocá[23] begins by declaring that "Before the Invasion of the Spanish, the communities had its way of life and they lived in harmony and had their own laws, they governed themselves by authorities composed of chiefs, principals and the elders", and consequently there is a persistent need to "reckon with a legal instrument" in order to "achieve living in harmony and that services should be equal without any discrimination". Paxtocá has even put up road signs and established a community treasury in order to enforce its order. Other cantons have chosen to invoke the need for development, and the preamble to the Rules of Canton Xolsacmaljá[24] reads: "It is urgent to define the functions and attributions of the authorities … thereby pursuing the equality of rights and obligations, with a view to communitarian development". Often human rights instruments such as ILO Convention 169/1989 on the Rights of Indigenous and Tribal Peoples are called upon as well because people realise that this document is a legally powerful defence of community autonomy, perhaps comparable to how individuals seek out support by visiting alien authorities in the town centre.

Taken together, the orders expressed in the written Mayan constitutions and in the oral traditions passed on every year on issues like community justice and government, migration and public services reveal a notion of political sovereignty that in many ways puts the community on a par with the state. That there are frequent clashes with Guatemalan authorities cannot come as a surprise, and in the next section we shall take a closer look at one such incident. It will be seen that the decisive factor is precisely the moral and consequently the political sovereignty of the Mayan community.[25] The constant tension

[23] The document is on file with the author.

[24] The document is on file with the author.

[25] The same point about the centrality of community political sovereignty is vividly demonstrated by Shannon Speed and Jane Collier in their article about the policies of the Mexican

between the Indigenous Mayoralty and the municipality is moreover a recurring theme in the history of the Mayan areas of Guatemala. The gradual erosion of the powers of the Indigenous Mayoralty in the 1970s and 1980s might have undermined the power of the elders and the tradition-based rule of the principals of Totonicapán, but today the struggle for sovereignty continues under the leadership of the vice-mayors, now presenting themselves as Communal Mayors. The making of Internal Rules is a good example.

HUMAN RIGHTS, VISITING

In spite of its good intentions, "human rights", personified by the Human Rights Ombudsman and the UN observer mission to Guatemala (MINUGUA), have so far not succeeded in overcoming the profound division between the Guatemalan state and the Mayan community. On the contrary, generally speaking human rights are categorised as yet another "alien authority" (*q'atb'al tzij*), on a par with the Guatemalan state and its Ladino tribunals.

In May 2000, when the communal authorities of Chuculjuyup became aware that a resident had sold a certain quantity of piped water to a neighbour without giving notice neither to the authorities nor to the water committee that had installed the water pipe, it was decided to fine him. However, the wrongdoer refused to pay whereupon the water committee decided to disconnect the water supply. In this situation, the man went to the Provincial Delegation of the Human Rights Ombudsman, pleading that to cut him off from the "holy liquid" (as the expression goes) was a human rights violation. The local representative of the Ombudsman agreed that the right to water is a human right, but when the Communal Mayoralty received this verdict, the Mayor and his team responded that "here there are two types of water, public and private", and pointed out that the committee already had very clear rules that prohibited any trading of its services. In the words of the mayoralty, the man might as well "go to the river, like we did before". When I investigated the case a few months later, they added: "What have human rights given us to meet the expenses of [installing piped] water?"

---

state v. Mayan communities in Chiapas, see Shannon Speed & Jane F. Collier, "Limiting Indigenous Autonomy in Chiapas, Mexico: The State Government's Use of Human Rights", in *Human Rights Quarterly*, Vol. 22, no. 4, 2000.

Shortly afterwards, another family refused to contribute a sum of money for the construction of a new school building, asserting that since they no longer had children of school age, they did not have to pay. After a phase of inconclusive negotiations, the mayor decided to disconnect the water in this case, too. The family went to the Human Rights Ombudsman, who decided to investigate the matter. He notified the Communal Mayor that he would soon visit Chuculjuyup, and that the presence of the authorities was indispensable. To demand a meeting at an already established hour without previous negotiation was interpreted as an insult and an example of the arrogance of "alien (Ladino) justice". Nevertheless, during his visit, the Ombudsman's representative succeeded in taking copies of the community's record books in which it was acknowledged that the sanction was in conformity with previous decisions, and that the procedure had been accepted and signed by all.[26] In his speech to the assembly, the human rights representative chose to refer to the "right to due process" rather than the "right to water", and he argued that the family in question had refused to pay primarily because of lack of confidence in the communal authorities. The people who had collected the money had not given any receipts. The mayor admitted to this practice and promised to set it right.

An exhaustive human rights analysis of this case is beside the point here, but it must be pointed out that there is no such thing as a "right to water". From a human rights perspective, what is at stake is the responsibility of the state (and its local representatives, including the Communal Mayoralty) to respect and protect the accused against abuse both while the case is pending and with regard to the form of sanction. Considerations as to how a state chooses to implement social and economic rights that deal with the "highest attainable standard of living" are not relevant inasmuch as general access to water is already in place and the case is in actual fact a conflict between an authority and an individual. However, for a Human Rights Ombudsman that sees itself as a provider of free legal aid as well as a watchdog on state action and legislative matters—its mandate allows for this—it is tempting to intervene in any case.

In national society, this type of human rights defence is an efficient way of accumulating political capital, but in Totonicapán such interventions might as well work to the contrary. There have been many similar cases, and there is

[26] These documents are also on file with the author.

much annoyance—but also anxiety—about how national authorities disapprove of traditional practices of sanctioning. In general, people are quick to say that "human rights only serve to defend delinquents" and that they "are of little value" (*no trae ningún beneficio*). However, it is necessary to add that most Communal Mayors and other leaders, too, are very much aware that the same human rights—cf. above about the use of the ILO Convention no. 169/1989 as the basis for local constitutions—are their best ally in the struggle to keep communal sovereignty as against the state of Guatemala.

CONCLUSIONS, CONTRASTS, AND BRIDGES

Through this comparison of the ethno-political discourse of the K'iche'-Mayan community and the discourse of human rights, we have uncovered a series of quite profound contrasts. We have also seen how this situation produces contradictions and confrontations that replicate the rupture between the Guatemalan state and the Mayan communities, and the corresponding cleavage between Ladinos and Mayas. In order to arrive at this deduction, we identified a distinct Mayan polity, based on specific ideas about personhood and a particular constellation of collective identities that are markedly different from the corresponding social realities of a modern nation-state. Given that human rights as a discourse tend to reproduce the social realities of societies based on nation-states rather than those of an indigenous community at the margins of a national society, in principle we have a situation of two distinct cultures meeting each other. Moreover, both consider themselves to be sovereign, even if at the same time they are conscious of having an intimate and asymmetric mutual relation.

At one side stands the K'iche'-Mayan community, represented through a collectivist identity, and whose own survival is imperious. Individuals are not equal, but differ in accordance with sex, personality and amount of accumulated respect. However, everyone complement each other within a compulsory enterprise to maintain the community. Rights or freedoms cannot be discussed in isolation from corresponding obligations. Individuals are credited with respect in accordance with their behaviour and compliance with communal duties.[27] It is the task of a communal authority to see to it that the

[27] For an insightful discussion of how to translate the Universal Declaration of Human Rights into a Mayan language, see Pedro Pitarch, "El laberinto de la traducción: la Declaración

inhabitants of the community submit to this order. This authority is unique and indivisible and based on a mixture of tradition and locally sanctioned innovation.

At the other side stands the ideal human rights-compliant state formation, represented by the sovereign individual whose freedoms and personal development the state is obliged to respect, protect and fulfil. To that end, its powers have been divided, and it has been subjected to a series of limitations in its conduct towards the individuals under its jurisdiction. These limitations are given as a set of fundamental rules that accept all human beings all over the world as inherently equal irrespective of sex, ethnicity, and social behaviour. Therefore a fundamental contrast is located in the concepts of citizenship ("respectable persons" v. "human beings") of the two communities. The Mayan community does not accept the idea that a person can put his/hers own interests first. Within human rights it cannot be accepted that persons are considered unequal and only subject to a gradual acquisition of full political rights—even as there is full acceptance of a whole range of lifestyles that in a Mayan community would violate the fundamental obligation to respect and protect community harmony.

The list of differing characteristics can be made much more extensive. However, by keeping in mind the distinct conceptions of personhood and differing ideas about how to order relations between the community and its individual members, it is easy to identify situations that will give rise to alienation and confrontation. Because ideas about personhood and a right order are based on morally grounded identities, disagreements may rapidly turn into conflicts about political sovereignty. In other words, the conflicts are real and profoundly rooted, but not insurmountable.

In much contemporary human rights literature, there is widespread talk about the need for respecting "different cultures", or as a Maya might put it, "different ways of being". The above observations about the production of disagreements and conflicts between communities ought to be taken as points of departure when bridges of mutual understanding are constructed between cultures. Good-willed but superficial efforts may only lead to increased levels of mistrust. In a situation of asymmetric power relations, entrenched by

Universal de Los Derechos Humanos en tzeltal", Pedro Pitarch and Julián López García, *Los Derechos Humanos en tierras mayas. Política, representaciones y moralidad*, Sociedad Española de Estudios Mayas, Madrid, 2001, pp. 127-160.

centuries of domination, it is only too easy to detect what Guatemalans routinely call "lack of seriousness" in the proposals of the adversary. Moreover, some contradictions are simply impossible to solve except as part of larger changes such as the weakening and eventual irrelevance of a community rule grounded in a single religious tradition.

Acknowledging all this, pragmatism seems to be the answer. It is necessary to enter into a series of temporary agreements without trying to impose the perfect solution from the first moment. The preambles of the Mayan canton constitutions that invoke ILO Convention 169/1989 and the ratification of the same treaty by the Guatemalan state are good beginnings. At the local level, we might also get support from the piece of Mayan everyday philosophy that concedes that "we respect each other in our different ways of being", as well as from the references to reciprocal love that routinely are invoked by the various Christian churches that predominate in Guatemalan society on both sides of the ethnic boundary. On the other hand, it is not hard at all to detect arrogant and myopic patterns of behaviour on both sides. For this reason pragmatism focuses on taking small steps. What happened between the Human Rights Ombudsman and the Communal Mayor in Chuculjuyup is a case in point. Both parties ceded something, but at the same time there remained a lot to be done. The establishment of a permanent dialogue between human rights and the indigenous authorities of Guatemala is an urgent task for anyone involved in constructing a more just society in Guatemala.

BIBIOGRAPHY

Barrios, Lina, 1998. *La Alcaldía Indígena en Guatemala: de 1944 al presente*, Guatemala, IDIES, Universidad Rafaél Landívar

Brintnall, Douglas, 1979. *Revolt Against the Dead. The Modernization of a Mayan Community in the Highlands of Guatemala,* New York, Gordon & Breach

Carlsen, Robert S., 1999. *The War for the Heart and Soul of a Highland Maya Town*, Austin, University of Texas Press

Carmack, Robert, 1995. *Rebels of Highland Guatemala. The Quiche-Mayas of Momostenango*, Norman, University of Oklahoma Press

Dembour, Marie Bénédicte, 1996. "Human rights talk and anthropological ambivalence: the particular context of universal claims", in Olivia Harris (ed.), *Inside and Outside the Law. Anthropological Studies of Authority and Ambiguity*, London, Routledge

Esquit Choy, Edgar and Carlos Ochoa García, 1995. *Tiqalil q'anej, kunimaaj tziij, niman tzij. El respeto a la palabra. El orden jurídico del pueblo maya*, Guatemala, CECMA

Falla, Ricardo, 1995 [1970]. *Quiché Rebelde. Estudio de un movimiento de conversión religiosa, rebelde a las creencias regionales, en San Antonio Ilotenango, Quiché (1948-1970)*, Guatemala, Editorial Universitaria

Foucalt, Michel, 1972. *The Archaeology of Knowledge*, New York, Pantheon Books

Foucalt, Michel, 1980. *Power/Knowledge: Selected Interviews & Other Writings 1972-1977*, New York, Pantheon Books

Hansen, Thomas Blom and Finn Stepputat (eds.), 2001. *States of Imagination. Ethnographic Explorations of the Postcolonial State*, Durham and London, Duke University Press

Pitarch, Pedro, 2001. "El laberinto de la traducción: la Declaración Universal de Los Derechos Humanos en tzeltal", in Pedro Pitarch and Julián López García (eds.): *Los Derechos Humanos en tierras mayas. Política, representaciones y moralidad*, Madrid, Sociedad Española de Estudios Mayas

Risse, Thomas, Stephen C. Ropp, and Kathryn Sikkink, 1999. *The Power of Human Rights. International Norms and Domestic Change*, Cambridge, Cambridge University Press

Speed, Shannon, and Jane F. Collier, 2000. "Limiting Indigenous Autonomy in Chiapas, Mexico: The Government's Use of Human Rights", in *Human Rights Quarterly*, Vol. 22, no. 4

Juvenile Justice and the Law in Uganda: Towards Restorative Justice

Lillian Tibatemwa-Ekirikubinza

INTRODUCTION

The paper is a critical analysis of the law and practice of juvenile justice in Uganda. Apart from a discussion of the written law the paper involves a discussion of the findings of a pilot study on the implementation of the Children Statute carried out between June and August 2003.

On the one hand, the paper attempts to evaluate the extent to which Uganda's law is in line with norms and values of a child rights based juvenile justice system. It then discusses societal perceptions towards the basic principles underpinning juvenile justice law: childhood and diversion. A discussion of societal perception is relevant on the premise that the enjoyment of rights depends as much on what is contained in the statute books as it does on what the actors perceive to be the accepted norms and values. In other words, the perceptions of the various stakeholders have an impact on the extent to which paper rights and black letter law are actualised.

On the other hand, the paper analyses the extent to which Uganda's law and practice are based on a trend which has emerged in several progressive juvenile justice systems; restorative justice, a notion which "eschews retribution and punishment as primary motivators for exacting compliance and relies on the innate capacity of individuals, families and communities to work out solutions which suit their situations."[1] In making suggestions for a model/process of restorative justice suitable for Uganda, the paper argues for a revisiting of indigenous justice traditions in order to ensure that the resulting model is cognisant of cultural sensitivities and is appropriate and acceptable to the community.

While bearing in mind, the limited nature of the study, the paper attempts to throw light on the following questions:

- To what extent are the principles underpinning a child rights based juvenile justice system in line with the perceptions of Ugandan society?
- To what extent are the principles underpinning restorative justice in line with society's perception towards justice?

---

[1] Ann Skelton, "Developing a juvenile justice system for South Africa: International instruments and restorative justice" in *Acta Juridica*, Juta & Co. Ltd., 1996, p. 180.

- How are children in conflict with the law *actually* treated by the various actors?

BACKGROUND

Uganda is a former British colony that gained political independence in 1962. Among the things introduced during the colonial period were English laws, which were applied in addition to the people's "customary laws." The 11 August 1902 Order-in-Council specifically stipulated that the law to be applied by the courts shall comprise, inter alia, various named legislation of the United Kingdom in force at that date, the substance of the English Common Law, Doctrines of Equity and Statutes of General Application, as well as indigenous laws and customs.

The co-existence of received laws based on the colonial legal system side by side with "customary law" created a phenomenon of legal pluralism in Uganda's legal framework. This plurality of laws continues to characterise the legal system of post-colonial Uganda.[2]

In addition to the above, there exists some kind of "living law", which is a rough combination of practices, attitudes, ideas, cultures and norms that are more or less a compromise to the social dictates. Formal laws influence living laws although they too generate their own rules and norms. It is for this reason that Nathalie Des Rosiers[3] adds that *living law is the relationship between official law and the law that emerges in the everyday interaction of people with each other.* Living law is influenced by, but does not necessarily conform to the formal legal system. It is for this reason that this study looked beyond the boundaries of legal centralism and considered other social and legal institutions (the semi-autonomous social fields) when assessing the operationalisation of juvenile justice law in Uganda.

Uganda's 1995 Constitution recognises the vulnerability of children, and Article 34 specifically dedicates some articles under the Bill of Rights, to children's rights. In 1996, the Children Statute was enacted by parliament.

---

[2] Women and Law in East Africa [WLEA] 1998.

[3] Reforming or rethinking the law? Canada's experience of law reform http://www.lcc.gc.ca/en/pc/speeches/2000629.asp

This piece of law has often been applauded as one of the most elaborate pieces of law on children on the continent of Africa. In addition to specific rights contained therein, the Statute incorporates all rights set out in the UN Convention on the Rights of the Child (CRC) and in the African Charter on the Rights and Welfare of the Child (the African Child Charter). It provides that:

> A child shall have the right to exercise, in addition to all the rights stated in this Statute, all the rights set out in the UN Convention on the Rights of the Child and the O.A.U. Charter on the Rights and Welfare of the Child with appropriate modifications to suit the circumstances in Uganda that are not specifically mentioned in this Statute.[4]

In effect, Uganda adopted the values and norms reflected in the 2 international human rights instruments. These universal norms and values could therefore be considered to have become national norms and values by law.

A close look at the Statute reveals that one can safely contend that the law is more detailed on the treatment and rights of children in conflict with the law, than on any other area of children's rights. The Statute directly logs into the provisions of the United Nations Standard Minimum Rules for the Administration of Juvenile Justice (Beijing Rules). It can thus be said that Uganda recognises the need to deal with children in conflict with the law, within a framework of international human rights standards. The Act is firmly placed within the ambit of children's rights and aims at a juvenile justice system centred on the rights of children.

NATURE OF THE EMPIRICAL STUDY

The study was conducted in the city district of Kampala, which is also Uganda's capital city. The research among other things involved in-depth interviews with groups of people who have a stake in juvenile justice: judicial officers, the police, local council executives, probation and welfare officers, parents whose children have been in conflict with the law, children who have been in conflict with the law as well as members of the community who have been victims of juvenile crime.

---

[4] See Rule 4 (c) of the First Schedule to the Children Statute.

The opinions and experiences specifically referred to in this paper revolve around in-depth interviews with 10 parents of children who have been involved in criminal activities; 10 children who have been in conflict with the law; 8 members of the community who have been victims of child offenders as well as 6 members of the community who have never been victims of child offenders on the one hand, and whose children have never been involved in criminal activity on the other hand.

The geographical area of the study and the sample of respondents were purposively selected. Kampala District was chosen because of its cosmopolitan nature. Katwe Police Station, located in Kampala District was selected for the study because it reportedly has a high incidence of juvenile crime.[5] I was introduced to the officer in charge of the Katwe Child and Family Protection Unit by an officer from the national headquarters. A look at the official records enabled me to identify children who had either been reported to or arrested by the Katwe police for involvement in criminal activities. Records at the police unit indicate the name of the child as well as the area of residence. I deliberately picked out children who reside in the village (zone) nearest to the police station.[6] With the help of the Local Council Executives of the area I was able to locate the residences of the relevant respondents. In each category of people interviewed I aimed at interviewing both male and female respondents.

THE WRITTEN LAW VERSUS SOCIETAL PERCEPTIONS

In this section of the paper I will discuss international and domestic law provisions relating to the three principles underpinning Uganda's juvenile justice law: childhood, diversion and restorative justice. I will also present the study findings on the perceptions of members of the community towards each of the said principles. The discussion also throws light on what is happening on the ground: the extent to which the said principles are followed in the handling of children in conflict with the law.

---

[5] I was informally given this information by colleagues at the National Police Headquarters.

[6] Makindye Zone.

The concept of childhood

Placed as it is within the ambit of children's rights, Uganda's juvenile justice law has as a major aim, the recognition of the age status and level of development of young persons. According to Section 3 of the Statute, a child is a person below the age of 18 years.[7] And under Section 89 of the Children Statute, the age of criminal responsibility was raised from 7 years to 12 years.

The raise in the age of criminal responsibility by the statute conforms to the principle in the Beijing Rules that the age of responsibility for crime should not be set at too low a level and should in any case reflect emotional, mental and intellectual maturity.[8]

To what extent is the legal definition of childhood in line with societal perceptions?

As already mentioned, the study involved in-depth interviews with parents of children who have been in conflict with the law. Asked who a child is, individual parents mentioned different ages as the turning point from childhood to adulthood (14, 15, and 16). Nevertheless, they all shared one common opinion; only an adult should be held responsible for her or his conduct. It thus comes out that they link the notion of childhood with that of immaturity. It is interesting to note that under Uganda's principal penal law, the section which establishes the minimum age of criminal responsibility is entitled 'Immature Age.[9]

Some members of the community defined childhood from a relationship perspective: a person remains a child indefinitely in the eyes of her or his parent. It was emphasised that within this context, age is irrelevant. Some respondents contended that childhood connoted the status of being controlled or perhaps controllable and thus capable of being punished by a parent. This

[7] The definition is in line with Article 257 of Uganda's constitution, Article 1 of the Convention on the Rights of the Child (CRC), and Article 2 of the African Child Charter.

[8] This principle was adopted by Article 17(4) of the African Child Charter wherein it is provided that there shall be a minimum age below which children shall be presumed not to have the capacity to infringe the penal law. And according to Article 40 (3) of the UN Convention on the Rights of the Child: States Parties shall ensure the establishment of a minimum age below which children shall be presumed not to have the capacity to infringe the penal law.

[9] Section 14 of the Uganda Penal Code.

notion of childhood fits in well with the concept of family responsibility for the wrongful actions of a child offender, one of the concepts at the centre of restorative justice programmes. Family responsibility also fits in well with one of the definitions of childhood put forward by the respondents i.e. that a child is a person who is still dependent on her parents, a person for whom the parent is still 'responsible'. If a person is responsible for another, it is likely that the former can influence the latter in keeping 'promises' arrived at in a restorative justice conference. It is to be noted that in the various definitions of childhood put forward by members of the community, the notion of parental responsibility was often emphasised.

Definitions from interviews with children who have been in conflict with the law were very similar to those of other groups. The most common answer, however, was that a child is a person who is still dependent on his or her parents. Dependency for this group was seen in terms of sustenance as well as guidance. According to the children, a person who needed guidance from the parent was still a child. If we assume that a person will only seek advice from a person she or he respects, this would offer support to the opinion that where a young person has broken the law, the involvement of the family (parents) in a restorative justice process is invaluable.

It is noted that among all the groups of respondents interviewed, the age of a person, as a standard of determining adulthood, was mentioned as an after thought. What is, however, most important is that among the various groups, it was agreed that a person should only be responsible for her or his actions after reaching maturity. This may form a basis for acceptance of the principle that a young person who infringes the law should be handled differently from an adult offender. Although there seems to be divergence between the parameters of childhood as defined by the law on the one hand, and as defined by members of the community on the other hand, the community is in agreement with the law that childhood (however defined) is synonymous with lack of criminal culpability. To that extent, societal perceptions and practice are at par with statutory law. It is perhaps for this reason that in several case studies to be discussed later, the victims looked to the parents of the erring children for restoration rather than to the formal agencies of the criminal justice system.

Diversion and the best interest of the child principle

As already mentioned, inherent in the Children Statute is a call to view juvenile justice through the discourse of children's rights. Perceiving children in conflict with the law through the window of children's rights means that, the child offender is recognised as first and foremost a child and then as an offender.

A *basic* premise of children's rights is that in all decisions concerning children, the guiding principle should be the best interest of the child. Section 4 of the Children Statute[10] provides that the welfare principles shall be the guiding principles in the making of any decision based on the provisions of this statute.[11] Uganda's juvenile justice law is premised on the belief that it is in the best interest of the child (and of society), that a child who has transgressed the law is re-habilitated and re-integrated into society. It is presumed that this will best be done outside the formal justice system and thus the diversion of a child from the formal justice system is a central aim of juvenile justice law and not peripheral to it. This is in line with the Beijing Rules, which provide that:

> Consideration shall be given, wherever appropriate, to dealing with juvenile offenders without resorting to formal trial[12]

Similarly, the UN Child Convention provides that in any dealings with a child in conflict with the law:

> States parties should whenever appropriate and desirable, promote measures for dealing with children in conflict with the law, without resorting to judicial proceedings. (Article 40 (3) (b).[13]

---

[10] Entitled 'Guiding Principles'.

[11] See also Article 4 (1) of the African Child Charter, which provides that: In all actions concerning the child undertaken by any person or authority the best interests of the child shall be the primary consideration. Article 3 (1) of the Convention on the Rights of the Child, which states that: "In all actions concerning children, whether undertaken by public or private social welfare institutions, courts of law, administrative authorities or legislative bodies, the best interests of the child shall be a primary consideration."

[12] Rule 11.1.

[13] The African Child Charter does not specifically provide for diversion although it states that the essential aim of the handling of a child within the criminal justice system shall be re-integration into the family and social rehabilitation. (Article 17(3)).

Historically, diversion referred to a mechanism for removing young persons from the juvenile court process before they were formally adjudicated. However, the term has taken over a wider meaning and is used to refer to any alternatives to the further advancement of an individual child into the juvenile justice system. Thus, diversion may occur at any point and could in fact prevent the child from entering the juvenile justice system. In the commentary to Rule 11 of the Beijing Rules, diversion is referred to as removal from criminal justice processing. It is observed in the commentary that in many cases non-intervention would be the best response and that diversion at the outset and without referral to social services may be the optimal response. The rule is thus calling for informal as opposed to formal social control.

In its emphasis of the need to divert children from the formal justice system, and in line with the Beijing Rules, Uganda's 1996 Statute provides alternatives to the formal justice system at *every* stage of the process.[14] First, it empowers the Local Committee Courts (LCs in local parlance) to hear and dispose of some matters concerning child "offenders". Furthermore, the law gives wide discretionary powers to the police to divert children from court proceedings. Further still, where a child must be processed through the court system, judicial officers are expected to ensure that institutionalisation of a child against whom an offence has been proved, is only a last resort. Below I discuss diversion at each of the three stages: the Local Committee Courts, the Police and the Family and Children Courts.

The Local Committee Courts

According to the Local Governments Act, all adults residing in a particular geographical area are automatically members of such village, parish and sub-county local councils. Under Section 48 (2) of the same enactment, Local Councils (LCs) are administrative units based on sub-counties, parishes and villages. All adults residing in an area periodically elect a 9 person committee as the administrative body of the area. The committee consists of the following offices: a chairperson; a deputy chairperson who is also responsible for children's affairs; a secretary for the youth; a secretary for finances; a secretary for education and mass mobilisation; a secretary for information; a secretary for security (defence) and a secretary for people with disabilities. These

[14] Under rule 11.2 of the Beijing Rules, diversion may be used at any point of decision-making without recourse to formal hearings.

administrative bodies were given judicial powers by the Resistance Committees (Judicial Powers) Statute of 1988. Section 1 of the Statute provides:

> The Resistance Committees in every village, parish, and sub-county are hereby established as courts.

And under Section 2 of the same Statute it is provided that:

> A Resistance Committee Court shall consist of members of the Resistance Committee of the village, parish, or sub-county as the case may be.

The Resistance Committees have been re-named Local Committees and thus we have Local Committee Courts.

Under Section 93 (2) of the Children Statute, Local Committee Courts are empowered to handle various types of criminal cases if perpetrated by persons under18 years.[15] For such offences, the village committees are the courts of first instance. The section is thus aimed at ensuring that children engaged in relatively non-serious crimes are completely kept out of the formal criminal justice system.

In furtherance of the aim of keeping children out of the criminal justice system, the orders which the Local Committee Courts are empowered to make are not institutional. Rather they re-locate the child back into the community. The orders are: reconciliation, compensation,[16] restitution,[17] apology, or caution. In addition, the courts can make a guidance order under which a child is called upon to submit himself/herself to the guidance, supervision, advice and assistance of a person designated by the court.

At the village level, the law specifically provides that no person shall be disqualified from membership of the committee on account of being illiterate

---

[15] Affray, common assault, assault occasioning actual bodily harm, theft, criminal trespass, malicious damage to property, soliciting or loitering for immoral purposes.

[16] Under Section 19 of the Resistance Committees (Judicial Powers) Statute, the order for compensation can constitute the handing over by the "offender", either property or cash to the aggrieved party as the court may deem to be the equivalent of the complainant's property or right which was damaged, lost or injured.

[17] Under section 20, restitution involves the return of the relevant property to the person entitled thereto.

in the official language (English). The underlying intention is to include all categories of people regardless of educational achievement. It therefore follows that legal knowledge is not a pre-requisite to membership of the committee. As reported by John-Jean Barya and J.Oloka-Onyango [18] procedural issues of a typical judicial hearing are dispensed with as the Courts essentially apply rules of Natural Justice. It is noted that the under section 12(2) no party to a suit before the LC court may be represented by a lawyer. This is aimed at preventing professionals from having access to these courts. The composition of these courts makes it more likely that they are more representative of community perceptions than are formal courts of law.

Under Section 106 of the Children Statute, decisions of the village committee courts can be appealed against as indicated in Table A. It is noted that Parish Local Committees, Sub-County Local Committees, the Court of Appeal as well as the Supreme Court are strictly appellate courts. It is for this reason that my discussion of diversion is limited to what happens at the village level.

Table A indicates that when a crime is committed within a particular village, members of the community can report the case to a member of the village executive committee. This is usually the chairperson of the committee or the secretary for defence. If the offence is beyond the jurisdiction of the village committee court, the case should be forwarded to the police. The police will then forward the case to the appropriate court of first instance. This can be either the Family and Children Court or the Chief Magistrate's Court or the High Court, depending on the seriousness of the offence and/or the circumstances surrounding its commission.

At times, however, cases are reported to the police without involvement of the village committee. If the case in question is one which the police has jurisdiction to handle (see discussion on police powers below) the police will use its discretion to caution and release the child. The police can also use its discretion and refer the case back to the village committee. Where the case is beyond the jurisdiction of the police and the village committee, the police will forward the case to the appropriate court of first instance.

---

[18] John Jean Barya and Oloka Onyango, *Popular Justice and resistance Committee Courts in* Uganda, Kampala, Friedrich Ebert Stiftung, 1994.

The Police

In line with the need to keep a child's contact with the formal criminal justice system at a minimum, Section 90 (2) of the Children Statute empowers the police to dispose of cases at their discretion without recourse to formal court hearings in accordance with criteria laid down by the Inspector General of

Table A

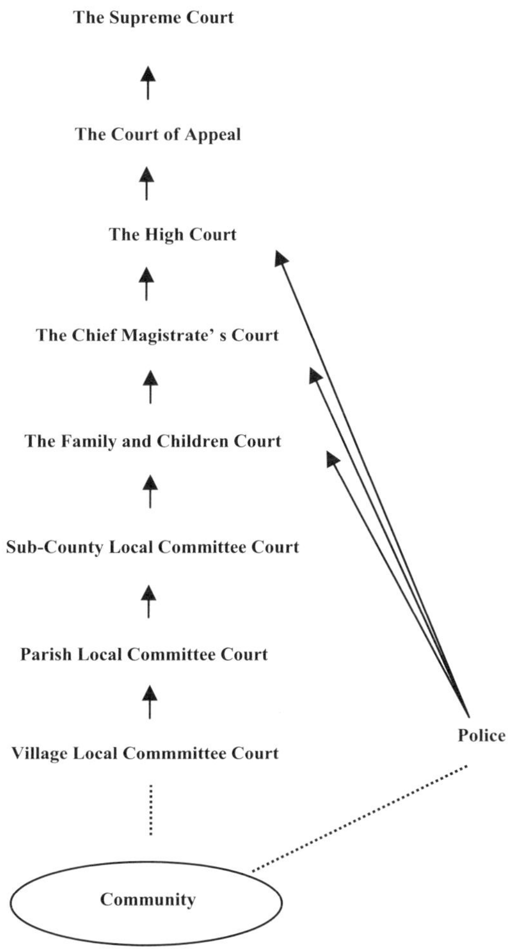

Police.[19] It is because police action can prevent a child from getting to court that I discuss the police before the Family and Children Court.

In order to ensure that children are handled by personnel with specific knowledge of the needs of children, it is provided by the police guidelines that cases involving children in conflict with the law shall be handled by the Child and Family Protection Unit. In line with section 90 (1) of the Statute,[20] the guidelines recognise caution by the police as a legitimate disposition of handling a child offender. The guidelines have specifically provided that where an offence is not serious, where a child shows remorse, where a child is a first offender, the police *shall* caution and release the child. Although the term "serious" offence is not defined by the guidelines, guideline 5.0 (x) specifically mentions some of the offences where the police *shall* caution and release the child.[21] The word shall indicates that the guideline is mandatory, this view is further supported by a latter paragraph of guideline 5.0 wherein it is stated that no child shall be charged with the aforementioned offences. It is to be noted that these are the very offences which the Local Committee Courts are empowered to try as courts of first instance. When a police officer is of the view that the circumstances surrounding the offence and the offender will not be appropriately dealt with through a caution, the case must be referred to the relevant local council. The police refer the child to the Secretary for Children Affairs without a formal charge.

Where a child is involved in a case beyond the jurisdiction of the village committee court and thus has to stand trial, the police is empowered to release the child on police bond, as long as the child's safety will not be at risk and the child will not be a danger to the community. Release can be on a child's own recognizance i.e. a promise made to the police officer that s/he will appear on a certain date and time at a particular place (e.g. the police station) as required.[22] The rule on police bond is in line with the general principle in juvenile justice law that detention of a child should only be used as a last resort. By recognition of a promise unaccompanied by monetary requirements, the

[19] The guidelines have been issued and are entitled "Implementation of the Children Statute: Police Guidelines."

[20] It is provided that: Where a child is arrested, the police shall under justifiable circumstances caution and release the child.

[21] Affray, malicious damage to property, criminal trespass, theft, common assault and prostitution.

[22] As defined by Guideline 11.5.

guidelines enable children from economically disadvantaged backgrounds to enjoy the same rights as children who are able to pay.

The Family and Children Court

The statute has made provision for special courts to handle offences beyond the jurisdiction of the Local Committee Courts – The Family and Children Court. The creation of special courts is a fulfilment of an obligation created under Article 40(3) of the CRC for state parties to establish authorities and institutions specifically applicable to children in conflict with the law.[23] The Family and Children Court is the court of first instance for cases that cannot be tried by the Local Committee Courts. It is empowered to determine *all* criminal cases against a child except offences punishable by death and offences for which a child is jointly charged with a person over the age of 18 years.[24]

Where a child is engaged in criminal conduct jointly with an adult, or is engaged in a capital offence, the case will be handled by a court with the appropriate jurisdiction to try the case. This will be either a Magistrate's court or the High Court. If an offence is proved against a child in a court "superior" to a Family and Children Court, the trial court must remit the child to the Family and Children Court for an appropriate order to be made.[25]

The Family and Children Court is empowered to issue various types of orders; absolute discharge,[26] caution, conditional discharge,[27] binding the child over to be of good behaviour, compensation, restitution, fine, probation,[28] detention.[29]

[23] The African Child Charter does not address the need for specialised institutions to deal with children in conflict with the law.

[24] Section 94 of the Children Statute.

[25] Section 101 (3) of the Children Statute.

[26] A sentence in which, although the offence against the juvenile offender is proved, no conviction is recorded and the offender is free to go without conditions.

[27] A delayed or held-off sentence; if the offender meets certain conditions, the court never decides on a penalty and the offender will have no criminal record.

[28] This order allows the offender provisional freedom rather than detention. It requires good behaviour and other conditions that the court may impose. The freedom is granted to the juvenile as long as he/she meets certain conditions of behaviour. The juvenile must report periodically to a probation officer.

[29] Section 95 (1).

The need for alternative orders is set out in Article 40 (4) of the CRC.[30] But although detention is mentioned the law clearly provides that detention or institutionalisation shall be a matter of last resort.[31] Just as is the case with orders given by a Local Committee Court, some of the orders that can be given by the Family and Children Court are premised within the restorative justice paradigm. Their focus is on reparation of the harm suffered by the victim. The need to keep a child's contact with the formal justice system at the very minimum is also apparent in the fact that almost all the orders re-channel the child back into the community.

Diversion and the Labelling Theory of Crime

It is noted that the aim of keeping children away from the formal justice system is consistent with the labelling theory of crime which draws attention to the potentially negative consequences for a young person to be formally labelled as an offender. It is argued that a child's contact with the formal justice system may increase the likelihood that the young person will engage in further anti-social behaviour. The labelling theory of crime was provided by Howard Becker way back in the 1960s.[32] Becker argued that:

> Deviance is not a quality of the act a person commits, but rather a consequence of the application by other rules and sanctions to an "offender". The deviant is one to whom the label has successfully been applied; deviant behaviour that people so label. (p. 9)

According to the theory, the act of labelling a person as deviant becomes a self-fulfilling prophecy. Once labelled, a person will tend to behave accordingly. Contact with the juvenile justice system is said to burden young people with just such a label.

In a commentary on the Beijing Rules[33] it is contended that diversion involving removal of a child from criminal justice processing serves to hinder

---

[30] The CRC provides inter alia that a variety of dispositions, alternatives to institutional care, shall be available to ensure that children are dealt with in a manner appropriate to their well being. The African Child Charter does not make mention of the issue.

[31] Section 95 (4).

[32] H.S. Becker, *Outsiders: Studies in the Sociology of Deviance*, New York: The Free Press, 1936. See also Stanley Cohen, *Folk Devils and Moral Panics*, London: Mac Gibbon and Kee, 1972.

[33] By Geraldine Van Bueren and Anne-Marie Tootell.

the negative effects of subsequent proceedings in juvenile justice administration such as the stigma of conviction and sentence.[34] In other words, labelling produces stigma, stigma lowers self-esteem and lowered self-esteem prompts anti-social behaviour.

But what are the perceptions of society towards diversion?

Interviews with the various categories of respondents revealed a general view that children's "criminal" behaviour should to the farthest possible extent be dealt with outside the formal criminal justice system. Several respondents opined that once a child is reported to the LC, the committee should make arrangements for the parents (family) of the child to meet with the victim of the offence so that a solution to the problem could be found. This idea has a lot of similarities with the Family Group Conferences (FGC) run by the National Institute of Crime Prevention and Reintegration of Offenders (NICRO) in Cape Town, South Africa.[35] The project is guided by the principle that work with young offenders should be rooted in the restorative justice paradigm. Under the FGCs, the victim, the offender and their families are brought together to redress the harm caused by the crime. The system also acknowledges that the offender's family, as the primary guardians of the offender, should be given the chance to deal with the situation in their own "family way".

According to Lukas Muntingh and Anne Monaheng,[36] FGCs are similar to the traditional way in which African communities used to deal with community and domestic problems. If a family member offended the community in some way, the whole family was shamed and ordered to pay for their member's actions or leave the village. Families took collective responsibility for each other. It is also contended by Muntingh and Monaheng[37] that families have unparalleled strengths to deal with their youth-in-trouble, but in many cases have relinquished their power.

---

[34] http://child-abuse.com/childhouse/childrens-rights/dci-be29.html

[35] Lukas Muntingh and Anne Monaheng, Family matters: How young offenders' families engage in restorative justice, http://ccrweb.ccr.uct.ac.za/two/7-3/p13.html

[36] Family matters: How young offenders' families engage in restorative justice http://ccrweb.ccr.uct.ac.za/two/7-3/p13.html

[37] *Ibid.*

I would however say that families have not deliberately relinquished their power. Rather social, economic and political changes that have occurred in society have forced families to take a back seat. In regard to criminal law, statutes have specifically provided that customary law has no place in the criminal justice system and it is in fact a crime to settle criminal cases outside the formal justice system.

Through processes similar to the FGCs, the family can be empowered to play their rightful role in supporting their children. As succinctly put by the two authors:

> When a family member is involved in criminal activity, the entire family is affected. Their reputation and dignity are at stake. It is logical to bring them into the process of restoring justice between the victim's family and their own. (p. 3).

This type of diversion also fits in neatly with the notion of childhood as presented by the various respondents in the pilot study; childhood connotes dependence on parents, childhood denotes a state when somebody is not fully responsible for her/his actions.

What do the children say?

The child offenders who were interviewed were strong in their opinion that the LC system is better suited to deal with child matters than are the police. Their view was based on the belief that since members of the LCs were part of the community, they know the individual children well enough to know the most appropriate way of dealing with a particular problem. It is interesting to note that what the children were proposing is in line with the need (expressed by the Beijing Rules) to focus on the offender rather than on the offence. I opine that this is likely to be most successful if the child is dealt with within the community where she or he comes from. The children also reported that the police are extremely harsh.

For example, there is the story of a male child aged 14 years who ran away from school. Although the act does not constitute an offence, his mother contacted the police who located the child at his aunt's place and arrested him. The police did not involve the LC but locked up the boy in a police cell. He was made to clean the filthy place, caned and then released. Asked for his views about the involvement of the LC officials in children's cases, he was emphatic that:

> .. If LCs settle children's cases, they do not punish children as much as the police do. ...My mother should never have involved the police. She should have involved my aunt instead. ...Police should be totally out of children's issues.

Another case involved a 17 year old boy who was arrested by the police for the "attempted murder" of his mother. Comparing the LCs with the police he said:

> When cases are settled by LCs, children are not as heavily punished as happens with the police. One escapes the kind of beating I got. LCs are more sympathetic because they are members of the community. They counsel rather than punish.

A 16 year old girl was rounded up by the police on the "mistaken belief" that she was a prostitute. According to the girl and to her mother, the girl just happened to be passing by a place frequented by prostitutes. She spent a night in a police cell and three nights at a women's prison, before she was eventually released by court. Her view about the involvement of the LCs was that:

> The police should always involve LCs in arrests. Before taking a child to the police station or to court, children should first be taken to their respective LCs. The LC should call the parents of the child offender and the victim and the case should be settled without the police or court involvement.

A 12 year old girl took views similar to those of the other children: a child should first and foremost be reported to its parents even before involving of LCs, and certainly before involving of the police.

What do the parents of child offenders say?

The parent of a 9 year old who was implicated in a theft together with an adult said:

> In cases which are not serious, the first step should be for the parents of the child to settle the matter with the aggrieved party. Only if this fails, should the matter be referred to the LCs. However, in serious cases such as defilement, the case should be handled by the police.

The father of a 17 year old boy who was arrested for defiling his 13 year old girl friend also said that the father of the girl should have involved his fellow parent first, "so that we could reach an understanding", instead of rushing to the police.

The parents were of the view that sending children to prison is counter productive because they come out of the institution hardened, they acquire bad behaviour and in fact do not reform. It was argued that harsh punishment by the police and prison personnel harden children and push them into more serious crime. The parents further explained that once a child has been in the hands of such personnel, that child is no longer in fear of anything. The child's opinion would be:

> What worse conditions can I ever be made to face?

The study shows that whereas the general view is that local committees are well suited to deal with children in conflict with the law, the police are negatively painted, not only as too harsh with children but also as corrupt.

Nevertheless, some parents expressed concern that at times, LC officials are bribed and their decision on whether to forward the case to the police or not sometimes depends on who among the family of the child and the victim has money. If the child's family gives money to members of the LC, even cases that are serious may never get to the police.

To what extent is practice in line with the avowed perceptions?

The study revealed that the majority of respondents were in agreement with the legal principle that children are more appropriately handled outside the formal justice system. Support for dealing with children outside the formal criminal justice system was so strong that some respondents held that even reporting of the child to LCs is not the appropriate first step. In the view of those respondents, a case should not be referred to LCs unless the victim and the parents of the child offender have failed to solve the problem. To such respondents, even the LCs constitute "authorities". For such people the commentary to Rule 11 of the Beijing Rules makes sense: in some cases non-intervention would be the best response and what is needed is informal as opposed to formal social control. Indeed in some of the cases in this study, some victims of juvenile crime chose not to involve the LC and resolved the disputes with the parents/guardians of the child offenders.

In some of the cases unearthed by the research, victims of juvenile crime went straight to report the erring child to the guardian/parent but made it clear to the concerned adult that should the conflict not be resolved, the matter would be brought either to the LC or even the police. As long as the victim was satisfied by the reaction of the child's guardian, the case was never forwarded to any other forum.

The law empowers LCs and the police to deal with relatively minor offences without involvement of the court system. But the study revealed that at times, it is not the seriousness of the offence but rather the extent to which a victim is appeased at these "lower" levels that determines whether a case enters the formal criminal justice system or no. For example a woman whose chicken house was regularly broken into at night by a 16 year old boy merely reported the boy to his grandmother. Having made the boy's grandmother pay for the birds at a price higher than the market price, the victim chose not to forward the case neither to the LC nor to the police. In legal terms, the boy had committed the offence of burglary, a felony which earns an adult offender a maximum sentence of 10 years imprisonment.[38] In another case in which a boy conspired with adults to break into his employer's house, the employer reported the case to the village committee. As soon as the parents agreed to compensate the employer for the property which had been stolen from the house, the case was concluded. A strict interpretation of the law would indicate that the village committee had no jurisdiction to handle such a serious case. It was not a case of simple theft but of house breaking, a felony which could earn an adult offender a seven year imprisonment term.[39] The fact that the boy had committed the crime together with adults would in fact confer jurisdiction on a Grade 1 Magistrate and not the Family and Children Court. Nevertheless, the parties involved "conferred jurisdiction" on the village committee court where it actually had none. Such a case reveals that as long as the parties to a crime agree that the relevant Local Committee Court will handle the case to their satisfaction, legal restrictions may be ignored.

The general view elucidated by the interviews was that local committees were considered more suited for dealing with juvenile crime than are the police. Nevertheless, the study revealed that some children who engaged in crime were taken to the police without prior involvement of the village committees. The findings indicate that it is not only the victims of crime that may hand over a child to the police, even parents/guardians of erring children sometimes involve the police in child behaviour which is not criminal and/or in offences which could legally be disposed of by the village committee court. A guardian

[38] Section 295 (2) of the Uganda Penal Code Act.
[39] Section 295 (1) of the Uganda Penal Code Act.

of a 10 year old who took his brother to the police for simple theft explained his action thus:

> I could have punished the boys myself indeed I caned them. … But the act of taking them to the police would act as a strong deterrent to such acts in future. One cane from a policeman sends a clearer message than 10 canes from a parent.

Another guardian, expressing a similar view, said that since some children do not obey their parents and have no fear for the LCs:

> The police should be involved because it has coercive machinery for enforcement of orders. Involvement of the police intimidates the child and minimises feelings by the child that nothing significant can be done to her or him. Fear of being taken to the police again deters future misconduct.

The study also revealed that the police itself sometimes take the initiative to handle children in conflict with the law and ignore the role of local committees. Some children ended up in court for offences which the police had power to dispose of. Such cases indicate that despite their wide discretionary powers, the police sometimes act contrary to the spirit and letter of juvenile justice law.

Restorative justice as a guiding principle

The theory of restorative justice

The theory of restorative justice has more or less gained worldwide acceptance. In 2002 the United Nations Economic and Social Council endorsed the UN Basic Principles on the Use of Restorative Justice in Criminal Matters and urged governments to create guidelines and standards for the use of restorative justice programmes. Although technically the principles are not legally binding, they express generally accepted principles and represent a moral and political commitment by States. They can also be used as guidelines for States in enacting legislation and formulating policies on the relevant matter.

A review of the literature reveals that there is not just one model, but various types of programmes and/or processes based on restorative justice. In line with that acknowledgement, K. Daly and R. Immarigeon [40] note:

---

[40] K. Daly and R. Immarigeon, "The Past, Present, and Future of Restorative Justice: Same Critical Reflections", in *Contemporary Justice Review*, Vol. 1, 1998.

> Over the last two decades "restorative justice" has emerged in varied guises, with different names, and in many countries; it has sprung from sites of activism, academia, and justice system workplaces. The concept may refer to an alternative process for resolving disputes, to alternative sanctioning options, or to a distinctively different, "new" mode of criminal justice organized around principles of restoration to victims, offenders, and the communities in which they live. It may refer to diversion from formal court process, to actions taken in parallel with court decisions, and to meetings between offenders and victims at any stage of the criminal process (from arrest, pre-sentencing, and prison release). It is a process used in juvenile justice, criminal justice, and family welfare/child protection cases. The concept has many aliases: reparative justice, transformative justice, informal justice, among them. (p. 21)

Daly and Immarigeon usefully add that:

> Although restorative justice is a capacious concept with multiple referents, there is a general sense of what it stands for. It emphasizes the repair of harms and of ruptured social bonds resulting from crime; it focuses on the relationships between crime victims, offenders, and society. (p. 22)

According to Daniel Van Ness it is due to the lack of a general agreement on a definition of restorative justice that the UN Basic Principles on the Use of Restorative Justice in Criminal Matters do not attempt to define the term but instead define "restorative justice programme" and "restorative justice outcomes".[41]

In Uganda, a look at the dispositions which the Local Committee Courts, the police and the Family and Children Court are empowered to order under the Children Statute reveals that society is being called upon to embrace principles of restorative justice. Rather than focus on punitive measures, which are usually at the centre of criminal justice, the orders are more focused towards repairing the harm done to the victim of the crime. As succinctly explained by Ann Skelton:[42]

---

[41] Daniel W Van Ness, "Proposed basic Principles on the Use of Restorative Justice: Recognising the Aims and Limits of Restorative Justice" in Andrew Hirsch et al. (eds.) *Restorative Justice and Criminal Justice*: *Competing or Reconcilable Paradigms?* Hart Publishing. Oxford and Portland, Oregon, 2003.

[42] Ann Skelton Ann, "Juvenile Justice Reform: Children's Rights and Responsibilities versus Crime Control" A paper prepared for the conference on 'Children's Rights in a transitional society' held by the Centre for Child Law, University of Pretoria, 30 October 1998. (http://www.lhr.org.za/projects/childrights/publications/juvenile.htm)

> Restorative justice is a theory of justice which relies on reconciliation rather than on punishment. It begins with the notion that a society which is functioning well operates within a balance of rights and responsibilities. When an incident occurs which upsets this balance, methods must be found to restore the balance, so that community members including the offender and the victim, can come to terms with the incident and can carry on with their lives. In order for this to occur the offender must accept responsibility for the fact that his or her behaviour has caused harm to the victim, and the victim must be prepared to negotiate and accept restitution and compensation for the offender's wrongdoing. Thus the purpose of restorative justice is to identify responsibilities, to meet needs and to promote healing. (p. 3)

Beale Sun Sara in her "Still Tough on Crime: Prospects for Restorative Justice in the United States"[43]defines restorative justice as:

> … 'a process of bringing together the individuals who have been affected by an offense and having them agree on how to repair the harm caused by the crime,' with the goal of restoring victims, offenders, and communities in a way that all stakeholders can agree is just. The system is based upon the recognition that crime harms individuals (victim) and relationships (the victim and offender's respective communities). (p. 3)

And in the words of John Braithwaite "restorative justice is deliberative justice; it is about people deliberating over the consequences of a crime, how to deal with them and prevent their recurrence. … So restorative justice restores the deliberative control of justice by citizens."[44]

Sara Beale[45] later adds:

> The aim of restorative justice is to establish accountability for the harm, promote mutual understanding of its causes and effects, and develop a process to make amends. In the restorative justice paradigm, the offender is not ordinarily incarcerated, but instead is obligated to apologize and otherwise compensate their victim, ideally receive forgiveness, and be reintegrated into the community. (p. 3)

Similar to Beale's definition, A. Duff states that "restorative justice is a process whereby parties with a stake in a specific offence collectively resolve

---

[43] http://leda.law.duke.edu/leda/data/99/bealeutah.html

[44] John Braithwaite, Restorative Justice and a Better Future, http://www.realjustice.org/pages/braithwaite.html

[45] *Ibid*, p. 43.

how to deal with the aftermath of the offence and its implications for the future." (p. 44)[46]

And in his "Restorative Justice: A Parallel System" Jim Consedine[47]states that:

> Restorative justice offers a process whereby those affected by criminal behaviour, be they victims, offenders, the families involved or the wider community, all have a part in resolving the issues that flow from offending … a shift from state power to community power. (p.183)

Consedine adds that the three key components of the restorative justice equation are the offender, the victim and the community.

I argue that the restorative justice paradigm is more suitable for a juvenile justice system because it has more potential to fulfil *the* main goal of juvenile justice: rehabilitation and re-integration into the community. This is through the following principles of restorative justice:

- Accountability (by the young person) for wrongdoing
- Family responsibility towards an erring young person
- Shaming
- Rehabilitation
- Community participation
- Diversion/Phasing out the formal justice system

I will thus discuss the extent to which Uganda law and practice is in line with each of the above principles underlying restorative justice.

1. The need for accountability/accepting responsibility

To what extent does Uganda law and practice require the child offender to be accountable for the wrong done?

[46] Antony Duff, "Restoration and Retribution" in Van Hirsch, 2003, *op.cit.*

[47] Jim Consedine , "Restorative Justice: A Parallel System" in Jim Consedine and H. Bowen (eds.), *Restorative Justice: Contemporary Themes and Practices*. Ploughshares Publications. New Zealand, 1999.

Restorative justice is premised on the need for the offender to acknowledge her/his accountability to the community. McElrea [48] explains the principle as follows:

> ... 'accountability' means understanding what you did and, then taking responsibility for it; and taking responsibility for it means doing something to make it right, but also helping to be part of that process. (p. 58)

Similarly Jim Consedine[49] says of accountability:

> Genuine accountability means, first, that when you offend, you need to understand and take responsibility for what you did. Offenders need to be encouraged to understand the real human consequences of their action. But accountability has a second component as well: offenders need to be encouraged to take responsibility for making things right, for righting the wrong. (p. 189)

Emphasis on the accountability of a child in conflict with the law towards the community is in line with the values expounded in the African Child Charter. The charter emphasises a child's responsibility as well as rights within the community and in Article 31 provides that:

> Every child shall have responsibilities towards his family and society, the State and … the community.

As Ann Skelton[50] notes, the African Charter blends children's rights with respect and responsibility for family and community and thus accords well with the concept of restorative justice.

It is therefore crucial that any alternative to the formal justice system emphasises the need for the child to be held accountable for her/his actions.

Although the interviews with adults as well as with the children emphasised the need for the involvement of the parents of a child in conflict with the law in making reparation to the victim, I noted that there was no mention of the fact that the child should take responsibility for his or her wrongful acts. There

---

[48] Freda McElrea, "Taking Responsibility in Being Accountable" in Consedine and Bowen, 1999, *op. cit.*

[49] Consedine, in Consedine and Bowen, 1999, *op. cit*

[50] Ann Skelton, Juvenile Justice Reform: Children's Rights and Responsibilities versus Crime Control, http://www.1hr.org.sa/projects/childrights/publications/juvenile.html.

was no mention of the need for the child to acknowledge the negative impact of his conduct on his victim. And yet one of the principles central to restorative justice is that the offender must be accountable and take action to repair the harm done. There is even a possibility that, indeed as noted by Lukas Muntingh and Anne Monaheng,[51] if the young person walks away with the perception that nothing has happened (to him or her) there is a likelihood that the child will re-offend.

It is worth of note that the need for the child's accountability is not specifically mentioned by Uganda's Children Statute. This can be contrasted with New Zealand's Children, Young Persons and their Families Act, which in its section 4 (f) propounds the principle that young people committing offences should be held accountable and encouraged to accept responsibility for their behaviour.

I, however, argue that meaningful accountability is only possible if the child offender actively participates in the conflict resolution process and thus, together with others, 'owns' the outcome. A young person will only participate actively in a context where her/his views are taken seriously. This would be consistent with a child's participatory rights enshrined within child rights law, e.g. Article 4 (2) of the African Child Charter, [52] and Article 12 of the UN Child Convention.[53] It is noted that both the African Child Charter and the UN Convention particularise the need for the child's voice in the context of judicial and administrative proceedings. On the other hand, Uganda's Children Statute does not make specific mention of this right. There is thus need to investigate the extent to which the notion of a child's participatory rights is acceptable in contemporary Ugandan society and how this impacts on the work of Local Committee Courts. It is also important to answer the question: is the

---

[51] Lukas Muntingh and Anne Monaheng, "Family matters: How young offenders' families engage in restorative justice (http://ccrweb.ccr.uct.ac.za/two/7-3/p13.html)

[52] Article 4 (2) provides that: In all judicial or administrative proceedings affecting a child who is capable of communicating his/her own views an opportunity shall be provided for the views of the child to be heard ... and those views shall be taken into consideration by the relevant authority in accordance with the provisions of appropriate law.

[53] Article 12 (1) calls upon states parties to ensure ' to the child who is capable of forming his or her own views the right to express those views freely in all matters affecting the child, the views of the child being given due weight in accordance with the age and maturity of the child. Article 12 (2) provides that: For this purpose, the child shall in particular be provided the opportunity to be heard in any judicial and administrative proceedings affecting the child ... in a manner consistent with the procedural rules of national law.

voice of an offender given space in the adjudication process of Local Committee Courts?

2. Shaming the offender

Another principle, often said to be crucial in a restorative justice, is shaming the offender, but is it necessary?

It has been claimed by scholars such as John Braithwaite[54] that a central feature of African legal systems was a concern to shame the offender. But within the child rights discourse, using shame to instil responsible behaviour is a rather controversial issue. As noted by Allen Campbell H. and Andrew Revering[55] this is because "... shame has picked up a finger-wagging moral connection considered to be detrimental to a person's ego." An important question to ask is therefore: Are there ways in which conduct which shames can be regarded as a violation of a child's right to protection from degrading treatment, a concern central to the rights of children as envisaged by Article 37 of the CRC and Article 16 of the African Child Charter?[56] Or can shaming be regarded as positive?

In a study of the use of corporal punishment as a method of disciplining children used by teachers and parents in rural Uganda,[57] I reported that the child respondents expressed the view that the humiliation felt in being caned in *public* was worse than the physical pain arising out of the act. On the other hand, most of the children saw nothing wrong with being caned "behind doors." The children also had very strong feelings against being told to wear placards as a way of announcing to the "whole world" that they had misbehaved in one way or the other. In a discussion with the teachers, it was revealed that the teachers were aware of the humiliation felt by the children in the above mentioned situations, but added that this in fact was the value in

[54] John Braithwaite, *Crime, Shame and Reintegration,* Cambridge University Press, 1989.

[55] Allen Campbell and Andrew Revering, "Holding Kids Accountable: Shaming with Compassion." In *Reclaiming Children and Youth* Volume 6, Number 3, Fall 1997.

[56] Article 37 CRC: No child shall be subjected to ... degrading treatment or punishment. Article 16 of the African Child Charter: States Parties shall take specific ... measures to protect the child from all forms of ... degrading treatment ...

[57] Lillian Tibatemwa-Ekirikubinza, "Understanding Children's Rights: the use of corporal punishment in rural Uganda", in *East African Journal of Peace and Human Rights*, Vol. 1, 2003.

corporal punishment. By shaming the child, it was believed that the child would resist from engaging in the same conduct in the future.

In his "African Justice: Compensating, Healing, Reconciling" Jim Consedine[58] writes that although shaming was seen as necessary in African adjudication, once that initial expression of community repugnance had been demonstrated, the next immediate concern was to reincorporate the wrongdoer into the community. According to John Braithwaite,[59]shame plays a key role in the regulation of social behaviour. The argument is that people are generally deterred from committing crime through fear of disapproval of their conduct by the people whose acceptance and opinion they value. Since it is the family and friends that we value, reparation agreements imposed by family and friends are more effective than punishments imposed by an unknown authority - courts. Braithwaite[60] explains that in traditional society the shaming was (and should be) done "within a continuum of respect for the offender." This would be followed by re-acceptance into the 'fold'. Referring to restorative justice conferences in which the offender and those he/she loves and/or respects meet with the victim and his/her supporters, Braithwaite contends that:

> The group discusses the consequences of the crime, drawing out the feelings of those who have been harmed. Then it discusses how that harm might be repaired and any steps that should be taken to prevent reoffending. In terms of reintegrative shaming theory, the discussion of the consequences of the crime for victims (or consequences for the offender's family) structures shame into the conference; the support of those who enjoy the strongest relationships of love or respect with the offender structures reintegration into the ritual. (p. 74)[61]

In "Restorative Justice and a Better Future" Braithwaite (1996)[62] distinguishes between reintegrative shaming and stigmatization as follows:

---

[58] In Jim Consedine, *Restorative Justice: Healing the Effects of Crime*. Ploughshares Publications. New Zealand, 1999.

[59] Braithwaite, 1989, *op. cit.*

[60] John Braithwaite, *Restorative Justice and Responsive Regulation,*. Oxford University Press, 2002.

[61] See also John Braithwaite "Shame and Criminal Justice" in *Canadian Journal of Criminology*;; Academic Research Library, July 2000; 42, 3. John Braithwaite and Stephen Mugford, "Conditions of Successful Reintegration Ceremonies: Dealing with Juvenile Offenders", in the *British Journal of Criminology,* Vol. 34 No.2, Spring 1994.

[62] John Braithwaite (http://www.realjustice.org/Pages/braithwaite.html)

> While reintegrative shaming prevents crime, stigmatization is a kind of shaming that makes crime problems worse. Stigmatization is the kind of shaming that creates outcasts; it is disrespectful, humiliating. Stigmatization means treating criminals as evil people who have done evil acts. Reintegrative shaming means disapproving of the evil of the deed while treating the person as essentially good. Reintegrative shaming means strong disapproval of the act but doing so in a way that is respecting of the person. (p. 3)[63]

Braithwaite argues that shame is difficult to avoid when a victim and her supporters, as well as the family of the offender, all talk through the consequences that have been suffered, emotionally as well as materially, as a result of the crime. It is further argued that appearance in a court of law does not have the same effect on an offender since the police or judges or the media have no relationship with the offender. These are people that the offender need not ever meet again. In agreement with Braithwaite, Allen Campbell H. and Andrew Revering[64] contend that:

> People are deterred less by the threat of official punishment than the threat of public disgrace. The loss of status, respect, and affection is significant, but it is not a threat that state officials can make. It can only be made by those who have a significant personal relationship with the offender. (p. 182)

It can be concluded from the above arguments that it is the presence of the people trusted and respected by the offender that can create feelings of shame. It is the people who are significant in the life of the offender that communicate the *shamefulness* of what he/she has done. Once it is followed by re-acceptance, it produces remorse and prevents re-offending. Thus shaming is not an end in itself it merely serves to communicate a message of disapproval of the act. Following it by re-acceptance implies that the group sees a clear distinction between the unacceptable behaviour and the potentially good person in the offender. A combination of accountability and respect is the key to deterrence. It can also be said that the notion of shaming is closely linked with the individual's accountability to the community.

In his support of shaming as a necessary component in juvenile justice, Braithwaite draws support from child development literature and contends that whereas both laissez-faire parenting that fails to confront and disapprove

---

[63] John Braithwaite Crime, *Shame and Reintegration*. Cambridge: Cambridge University Press. 1989.

[64] Campbell and Revering, 1997, *op. cit.*

children's misconduct and punitively authoritarian parenting produce a lot of delinquents; delinquency is less likely when parents confront wrongdoing with moral reasoning. He then concludes that in the same way, the justice system will do better when it facilitates moral reasoning by families as an alternative to punishment by the state.

Hopefully local committees acting as juvenile courts can adopt appropriate procedures geared towards re-integrative shaming rather than stigmatisation and exclusion.

3. Community participation

Another question to answer is: to what extent is the community given responsibility for a child offender in Uganda?

Linking restorative justice to community participation, Kay Pranis[65] states:

> A restorative response to crime is a community-building response. It is necessary to build a broad base of support for restorative justice principles and practices. Because restorative justice is grounded in community involvement, it is not possible to implement a comprehensive restorative system without community ownership and support. A comprehensive restorative response to crime engages the community as a source for reconciliation of victim and offenders and as a resource for monitoring and enforcing community standards of behaviour. The restorative justice framework calls for the inclusion of all stakeholders, especially victims and community members, in designing and implementing local justice practices. It is an empowerment model that must clearly be grounded in grassroots commitment at the local level. (p. 1)

Similarly McElrea[66] pointes out:

> Restorative justice is essentially a community-based model that encourages the acceptance of responsibility by all concerned and draws on the strengths of the community to restore peace. (p. 56)

[65] Kay Pranis, How to Build Community Support for Restorative Justice http://www.ojp.usdoj.gov/nij/rest-just/ch4/how2build.htm.

[66] McElrea, in Consedine and Bowen, 1999, *op. cit.*

In reference to restorative justice Hickey C.[67] points out:

> Central to restorative justice is recognition of the community, rather than criminal justice agencies, as the prime site of crime control. (p. 85)

Within the paradigm of restorative justice, it is not only the offender but the community as well which must take responsibility for the crime. "Crime is viewed as a social phenomenon that is best addressed through social processes; individuals must take responsibility for their crime, but so too must the communities to which they belong."[68]

The Children Statute is in line with the notion of community responsibility. For example Part III of the statute, entitled "Support for Children by Local Authorities", creates responsibilities not only for the "authorities" but also for individual members of the community towards children. Under Section 11(1) (a), it is the general duty of every local government council, from village to district level, to safeguard and promote the welfare of children within its area and (b) to designate one of its members to be the person responsible for the welfare of children. It is provided that the designated person shall be referred to as the Secretary for Children's Affairs. In the same vein Section 48 (2) of the Local Governments Act provides that the vice chairperson of each parish and village executive committee shall also be Secretary for Children Welfare.

As already mentioned, the Children Statute recognises the value of enabling the community to deal with children by, among other things, empowering the Local Committee Courts to hear and dispose of some matters concerning child "offenders".

The alternative orders at the disposition of the court re-locate the child into the community. Community based methods of handling children in conflict with the law offer the community the opportunity to provide appropriate support and guidance.

---

[67] Hickey C, "Alternative Dispute Resolution Within Criminal Justice", in Consedine and Bowen, 1999, *op.cit.*

[68] Page 3 of "Chapter 1: Origins and Implementation" http://www.aic.gov.au/rjustice/jjustice/chapter1.pdf. Citing T.F.Marshall "Grassroots Initiatives towards Restorative Justice: The new paradigm", paper presented to Fulbright Colloquium, University of Stirling, 1-4 September 1992.

It is assumed that a child's offending does not bring to an end the community's responsibility towards her/him. Within the context of contemporary Uganda, the Secretary for Children's Welfare should, together with the child's parents, be the primarily responsible for ensuring that the child respects the decisions made at a restorative justice conference.

As already noted respondents in the pilot study were of the view that children should to the farthest possible extent be dealt with by the community. This is in line with restorative justice in that one of the central principles of restorative justice is "the recognition of the community, rather than the criminal justice agencies, as the prime site of crime control."

4. Rehabilitation and re-integration

It is also noted that the avowed primary aim of juvenile justice is the rehabilitation and reintegration of the child into the family and community, so as to ensure that the young person assumes a constructive role in society.

Re-socialisation of a child offender is the major aim within the child rights discourse at the global level as evidenced in the African Child Charter and the UN Child Convention. Article 17 of the African Child Charter deals with Administration of Juvenile Justice and under Article 17 (3) provides that:

> The essential aim of treatment of every child during trial and also if found guilty of infringing the penal law shall be his or her reformation, re-integration into his or her family and social rehabilitation.

And Article 40 (1) of the CRC provides inter alia that:

> States Parties recognize the right of every child alleged as, accused of, or recognized as having infringed the penal law to be treated in a manner consistent … with the desirability of promoting the child's reintegration and the child's assuming a constructive role in society.

If rehabilitation and re-integration are major aims, any decisions on the handling of the child should focus on addressing the difficulties in the young person's circumstances, rather than on the offence. It therefore follows that the forum handling the young offender should, among other things, focus on the "causes" of /motive for the child's misbehaviour. One of the merits associated with "informal justice" is that it allows a wider, unconstrained discussion of the problems existing in the offender's life. In reference to restorative justice, Hickey C[69] contends that restorative justice, among other things, is:

> A way of dealing with conflicts arising from crime *and resolving the underlying problems which cause it.* (p. 85) (My emphasis)

In addition, the consequences of as well as remedies for the crime are discussed. In such a system, the needs of both the child offender and the victim are likely to be met. It is possible to ensure that rehabilitation, as a major goal of child rights law on the one hand, and restitution, as a goal of restorative justice on the other, are merged. It is thus important that studies examine the extent to which the Local Committee Courts and indeed other actors inquire into, and are guided in their decisions by, the causes of a particular child's infringement of the law.

To what extent is the rehabilitation of the child given centre stage in Uganda's law and practice?

In an interview with a Probation and Social Welfare Officer, I was disheartened to learn of her obvious lack of interest in the social economic background of the children who she comes in contact with as a result of their breaking the law. When specifically asked whether orphans are disproportionately represented among children who come in conflict with the law, her answer was:

> We never ask the children whether they are orphans or not. ... In any case these children tell a lot of lies. They could say that they have no parents when in fact their parents are alive.

Due to the limited nature of the research, it is not possible to know whether the other actors within the juvenile justice system are more aware of the value of evaluating a child's offending within the context of his/her wider environment. It is, however, pertinent to note that a study of the Children Statute reveals that successful operationalisation of the rights of children in general, and juvenile offenders in particular depends heavily on the office of the Probation and Social Welfare Officer. For example, it is provided under Section 96 that before a court can make a decision to detain a child in conflict with the law, a written social background report must be prepared by a Probation and Social

[69] Hickey, in Consedine and Bowen,1999, *op. cit.*

Welfare Officer. The court is obliged to take the report into account before making any order. The section further provides that the report shall include, among other things, *the social and family background of the child.* And under section 90 of the Statute, a Probation and Social Welfare Officer stands in the place of a guardian, to a child who has been arrested by the police, where the parent cannot be present to attend the police interview. It can thus not be taken lightly that a person occupying an office on which a successful implementation of child rights law depends heavily reveals total lack of knowledge of one of the principles underpinning juvenile justice: focus should be more on the offender than on the offence.

I argue that rehabilitation by and within the community partly depends on the public's receptivity to restorative justice principles rather than punitive policies. The public's receptivity, on the other hand, depends on whether the public is convinced that it is in the best interest of the community, that children in conflict with the law are handled outside the formal justice system. Writing about victim-offender mediation in Austria, Losching-Gspandi and Kilchling report that offenders can be required to offer community service or payments to a public welfare organisation as a form of symbolic restitution.[70] Symbolic restitution can be imposed instead of or in addition to restitution to an individual victim. It is noted that community service is now closely linked with restorative justice. Thus the UN Basic Principles on the Use of Restorative Justice Programmes in Criminal Matters gives community service as an example of "restorative outcomes". In Uganda this will necessitate minor amendments to the Children Statute to empower both the Local Committee Courts and the Family and Children Court to use community service as one of the dispositions available within juvenile justice.[71]

---

[70] Cited in Beale ibid

[71] Under the Community Service Act, Act 5 of 2000 community service is recognised as non-custodial punishment which a court can order on conviction of an offender. Its effect is that the offender is obliged to perform work within the community for a specified period of time. Currently due to the fact that community service is not mentioned by the Children Statute as one of the orders available to a Local Committee Court under Section 93 (4) or to the Family and Children Court under Section 95, it is presumed that community service cannot validly be imposed on a child in conflict with the law.

Other principles relevant to restorative justice

- The need for cultural sensitivity

Fully aware that the success of a restorative approach is dependent upon community support and involvement, it is imperative that whatever model is adopted ensures cultural sensitivity and cultural appropriateness in as far as they are not in conflict with basic human rights principles. It is perhaps not debatable that successful implementation of any law largely depends on societal perceptions.

Uganda is not culturally homogeneous, and it is therefore likely that the detailed procedures of a Local Committee Court will be determined by the cultural and traditional practices of a particular geographical area. It is thus important that the legal framework allows for flexibility. There is also need to take recognisance of the rural-urban dichotomy. A model which is appropriate in a rural environment may not be successful in an urban environment. Indeed in questioning several respondents as to what they perceived to be the possible role of clan heads on the one hand, and religious leaders on the other, in solving cases of children in conflict with the law, several of them were emphatic that in an urban set up such institutions have no meaningful roles. A 35 year old man said that:

> Traditional institutions are no longer functional, for they have no power. One can afford to ignore their decision and what would they do to enforce it? Nothing.

A 47 year old woman answered:

> Clan leaders can only be useful in rural areas where residents belong to the same ethnic group. They have no legitimacy in an urban area for we belong to different tribes.

And when asked if people ever take such problems to religious leaders rather than to LCs, the 47 year old woman said:

> It is only LC. Religious leaders are not effective because the offender and the offended may belong to different religious faiths. Such is only possible if both parties belong to the same religion. And even then, some people are nominal believers whereas others are more serious with their faith. A religious leader will only have 'authority' in the eyes of an ardent believer, whatever the religion.

The above answers draw attention to the fact that any model of conflict resolution should take into account the dynamics of a particular community. In fact when asked whether there is a formula for setting up a restorative justice conference, Hayden A and Henderson P. (1999:78)[72] answered:

> It is not desirable to define a process for setting up a restorative justice conference as the dynamics of conferences are as diverse as the people who take part.

What is required of the state is therefore to provide a framework and leave the details to the communities. This is what the Uganda legislature has done by giving Local Committee Courts wide discretionary powers

- The needs of the victim

Although not specific to juvenile crime, another principle on which restorative justice is premised is the need to cater for the needs of the victim. But is it possible to cater both for the needs of the victim as well as the needs of the young offender?

The African Charter calls for treating children in conflict with the law in a manner consistent with the child's sense of dignity and worth. The charter also states that *the treatment should also reinforce the child's respect for the human rights and fundamental freedoms of others.*[73] (My emphasis) Inherent in the charter is therefore acknowledgement of the needs of the victim and of what is often referred to as the "righteous anger" of victims of crime.

Adoption of a restorative justice model for young offenders fits well with Article 17 of the African Child Charter, above mentioned, more than does a formal criminal justice system. For as observed by Fred McElrea:[74]

> Under a restorative justice model the victim is not just a faceless, nameless entity. His/her anger and hurt is witnessed in a face-to-face encounter ... the victim is experienced as a living, hurting human being. (p. 57)

---

[72] A. Hayden and P. Henderson, "Victims: The invisible People" in Consedine and Bowen, 1999, *op.cit.*

[73] Article 17 (1).

[74] McElrea, in Consedine and Bowen, 1999, *op. cit.*

In contrast to restorative justice, it is noted of the formal justice system: "the offender often does not realise the real impact of what he has done." (p. 7)[75]

The near total absence of the victim's voice in the 'retributive' criminal justice system has been decried by many. For example, Hickey C[76] states that:

> ... victims are marginalised and their interests subsumed to society's wider interests. ... the state has stolen the victim's conflict with the offender. (p. 85)

And Hayden and Henderson[77] note that although victims are the proximate if secondary cause of all criminal justice proceedings, they are secured little if any recognition. Hayden and Henderson, however, happily note that on the other hand, victims are at the centre of restorative justice processes.

To the question "what does restoring victims mean?" Braithwaite[78]gives the answer:

> It means restoring property loss or the personal injury, repairing the broken window or the broken teeth. It means restoring a sense of security. Even victims of property crimes such as burglary often suffer a loss of security when the private space of their home is violated. (p. 4)

Interviews with community members who had been victims of child offending all agreed on one thing: what they wanted most was reparation. Among 9 respondents who were victims of property related crime the common statement was:

> All I wanted was that the parents of the child give me money to compensate my loss. Once that was done, I did not find any reason for following up the matter to see whether the child had been given any punishment. I do not know what happened thereafter.

There is also the story of a housewife who was assaulted and injured by a 16 year old girl. She demanded that the grandfather of the girl should give her money for medical treatment if the police were to be kept out of the case. After receiving the money she never found out whether the girl's grandparent ever 'did anything' to the girl thereafter.

---

[75] Sir Michael Hardie Boys in his "Foreword" to Consedine and Bowen, 1999, *op.cit.*

[76] Hickey, in Consedine and Bowen, 1999, *op.cit.* "

[77] Hayden and Henderson, in Consedine and Bowen, 1999*, op.cit.*

[78] (http://www.realjustice.org/Pages/braithwaite.html).

It is understandable that the victims' focus was on being 'compensated' but it is unfortunate that the voice calling for measures to ensure that children are kept out of further crime was almost totally silent. This was so even in cases which were relatively dangerous to the child and to society. For example, a 35 year old woman narrated a story in which she was a victim of 'house breaking' as follows:

> I rear chicken but one time the number kept on reducing. Every other day, I would find less and less birds in the house, which was adjacent to my house. The door to the chicken house was always locked at night. ... One day at 2.00 A.M my neighbour's grandson aged about 15-16 years old was caught red-handed breaking into the chicken house. We took the boy to his grandmother. He admitted responsibility for all the stolen chicken. She paid for all the chickens at a price higher than the market price, because she did not want her child taken to the police. Nobody reported the matter to any other authority. I had been compensated; I had no interest there after.

And in another case involving a 32 year old woman as the victim, it was said:

> A friend gave me a young boy of about 10 years to come and stay with me because I am a single woman and I was staying alone in the house. I am a trader so I leave home very early and come back rather late ever day. I would leave the child home ... One day the boy asked for permission to go and visit his parents. I bade him farewell and locked the house with the only available key. On that day I came home earlier than usual. I was surprised to find the boy at home and inside the house since I had locked up the house and gone off with the key. I then immediately realised that some of my property was not in the house. The boy denied knowledge of the whereabouts of the missing property. I contacted local security personnel who threatened to burn the child if he did not tell the truth. Eventually the child revealed that some young men from the neighbourhood had contacted him and in exchange for some money, he had given them the key to the house. They made duplicates to the house and were planning to come and "clear" the house that night.

Asked what eventually happened to the boy, the woman answered:

> The parents of the child agreed to replace whatever had been taken. The case was not taken any further.

Although it is agreeable that children should, to the farthest possible extent, be kept out of the formal justice system, it is necessary for society impress upon the child that what he has done is not acceptable. In engaging into criminal activity at night, the boy who stole chicken exposed himself to great danger. In associating with adult criminals the boy in the latter story could have been on a sure path into a violent criminal career. Yet there was no evidence that the community took any steps to protect each child from the criminal path. The needs of each of these children were not a concern.

In the one and only case where the victim was concerned about the possibility of children taking on a permanent criminal career, one of the children engaged in the offence was the victim's younger brother. In this particular case property disappeared from the respondent's home. On questioning the young brother (aged 15), the victim learnt that together with another 15 year old boy, the brother had ferried the things out of the house. The 36 year old man took the young persons to the police and asked the police to subject them to corporal punishment. Asked why he had not personally administered the cane, the man replied:

> I gave them a few canes but I knew they would not take my punishment as seriously as they would the police. These were young children who were at the risk of turning into thugs if they were not immediately dealt with. Punishment by the police would send a clear message. It would be a deterrent. The mere fact of facing the police would act as a deterrent.

It is noted that although the orders provided for under Uganda's Children statute clearly focus on reparation of the harm done to the victim, the enactment does not specifically provide for the involvement of the victim in the process of decision making. The question therefore remains: in proceedings before a Local Committee Court, where is the voice of the victim? But perhaps absence of direct mention of the victim must be understood from the context within which the law under discussion came to be. The law on juvenile crime is but a part of a statute concerning the rights of children. It is not an enactment aimed at reforming criminal justice. It is therefore just a coincidence that with a little innovation, both the needs of the child offender and the victim can be met. With a little innovation the law can be used to re-integrate the child into society on the one hand, and repair the harm caused by the crime on the other. And the extent to which a successful merger occurs depends on the specific process that a particular Local Committee Court will adopt.

Criticism of a system which marginalises the victim is legitimate. And indeed the needs of the victim must be recognised and accommodated. However, I must emphasise that while using restorative justice processes within juvenile justice, one must ensure that focus on the needs of the young person is not lost and that his/her well-being remains a primary concern. But perhaps if we accept that "restorative justice means restoring *victims*, restoring *communities* and restoring *offenders*",[79] the needs of all the various stakeholders will be met.

RESTORATIVE JUSTICE: RE-VISITING INDIGENOUS JUSTICE TRADITIONS IN AFRICA.

It has been contended that reconciliation, restoration and harmony, negotiation and arbitration, rather than adjudication, guide African customary courts.[80] It has also been said that in Africa, the central purpose of a customary law court was to acknowledge that a wrong had been done and to determine what amends should be made.[81] In the traditional societies, the first questions to be asked would be how can this damage be repaired, how can we restore the relationship?[82] Bennie Goldin and Michael Gelfand[83] report that:

> In Shona traditional society, the aim of the law is primarily to compensate the person or family wronged by the crime, rather than to inflict punishment on the criminal, although punishments are imposed as well in some cases. (p. 23)

Goldin and Gelfand further state that the award of damages to the wronged person is of more interest to the judges than the application of punitive measures to the wrongdoer.

Writing about the Barotse of Northern Rhodesia, Gluckman[84] states that they disapproved of any irremediable breaking of relationships. Gluckman further notes that for the Barotse traditional society, it was a supreme value that villages should remain united; kinfolk, families and kinships should remain associated. Consequently, throughout a court hearing, the judges tried to

[79] Braithwaite, 2000, *op.cit.*

[80] A.N Allot, "The people as Law-makers: Custom, Practice, and Public Opinion as Sources of Law in Africa and England.", in *Journal of African Law*, Vol. 21 No 1, 1977.

[81] Dlamini C. "The Role of Chiefs in the Administration of Justice" (Unpublished LLM Thesis), University of Pretoria, 1998) cited in Skelton, 1998, *op. cit.*

[82] Michael Lapsley, "The Heart of Justice: Truth, Mercy, Healing, Forgiveness" in Consedine and Bowen, 1999, *op.cit.*

[83] Bennie Goldin and Michael Gelfand, *African Law and Custom in Rhodesia*, Juta and Co. Ltd. Cape town 1975.

[84] Max Gluckman, *The Judicial Process among the Barotse of Northern Rhodesia,* Manchester University Press, 1955.

prevent the breaking of relationships, and to make it possible for the parties to live together amicably in the future. In his words:

> The court tends to be conciliating; it strives to effect a compromise acceptable to, and accepted by all the parties." (p. 21)

Gluckman further asserts that because the task of the judge is to encourage conciliation, he constantly has to broaden the field of inquiry and consider the total history of relations between the litigants, not only the narrow legal issues raised by one of them. I contend that within juvenile justice such an approach would be invaluable for, as pointed out earlier, meaningful rehabilitation and re-integration into society call for a discussion of the causes of the child's misbehaviour/ the circumstances under which a child infringed the law.

In their analysis of Resistance Committee Courts in Uganda as a form of "popular justice", John-Jean Barya and J. Oloka-Onyango state that conciliatory systems of dispute resolution are believed to have prevailed in pre-colonial Africa.[85]
In her "What Can Indigenous African Customs Teach Contemporary Juvenile Justice?" Karen Van Eden[86] throws in a word about the handling of child wrongdoers according to traditional African justice. Eden reports that within the Thembu community of the Eastern Cape, when a child offended against an adult member of a community, the parents would be expected to accompany the child to apologise to the offended person.[87] If property had been damaged or stolen, negotiations took place between the parents of the child and the offended family in order to decide how to correct the problem.

Writing about the customary law of the Shona of Zimbabwe, Goldin and Gelfand[88] reported that under Shona customary law, a father[89] is liable for the

---

[85] Barya and Onyango, 1994, *op. cit.*

[86] Cited in Consedine, 1999, op.cit. p. 175.

[87] There is a possibility that the social status of the child's family may affect the way a case is handled. Nevertheless, the aim of citing Van Eden's observation is merely to emphasise the point that restorative justice is not an entirely new concept in African societies. And since I did not specifically focus on the impact of social status on the use of restorative justice i.e. social status was not one of the demographic characteristics focused on, neither was it present in any of the research hypotheses which guided my research, I am in no position to come up with meaningful conclusions.

[88] Goldin and Gelfand, 1975, *op. cit.*

wrongdoing of his children. The father is held liable for the actions of his children until and unless the child is no longer under his control.[90]

According to Lukas Muntingh and Anne Monaheng,[91] the modern Family Group Conferences are similar to the traditional way in which African communities used to deal with community and domestic problems. If a family member offended the community in some way, the whole family was shamed and ordered to pay for their member's actions or leave the village. Families took collective responsibility for each other.

It is possible that in Uganda, parental responsibility for a child's wrongdoing is not just a notion of pre-colonial African society but prevails even today. As earlier mentioned, in the interviews with adults and children in the pilot study, respondents emphasised the need for the involvement of the parents of a child in conflict with the law in making reparation to the victim. It is therefore no surprise that when one father in the pilot study "handed" over his child for punishment to the owner of a car destroyed by the child, the victim felt that the father was being dishonest. The 29 year old woman told her story as follows:

> I parked my car by the side of the road and went into the market. I came back to find its windscreen shattered. The market vendors handed over to me a 9 year old boy. They told me it was the little boy who had thrown stones at the vehicle. The boy did not deny the act. I took the boy to the nearest police station. I was informed that since the child was below 12 years, the police had no power to deal with the case. The police officer on duty gave me a letter of introduction to the local council executives of the area where the child lives. ... The local authorities summoned the father of the boy. But all he said to me was: "I have no money to pay to you, take the boy and do whatever you can with him." Under those circumstances what could I do? I believe the father of the boy realised that the police could not force him to do anything. He was being dishonest. He was abdicating his duty.

The above story also clearly reveals that the use of restorative justice can only succeed if the child's family is willing to co-operate.[92]

---

[89] It should be no surprise that it is the father that is mentioned rather than the parent since the society in question is patriarchal.

[90] I note that the concept of having "control over a child" does not augur well with the modern child rights discourse. In this context, however, I presume the phrase has more to do with dependence on a parent, with a parent's responsibility for the child, than denial of self-will.

[91] Lucas Muntingh and Anne Monaheng, Family matters: How young offenders' families engage in restorative justice, http://ccrweb.ccr.uct.ac.za/two/7-3/pg13.html

[92] And although the issue was not investigated in any detail, it is hardly likely that restorative justice can work in dysfunctional families.

THE WAY FORWARD FOR UGANDA

Uganda has, through the Children Statute, made long strides towards a progressive juvenile justice system, which provides opportunities for restorative action. One major step has been the involvement of a grass root institution[93] – the Local Committee Court – in the "adjudication" of cases involving children. This holds out hope for a renewal of community responsibility for the children. The statute, however, gives little guidance on the involvement of the victims of crime. Similarly, it is silent on the need to ensure that the child offender is not only held accountable for the unlawful conduct but also directly participates in repairing the harm done to the victim and to society. Absence of a particular direction may be advantageous for as observed by Kay Pranis:[94]

> There is no single road map or blueprint for building a restorative system; nor do we have answers to all the questions raised by the principles of restorative justice. The process of searching for answers should involve dialogue with all who have an interest in the question. (p. 1)

As already mentioned, Uganda is not culturally homogeneous. Furthermore one cannot ignore the rural-urban dichotomy. The consequential complexity of using restorative processes in urban communities is noted by several scholars. John Braithwaite[95]advises that the institutions of restorative justice we build in the city must be culturally plural, quite different from one community to another depending on the culture of the people involved. In her literature

[93] Local Council Courts are considered grass root institutions due to the fact that they operate at the lowest levels of society: villages. They represent a bottom-up approach to community governance. It need also be mentioned that although they are created by statute, they are voluntary in nature and the members are not remunerated by the state. They offer a peculiar type of participatory democracy in that eligibility to serve on the committee does not depend on political affiliation but rather on individual merit. In fact it is not uncommon to find a village committee on which members belong to various political affiliations. Also note that there is no requirement for any minimum education standard. All one needs to be eligible for election is residence in the particular geographical location. It is in that context that they are popularly referred to as grass roots institutions.

[94] Kay Pranis, "How to Build Community Support for Restorative Justice" http://www.ojp.usdoj.gov/nij/rest-just/ch4/how 2 build.htm

[95] John Braithwaite, "Restorative Justice and a Better Future" http://www.realjustice.org/pages/braithwaite.html

overview of mediation processes in pre-industrial societies, Merry Sally[96] offers a warning about the simple transplantation of mediation practices from one social context to another. She cautions thus:

> The efficacy of mediation depends on the existence of a cohesive, stable, morally integrated community whose powers of informal social control can be harnessed to informally achieved settlements. ... [But in contemporary America] disputants are rarely embedded in a close, cohesive social system where they need to maintain cooperative relationships. Even when disputants come from the same neighbourhood, unless they are integrated into a unitary social structure their conflicts in one relationship do not have repercussions for others. (p. 34)

What Merry Sally observes about American society can also be said about urban communities in Uganda – they can hardly be described as morally integrated. The earlier discussion on the relevance[97] of clan leaders in conflict resolution in an urban setting in Uganda gives credence to this contention.

In light of the heterogeneous cultures of Uganda as well as the rural urban dichotomy it is important that the legal framework allows for flexibility. It is also noted that flexibility increases the ability of the parties to tailor a response to the crime, the offender, the victim and others who have been affected.[98] I am once again persuaded by the observations of Kay Pranis[99] thus:

> The appropriate role of the state ... is to articulate the vision, disseminate information, and provide support and technical assistance (in attempts to evolve a more restorative approach). (p. 1)
>
> As observed by Braithwaite[100] the role of the restorative justice movement is to help the people recover *their own restorative traditions*. Indeed as he further contends, we need a culturally specific *investigation* of how to revive the restorative justice practices that may be lying idle in our society.

Nevertheless there may be a reason for providing guidelines to LC courts in their role as juvenile courts. This is because, as suggested by Pranis,[101] lack of

---

[96] Cited by Anthony Bottoms "Some Sociological Reflections on Restorative Justice" in Van Hirsch, 2003, *op.cit.* p. 108.

[97] In fact their irrelevance.

[98] Van Ness, in Van Hirsch, 2003, *op. cit.*

[99] Kay Pranis; "How to Build Community Support for Restorative Justice" http://www.ojp.usdoj.gov/nij/rest-just/ch4/how 2 build.htm

[100] Braithwaite, 2002, *op. cit.*

[101] *Ibid* p. 98.

understanding of underlying values often leads to undesirable results. I am convinced that, at the very minimum, the local courts need guidelines on the importance of the following:

- The needs of the child offender arising from her or his status as a child
- The need for the child offender to accept responsibility
- Family responsibility towards the erring young person
- Community participation
- The voice of the victim

By its very nature, a Local Committee Court can easily adopt the above guidelines. As earlier mentioned, the court consists of the (9) members of the village executive committee. Section 3 (1) of the Judicial Powers Statute provides that at each sitting of the court, the minimum number of members present must be 5. Under Section 3 (4), the court has power to co-opt other members of the council so as to enable the court to realise a quorum. These provisions make it possible for a court to co-opt members of the child offender's family as well as members of the victim's family? at any sitting. Section 3 (5) provides that every question arising before the court shall be determined by consensus. It is only in default of a consensus that a majority vote is required. The fact that decisions are principally based on consensus also fits in well with restorative processes since they are inherently founded on negotiation.

One of the characteristics of restorative justice processes is that they are inherently flexible. It is perhaps partly for this reason that the United Nations opted to issue basic principles rather than standard minimum rules[102] or even come up with a convention. As observed by Daniel Ness[103] basic principles provide governments with general guidance related to a particular topic, but they do not address in detail how the principles should be implemented. The legal effect is that no country is required to use restorative justice programmes. However, the document makes it permissible for countries considering

[102] Standard minimum rules are more comprehensive directives to member states and provide detailed guidance. Being more specific than basic principles and offering less flexibility once promulgated, they are perhaps not appropriate for the development of community specific restorative justice programmes.

[103] Van Ness, in Van Hirsch, 2003, *op. cit.*

restorative justice programmes to draw upon the experience of other countries. [104] It is also noted that the Children Statute has given the Local Committee Courts wide discretionary powers. Caution must be taken of the fact that flexibility and discretion can easily lead to abuse of power and could undermine existing protection of individual rights. The danger is even more imminent when dealing with vulnerable groups such as children. It would indeed be ironical if a law enacted for meaningful protection of children's rights led to increased violation of their rights. There is therefore a need to provide guidelines which emphasise principles that are basic to a humane criminal justice system as well as to children's rights. For example:[105]

- The decision arrived at must consider the issue of the child's inability to make reparation, e.g. in financial terms, in light of the lack of maturity.[106]
- The need to protect the child from cruel, demeaning or degrading punishment[107]
- Proportionality of reparation of the harm caused.
- Reintegration is the primary objective and punishment should only be inflicted when justifiable.
- The child must **not** be forced to accept responsibility. It should be emphasised that the adoption of informal processes does not abolish the presumption of innocence. Consequently, the child must be enabled to tell his/her side of the story in an atmosphere where the child does not feel intimidated. This would be in line with the fact that the principle of restorative justice is in fact premised on an accused person pleading guilty.
- The child's right to meaningful participation in the process must be respected.

Provision of guidelines to Local Committee Courts would not be a departure from the norm since the police as well as the Family and Children Court have

[104] *Ibid.*

[105] Some of the examples have been adopted (and modified) from Duff, 2003, *op. cit.*

[106] Innovative approaches can ensure that where it is feasible, appropriate and agreeable to the victim, a child can perform work for the victim.

[107] Such as corporal punishment, which is seen by many adults as a time-tested way of instilling discipline in children.

been, in spite of their wide discretionary powers, been issued with guidelines.[108]

As already noted, it is very likely that the process of adjudication is dependent on the cultural practices of the people living in that particular area. There is a possibility that the majority of the people conduct their activities in accordance with customary procedures. We also know that customary law is largely tribal in origin. It is necessary therefore that "the government monitors the outcomes to insure fairness, equity, and effectiveness of processes" designed at the local level. It is only if the process is monitored that the child will enjoy the minimum procedural rights necessary in adjudication. This calls for periodic situation analyses. The UN Basic Principles on the Use of Restorative Justice Programmes in Criminal Matters urge member states to promote research and evaluation of restorative justice programmes in order to assess the extent to which they result in restorative outcomes, serve as an alternative to the criminal justice process and provide positive outcomes for all parties.[109] The rules acknowledge that restorative justice processes may need to undergo change in concrete form over time and member states are urged to encourage regular, rigorous evaluation and modification.[110] It is hoped that all this would increase the likelihood that the purpose of restorative processes will be accomplished and that, as stated by Daniel Van Ness,[111] "restorative justice processes do not become one more fad in the history of criminal justice reform."

In Uganda it is imperative that the vital role of record keeping is impressed upon the Local Committees. Currently, although Section 14 of the Judicial Powers Statute makes mention of court records, it is not uncommon to come across local council committees which admit total absence of any court records. In the pilot study mentioned above, I was unable to access any Local Committee Court records precisely because they were none. According to Policy Statement by the Ministry of Local Government for the Year 2002/2003,[112] a Local Council Courts Bill has been developed to amend the current law. Among its strong points will be "the introduction of the recording

[108] The Police Guidelines issued under Section 90 (2) and the Family and Children Court Rules (1988) issued under Sections 17, 19 and 84 of the Children Statute.

[109] See Principle 22.

[110] See Principle 23.

[111] Van Ness, in Van Hirsch, 2003, *op. cit.*

[112] (http://www.molg.go.u/policies/exsummary2003.htm).

of court proceedings and the keeping of court records." The new law will provide and co-opt a person who is able to read and write the local language of an area at village and parish levels and English at the sub-county level, for the purpose of recording court proceedings. If these proposals are adopted there is hope that it will be possible to monitor the processes.

CONCLUSION

It is clear that Uganda's statutory juvenile justice law is a par with international human rights standards on the treatment of children who have infringed the penal law. The study has revealed the possibility that a significant number of actors within juvenile justice are in agreement with the major principles underpinning a rights-based juvenile justice system – that a child should be handled differently from an adult offender, that a child who has infringed the law should to the farthest possible extent be dealt with outside the formal criminal justice system. Consequently, there is a tendency to handle child offenders at the family level and/or at the more informal forum- the Local Committee Court - rather than involving the police. Thus statutory law, societal perceptions and practice are a par.

An analysis of statutory law has also revealed that all the institutions empowered to handle child offenders are expected to be guided by the notion of restorative justice rather than retributive justice.

Due to the limited scope of the research, it was not possible to establish the extent to which Local Committee Courts emphasise reconciliation between the victims of juvenile crime and the child offenders. The study however brought out the fact that monetary compensation is often the driving force behind the negotiations. The findings also indicate that the need for the child to accept responsibility for the wrong done to the victim and to the community, the need for the child to take action to repair the harm done, is often ignored in the negotiations. Thus whereas victims were financially compensated (by the child's parents/guardians) for the wrong done to them, no child was formally called upon to apologise for her/his wrongdoing. The process seemed to emphasise parental responsibility for the child's misbehaviour and ignored the need for the individual child to be held accountable. In a similar vein, there was no evidence that the actors give serious thought to the need to rehabilitate the child. Thus no questions were geared towards unearthing what could have led to the crime in question. This seemed true of cases involving violence as well as those involving property related crime. And yet the law expects actors to focus on the need to rehabilitate rather than to punish the child. It need to be pointed out that accountability and rehabilitation both call for active participation of the child in the process of dispute resolution. It is thus necessary to investigate whether it is acceptable to Ugandan societies that a child - child *offender* - can have a voice in such a process.

It can thus be concluded that in as far as the operationalization of the principle of restorative justice is concerned; some aspects of a restorative justice process were being adhered to. However, some aspects of the principle did not feature at all in the few cases investigated.

Literature suggests that in several pre-colonial African societies, restorative justice was the guiding principle in dispute resolution. It is also suggested that children were treated differently from adult offenders; that children were not held fully responsible for their wrongdoing.

If indeed, justice *principally* based on retribution came to Africa only with the advent of colonialism, the philosophy could still be foreign to a large majority of the people. This would make a juvenile justice system based on restorative justice principles acceptable to African communities, for it would be culturally appropriate. What is, however, needed is a full investigation into the extent to which each of the principles underpinning restorative justice is acceptable to *contemporary* Ugandan society. If restorative justice already exists informally or indigenously in contemporary societies, all that is needed is to develop it to suit notions of justice within universally accepted human rights norms. For the moment what needs to be done is an investigation into 'how to revive traditional restorative justice practices *but* in a way that helps them become procedurally fairer, in a way that respects fundamental human rights, that secures protection from domination.'[113] And as earlier mentioned, the value in applying restorative justice to children in conflict with the law lies in the fact that its principles have the potential to fulfil the main goal of a modern juvenile justice system: rehabilitation and re-integration of the child offender into the community.

[113]John Braithwaite, Restorative Justice and A Better Future http://www.realjustice.org/Pages/braithwaite.html

BIBLIOGRAPHY

Allot, A.N, 1977. "The People as Law-makers: Custom, Practice, and Public Opinion as Sources of Law in Africa and England", In *Journal of African Law,* Vol. 21 No. 1

Barya, John-Jean and Oloka-Onyango J., 1994. *Popular Justice and Resistance Committee Courts in Uganda*, Kampala, Friedrich-Elbert-Stiftung

Beale, Sun Sara, Still Tough on Crime: Prospects for Restorative Justice in the United States,
http://leda.law.duke.edu/leda/data/99/bealeutah.html

Becker, Howard, 1963. *Outsiders: Studies in the Sociology of Deviance*, New York: The Free Press

Bottoms, Anthony, 2003. "Some Sociological Reflections on Restorative Justice" in Andrew Van Hirsch et al (Eds.), *Restorative Justice and Criminal Justice: Competing or Reconcilable Paradigms?* Hart Publishing, Oxford and Portland, Oregon

Boys, Michael Hardie, 1999. "Foreword" in Jim Consedine and Bowen H. (Eds.), *Restorative Justice: Contemporary Themes and Practice,* Ploughshares Publications. New Zealand

Braithwaite, John,

"Restorative Justice and a Better Future"
http://www.realjustice.org/pages/braithwaite.html

1989. *Crime, Shame and Reintegration,* Cambridge University Press

2000. "Shame and Criminal Justice" in *Canadian Journal of Criminology*, Academic Research Library, July

2002. *Restorative Justice and Responsive Regulation,* Oxford University Press

Braithwaite, John and Stephen Mugford, 1994. "Conditions of Successful Reintegration Ceremonies: Dealing with Juvenile Offenders" in *British Journal of Criminology*. Vol. 34 No. 2 spring

Campbell, Allen H. and Revering Andrew, 1997."Holding Kids Accountable: Shaming with Compassion" in *Reclaiming Children and Youth,* Volume 6, No.3 Fall

Cohen, Stanley, 1972. *Folk Devils and Moral Panics,* London: Mac Gibbon and Kee

Consedine, Jim,

1999. "African Justice: Compensating, Healing, Reconciling" in Consedine Jim (ed.), *Restorative Justice: Healing the Effects of Crime*, Ploughshares Publications, New Zealand

1999. "Restorative Justice: A Parallel System" in Jim Consedine and H. Bowen (Eds.), *Restorative Justice: Contemporary Themes and Practices,* Ploughshares Publications, New Zealand

Daly, K and Immarigeon R., 1998. "The Past, Present, and Future of Restorative Justice: Same Critical Reflections", in *Contemporary Justice Review*, Vol. 1

Duff ,Antony, 1955. "Restoration and Retribution" in Andrew Van Hirsch et al. (eds.), *Restorative Justice and Criminal Justice: Competing or Reconcilable Paradigms?* Hart Publishing. Oxford and Portland Oregon, 2003.
Gluckman Max, *The Judicial Process among the Barotse of Northern Rhodesia*, Manchester University Press

Goldin, Bennie and Michael Gelfand, 1975. *African Law and Custom in Rhodesia*, Juta and Co. Ltd. Cape Town

Hayden, A. and Henderson P., 1999. 'Victims: The invisible People' in Jim Consedine and H. Bowen (Eds.), *Restorative Justice: Contemporary Themes and Practice,* Ploughshares Publications. New Zealand

Hickey, C., 1999. "Alternative Dispute Resolution Within Criminal Justice" in Jim Consedine and H. Bowen (Eds.), *Restorative Justice: Contemporary Themes and Practice,* Ploughshares Publications, New Zealand

Lapsley, Michael, 1999 "The Heart of Justice: Truth, Mercy, Healing, Forgiveness" in Jim Consedine and H. Bowen (Eds.), *Restorative Justice: Contemporary Themes and Practice,* Ploughshares Publications, New Zealand.

McElrea, Freda, 1999. "Taking Responsibility in being Accountable" in Jim Consedine and H. Bowen (Eds.), *Restorative Justice: Contemporary Themes and Practice,* Ploughshares Publications, New Zealand

Muntingh, Lukas and Anne Monaheng, Family matters: How young offenders' families engage in restorative justice, http://ccrweb.ccr.uct.ac.za/two/7-3/pg13.html

Pranis, Kay, How to Build Community Support for Restorative Justice http://www.ojp.usdoj.gov/nij/rest-just/ch4/how 2 build.htm

Skelton, Ann, Juvenile Justice Reform: Children's Rights and Responsibilities versus Crime Control
http://www.1hr.org.sa/projects/childrights/publications/juvenile.html

Skelton, Ann, 1996. "Developing a juvenile justice system for South Africa: International instruments and restorative justice" in *Acta Juridica*, Juta & Co. Ltd.

Tibatemwa-Ekirikubinza, Lillian, 2003. "Understanding Children's Rights: The use of corporal punishment in rural Uganda", in East African Journal of Peace and Human Rights, Vol. 1.9:1

Van Bueren, Geraldine and Anne-Marie Tootell, Commentary on the Beijing Rules, http://child-abuse.com/childhouse/chldrens–rights/dci-be29.html

Van Hirsch, Andrew et al (eds.), 2003. *Restorative Justice and Criminal Justice: Competing or Reconcilable Paradigms*? Hart Publishing, Oxford and Portland Oregon

Van Ness, Daniel W, 2003. "Proposed Basic Principles on the Use of Restorative Justice: Recognising the Aims and Limits of Restorative Justice" in Hirsch Andrew et al (eds.), *Restorative Justice and Criminal Justice: Competing or Reconcilable Paradigms*? Hart Publishing. Oxford and Portland Oregon

Women and Law in East Africa [WLEA] 1998.

LEGAL INSTRUMENTS

1. The Children Act, Chapter 59, Laws of Uganda, Revised Edition, 2000.

2. The UN Convention on the Rights of the Child.

3. The O.A.U Charter on the Rights and Welfare of the Child.

4. The United Nations Standard Minimum Rules for the Administration of Juvenile Justice (Beijing Rules).

5. The Constitution of the Republic of Uganda.

6. The Penal Code Act, Chapter 120, Laws of Uganda, Revised Edition, 2000.

7. The Local Governments Act, Chapter 243, Laws of Uganda, Revised Edition, 2000.

8. The Resistance Committees (Judicial Powers) Statute of 1988.

9. UN Basic Principles on the Use of Restorative Justice in Criminal Matters

10. The Community Service Act, Chapter 115 Laws of Uganda, Revised Edition, 2000.

11. The Executive Committees (Judicial) Powers) Act, Chapter 8, Laws of Uganda, Revised Edition, 2000.

Legal Pluralism and Transitional Justice in Afghanistan: A Gender Perspective

Karin Ask

They took all the women and girls to another room and started with my fourteen-year-old daughter. Then... they tried to rape my twelve-year-old daughter. The commander said, 'It is our choice. You are Talib [a member of the Taliban] and you are Pashtun.' I am concerned about the future of my daughters. No one will marry my daughters. There is nothing left for us; marriage and honour is gone"[1] Excerpt from a mother's testimony to Human Rights Watch.

Perhaps at no other time in Afghanistan's history were women's human rights so widely debated – at least outside the country - as during the time of Taliban. While it may be premature to pass a judgement on the Afghan Transitional Administration (ATA) for how they handle human rights abuses of the past it is high time to focus international attention on the demands raised by female citizens in the post-Taliban Afghanistan.
The despondency created among many Afghan women by the lack of priority given to the legal protection needed to enjoy the human rights and freedoms promised, is captured succinctly in the words of another female respondent ,"During the Taliban era if a woman went to market and showed an inch of flesh she was flogged; now she is raped.[2]

INTRODUCTION[3]

I have chosen to build this article closely on appraisals and journalistic reports about the types of demands for justice raised by Afghan women. A main reason is to try to get as close as possible to assess the female actors points of view, and to contextualise the meagre resources we have about how they understand and conceptualise access to justice and human rights. The empirical data I draw upon is compiled from several sources: first weekly news bulletins on Afghan recovery written by Afghan Journalists during the years 2002 and 2003;secondly, material from the Afghanistan Independent Human Rights Commission (AIHRC); thirdly from select reports by Human Rights Watch (HRW), International Crisis Group (ICG) and Amnesty International (AI). The cases presented are interpreted against the background of experience from own anthropological fieldwork in 1992 and 1999.

---

[1] Interview with N. aged thirty in *Paying for the Taliban's Crimes: Abuses against ethnic Pashtuns in Northern Afghanistan.* Human Rights Watch 2002:22, Vol.14, No.2 (c) Available at http://www.hrw.org/reports/2002/afghan2/

[2] *"No one listens to us and no one treats us as human beings": Justice denied to women,* Amnesty International 2003. Available at http://www.web.amnesty.org/library/index/engasa110232003.html

[3] Sindre Bangstad, Are Knudsen and Tone Bringa have given critical comments to earlier versions of the text. I have benefited from their advice, however, one of them are responsible for the assessments made which are solely my own.

For all Afghans, rural and urban, the family is the paramount institution to which they look for rights and owe obligations, and the women who claim divorce capture the tension of conflict between, national law and the international human rights regime. The key words marriage and honour in the first quotation foreground two basic values in the moral order of the Afghan society which also relates to the general principles of human rights. I have also chosen examples from the field of family law because this is a field where well-known Afghan scholars[4] have published studies on the historical developments and conflict between local law and the codification of family law, where the event of divorce is an entry to discuss conflicts between the conceptualisation of gender rights in local law or customary law, national law and the international human rights in post Taliban Afghanistan. And last, but not least women's rights in marriage open for reflection which confronts us with basic challenges of translating between the particular local conceptualisation of women's rights and the universal human rights, in this case exemplified by the rights given in the declaration on marriage in the Universal Declaration of Human rights (UDHR).[5] Anthropological theory of legal pluralism (e.g. processes of adjudication in states that maintain both customary and received legal codes) provides a framework to assess how the types of interaction between local law, religious law and state law enable or constrain women's rights in marriage in the semi-autonomous field of family law. [6]

A HISTORY OF LEGAL PLURALISM IN A WEAK STATE

Most contemporary legal systems, both in developing countries as well as modern developed nation states contain parallel and contradictory regulations,

---

[4] Mohammed Hashim Kamali (1985) *Law in Afghanistan. A Study of the Constitutions, Matrimonial Law and the Judiciary.* Leiden, E.J. Brill. Ashraf Ghani (1983) "Disputes in a court of Sharia, Kunar Valley, Afghanistan, 1885 -1890". *Int. J. Middle East Stud.* 15 pp. 353-367. Helena Malkiyar (1997) discusses the subject matter in the article "Development of family law in Afghanistan: the roles of the Hanafi Madhab, customary practices and power politics", in *Central Asian Survey* Vol.16 (3), pp.389-399.

[5] Article 16 (1) Men and women of full age, without any limitation due to race, nationality or religion, have the right to marry and to found a family. They are entitled to equal rights as to marriage, during marriage and at its dissolution.(2) Marriage shall be entered into only with the free and full consent of the intending spouses.(3) The family is the natural and fundamental group unit of society and is entitled to protection by society and the State.

and so is also the case with Afghanistan. Below I synthesise main shifting points in the state's attempt to subordinate local law to national law with reference to the codification of female citizens rights in marriage.
At the beginning of the 20th century Afghan rulers sought to curtail the use of Local law by the tribal Khans and local tribal councils (Jirga). King Abdur Rahman (1880-1901) sought to consolidate the central power of the state by giving Sharia pre-eminence over local law, and appointed religious judges (*qadi*) who got their pay from the king in a way which made them state functionaries[7] rather than independent judges within the western liberal tradition. It is interesting to note that jurisdiction on marriage and divorce were among the issues that received special attention in the processes of modernisation and centralisation of the Afghan state.[8]

In 1923 when Afghanistan received its first written constitution (Nizamnama) religious law, Sharia, was given a supplementary and subordinate role to other laws, except in the domain of personal law and family law. King Amanullah (1919 – 1929) tried, nevertheless, to introduced restrictive law reforms to outlaw child marriage and polygamy. These reforms met with strong resistance from the conservative feudal elite and were among the significant political factors which were used to rally the rebellion which led to the downfall of Amanullah. The conservative regime which followed after Amanullah emphasised its conformity to Sharia and the1931 constitution also returned to more restrictive government policy on family law. The 1964 constitution given under the reign of king Zahir Shah made parliamentary law the principle basis for national laws in place of royal decrees (*Farman*), issued by the court. Sharia Courts were no longer mentioned in the constitution; instead Article 98 gave the Supreme Court the ability to allocate Sharia power to other courts and the national *Ulema* (Scholars of Muslim Jurisprudence) were given formal control to ensure that secular parliamentary laws were compatible with Islam. (Art. 54, Constitution of 1964). The current marriage laws set the age of majority to enter marriage to 16 years of age for girls and 18 years for boys.[9]

---

[7] Ashraf Ghani, op.cit., p.345.

[8] The religious judges were for example given the responsibility to control that the spouses met Sharia requirements to enter into marriage. Ghani, Ashraf op.cit., p.356.

[9] Resistance and discussion about child marriage also illustrates a principal difference in interpretation of religious law (Sharia) and national secular laws. A valid interpretation of religious law that meets Sharia requirements may define girl child as adult upon her first menstruation while national law will codify a definitive age to enter into marriage.

It is also interesting to note that the Ministry of Justice in the 70s took the initiative to suggest the new adjudication mechanisms *Jirga-e sulh* (lit. peace councils) which sought to develop local law to settle family conflicts. This innovative collaboration between local law and the national judiciary was however short-lived as national political crisis brought the People's Democratic Party of Afghanistan (PDPA) to power through the coup d'état in 1978.

The rhetorical importance given modernisation of family laws by shifting Afghan regimes is also evident in one of the first decrees given by PDPA, Decree No.7, which declared that "unjust patriarchal feudalistic relations between husband and wife" was illegal and outlawed the traditional payment of bride price or dowry which is a major transaction between the families of groom and bride in local law. The decree did not, however, outlaw the Sharia dower (*Mahr*) which is explicitly mentioned in the Koran as necessary gift to the bride to contract a legal marriage. The new legal regulations on marriage was nevertheless quoted as "un-Islamic" by the Afghan Mujahedin parties , and when they came to power in 1992 they abolished all the reforms of the marriage laws introduced by the PDPA . In addition, the interim government headed by President Rabbani also chose to demonstrate its commitment to Islam and Afghan identity by imposing new legal restrictions on women. In September 1993 the Supreme Court issued a *fatwa* (legal opinion issued by religious authority) demanding that the government "immediately enforce all the commands of Allah, especially concerning the veil, drive all women out of government offices and close schools for girls".[10]

When the Taliban emerged as new contenders for power in 1994, it was at a time of internecine fighting between shifting alliances of *mujahedin* parties which added to the general lack of law and order by an increase in the threat to women of sexually related crimes, rapes and abductions.[11] The initial welcoming of the Taliban among rural Afghans in Pashtun dominated communities should be appreciated against this background. The mythical restoration of law according to the principles of Pushtunwali is also embodied

---

[10] Court of the Islamic State of Afghanistan, "Fatwa on Veil" Kabul 1993. The enforcement of these restrictions remained unsystematic and many women were able to continue to work in government departments, education and health care at their own risk, till the Taliban established their rule in Kabul in 1996.

[11] Documentation on the scale of these crimes are available at http://www.afghanjustice.project.org

by[12] the story of how Amir Mullah Omar the leader of Taliban killed two warlords who had abducted and raped women outside Kandahar , using the traditional rules of vengeance (*badal*) to restore honour.

To sum up, during the last quarter of the 20th century the changing Afghan regimes have *de facto* operated on the principles of the 'rule of the gun' at the same time as shifting regimes in Kabul also have used differing and contradictory ideologies to legitimate their administration of law.

After the establishment of the Afghan Interim Administration (AIA)[13] in December 2001,the Bonn agreement reinstated the 1964 Afghan Constitution and "existing laws" as the interim legal framework for Afghanistan. Key dimensions of existing law include local law and Sharia law as well as international conventions acceded to the Afghan regime acced to. The Bonn agreement also established the Afghan Independent Human Rights Commission (AIHRC) to incorporate international human rights principles into Afghan justice institutions.

LOCAL LAW

My use of the term local law in this article refers primarily to Pashtunwali, the customary unwritten law (*riwaj*) that is also living law in the border regions of Pakistan where more than three million Afghan lived as refugees for more than twenty years. From the point of view of the refugees who shared the values in Pashtunwali[14] with their host local law extended beyond the territorial borders

[12] For a discussion of the shifting priorities given to human rights programming during the Taliban regime see Arne Strand "Bombs and Butter: Compensation Issues in Protracted Conflicts and the Case of Afghanistan" (pp. 124-128)in George Ulrich and Louise Krabbe (eds.) *Human Rights in Development Yearbook 2001,* The Hague: Kluwer Law.

[13] The terms used to refer to the Afghan authorities after the fall of the Taliban reflects the different stages set by the Bonn agreement (2001), Agreement on Provisional Arrangements in Afghanistan Pending the Reestablishment of Permanent Government Institutions, Bonn, December 2001. After the Emergency Loya Jirga in June 2002 the national authorities name changed to Afghan Transitional Administration (ATA). The Constitutional Loya Jirga in 2003 adopted the official designation The government of the Transitional Islamic State of Afghanistan.

[14] I ignore variations in customary law among the different ethnic groups in Afghanistan. Hazara. The position of Pashtunwali in Afghanistan is to be appreciated against the historical background of the domination of the Pashtun tribes in the historical nation building The application of local law at the micro-level emphasises local law as an unwritten code of honour.Cf. Asta Olesen *Islam and politics in Afghanistan,* London, Curzon Press 1995. A detailed analysis of the political status of Pashtunwali in the border region between Afghaniatan and Pakistan is to be

of Afghanistan. The perceptions on local law between refugees with a rural as opposed to an urban background differed but both categories recognized local law and religious law (Sharia) as a basic legal perception.

The symbol of *jihad*[15] invoked by the refugees emphasises the religious legitimacy of their identity as refugee-warrior (*mujahedin*). The metonym draw on key text in the Koran, in which believers are reminded of the religious obligation to receive Muslims who flee[16] from nations invaded by non-believers. The customary obligation in local law Pashtunwali to give asylum and hospitality (*melmastia*) were also brought to mind.

Sharia in its broadest terms refers to the accepted customs of Muslim communities in doctrinal belief, ritual action, civil jurisdiction, commercial transactions and criminal punishment. The Koran and the tradition (Sunnah) of the Prophet Muhammad establish the general principles and some specific rules to make legal descisions.[17] Even if *Sharia* is a divinely revealed law that cannot in principle be changed by human intervention, there is ample historical evidence which show that all Muslim nations (with the partial exception of Saudi Arabia) have codified religious law as part of their nation building project. In the case of Afghanistan the legal school of Hanafi is used as the exemplary norm in family law for the overwhelming majority of Sunni Muslims while the Shii minority follow the Jafari school.

Different layers of religious law and local law were activated as regulatory norms of gender interaction in every day life during the war and exile. Female perspectives on the authority of the resulting amalgam between local law and religious law were brought up in interviews with female refugees in Pakistan who distinguished between fields where the local customary law (*riwaj*) applied in distinction to norms derived from religious law (*mazab ki bat*).

This distinction was brought up by women as a critical reaction to a *fatwa* given by a group of Afghan religious leaders in Pakistan representing the seven Afghan *mujahedin* parties in further restricting the social and economic

found in Ahmed S. Akbar, *Millennium and Charisma among Pathans*, London, Routledge and Kegan Paul 1976.

[15] *Jihad* literally means "little" struggle, while the reinvention of tradition that involves changing of personal mores is what is classified in Islamic theology as the "large" struggle.

[16] This historical event, the Hijra, is described in the Koran (S:6:41-42), and a common term for refugees of this category is *muhajir*.

[17] These general rules analogical reasoning (*Qiyasas*) and consensus (*Ijma*) are applied by Islamic jurists to arrive at descisions. These are compiled as exemplary references in Islamic jurisprudence (*Fiqh*).

mobility of female refugees.18 The way the 'refugee warriors' controlled the internal organisation of the Pakistani camps 19 was brought up by female refugees who told me how they sought help from the tribal leaders against what they regarded as usurpation of the religious law to gain admission to income-generation projects.[4]

The initiatives taken to resist the cementing of restrictive interpretations of local traditions of gender segregation by reference to religious law, was also a subject where the international humanitarian community bargained over the interpretation of local law with the refugee community. The understanding of the justice of interpretations and solutions made with reference to local law was also impacted by the negotiation with different actors in the refugee environment.

The neighbouring countries where Afghan refugees spent years in exile were also undergoing processes of political process of Islamisation which affected the national laws. The refugees who entered Pakistan during the military dictatorship of Zia-ul-Haq for example, arrived at a time in the 1980s when female seclusion and patriarchal control was strengthened by the Islamization of national law. Local law gives a woman her rights through her ascribed social identity in the larger kin group collective. Her rights in the community are established by default, or in other words, by the exclusive rights relevant personalities in the patriarchal family structure hold in her as against the world. This mode of ascribing rights to women in local law also refuse to go along with individual obligations between the state and its female citizens, and is diametrically opposed to the basic principles of human rights, where the person has rights as an individual human being. This mode of ascribing rights to female citizens is diametrically opposed to the basic principles of human rights, where the person is accorded her rights *qua* individual human being.

The authority of local law was also upheld by the tribal councils (*Jirga/Shura*). A *Jirga* is a local/tribal institution of decision-making and dispute settlement. This is an informal institution which utilises local

---

[18] Diana Cammack characterises the changes in policy between the Taliban and other *mujahedin* groups "not so much a matter of substance as of degree", "Gender relief during the Afghan war" in Indra, Doreen (Ed.) *Engendering Forced Migration Theory and Practice*, Berghahn Books, New York, Oxford, 1999:pp.94 - 95.

[19] Matthew B. Fielden describes how *mujahedin* leaders became powerful gatekeepers to channels for distribution of refugee relief, "The geopolitics of aid to Afghan refugees in Northwest Frontier Province, Pakistan", *Political Geography,* Vol. 17, No.4, 1990, p. 471.

customary law to arrive at collective decision about the resolution of a dispute (or local problem) is binding on the parties involved.[20]

The membership of these councils varies according to the issue being handled but they are in principle open to any *male* household head on the basis of membership in the tribe. During the war the traditional tasks for deliberations in these councils also changed in response to pressure put on them by international humanitarian organisations. As a result of the *ad hoc* expansion of responsibilities taken on by the local councils for example to "gender mainstream" humanitarian assistance their knowledge and competence expanded and resulted in innovations like the female *shuras* [21] that open the local councils for women.

The main contrasts between the local councils (*Jirga/Shura*) and a court of *Sharia* may be summarised as the difference between negotiations to restore an equilibrium between two contestants and adjudication to restore justice. In a Jirga the adjudicator is a well-regarded member of the community whose identity is agreed upon by the disputant. This is often a person who is reputed to have a lineage with an accepted claim to descent from the Prophet Muhammad. He (this person is invariably a male) is expected to utilise both his religious and his personal influence and knowledge about the conflict to settle disputes, while in a Sharia court the judge (*Qadi*) is an religious expert who passes judgements on the basis of interpretations of general rules .

The Taliban institutionalised the operation of religious law (Sharia) at the state level for example through the government department known as the Ministry of the Promotion of Virtue and the Elimination of Vice (*Amr el-Maruf WA el-Munkir*)[23] the same name they gave the infamous religious police who were authorised to administered corporal punishment (whipping) on the spot for transgression of rules on appropriate Islamic clothing, etc.

---

[20] Wardak, Amin (2002b) " Jirga: Power and Traditional Conflict Resolution in Afghanistan" in *Law after Ground Zero.* Ed. John Strawson, London Cavendis.

[21] Even if these female *shuras* did not open for full participation in communal dispute resolutions they did increased formal influence for women in negotiation of norms for humanitarian assistance, cf. *Afghanistan and Civil Society,* Kristian Berg Harpviken, Arne Strand, Karin Ask, Chr. Michelsen Institute, Bergen, December 2002.

[23] The religious legitimacy for this special ministry is based on the Islamic legal doctrine of *Hisbah,* which aims to guard public order through social vigilance. Similar police exists in Saudi Arabia and comparable agency has reappeared inside the ATA administration as an office in the Ministry of Religious Affairs.

Figure 1[22]

Jirga/Shura	*Sharia*
Decision according to particular tribal values (*Pashtunwali*)	Interpretation/decisions made according to universal rules (*Fiqh*)
Well-regarded members of community	Judge an externally appointed expert
Context-sensitive resolutions	Rule-specific judgements

The so-called *Mahram* decree given by the Taliban authority of 16 July 1997 was the first among a series of decrees that restricted Afghan women's legal rights which caught the attention of the international assistance community. Sharia classifies cross-sex relationships within two categories, i.e. lawful, *mahram*, and unlawful, *na-mahram*. In customary law the norms for how men and women of these two categories may associate in everyday life are related to institutionalise gender segregation between men and women in the category of marriageable *na-mahram*. The arguments over this decree between the international assistance community and Taliban was both caused by its blatant violation of the basic human rights of freedom of movement and because of the practical hindrances it caused for foreign organisations to employ Afghan women.

During field work in 1999 I had the chance to observe at close quarters how women at the same time as they disagreed with the religious justification (*mazab ki bat*) for the engaged in skilful bargaining process with reference to customary law (*riwaj*) to increase their opportunities for jobs with humanitarian organisations.

To summarise, the laws the Taliban promulgated during their years in power entered into idiosyncratic arrangements of local law and Sharia. The decrees represented an inversion of the main historical trend where central authorities had endeavoured to subordinate local law by the use of Sharia and secular national law. Another example of this inversion is the way they enforced selected practices of local law such as the strict enforcement of gender segregation with reference to religious law and the use of veil. Their policy on veiling was criticized by the Organisation of the Islamic Conference (OIC) for lacking a sound basis in Sharia. The consequences of Taliban laws on gender segregation lead several international aid organisations together with

[22] Adapted from Harpviken et.al 2002, p.6.

UN agencies to impose strict criteria of gender conditionality in order to protect the basic rights of Afghan women.[24]

HARAMISATION OF LAW

Albeit that Taliban interpretation of Sharia was idiosyncratic, and its ideological basis was founded on an unusual relationship between Islamic faith and legal power, the way moral norms were made legally binding rules, is comparable to historical development in other Muslim countries. I have adapted the term *Haramisation* from Andre Gingrich [25] to refer to the processes where acts are converted to religiously binding obligations (*farz*) by far-reaching disciplinary control of the female to mark the forbidden category (*haram*).

The way Taliban tried to discipline within the realm of personal morality (*adab*) by imposing standards of dress and bodily appearance with reference to Sharia law, (for example a particular local form of veil (*burkha*) and the mandatory growing of beards for men) is apt illustrations of the processes of *haramisation*.

DILEMMAS OF ADJUDICATION BETWEEN LOCAL LAW AND NATIONAL LAW –THE CASE OF DIVORCE

In June 2002 the Afghan Recovery report carried news about hundreds of women who approached judges at the local courts in Kabul with claims that their marriages should be annulled on the grounds that they were forced. The courts in the capital gave notice that they were unable to process the cases adequately and asked for guidance and a decision from the Supreme Court.[26]

---

[24] For a comprehensive discussion see Nancy Dupreé Hatch (1989) "Afghan women under the Taliban", in *Fundamentalism Reborn?* Ed. William Maley, London: C. Hurst & Co and Centilivres-Demont, Michelene (1994) "Afghan Women in Peace, War and Exile", in Banuaziz, Ali and Weiner, Myron (eds.) *The Politics of Social Transformation in Afghanistan, Iran and Pakistan*, Syracuse: Syracuse University press. Mohammed Haneef Atmar, "Politicisation of Humanitarian Aid and its Consequences for Afghans", in *Disaster,* Vol. 25, No.4, 2001.

[25] André Gingrich analyses comparable processes in Yemen in his article "Inside an exhausted community: An essay on peripheral moralities", in Signe Howell (Ed.), 1997: p.160, *The Ethnography of Moralities,* London: Routledge.

[26] Afghan Recovery Report, no.17, 3. July 2002. Source available at http:// www.iwpr.net.html.

The Supreme Court advised the lower court to imprison the women under the charge of "social crime", a catch-all term for breaches of the honour code in local law that is also used to raise charges against women for the offence of "running away." Reports about this crime are recurring from several sources and a female judicial officer at police headquarters in Kabul estimates that 30 percent of women arrested are linked to cases of running away to avoid forced marriages.[27]The way this charge is regularly used seem also undermine women's faith in the legal process as demonstrated by the answer given by a women's rights activist interviewed by Amnesty International in Kabul "Judges will chose between written law, custom and Sharia according to which suits the interests of the man".[28]

Another dilemma created by the way these cases were handled by the court is the way the principled difference between women rights and status in local law and the national law justice system is blurred. This is graphically demonstrated by the way the formal justice system may order virginity tests to ascertain a woman's sexual characteristics, in other words how she embodies her male relatives' honour, before she is given the right to present her claim before the court.[29]

The women who sought divorce in different courts in Kabul June 2002 remained in prison until October 2002, when President Hamid Karzai availed himself of the traditional amnesty given to prisoners at the start of the holy month of fasting, Ramadan, to release the women. This descision was publicly criticised by the Supreme Court Chief Justice, Fazl Hadi Shinwari.[30]

The women who were released from prison had sought divorce on the grounds that their families had forced them to marry under duress. This is a valid ground for divorce under the Hanafi School of religious law, where the marriage of an adult and sane person is null and void if she/he is forced to marry without her/his consent. Even if the imprisonment of the women contravened Sharia as well as national law, the descision to take the women into custody reflects a pertinent awareness of the force of local law. The traditional way to restore family honour where female kinswomen's sexual

[28] Amnesty International 2003, *op.cit,*. p. 23. See also "Afghanistan women and reconstruction", March 2003, p. 22, Brussels/Kabul

[29] This practice has been reported from several towns in 2002. The recent Amnesty report describes how young women are detained and subjected to forcible virginity tests on the instigation of their families. Amnesty International 2003 *op.cit.*, p22.

[30] Afghan Recovery Report, No.37, November 22, 2002.

behaviour is questioned in ways that tarnish the family reputation is to remove the blot through eradication of the offending part, and a woman who initiates divorce is also vulnerable to punishment exacted by so-called honour killings. The imprisonment of the women was thus also made to protect the women from possible vengeance under local law, a "force" that reflects the moral dilemma for the judges who need to asses plural legal system with clear thought. [31]

FAMILY LAWS AND THE FACTS OF FAMILY

The national Law on Marriage of 1971/1350 set the legal age to enter into marriage at 18 years of age for boys and 16 years for girls. However, according to the Ministry of women's affairs, approximately 57 percent of girls are married before the age of sixteen. As mentioned above, there is no formal restriction on adult women and men to contract their marriage individually . The traditional practice in most Afghan communities, however, follow s the logic of local law where a first marriage for both women and men is arranged by the legal guardians (*wakil*) of the bride and groom where the overarching concern is to create links between appropriate families in larger kinship networks.[32] Endogamous marriages are common and it is seen as dishonourable for the family to give a women in marriage to a family who is socially inferior, while it is acceptable to take a wife from an "inferior group". The traditional payment of bride price means that there is also an economic incentive to control of marriage by the families.

Women are obliged to seek dissolution of the marriage through national courts if the right to divorce (*talaq-i-tafwid*) has not been granted to the woman in the marriage contract and if she applies for a divorce on grounds other than those stipulated in the contract she forfeits her dower (*Mahr*).[33] A

[31] I do not imply that honour killings are an automatic reaction to infringements of family honour. The young girls who refused to leave the prison upon release nevertheless demonstrate the fear of this type of vengeance from the family. See Are Knudsen in this volume for an in depth ethnographic analysis of circumstances of honour killing.

[32] Nancy Tapper argues on the basis of her detailed ethnographic case studies that divorce "is rare, shameful"..."A wife who misbehaves should ideally be killed rather than divorced" Nancy Tapper, *Bartered Brides. Politics, Gender and Marriage in an Afghan tribal society.* Cambridge, Cambridge University Press, 1991: pp.16-17.

[33] In Afghan law of marriage the *mahr* is the right of the bride to be written down in the marriage certificate, the civil marriage contract *Nikha Khat*.

man's right to divorce is easily obtained both under local law and in religious law (Sharia) where the husband has a unilateral right to dissolve a marriage by pronouncing "I divorce thee" (*talaq*) three times.

To understand the significance of legal rights in marriage to Afghan women we should also appreciate the national statistic which shows that marriage is a universal fact for Afghan women and men. In the 1970s, one-third of the population was estimated to have married before the age of 20, and only one to two percent is estimated to remain unmarried.[34] This statistical norm set the basic frames and prospects for living for both women and men. However, while men may marry all along their life span, the marriageable age for women is generally restricted to their reproductive life cycle. This context is another reason why women are more vulnerable than men to infringement on their rights of marriage. There are also unexpected consequences of regulations attached to the marriage laws. An example is a mid 1970s regulation which provided that married women could not attend high school classes which was upheld in November 2003 by Karzai's government to protect unmarried girls from hearing "tales of marriage".[35]

These and similar reports illustrate some of the challenges law givers met when confronting the ingrained unwritten patriarchal control in local law as well as national regulations of marriage law.

CONSTITUTIONAL CHANGES

The importance Afghan women give to legal rights in marriage is also demonstrated by the fact that the female delegates to the Constitutional Loya Jirga in December 2003 choose to focus on women's rights in marriage in constitutional law. The State Minister of Women's Affairs, Mahbooba Hoquqmal, moved a proposal that the issue of forced marriage and the equality of men and women before the law and in court be dealt with in separate Articles in the Constitution. The unofficial English translation of the Constitution[36] does not include any paragraphs on marriage, but Article 22 states that the citizens of Afghanistan, whether man or woman have, equal

[34] *Government of the Democratic Republic of Afghanistan*, 1981.

[35] Supporters of the law said it was necessary to protect unmarried girls from hearing "tales of marriage" - in other words explicit details about sex from their wedded classmates." Afghan Recovery Report, No.80, November 10, 2003.

[36] The Constitution of Afghanistan (unofficial translation), Year 1382 (2004). Available at (http://www.constitution-afg.com/Adopted%20Constitution.htm)

rights and duties before the law and the Constitution expressy requires the state to abide by the UDHR and the international conventions that Afghanistan has signed.

The Afghan Independent Human Rights Commission (AIHRC) has also raised the issue of forced marriage in follow up workshops for the delegates to the Constitutional Loya Jirga. In response to reports of high numbers of suicide attempts among women forced marriage was identified as a major cause. AIHRC estimates that 60 - 80 per cent of all marriages are forced in the sense of being under aged, or arranged as marriages of a women "in repayment of debt". [37]

Under the new Constitution every member of the Supreme Court must take an oath to support judicial justice and righteousness in accordance with the sacred religion of Islam, and recommendations to solve possible contradictions between *Sharia* and National law, "No law can be contrary to the sacred religion of Islam and the values of this Constitution.", rests with the Supreme Court presided over by the conservative Chief Justice Fazl Hadi Shinwari and it is a regrettable fact that no female judges have a seat in the Supreme Court. The Chief Justice who is a prominent religious conservative38 was originally appointed by the Afghan Interim *mujahedin* government of Rabbani who reappointed him in December 2001 just before the Bonn Agreement was adopted. He is also reported to have been instrumental in the removal of Dr. Sima Samar (the chairperson of AIHRC) from the office as Minister of Women's Affairs, after she expressed independent views on Sharia and women's rights in an interview with a Canadian magazine.[39] It is against this background that every constitutional guarantee for equal gender rights such as the semantic meticulousness in wording of the Constitution 'The word Afghan

---

[37] AIHRC: Women rights http://www.aihrc.org.af/womenrights.htm

[38] The Chief Justice Shinwari is 74 years thus 14 years older than the required age limit of 60 years set in the 1964 constitution. The 2003 Constitution requires that the Supreme justice have higher education in law or in Islamic jurisprudence, and sufficient experience in the judicial system of Afghanistan. Shinwari is a graduate from the prestigious Deoband *Madrasa* in India but has no formal training in secular law. In a rare interview he states that "I think the knowledge I have in Islamic studies and principles is enough for a Chief Justice, I will never accept and I am not obliged to learn any law or regulation opposing Islamic law." However, "there are some foreign rules and regulations that are similar to Islamic laws, such as human rights, and I will never oppose them." Available at http://www.iwpr.net/sub_form.html

[39] The case was reported in a press release from Human Rights Watch in June 2002 at http://hrw.org/press/2002/06/afghan0626.htm and was also commented in the Kabul based national press.

applies to every citizen in Afghanistan, woman and man'[40] is to be appreciated. The Supreme Court has also created a *Fatwa* Council of religious clerics who may issue rulings on its own initiative. Among their positive religious interpretation (*fatwa*) is to allow women to remarry if their husbands have been missing for more than four years, reducing the 70-year wait required under the Hanafi School of religious interpretation.[41]

THE MIX: LOCAL LAW, SHARIA, NATIONAL LAW AND INTERNATIONAL LAW;

The subordination of national law to local law is also evident in the way women sometimes are used as pawns in local litigation where they may be given in marriage to end enmity and feuds between two families; the term in local law for this type of marriage is *bado shaza /swara*. These and other practices of local law such as the remarriage of a widow to her late husband's brother (*levirate*) conflict with Islamic law (Sharia) as well as secular national law and have been declared illegal by several Afghan governments, also the Taliban who gave *fatwa* to outlaw the levirate and the exchange of women in marriage to end feuds as un Islamic.[41]

BETWEEN LOCAL AND GLOBAL CONCERNS

Once the idea that individuals have inalienable human rights is accepted, governments and other agents have corresponding legal and moral obligations for which they may be held accountable. The case of the women seeking divorce in June 2002 illustrates in a small way the judicial as well as the moral dilemmas of honouring human rights and simultaneously balance between the conflicting norms of justice in a plural legal system. In a society like

---

[40] The Constitution of Afghanistan Kabul year 1382 (2003) Available at http://www.constitution-afg.com/Adopted%20Constitution.htm

[41] This example show the possibilities of choosing rulings and precedence that are more favourable to women if one choose among different Schools of Sharia law. The fatwa was given based on the interpretation of the Maliki school of Sharia.

[41] Ghulam Rabbani Adeeb general director in the Justice ministry, explains that the tradition continue because "it is the best way to prevent blood feuds" and concludes this is "only part of people's culture" not "part of our legislation." Afghan recovery Report No.39, December 6, 2002.

Afghanistan where gender segregation is of high importance culturally, the lack of female staff in the judiciary is also a major hindrance to fulfil these obligations. According to UN figures there are only 50 female judges in the whole country,[42] most of them working and residing in Kabul. In October 2003 representatives of the Supreme Court provided an even smaller number, out of a total of 2006 judges in the country approximately 27 were female.[43]

However, more important than the exact numbers number of female judges is how the attention paid to gender in the conceptualisation of the framework set to restore a functioning judicial system.44Some international experts have suggested a "three pronged approach" to rebuilding the judicial system in Afghanistan where "the customary system should function in most of the country, while the formal pre-1978 legal system should apply in Kabul and a few major cities." The international community should provide direct assistance in the handling of only a very limited number of specific major crimes".45 International experts also suggest "giving the customary system... such as the *Qadi* courts" ...prerogative in rural areas where "no attempt should be made to impose any other legal system or structure ."[46] While these propositions are not to be understood as an officially endorsed plan by the national authorities, the lack of trained staff in the formal judiciary may lead to a state of affairs where the administration of justice can differ in two ways: first as between the use of local law and formal law, and, secondly as between urban and rural areas. The gender consequences of such a system will hamper women's access to justice under national law leaving the majority of women to the mercy of the justice of local law.

In a society in which the overwhelming majority of female citizens is illiterate (85 percent) and e.g. unable to follow up paperwork to access to the formal court system the association of women judges in Afghanistan (AWJA) has undertaken a formidable task to defend and protect women's rights under the national laws . The work they do to increased female legal capacity is also

---

[42] This number is given by the UN Office of Humanitarian Affairs, IRIN. Accessed on 4.04. 2003.

[43] AI, *op. cit.* 2003 : 25p.

[44] "Establishing the Rule of Law in Afghanistan" United States Institute of Peace, Special report 117, March 2004.

[45] *Rebuilding Afghanistan. A framework for establishing Security and rule of Law.* Washington January 2002 United States Institute of Peace. Available at http://www.usip.org/ruleoflaw/rebuilding/afghan_mainreport.html

[46] *Rebuilding Afghanistan. A framework for Establishing Security and the Rule of Law*, 2002, United States Institute of Peace, Washington. Available at http://www.usip.org/ruleoflaw/rebuilding /afghan_mainreport.html

critical for better responsiveness to women's claims for justice in the formal courts.

The case of women seeking divorce is a prism that highlights one important part of the problem of reaching equitable process of gender justice in Afghanistan, namely the way local law subordinates individual rights under collective rights. The reports about women who claim divorce in Afghanistan is thus one gauge to the uphill struggle required to transform ideas about human rights "into juridical binding norms and reach a phase where these norms are put into practice."[47]

INTERNATIONAL LAW

The Afghan state became a party to several UN charters and conventions during the years of war and conflict between 1980 and 1994[48] and the Convention on the Elimination of All Forms of Discrimination against Women (CEDAW) was signed in August 1980 by the Karmal regime and reaffirmed by President Karzai in March 2003.[49]

The Universal Declaration of Human Rights (UDHR) states that the family is the foundation stone of society and that marriage should be freely contracted by adult individuals. In Afghan society the institution of family is precisely such a foundation unit making marriage (and divorce) of instrumental concern to the larger kinship units. Afghanistan has also ratified CEDAW without reservations and is obliged to ensure that men and women have "the same right to enter into marriage...the same rights during marriage

[47] Asbjørn Eide, Quoted in Andreas Føllesdal "Menneskerettigheter og normative politisk teori. Premisser og paradokser" [Human Rights and Normative Political Theory. Premisses and Paradoxes]. In 'Mennesker & rettigheter', *Nordic Journal for Human Rights*, Vol.1, No 1, 2001.

[48] Afghanistan acceded to the International Convenant on Economic, Social and Cultural Rights (CESCR) in January 1983, the International Covenant on Civil and Political Rights (CCPR) in January 1983, and the International Convention on the Elimination of All Forms of Racial Discrimination (CERD) in July 1983. The Convention against Torture and Other Cruel Inhuman or Degrading Treatment or Punishment (CAT) was signed in April 1987 and the Rabbani regime acceded to the Convention on the Rights of the Child (CRC) in May 1994. Source: Office of the United Nations High Commission for Human Rights *Status of ratification of the principal international human rights treaties*.

[49] President Karzai also signed the treaty on the International Criminal Court (ICC) in February 2003. The treaty came into force from 1 May 2003, since which date the ICC has had the authority to investigate and prosecute serious war crimes, genocide and crimes against humanity committed on Afghan soil.

and at its dissolution"[50]. The resolute resistance made in Afghan societies to implement this right illustrates the conflict that does exist between the ways some humans rights are defined by the Universal Declaration of Human Rights and the ways they are understood in an Islamic and local cultural context. The 'universal' human rights need to be translated and properly understood within the 'particularistic' Afghan context at grass roots level.

CONCLUSION

> I can't say what human rights are, but I know that we have been deprived of them and need them urgently". Afghan villager's answer to a question about his opinion on human rights.[51]
>
> The Afghan Independent Human Rights Commission (AIHRC) is given the mandate "to monitor human rights, investigate human rights violations, the development of domestic human rights institutions and institute a program of human rights education.

With this wide-ranging mandate, the way in which the commission has been able to impact on women and men's rights awareness through educational campaigns and cooperation with likeminded groups, is, indeed commendable. In a recent survey carried out on Afghan attitudes and knowledge about human rights and women's political and civil rights, more than seventy-two percent of those surveyed thought that women should be involved in community decision making.[52] Afghan women's awareness of the ideas of the international human rights were shaped and sharpened by experience made during years of war, and by the expectations raised by the international community for post-war reconstruction. In the current situation where the universal human rights need to be legitimised and properly understood within the particularistic context of Afghan society at grass roots level, the women who pursued their claims for divorce represent a small illustration of the challenge to restore a sense of justice acceptable to the people of Afghanistan.

---

[50] CEDAW Article 16 (a) and (c).

[51] "Human Rights and Reconstruction in Afghanistan", New York, 2002 available at http://www.cesr.org

[52] *Speaking out: afghan Opinions on rights and responsibilities*. The Human Rights and Advocacy Consortium. Kabul November 2003.

BIBLIOGRAPHY

Akbar, Ahmed S., 1976. *Millennium and Charisma among Pathans*, London, Routledge and Kegan Paul

Atmar, Hanif (2001) "Politicisation of Humanitarian Aid and its Consequences for Afghans" in *Disasters*, Vol.25, No.4.

Cammack, Diana, 1999. "Gender relief during the Afghan war" in Doreen Indra , *Engendering forced migration. Theory and practice*. New York: Oxford Berghahn Books

Centilivres-Demont, Michelene, 1994. "Afghan Women in Peace, War and Exile", in Banuaziz, Ali and Weiner, Myron (eds.) *The Politics of Social Transformation in Afghanistan, Iran and Pakistan*, Syracuse: Syracuse University press.

Eide, Asbjørn, quoted in Andreas Føllesdal, 2001. "Menneskerettigheter og normative politisk teori. Premisser og paradokser" [Human Rights and Normative Political Theory. Premisses and Paradoxes]. In 'Mennesker & rettigheter', *Nordic Journal for Human Rights*, Vol.1, No 1

Fielden, Matthew B., 1990. "The geopolitics of aid to Afghan refugees in Northwest Frontier Province, Pakistan", *Political Geography,* Vol. 17, No.4, p. 471.

Ghani, Ashraf, 1983. "Disputes in a court of Sharia, Kunar Valley, Afghanistan, 1885 -1890". *Int. J. Middle East Stud.* 15 pp. 353-367.

Gingrich, André, 1997. "Inside an exhausted community: An essay on peripheral moralities", in Signe Howell (Ed.), *The Ethnography of Moralities,* London: Routledge.

Harpviken, Kristian Berg, Arne Strand and Karin Ask, 2002. *Afghanistan and Civil Society*, Oslo: Norwegian Ministry of Foreign Affairs.

Hatch, Nancy Dupree, 1989. "Afghan women under the Taliban", in *Fundamentalism Reborn?* Ed. William Maley, London: C. Hurst & Co.

Kamali Hashmi, Mohammad, 1985. *Law in Afghanistan. A Study of the Constitutions, Matrimonial Law and the Judiciary.* Leiden: E.J. Brill.

Malkiyar, Helena, 1997. "Development of family law in Afghanistan: the roles of the Hanafi Madhab, customary practices and power politics", *Central Asian Survey* Vol.16 (3), pp.389-399.

Olesen, Asta, 1995. *Islam and Politics in Afghanistan* , London: Curzon Press.

Strand, Arne, 2003. "Bombs and Butter: Compensation Issues in Protracted Conflicts and the Case of Afghanistan" (pp. 124-128)in George Ulrich and Louise Krabbe (eds.) *Human Rights in Development Yearbook 2001,* The Hague: Kluwer Law.

Tapper, Nancy, 1991. *Bartered Brides. Politics, Gender and Marriage in an Afghan Tribal Society,* Cambridge University Press: Cambridge.

Wardak, Amin (2002) "Jirga: Power and Traditional Conflict Resolution in Afghanistan", in *Law after Ground Zero.* Ed. John Strawson, London Cavendish.

Other sources:

Afghan Recovery Reports, Volume 2002 , 2003;
http://www.iwpr.net/sub_form.html

Amnesty International:

> *Afghanistan women and reconstruction*, March 2003, p. 22, Brussels/Kabul
>
> *"No one listens to us and no one treats us as human beings": Justice denied to women,* 2003;
> http://www.web.amnesty.org/library/index/engasa110232003.html

Center for Economic and Social Rights *"Human Rights and Reconstruction in Afghanistan",* New York, 2002; http://www.cesr.org

Constitution of Afghanistan, Kabul 1382 (12003); http://www.constitution-afghan.com/Adopted%20Constitution.htm

Court of the Islamic State of Afghanistan. *Fatwa on Veil*. Kabul 1993

The Human Rights and Advocacy Consortium. *Speaking out: Afghan Opinions on rights and responsibilities*. Kabul, November 2003.

Human Rights Watch.*Paying for the Taliban's Crimes: Abuses against ethnic Pashtuns in Northern Afghanistan.* Human Rights Watch 2002:22, Vol.14, No.2 (c); http://www.hrw.org/reports/2002/afghan2/

Office of the United Nations High Commission for Human Rights *Status of ratification of the principal international human rights treaties.*

United States Institute of Peace, *Rebuilding Afghanistan. A framework for establishing Security and rule of Law.* Washington January 2002; http://www.usip.org/ruleoflaw/rebuilding/afghan_mainreport.html

www.afghanjustice.project.org

Administering the African Society Through the Living Law

Michelo Hansungule

INTRODUCTION

When asked whether they have been to Africa, people in Europe like to answer: Not really, I have been to Algeria, Egypt or Tunisia but not really to Africa. And then they add: You know it is different! This is a ritual answer for most Europeans that have not yet crossed the Sahara, which separates the north from the African sub-continent. I don't really know to what extent Egypt can be described as different from sub-Saharan Africa or for that matter the rest of the Arab Africa. But they are right. Africa is different from other parts of the world. We no longer emphasise these differences today but all the same it is different. The way people live and generally conduct their lives is certainly quite different say from people in Western countries. A Swedish couple in Stockholm getting married will certainly conduct their marriage rituals differently from an African couple in Benin or in Malawi. Of course the end result is the same and therefore, oftentimes I do not really want to emphasise the differences. It is more like a French driver driving on the left-hand side inside the car while his English counter-part drives on the right-hand side but both will reach their destination, which may be the same.

The differences between Africa and the rest of the world manifest itself differently. Besides the marriage institution, the way Africans relate to one another in the family i.e. their roles and responsibilities, is different. As I am writing this article, I have just gone through on of these roles, which I am sure middle-aged men of my age in Europe would not bother about. Let me elaborate. You see, one of my 'silent' names is Lyambai. I mean I never use it in legal documents because the first government officer I encountered when I became public ignored it. I had to struggle to add one of my present names – Michelo – but that is another story. As I came to learn later, the name Lyambai was given to me by my grandfather. By our law, grandparents enjoy an overriding right to name their grandchildren, and often they will give them their own names. But Lyambai was not my grandfather's real name either. It was his nickname. In the Lozi language, a language of one of Zambia's four main ethnic groups inhabiting the western part of the country, the word Lyambai means a big river. You see, one of Zambia's four biggest rivers is called the Zambezi River. At the point where Zambia shares its borders with Zimbabwe, the Zambezi gives way to the world famous Victoria Falls, named after Queen Victoria by the English explorer Dr. David Livingstone in the middle of the 19th century. I would not be surprised if this is confusing you, the reader. It confuses me too and frankly, I don't really understand most of what lays behind our living law. Let me come to the point. Upon seeing a big tall towering man serving European colonial administrators as the police, or as they were known at that time – messengers – Lozis gave him the nickname Lyambai. They thought my grandfather was as big and tall or long as the river Zambezi. They named him after one of Zambia's famous rivers!

When I was born, my grandfather passed on his nickname to me. To this day, old men and women in my village only know me by this name. This is in spite of my attempts later, when I registered school, to adopt Christian or Western names, which I said is a story for another section. Now, my grandfather and father are both dead. Recently, I lost one of my favourite nieces. I am using the word 'niece' only in order to communicate in this article. Otherwise, it does not exist in my culture. She is my child just as if she was my own child. Somehow, I did not get to know about her sudden death from a suspected heart attack till the day after she was buried. Communications between South Africa, where I reside and work, and Zambia my home country are certainly not among the best. By the time, I raised enough money to fly to Zambia, I found that not only had they already buried her but all the mourners had returned to their homes. However, I found my cousin – my niece's mother - and of course my late niece's husband. After receiving me in the traditional way i.e. performing the traditional mourning, my cousin and I sat down for the traditional greetings. This is when you ask the 'hows' and 'whens' and 'whys' in relation to the deceased's death. After she had told my about the death, my cousin rather surprised me by saying the funeral was actually about me, and not my dead niece. I asked how? She said virtually everyone of our extended family was asking whether I knew about it, where I was and when I would come. I still had not got it. Then she reminded me of what I myself had forgotten – that I was *[the]* Lyambai – the head of the extended family after my grandfather and my father had passed on. By our 'law', I was bound to be there to play certain roles and assume responsibilities during my niece's death just as if my grandfather had risen from the dead. I am still to meet a European man subject to such legal duties to his nieces as I was.

And then a colleague of mine from Ghana reproached me for not replying immediately to her email. I explained that I had gone home to Zambia to attend to the funeral of my niece, who had suddenly collapsed and died on a Sunday, and was buried two days later on a Tuesday. My Ghana colleague was astounded. She asked me why the burial had taken place so quickly, only two days later. I said that normally, burials in Zambia took place anywhere from two to seven days after the death. By our law, we do not normally wait longer than that. My colleague was very surprised. She said in Ghana, it was a law in most communities to keep the corpse for up to as long as one, three, six months or even one year before the burial. During this time, a lot of things take place. In particular, rituals are performed. Very expensive preparations for the main day of the funeral – burial – take place during that time.

She explained to me that she had lost her mother-in-law only about a year earlier. According to their law, my colleague, a lawyer by profession, had to walk barefooted during the funeral of course dressed in black. She told me many other things, but one which still sticks to my mind is that she was asked or rather ordered to stay in a closed room throughout the night with the corpse of her mother-in-law during which time she conveyed messages to the departed from the living through the corpse. Something like: please mother, can you tell our ancestors that so and so in our family has no child. Please let her be blessed with a child. Please tell them that so and so is poor, let our spirits help him rise from poverty, etc. Talking to the corpse! I couldn't believe it, but that's their law.

In this article, I have set out to look at some aspects of African living law using relevant examples from selected African cultures and traditions, and, where possible, I will try to relate them to the notion of human rights. In particular, though not necessarily, I will try and look at the African family emphasizing distinctive roles and responsibilities of individuals, the notion of marriage in Africa especially some of its effects, broader subjects like property relations in Africa particularly the living law or land ownership and inheritance patterns, etc.

But before we go on, let me reiterate a warning initially sounded by a rather brave European. For a long time, Africa was seen in a bad light, its morals (or lack hereof) condemned out of hand in favour of a Euro-centric approach to law and morality. Today even the Africans themselves have a hard time acknowledging the value of their "living" law, rejecting it as inappropriate and inferior. Needless to say, I disagree, and, thankfully, I am not alone. At an early stage even a European, A.T. Culwick, showed rare courage in rejecting European chauvinism. He said:

> The plain fact is that we cannot reasonably pass judgment on African values without first doing so on our own. Only be recognizing our most deeply ingrained prejudices for what they really are, by discriminating honestly in the

> light of reason between the universal and the relative in moral values, can we formulate a valid philosophy of administration and education for Bantu Africa. The white man comes to Africa making the fundamentally unsound assumption that his moral ideas are in some way absolutely true, and his way of conducting life and arranging human relationships is therefore absolutely better than that of the African. Leaving aside the question whether his ideas of moral values have not in fact gone astray even in his own environment, what grounds other than his own opinion has he got for proclaiming them true for all times and places? [1]

At least as late as the 1980s, especially American writers[2] maintained the notion of the African society of not having standards on human rights till the advent of modern western society, which is exactly what Culwick and this author reject.

At this stage there is a need for Africa to re-invent its position in relation to the concepts of law and justice, moving away from the notion that just because something is European it is automatically the right thing, but at the same time also analysing critically the traditional elements of law and justice so as to ensure that the valuable elements are preserved.

1. THE AFRICAN FAMILY TREE

The family concept in Africa is very complicated. For one thing, it cannot be compared to anything in the West. It simply has no equivalence. So many studies have been conducted on the African family, as usual mainly by Western scholarship. Very little of it has come from Africans themselves. The danger is all too obvious. Imagine an African writing about the Danish family and writing about it *correctly*. Articulating all those intricacies as correctly as can be! Of course it is possible but the dangers of misinterpretations and distortions are simply too obvious. This is the problem with the African family as interpreted and presented by Westerners through Western tentacles. It is dangerous. With this caveat, however, we should now try sourcing the international standards on the family and see whether we can relate them to the actual situation in Africa.

---

[1] A.T. Culwick, "Good Out of Africa. A Study in the Relativity of Morals" in *The Rhodes-Livingstone Papers*, Number Eight, Manchester University Press, 1942, p. 1

[2] See e.g. Rhoda Howard, *Human Rights in Commonwealth Africa*,Totowa, Rowman & Littlefield, 1986; and Jack Donelly, *Universal Human Rights in Theory and Practice*, Ithaca, Cornell University Press, 1989.

Traditionally in Africa as well as Europe, the family was regarded as one of those enclaves protected from outside interference. The family was out of bounds to the law. What went on in the family had nothing to do with the state or society. However, with the growing realization that the state must protect human dignity and more especially individual status, it slowly dawned upon societies to extend the monitoring of the human rights standards right into the family and if necessary, take the standards right through to the bedroom. International human rights instruments together with domestic legal regimes are frequently used to secure the protection of the individual in family settings. Is this equivalent to interference in the family domain? Not necessarily. While the state has no business poking its dirty nose into the private lives of people, it has an obligation to protect the family, which by extension means not only protecting values but also the dignity of the individuals who constitute the family.

Of course, the state should not go about dictating moral values under the guise of protecting the family while ignoring the interests of individuals, particularly where these are in conflict with the interests of the collective. Similarly, the state must not over-emphasize individuals' interests at the expense of the collective. From an African perspective, the state fulfils its duty only when it balances its protection mandate between the individual and the collective. The argument here is that modern approaches are flawed to the extent that they overemphasize the individuality aspect at the expense of the collective. On the other hand, individualistic approaches conflict with collectivistic strands. Too much emphasis on the value of collectives easily ends up meshing the individuality all too apparent in a human being. The answer in both cases lies in the art of balancing.

The family clause, Article 16 of the Universal Declaration of Human Rights (UDHR), states:[3]

> Men and women of full age, without limitation due to race, nationality or religion, have the right to marry and to found a family. They are entitled to equal rights as to marriage, during marriage and at its dissolution.
> Marriage shall be entered into with the free and full consent of the intending spouses.

[3]Human Rights. A Compilation of International instruments, Volume 1. (Second Part) Universal Instruments. United Nations. OHCHR. Pp. 1-6 and the ICCPR is listed on Pp. 17-34

> The family is the natural and fundamental group unit of society and is entitled to protection by society and the State.

In a similar vein, Article 23 of the International Covenant on Civil and Political Rights (ICCPR) picks up the tune from the UDHR. It states:

> The family is the natural and fundamental group unit of society and is entitled to protection by society and the State.
> The right of men and women of marriageable age to marry and to found a family shall be recognized.
> No marriage shall be entered into without the free and full consent of the intending spouses.
> States Parties to the present Covenant shall take appropriate steps to ensure equality of rights and responsibilities of spouses as to marriage, during marriage and at its dissolution. In the case of dissolution, provision shall be made for the necessary protection of any children.

Regionally, the African Charter on Human and Peoples' Rights[4] was adopted by the Organisation of African Unity (OAU) in June 1981 and came into force in 1986. Article 18 of the Charter stipulates:

> The family shall be the natural unit and basis of society. It shall be protected by the State which shall take care of its physical and moral health.
> The State shall have the duty to assist the family which is the custodian of morals and traditional values recognized by the community.
> The State shall ensure the elimination of every discrimination against women and also ensure the protection of the rights of the woman and the child as stipulated in the international declarations and conventions.
> The aged and the disabled shall also have the right to special measures of protection in keeping with their physical or moral needs.

Significantly, paragraph 3 of article 17, which deals with education and culture, reaffirms the importance of preserving cultural values in these terms:

> 3. The promotion and protection of morals and traditional values recognized by the community shall be the duty of the State.

But all this is hardly surprising. It is hardly coming as a surprise that the Charter is so equivocal on the relevance of African tradition and culture in a modern human rights instrument. Right from the start, the forefathers of the

---

[4] Human Rights. A Compilation of International Instruments. Volume 11. Regional Instruments. United Nations. ST/HR/1/Rev.5 Cvol.11). Pp. 330-346

Charter left no doubt as to their bias towards the ancient African society and in particular family morals, which act as the living law that ties the family members together. The preamble to the Charter, in particular paragraph 5, summarized this preoccupation:

> Taking into consideration the virtues of their historical tradition and the values of African civilization which should inspire and characterize their reflection on the concept of human and peoples' rights

Earlier, when detailing instructions to the restricted group of Highly Qualified Experts chosen to draft the Charter, the African Heads of State and Government left no doubt as to the direction they wanted the treaty to lean towards. In the very first term of reference, they directed the experts:

> 1. to be inspired by the tradition of African society and the principles upon which such tradition are based.[5]

Clearly, the above standards don't speak the same language. In particular, the African Charter could be accused of unnecessarily tilting towards the side of traditional African society ignoring individual liberties. This accusation is buttressed by the eloquence with which the Charter speaks about what it calls 'duties of the individual' listed in articles 27 through to 29. Most of them are very concrete in nature, such as the reference made of the duty of children to look after their parents even to the extent of maintaining them in case of need, and the duty to pay tax, to the most overall such as the duty of the individual "to preserve and strengthen positive African cultural values". [6]

Article 28 embalms the principle of morality and makes its fulfilment pivotal to the exercise and enjoyment of the fundamental human rights. What does this mean? First, we should observe that the issue of morality begs for an extended explanation as the individual rights referred to seem to apply only to individuals that are demonstrably worthy of them. Moral worthiness of the individual is one of the gateway factors for being entitled to have individual rights. For instance, it is not expected of an African to speak loosely about sex in public or private in pursuance of his freedom of expression. Freedom of expression is severely restricted by the duty to respect morals. Recently, Mrs.

[5] Michelo Hansungule, "The African Charter on Human and Peoples Rights: A Critical Review" in *African Yearbook of International Law*, Volume 8, 2000, p.273.

[6] Article 29 (5), Article 29(6), and Article 29(7).

Mary Robinson, former UN High Commissioner for Human Rights, told an LL.M in human rights class in Pretoria: Journalists often ask me which human right standard I think often gets violated? She explained: I tell them that as far as I am concerned it is poverty. Poverty, she said, is the most serious obstacle to human rights. The former Irish President then said: then they (journalists) don't quote me. Poverty is not *[sexy]* enough for their reports.

The easy use of the word 'sex' would be shocking to a morally conscientious African. In the West, the word even appears regularly in newspapers and television, which anyone including children have access to. The other day, a British tabloid – the Sun – carried a story of an elderly couple praising the newly introduced viagra tablet saying that it had tremendously improved their sexual life. Prominently displayed on the front page, the woman was quoted for saying that as soon as her husband took it, he was all over her, and never gave her a break throughout the night. The subject was whether the British Government should subsidize viagra.

In Africa, an open discussion on the subject is generally frowned upon, as both the subject and the word itself is taboo, as in most other parts of the world, even Europe. Recently, when teaching the idea of human rights to chiefs or traditional leaders from the Southern African Developing Community (SADC) countries, I asked them to think of the word 'sex' in terms of their local tongues and culture. I asked their Royal Highnesses, as they are locally known, whether it is easy for them to put the word 'sex' on their lips in their mother tongue in private or public? No one would. Sex is an unspeakable word in local tongues. Related to human rights, this means that while opinion and expression is a fundamental human right, for instance, under Article 9 of the African Charter on Human and Peoples' Rights, this right is severely limited when it comes to sex, and in this way to the moral requirement under Article 27 of the Charter. Even careless expressions or expressions that are outside the moral limits anticipated in Article 27 may consequently not enjoy protection.

The idea is that a person can express an opinion without the use of the word sex. Similarly, it is not necessary to use words like 'stupid' or 'idiot' in order to express oneself. It is not a common sight on African streets to see young or old people kissing or in compromising situation. Kissing is associated with immorality and not viewed as a form of expression. In fact, anything perceived to be immoral is heavily censured in African culture. For instance, in public gatherings, culture dictates that men congregate among themselves away from their women. It is not allowed for a man, for example, at public events like funerals or marriage ceremonies, to be in physical contact with his wife. In fact, women and men are expected to go their separate ways according to their gender from sunrise until bedtime in the evening. I have tried it myself to be next to my wife in public, which has provoked public disapproval. A friend of mine, married to a German woman, has tried to keep his marriage vows finding time each working day to go and kiss her at her workplace, something that is sending giggles and disapproving gossips across town.

In some African countries like Nigeria, institutions have been introduced to see to the observance of moral prescriptions. For example, in Northern Nigeria, a morality police has been mandated to, among other things, ensure the criminal prosecution of persons caught in adulterous relationships. A number of young women, among them single women like Safia Hussein and Amina Lawal,[7] were charged with adultery with married men. As a consequence of the world attention the two cases attracted, Shariah judges in the two cases found it within their wisdom to drop the charges against these women either in the law or in their hearts. Significantly, however, none of the men committing adultery were similarly treated. This is only in keeping with the male-dominated society, in which legal equality between men and women as stipulated in the above instruments is illusory.

With the above, we cannot but observe that the Charter has accorded the family the pride of place. The only question that remains is what type of family exactly was in the minds of the framers of the Charter at the time they sat down to draft the instrument? The UDHR's article 16 is obviously a pious hope at developing a universal standard on family in spite of the different attitudes. The difference between this and the family clause in the ICCPR is only that the latter is legally enforceable, otherwise the spirit is the same. On the other hand, the African Charter is clearly for the African family defined in terms of traditional African society.

When measured against either UDHR or the ICCPR standards, the African family elicits plenty of controversies. Just the very notion of 'full age' in regard to the right of individuals to marry is problematic. Similarly, the right to marry, which by corollary asserts the right not to marry, is a big problem in

[7] See the following website for information and materials on Shariah and women's rights in Nigeria especially the two cases above: www.feminist.org/news

status conscience traditional societies. Very often, no status attaches to an unmarried adult. Finding a family is not conceived as a right but is taken as a duty jealously overseen by the elder members of the family. Equality of rights as to marriage, during marriage and at its dissolution is even more problematic. With the patriarchal notion, it is inconceivable that parties can in any sense be considered equal. I have tried to sell this idea to chiefs in human rights workshops, and obviously they are adamantly against it. We shall elaborate further. But equal access to family resources for couples that are dissolving their marriage is an illusion in typical African families. Similarly, freedom to exercise consent on the decision to marry is only recently becoming a reality.

2. WHAT IS FAMILY IN TRADITIONAL LAW?

Traditionally, an African family is a very large baobab-like institution, it is an extended family which excludes virtually no one, beside husband, wife and children, as in the Western sense, also the father and mother of both the husband and the wife as well as their children, who are regarded brothers and sisters, especially but not only of the husband. Grandfather, grandmother and their children i.e. brothers and sisters of the father of the husband, and I dare say their children too, are also included. In contrast to what I have heard, namely that Africans do not have the equivalent of the English word cousin or aunt, at least we do in my culture – the Tonga ethnic group in Zambia. I don't call my mother's brother's children brothers or sisters (Mwanaakwesu), I call them cousins (Mweenima). It is different both in words and in sense. The ones I call brothers and sisters, contrary to English culture, are my father's brother's children. These I must not only call brother and sister but also strictly treat as such. The point is that the word cousin is not alien to African culture. Of course there might be cultures and traditions devoid of such differentiation but this is not an absolute in all cultures.

Above, I have only given a simplified sample of the traditional African family structure. Very simplified I must say because a detailed description of the interlocking and interwoven structures of the ancient African family is beyond my competence, and, in any case it would definitely sidetrack the article. It is an obviously much more complicated issue than this simple illustration suggests. However, the fact is that these individuals are glued to one another and each one of them to the community in terms of a carefully elaborated set of duties and responsibilities recognized and enforceable by living law. I have already showed above how I was cornered in relation to the death of my niece. Each member of the family is expected [and I dare say by norms amounting to law] to carry out his or her share of familial duties to each other, to the elders, community, ethnic group, etc. When one member of the family dies, each member of the extended tree *must* attend the funeral.

Mzee[8] Jomo Kenyatta, Kenya's founding father, has demonstrated at great length the practice of some of these individual duties.[9] A child, according to Kenyatta, must never call his or her parent by their names. It is not only contrary to law but even more taboo. When we say a thing is taboo, it means we are invoking a higher law than ordinary man's law, which is possible to infringe. No child can call an adult man or woman, particularly those in marriage relationships, by their first names. It is simply unthinkable, which answers the next question what if she or he did? But there is a claw back clause. In order for an old man or woman to enjoy this respect, s/he must deserve it. It is a duty owed not just every man or woman but only those who deserve it. In fact, it is common to find children talking indecently about an old person without any restraints where the subject's conduct and behaviour is deplorable. The Bantu words "Tata" and "Mama", meaning father and mother, or corresponding terms in other tongues are frequently used by younger persons when referring to older relatives, and even total strangers. Again, as Kenyatta pointed out, this does not apply to an unscrupulous man or woman however old s/he may be.

Beside linguistic references, other forms of manifesting the duty of respect based on age include the manner in which one is conducting himself or herself to someone older than him or her. For example, I have frequently asked my Swedish class whether they would defer to an uncle if he were to come into a house where he finds you seated. Would you, for instance, give him the chair or not? In Africa, I cannot ask such a question because of its unmistakable superfluity. Each and every young African knows from childhood that the chair belongs to an uncle, aunt or any older person. It cannot be otherwise. Similarly, when serving an older person, children are bound to kneel while

[8] This is respectful way of addressing an old man in Kiswahili. You need not be old but simply compelling respect from the one who is calling you. Each time I am teaching in Kenya, I am to my surprise frequently referred to as Mzee. It terrorizes my nerves to imagine I deserve such honor.

[9] Jomo Kenyatta, *Facing Mount Kenya*, London, 1938, pp. 15-35

holding the thing being served in both hands. Similarly, one must give way (literary come out of the way and in small paths go into the bush) when an adult person is coming from the opposite direction. There are many examples to illustrate this, but the point is that individuals are subject to several duties qua individuals in traditional African society such as those based on age, sex, seniority, etc. This is one of the most interesting aspects of the African family.

It may be a question of maintaining the power of the elders, but it is first and foremost a question of dignity. While a child is not allowed to call an adult by name, let alone the first name, adults are encouraged not to call fellow adults, especially by their first names, in the presence of or to children. It is a duty that is exercised vice versa. This is not just a name thing. It is more. Behind is the idea of dignity. Others might dispute it and ask: But why? If it is a matter of dignity, is the duty not extended to children? The answer is yes, they will also be entitled to it, but only when they grow older. It is like the right to vote. In spite of the importance of this value to the dignity of a human being, children cannot exercise the right to vote because they are children. Similarly, children cannot exercise their right to work as adults. But the fact that children cannot work does not make it less a right in relation to others. Similarly, children are in the same position in African culture. Besides, we have referred to Jomo Kenyatta (above) with his injunction to the effect that an adult person not deserving of respect cannot expect it from children, which by implication means children too must be respected.

It has often been said that respect was only an entitlement of men who were the ones defining the boundaries as well as rules on etiquette. It may be so. As the African society is patriarchal, it should not be surprising that this is not the case. However, my own experience differs significantly. I do not know, and have never known, the first name of my senior mother. My father was polygamist and my mother was his second wife. Frankly, I grew up without ever knowing the name of my senior mother. Similarly and frankly, growing up I did not know the first names of my father's sisters until their names were given to children of my brothers and sisters or children of others in our extended family. This is how I came to know and to start using the names of very old women and men, i.e. through the children named after either the living or departed seniors. Most women are known after their children, especially their first-born. My mother was known as Ina-Malala or Ina-Thomas after my elder brothers Malala or Thomas, who was also the first-born in my mother's house. I naturally felt happier when she was called Ina-Michelo, after my name. More senior women especially but also men would call her by her own name but never junior women and men. Ina-Michelo in my tongue means 'mother of' Michelo.

African morals are very strict indeed. For instance, it is considered taboo for a child to look at naked women let alone adult women. I would consider suicide if I were caught glaring at my naked in-laws. Therefore, it is true as Max Gluckman recorded in the 1947 Lozi case of The Man who helped his Mother-In-Law Cross a Ford.[10] The poor man in this case thought he was doing his two mothers-in-law a favour helping them cross the crocodile infested river. As would be expected, they lifted their dresses up to their buttocks to ease their movements in the water. However, a man who saw the trio, i.e. the son-in-law and the two women, reported the incident to the husband and later to the elders of the village whereupon the case was tried and the poor fellow ordered to pay the aggrieved husband compensation. The Lozi court, the court of the Lozi people of western part of Zambia, upbraided the man for looking at the naked bodies of his mothers-in-law.

Similarly, the court found a young man liable for sitting in a closed hut with his sister.[11] Even though the boy insisted he had done nothing wrong, the court found him guilty and ordered him to pay a sacrifice to the tribunal observing: "I am sure you did nothing wrong with your sister, but you should not sit alone in a closed hut. You must give the beast for sacrifice". These are very high moral standards. More or less they are still being practiced today in traditional African societies. You can therefore understand my shock at the revelation by a friend of mine – a professor of human rights law in a western country – that he had gone on holiday, which included swimming, with his minus/plus 20 years old niece. To this day, I cannot seem to get over the shock I went through when introduced to a so-called 'naked colony' when I was studying in one of the European countries. I found whole families naked – father, mother, adult and young children, friends, etc!

Talking about according respect to mothers-in-law, I must share this incident. Long time ago, when I was somewhere around 10 to 12 years, one of my brothers-in-law, husband to one of my sisters in my senior mother's house,

---

[10] Case No. 37 in Max Gluckman, The Judicial Process Among the Barotse of Northern Rhodesia, 1955, pp. 148-151.

[11] Case 40: The Case of the Incestuous Action, in Gluckman, 1955, *op. cit.*, p. 154.

came from the town to pay us a visit in the village. I was the only young person at home. My father was away but both my two mothers were present. According to my culture, it is not allowed for my brother-in-law to talk directly neither to my mothers nor my father, nor vice versa. It would be a sign of disrespect on either side. As luck would have it on that day, it fell on me to relay the information on either side. Each of my mothers would greet my brother-in-law through me, I would then dutifully conveyed the greetings and return my brother's responses, and so on and so forth. The whole thing was fine to me but it went on and on. I exploited the situation. As time passed by, I faked fatigue until they gave me something in return. My brother-in-law had no choice but to concede to my demands. He bought me sweets and biscuits as compensation and only then did I continue my services. Each time, I ran out of my compensation, I withdrew my services until the sweets and biscuits were replenished!

A problem in African culture is when a woman has no child. Just like in Western societies, the woman (and her husband) could adopt a child, whom she would keep and raise at home and whose name she would become known by. The difference, however, is that in Africa adoption is limited to children of relatives within the extended family circle. It is not usual to adopt and bring into the family a total stranger. So, though we are calling it adoption, it is in actual fact rather an extending support, especially to disadvantaged family members.

3. RITE OF PASSAGE

After puberty but before marriage, teenagers will undergo rituals to announce their transition to adulthood. This is now creating lots of problems with human rights. In some cultures, the passage from child to adulthood is dramatized through male and female circumcision – the latter recently known as female genital mutilation (FGM). Among the Pokoti, on the border between Kenya and Uganda, the transition is, in addition, marked by sending boys to steal cattle from other Pokotis or other tribes like the Karamojong. Cattle-rustling is a demonstration that a boy has matured into adulthood. Others require the boys to kill a lion before being admitted into the adult world. In a process, which is a part of my culture, though I never went through it myself, boys are separated from girls and parents and taken away to some bush where they are confined for a month or two to learn the ABC of life from selected adult men, for the boys, or women, for the girls. I still vividly recall my elder brother being at one of these camps. The boys would build temporary shelters, which they would call their houses, and then built similar shelters at the girls' camp, each boy being required to build at least one particularly for the girl he loved. It is at these camps that boys and girls will be taught the family and community moral code such as respecting seniority or age.

In South Africa today, male circumcision camps is a controversial subject. As a result of some young men's unfortunate death at some of these camps, society is getting increasingly concerned with the practices. Government has now intervened to try to monitor these camps and ensure that they are operated within the bounds of the law. Similarly, some girls in FGM camps across Africa are reportedly dying from the effects of the botched operations. However, the concept is that a girl or boy must go through the rite of passage before being ready for marriage or other adult tasks. If a man, for instance, is not circumcised in circumcising communities, he will never be regarded as an adult. The Kikuyu of Kenya, for instance, and the many circumcising tribes of South Africa refuse to be addressed by uncircumcised men whether from their own or other tribes. For instance, a politician trying to drum up support for his candidacy cannot expect support from a circumcised community if he is not circumcised himself. Circumcised men have been known to mistreat uncircumcised men married to women from circumcised communities, sometimes forcing these women to divorce their men. Some tribes go as far as circumcising an uncircumcised man when departed as the group prepares to bury him!

4. AFRICAN MARRIAGE

Although a family can emerge without a marriage, society has since time immemorial dictated that partners should marry. It is in this respect that it comes as a matter of shock and complete disappointment that unlike the UDHR and the ICCPR, the African Charter does not mention the word marriage at all. It is disappointing because, between Africans and Europeans, the former no doubt have a lot of experience to share about marriages with the latter. In Africa, marriages still take place, even with modernization, and are regarded not as old-fashioned but relevant for the fulfilment of individual worth.

The African marriage ceremony is a climax of several days and even months or years of behind the scenes negotiations and other acrobatics. Anyone who has attended a ceremony of traditional African marriage would be full of praises of the various aspects that go with it. At the same time as being a very serious affair, the African marriage is also a tourist attraction. But how is marriage arrived at? What legal and social steps precede the big day?

African cultures seem to agree that the marriage ceremony is a culmination of a long-drawn process, which may span several months. This was the view of over forty chiefs or traditional leaders from SADC countries at a workshop held for them on human rights.[12] Previously, intending spouses did not choose their partners. Elders chose partners for them. But this is a long time ago, things have since changed and as a rule, intending parties choose their partners themselves. Even in those days, when parents chose partners for their children, cultures were not completely oblivious to the right of parties to choose their loved ones. Of course there are still cases of "arranged marriages" or marriages without the prior consent of the parties, but these are few and isolated. The very fact that they attract attention when they occur confirms this view.

[12] We have already made reference to this workshop. It took place in the tourist town of Livingstone from 24 to 31 May 2004. Over 40 chiefs attended from Angola, Botswana, DRC, Lesotho, Malawi, Namibia, Swaziland, South Africa, Zambia and Zimbabwe. The workshop was organized jointly by the Raoul Wallenberg Institute of the University of Lund in Sweden and a Zambian NGO called Women for Change. In an earlier chiefs' workshop held at Mpekweni Sun Resort in Eastern Cape in South Africa, in May 2003, an interesting development took place. I had divided the chiefs into groups and assigned them cases to discuss and come up with recommendations during plenary. An incident arose when one group that had been assigned the subject of Female Genital Mutilation (FGM) was making their presentation . Although the group itself felt FGM was a violation of human rights, and proceeded to present on those lines, other chiefs walked out of the plenary session. Those who walked out felt strongly that FGM was taboo and should not be discussed in public. Others thought that, since the subject of FGM was not commonly practiced in Southern Africa, it was only fair that it was discussed by people whom it concerned. One of the few women chiefs from Zambia took the flow. She insisted that the subject be discussed. Against catcalls from male chiefs, the Zambian chief castigated her fellow chiefs of being behind some of the cruel cultural traditions such as FGM because they served their interests. While male chiefs called on me to curtail her statement, which I of course ignored, the Zambian chief accused her male counterparts of being violating women's rights for instance by early and forced marriages. She spoke at length about forced and early marriages and pointed her finger of blame directly at traditional leaders, whom she said were among the beneficiaries. She accused them of engaging in and encouraging polygamy. It was an exciting moment. For me, it was important that I encouraged her and protected her right to speak out especially among traditional leaders and in view of her status as a woman – potentially one of the victims. I had no doubt the message went through.

Many years ago, when I was still at lower primary school, way back in the 60s, I had a grisly experience. A group of several men, some of them well known to me, were pulling and pushing a woman, who was very well known in the village. I simply did not understand what was going on. The woman was crying and fruitlessly trying to free herself from the crutches of hefty men. Later at home, I asked my mother what was happening. She explained to me that the woman was being married. I was told that this form of marriage was called *Kutizya* in my tongue or forced marriage in English. According to custom, the knot was tied once the woman was forced into the house of the abductor. If she managed to free herself, for instance, and successfully bolted back to her people, her parents would usually send her back. Since then, I have never heard or seen anything like it.

Above, we have addressed two practices under one subject. Marriages may be contracted by force, which, as we said, is virtually becoming extinct. A marriage may implicitly be considered as a forced one where for instance it is 'forced' upon the spouses by parents or other elders. The marriage of Prince Charles and Princess Diana is an excellent example. Prince Charles is alleged to have said he was forced by his father to marry Diana, a commoner. Such types of marriages are common among royalties in Africa. In a sense, they are examples of forced marriage.

One of my farm workers in Zambia recently told me that his seventy-plus father, living in a village, had married a twenty something girl. He of course was already married to three other women. There was no apparent force used in tying the knot between the old man and the young woman. These types of marriages are frequent in Africa. It has just been announced, for example, that King Godwin Zwelatini of the Zulu people in South Africa's Kwa-Zulu province, a grandson son of the proverbial King Shaka Zulu, will be marrying a young twenty something girl from Swaziland. The King is over 60 years and has already five other wives. Recently in Swaziland, a brave woman, Ms. Dlamin, [13] dragged the Monarch to the High Court on a habeas corpus application fighting for the return of her teenage daughter Zena, who had been abducted and taken to King Mswati in order to be married by the King's emissaries. This was the first case in the history of the Monarch of Swaziland, already husband to over ten wives. Unfortunately, before the presiding Chief

[13] Ms. Dlamin versus Attorney General & Police Commissioner. 2002. Swaziland High Court. Mbabane.

had the opportunity to rule, the case was adjourned *sine die* at the instance of the petitioner. This happened after the Monarch had arranged for the eighteen-year old school-girl Zena speake on phone to her mother confirming that she had married the King of her own freely will.

In normal situations, a marriage begins by informal negotiations usually by go-betweens. Recently, Friends in Pretoria and I drove to Venda on the Zimbabwan border to present a token payment of 500 South African Rand (100 USD) to a chief's family. A young man from Venda, who recently graduated in law and now is practicing as a lawyer in one of the law firms, decided he would marry the chief's daughter, who still studied law at the University of Venda. The girl and boy met at Church in Pretoria when the girl was there on vacation staying with her 'mother', the wife of my friend, working with me, who was cousin to the wife of the chief. After the boy made the decision to marry the girl, we advised him to go by the living law – the Venda law on marriage. In most other cultures, it is a requirement that a token payment be made by the groom-s family to the bride's family before anything can take place. In real traditional settings, I would not qualify to accompany the team as I come from a totally different family background. But in the towns it happens that any adult man or woman could represent the groom's relatives.

Once the token payment is made (which can be anything besides money), the relatives of the girl will ask her whether she knows the boy/man seeking her hand in marriage, and if she does, whether she loves him. Upon confirmation, the relatives of the wife-to-be will summon each other, i.e. maternal and paternal relatives, to discuss the proposal. Simultaneously, the relatives of the husband-to-be will convene similar meetings to discuss the same. Once the parties are ready, i.e. they have finished their respective discussions, the groom's family will approach the bride's relatives to open the negotiations. The two families assign the task of negotiating to a select group of their relatives, usually uncles and aunties. The groom's family has the difficult task of trying to make the bride's family interested in negotiating. They will have to know and be familiar with the personal law on the side of the bride in case the two parties come from different ethnic groups governed by different laws. The groom's family will shower the bride's family with money or various kinds of gifts in order to encourage them to talk and to smoothen the talks. In some families, the bride's family will not open the gate for the groom's relatives or allow them to set foot on their homestead without the latter first giving the former something. They (bride's family) will pretend that they do not know the groom's family? Even after the talks have started, the bride's family may suddenly halt them temporarily unless the groom's family comes up with 'something' to encourage the talks. That 'something' may be payment of money or buying beer, which the parties will drink while they talk.

What do they talk about? Initially, the parties try to explore the families in order to get to know each other. This is the time to know the family trees on both sides so as to avoid that the future spouses are relatives. It is also time to find out the standing of each of the parties. Some of the qualities the parties will be looking for are whether the member of the other family are hard working; whether they are talkative; whether they are notorious witches; whether they are hospitable, etc. In my culture, the end of negotiations will, among other things, be climaxed by the naming ceremony. During this ceremony, the relatives of the groom will give the bride a name by the relatives of the husband, which is added her original name, and by which she will be known especially by that family. This is to symbolize that she has joined a new family. It is a kind of a welcome practice. Once preliminaries are over, the parties will go into more serious issues like dowry.

Dowry, otherwise known as bride price, is one of the most criticized institutions of traditional African society. Most feminist organizations and individuals regard dowry as equivalent to selling the girl or putting a commercial value on her dignity. It is true that some people use the dowry concept to raise money and in this case, it is very close to selling the woman. A father in an African country had pegged his daughter's dowry at a brand new BMW car! However, it is important always to separate the activities of individuals from the concept. Conceptually, dowry was never meant to be a commercial sale. Originally, dowry was expressed in a token payment from the groom's family to the family of the bride. The payment differed from custom to custom, and from community to community. Even girls of the same family would attract different dowry payments depending on various factors. In my culture, the law is that the man's family must pay no less than four heads of cattle. Of course you can pay more if you have the means. Negotiations will centre on whether to pay four or less depending on the means at the disposal of the groom's family. In one of my chiefs' human rights workshop in the western part of Zambia in April 2001, a female participant, who had come to represent her father, a chief who could not attend due an indisposition, said that she would not attract much in dowry because she had a child before marriage. These are some of the factors taken into account during negotiations. Others would include things like the groom's educational status, which means claiming the expenses incurred by her family in educating her.

In my culture, each of the four heads of cattle has a distinct significance. For instance, one of them goes to the woman who acted as midwifery when the girl was born. One goes to the mother of the girl and is normally kept by the maternal uncles or extended family of girl's mother. The father is given one, which represents his chin, which his daughter used to play with as she was growing up. The last one goes to the father's kin. Once the cows give birth and multiply, the calves are shared among the maternal and paternal relatives. In the absence of cattle, payment could be made in money. But one important point is that dowry is never paid out all at once. It is generally understood that the obligation will be honoured gradually. This is important because what is at issue is the creation of a new family and not commodisation of a spouse. In countries like Malawi, Eastern Zambia, Zimbabwe, etc., there is a form of payment called *Lobola,* literally meaning fishing. If the cow, which is used as payment, does not change hands, the man has no right to claim custody of his children on divorce. Similarly, the man's relatives will lose their rights to the children if *lobola* has not been paid by the time of the man's death. Their rights resuscitate only upon the fulfilment of this obligation.

William Rayner[14]is one of the few European anthropologists who recognize the value of dowry in African culture. He has said that dowry payment, which varied in relation to the wealth of the community, dissuaded men from bullying or other forms of cruelty and encouraged the stability of marriages. Consequently, dowry or more specifically *lobola* was a promise that the husband would treat his future wife well. A man whose family has paid a lot of lobola will always bear in mind the special place of his wife and his wife's family and will not dare to touch her.

Dowry is the thread that ties the marriage contract together. It is to Africans what the blessing of the church or the legal acts of the state registrar is to a westerner. Frequently, the question arises in divorce cases whether dowry was or was not paid. Dowry is what seals the contract of marriage. Strangely, even spouses that choose to marry under western law of marriage, which provides

[14] William Rayner, *The Tribe and Its Successors: An Account of African Traditional Life and European Settlement in Southern Rhodesia.* New York, Praeger, 1962, p.58.

no dowry, nevertheless apply the dowry requirement. There are very few marriages in Africa where dowry is not paid, however 'westernised' the parties. In an earlier workshop for traditional leaders, I attended in Eastern Cape in South Africa, the chiefs asked me: if we abandon dowry on the grounds that it clashes with human rights, what alternative do we have for tying our marriages? Payment of dowry is what makes Africans identify themselves as such and the marriage as marriage. A female human rights activist from Zimbabwe in my human rights short course in Pretoria boldly stated that she did not understand Europeans marrying "just like that". Dowry, she said, was an important precondition to marriage and what legitimated the institution.

Once the negotiations are completed, a date will be set for the wedding. As already explained above, this is a big event in most cultures. Today, people combine African with Western culture and organize a white wedding, which was not required before. The wedding ceremony is fundamentally the same as in Western culture (regardless of whether it takes the form of a secular and relatively anonymous town hall wedding, or that of the much more elaborate church wedding with relatives and friends gathering for expensive festivities afterwards), save for interpositions necessary to articulate some aspects of African culture. For instance, in my culture, the bride is prodded to cry and expected to walk slowly from a distance to the high table. She must not look people in the face, but always bent as she is slowly helped by her bridesmaid towards her future husband. The walk, which is rehearsed several times, should be slow so as not to show people that she is happy to go into the marriage when in fact she is.

5. POLYGAMY

Once a man has married, he has exhausted this right to marry. Contrary to a widespread perception, African society is as monogamous as any other. In fact, the difference, as observed before, is that once married, it is very difficult in African culture to divorce, in contrast to the relative freedom to do so in the liberal Europe, especially Scandinavia.

African culture teaches people to be sure and to realize that they are grown up before making vows. Of course you do not forfeit your right to divorce after you are married although previously in some cultures you actually did, just like the Biblical Catholic marriage. But marriages in Africa used to be so respected that everything was done to preserve them, at least formally. This was particularly so where there were children. Article 4 of the Convention on the Rights of the Child (CRC) guarantees the principle of 'the best interest of the child' but African culture is a culture that already ensured this principle in more ways than one. If the chemistry between the spouses has completely dried up, polygamy would sometimes be recommended instead of divorce.

Polygamy was also recommended as a mechanism to replace the men that might have died in war. Rich men married polygamously to show off to poorer men. A titled man or one who was very famous in the community would be encouraged by is kin to marry more women to help in looking after the stream of visitors that called on him. Jealousy is another reason. Especially the mother-in-law would encourage her son to marry another wife as a device to check on the jealousy of his wife. There are many reasons. Moral weakness is another. The man may simply want another partner to satisfy his amorous needs, which never get satisfied anyway. Experience from polygamous men shows that the minute he marries one, he starts running after another, and so on and so forth.

The point about polygamy is that contrary to popular perception, African society does not in fact condone it. How do we know this? First, the community does not usually get involved in marriage negotiations, as in the first marriage we illustrated above. The second and subsequent marriages are really the man's own business. He might involve only one or two of his relatives, but there is no keenness such as we have highlighted above. It must be borne in mind that some of the man's relatives may themselves in fact disapprove of his intention to get more wives either because they themselves are monogamous or for any other reason. Another fundamental point is that polygamy is not a universal norm in cultures that practice it. While one man may be polygamous, his next-door neighbour may be a stout monogamist. Even brothers are known to split across the middle when it comes to marriage preferences.

Let me relate a real story about polygamy. Earlier on I disclosed my family status. I was born of polygamous union, and I must say it was hard. I am sure it would have been even harder had my brother and I been girls. It is not easy to be born of a second house. I am not only talking about attention here but about virtually everything. Though it might look harmonious from the outside, inside the polygamous marriage is more than hell particularly for the children, but this is a subject for another occasion. Recently, whilst attending a funeral at my village, I wanted very much to meet the wife of my cousin, who also acted as village headman. I did not see her on the first day and night even though the headman did not sleep far away from me outside the funeral house. As custom dictates, we sleep outside in what are called 'night vigils' during funerals, not on beds but on the ground using grass as mattresses, although today some people use real mattresses. When I finally saw her on the third day, I told her that I had been looking for her but could not see her with my cousin. I had great respect for my cousin. He was one of the first people in the village to get an education and to rise up to become headmaster of the mission school. His wife got educated too and became headmistress of the girls' school. They were my models. She told me she had stayed home on the first and second nights of the funeral because my cousin had come with his second wife. I was shocked, as I did not know he had become polygamous. And on seeing my shock, she added: " I am the one who told him to get a second wife after he retired from work and decided to go to the village to settle down while I was still teaching. It was convenient to both of us". From this, convenience is another reason. Wives in patriarchal traditional African society are supposed to maintain and look after the husband, children and the husband's kin. It is difficult but that is how it is.

6. SUCCESSION & INHERITANCE

The law on succession and inheritance has been equally controversial in African culture. In a very limited sense, succession relates to issues like succeeding to the throne of a king or chief. Royalty or chieftainship, all over the world, is limited to blood relatives. It is rare that this is passed on to outsiders, and as one outside the circle of the chieftainship in my community, I have never entertained the idea of one day finding myself on the throne. Doing what, if I may ask? However, monarchical or chieftainship title is often characterized with a lot of succession rows. In one sense, this is healthy because it proves the existence of competition in a community and especially a sense of clan or family democracy.

Inheritance has been the more problematic of the two as far as ordinary people are concerned. The issue of how to share the estate of the deceased is very problematic particularly in instances where the deceased dies intestate. There are cases, however, where even though the departed is testate, the relatives will fight over the estate or even ignore the Will. But it is first and foremost when the deceased in intestate that the problems come to the fore.

I remember one of my LL.B lecturer's favourite question was why Africans were not in the habit of making wills. It was so habitual a question that it was boring. Looking at it now, the question is fundamentally false. Africans do make wills according to their concept of a will. When a dying African makes an oral will, such as "I leave that cow to my daughter", it will be complied with to the letter. However, in instances where the deceased leaves behind no oral or written will, the practice is that the estate is shared according to customary rules and principles prevailing in the community. Paternal and maternal relatives take part in the sharing of the estates often to the exclusion of the deceased's children and his widow(s). We will not go too much into this but only point out that not all cultures are guilty of disinheriting the children and surviving spouse. However, this is the general trend in most African cultures. The only question we should address here is why African law is seemingly discriminatory of the children and spouse while favouring the deceased's extended family. The answer is very simple.

The African philosophical outlook is based on the group. Everyone is perceived to belong to a group or collective, the individual is only part of that group. Group-belonging as opposed to individuality is manifested in many ways. For instance, when a person is born, the whole group (extended family) joins in the celebrations. We have already discussed marriages, which we said are public affairs. When eating, Africans eat together, with their fingers, to symbolize the solidarity. Only a rascal would turn his back to others and eat alone.

Another example is land tenure. Africans only obtain distinct user rights, as private ownership of land is alien to African culture. [15] Consequently, when an individual dies, the collective asserts its right over the land. The individual, being only part of the collective, belongs to the collective and in death to the spirit of ancestors of the collective. Consequently, all of the deceased's worldly possessions are claimed by the collective, defined as the members of the extended family. In maternal societies, the children of the deceased inherit

[15] One example, where this collided with European views, is Kitok v. Sweden, Communication No. 197/1985. Human Rights Committee, Forty-third Session, Supplement No. 40 (A/43/40), annex VII, sect. G.

from their uncles and the maternal uncles' children from their maternal uncles, and so on. The surviving spouse, not being a blood member of the extended family, looks to her extended family for inheritance, and not to the estate of her husband. In paternal families, on the other hand, children inherit, though even they exclude spouses. One point, however, that has never been stated is that inheritors have no property rights to the pieces of estate assigned to them. They are only custodians of the inherited property and cannot sell it. This property is for all the survivors especially the children. My father had inherited one ox and two cows in addition to a grinding mill from his father, my grandfather. I remember that his sisters and nephews could at anytime get the two oxen to plough their fields. Similarly, the calves born of the cow were continually being shared among the members of the extended family. We didn't treat them as our property. The reason why it is different now is poverty and greed among people. The concept as it used to be is certainly different from the practice today. Before I leave this part, I must only mention one thing: widow inheritance. Indeed it used to be custom that a widow would be inherited by a male relative of her deceased husband. It is difficult to see the value of it today. But at that time, it was essential for the protection of women, especially the dignity of the widow. Widows actually asked to be inherited in order to get protection, especially when they were not able to fend for themselves for instance by having a job.

7. AFRICAN JUSTICE SYSTEM

There is no better way to wrap up our overview than a brief look at the African justice system. Before the advent of the current system of justice, how did Africans resolve their problems? We can ask the same question differently: how do Africans in traditional societies today resolve their disputes?

Until recently, this question would certainly not be relevant. However, Africa has had a rude wake up call only recently. The 1994 genocide in Rwanda made Africans start asking themselves basic questions such as whether the prevailing concept of justice is the right concept for the African people? It is ironic that it had to take genocide to make Africans start asking who they really are. But this is not at all strange. The present concept of human rights has its roots in the Second World War. Had the millions of Jews that that succumbed at the hands of Hitler not died, the world would probably not have woken up to the present reality.

Among others, the original process of justice in Africa is woven around the principles of inclusiveness, participatory and substantive justice. Inclusiveness is a reference to the fact that Africans try to include everyone in their search for justice. Every adult has a legal right to take part in proceedings and to be consulted before the final decision. The chief or elder never decides by himself.

It has been alleged, for instance, that women do not take part in traditional justice systems. This may be true but only in some and not all cultures. In my culture, the experience is vastly different. Women were very active participants at several sessions I witnessed in various villages in Zambia. The geography of these 'courts' or traditional adjudication assemblies of course gave men an edge over women. Village heads, chief or headman (usually men) would sit on the highest stools in a semi-circle with their front to men on stools, again sitting slightly higher than the rest of the male audiences, who would sit on anything they picked such as stones, bricks, root of the tree etc., but behind the chief/headman and his councillors. On the other hand, the women would sit facing the chief/headman, usually on the ground with their legs stretched or folded. An interesting observation I made was that resulting from this geography in all the audiences I attended, women contributed more than men. The geography rather than anything else tended to favour women. As they faced the headman, he would almost always see their hands each time he sought contributions while men were behind him, and therefore he could not easily see their hands. The men continuously protested that their hands were being ignored, but the fact is that they were behind the chief or headman. As I said, I never experienced the headman or chief deciding a case singly. In fact, I would get bored listening to long undulating interventions aimed at 'clarifying' this or that without anyone interrupting.

It has been said that African justice is short of universal justice to the extent that there is for instance no right of appeal, and even worse not everybody is allowed legal defence. All this is distortion. There is as much a concept of legal defence in African justice as in other justice systems. Of course people may not have gone to law school and then on to practice law, but this by no means suggests the absence of legal defence. Legal representation has always been part of the African justice system. Not necessarily a loquacious person will be called upon to help the defendant state the case but anyone who is familiar with the case or the parties. Before the village court, senior relatives of either of the parties will help state the case. On the other hand, the village head is expected to appear before the chief's court to state the case not for one but for both parties because the idea is not to see to one part winning or losing the case but simply to substantiate justice. Besides, the court itself acts as a kind of defence counsel. Though patently impartial, the court deliberately cross-examines the defendant as if it was against his side when in fact it is not.

Regarding the right of appeal, it is true that once a decision is made, it cannot be appealed. But this is because everyone present is given more than their fair share to state their viewpoints, which would only be repeated again and again.[16] If everyone in the community is afforded a chance to state their side, what else will remain for an appeal case? Allowing repeated interventions on the same points and applying less strict rules of evidence than e.g. in Commonwealth legal practice are intended primarily for the purpose which may otherwise be achieved by appeal,. Besides, in some communities, the possibility of appeal is not altogether totally out of bounds. A party, against whom a decision has been made, may on the basis of fresh evidence seek the indulgence of a senior relative of the chief or headman and a case decided differently. However, this is rare as the decision is made publicly by every member of the village. Besides this, however, the greatest advantage of African justice is that it is justice according to people's own standards. It is very unlikely that once a decision has been made, one would seek to avoid it. Second, the public nature of it is such that it is viewed as binding on all within its jurisdiction only on this account. Finally, it is not expected that there will be problems in ensuring enforcement. A person would ignore such decision at his peril.

Again, Rwanda is experimenting with African justice. More than forty thousand people, previously awaiting trial for genocide-related offences, falling in categories two to four, have been released from jail and are to face *Gacaca* trials. Gacaca or grassroots justice, like the name suggests, will be conducted before trees or on hills rather than before robed judges in

[16] See, for instance, the case of the Vague Complaint (1942) in Max Gluckman, supra. Pp. 78-79. On 7 August 1942, a woman appealed to the Saa-Katengo Kuta at Lealui from Prince Mwenekandala a decision arising from her husband's divorcing her. She began a long and rambling story about the marriage payment, how they had separated on a journey, and what her parents and relatives had said. The judges cut her short: "Come to the point. What are you claiming?" Again, she rambled and again she was told to state her claim: "We cannot understand your dispute." They told the clerk to take notes till he found out what she wanted, so that they could have a dispute into which to enter.

flamboyant buildings. Members of the community against which the genocide crimes were committed will be elected on the basis of standing in society to preside over the trials. The *Nyanga Mugayo*, or respected members of the community that will act as judges, are appointed among ordinary members of the community. The whole idea behind Gacaca is to use community principles to reconcile the community. Through community participation, it is hoped that society will gradually start to heal itself. Gacaca may not bring justice according to Geneva or New York but there is no doubt it will lead to healing, which is the most important point. But beyond this, Gacaca is an experiment for the rest of Africa.

CONCLUSION

The most important lesson above is that it is time for Africa to realize that it does not have to be Europe or America in order to do it right. From a legal perspective, Africa has been marked by colonialism as much as in other spheres, e.g. the way African institutions have been cast after the European models. The challenge is how to convince Africans that they can live by their living law without copying everything from others. Copying may be good if it is done to enrich your, copying for the sake of copying is not. If only Africa would take a second look at her own civilization, especially in the areas outlined above, she would be surprised not only to find that she has enough law to bank on within her own backyard, but also that in fact most of what is obtained in the world now has an original basis in Africa as well.

BIBLIOGRAPHY

A.T. Culwick, 1942. *Good Out of Africa,* "A Study in the Relativity of Morals", in *The Rhodes-Livingstone Papers* Number Eight Manchester University Press

Jack Donelly, 1989. *Universal Human Rights in Theory and Practice,* Ithaca, Cornell University Press

Max Gluckman, 1955. *The Judicial Process Among the Barotse of Northern Rhodesia*, Manchester University

Michelo Hansungule, 2000. "The African Charter on Human and Peoples Rights: A Critical Review", *African Yearbook of International Law*, Volume 8, Pp. 265-331.

Rhoda Howard, 1986. *Human Rights in Commonwealth Africa*,Totowa, Rowman & Littlefield

Jomo Kenyatta´, 1938. *Facing Mount Kenya*, London

Human Rights. A Compilation of International instruments, Volume 1. (Second Part) Universal Instruments. United Nations. OHCHR.

Human Rights. A Compilation of International Instruments, Volume 11, Regional Instruments, United Nations, ST/HR/1/Rev.5 Cvol.11).

William Rayner, 1962 *The Tribe and Its Successors: An Account of African Traditional Life and European Settlement in Southern Rhodesia*, New York, Praeger, p.58.

www.feminist.org/news

Wilson, Richard A., 2000. "Reconciliation and Revenge in Post-Apartheid South Africa: Rethinking Legal Pluralism and Human Rights", *Current Anthropology*, Vol. 41